S0-CPS-538

Maybe —
NOThing on
corine —

By Irving Babbitt

DEMOCRACY AND LEADERSHIP.
ROUSSEAU AND ROMANTICISM.
THE MASTERS OF MODERN FRENCH CRITICISM.
THE NEW LAOKOON.
An Essay on the Confusion of the Arts.
LITERATURE AND THE AMERICAN COLLEGE.
Essays in Defense of the Humanities.
ON BEING CREATIVE.

HOUGHTON MIFFLIN COMPANY
BOSTON AND NEW YORK

THE MASTERS OF MODERN FRENCH CRITICISM

THE MASTERS OF MODERN FRENCH CRITICISM

BY

IRVING BABBITT

Professor of French Literature
in Harvard University

BOSTON AND NEW YORK
HOUGHTON MIFFLIN COMPANY
The Riverside Press Cambridge

COPYRIGHT, 1912, BY IRVING BABBITT

ALL RIGHTS RESERVED

Published December 1912; reprinted January 1916;
February 1919; October 1923; January 1926;
February 1928; November 1930; June 1940

801
B112m

The Riverside Press
CAMBRIDGE · MASSACHUSETTS
PRINTED IN THE U.S.A.

"*La critique universelle est le seul caractère qu'on puisse assigner à la pensée délicate, fuyante, insaisissable du XIX*[e] *siècle.*"

RENAN.

193253, cop.3

PREFACE

WHAT I have tried to do in this volume is not to criticise criticism, at best a somewhat languid business, but to criticise critics, which may be a far more legitimate task, especially if the critics happen to be, as in the present case, among the most vital and significant personalities of their time. Matthew Arnold speaks in one of his sonnets of "France, famed in all great arts, in none supreme." Yet elsewhere he accords to Sainte-Beuve a supremacy in the art of criticism of the same order as that of Homer in poetry. That Arnold was the last man to underestimate a supremacy of this kind we may infer from the familiar sentence in his essay on translating Homer: "Of the literature of France and Germany, as of the intellect of Europe in general, the main effort, for now many years, has been a critical effort."

To study Sainte-Beuve and the other leading French critics of the nineteenth century is therefore to get very close to the intellectual centre of the century. We may thus follow the main movement of thought through this period and at the same time build up the necessary background for the proper understanding of the ideas of our own day, whether they continue this earlier thought or react from it.

The so-called anti-intellectualist movement of the present time especially can only be understood with reference to such a background; it is a reaction from the dogmatic naturalism that reached its height in the second half of the nineteenth century, a sign that the world is growing weary of scientific positivism and its attempt to lock up reality in its formulæ. The walls of that particular prison house of the spirit are plainly crumbling. Parts of the edifice have been collapsing of late with almost dramatic suddenness. We must rid ourselves of all forms of the metaphysical illusion (including the scientific form), says M. Bergson, perhaps the chief spokesman of the new tendency, and so make philosophy vital. This attempt of philosophy to escape from mere intellectualism is in itself highly laudable. With the older type of metaphysician ordinary mortals felt that they had very little in common. They could at most address to him the Virgilian query: —

> "Quid struis? aut qua spe gelidis in nubibus haeres?"

But the philosophers have of late been coming out of their chilling clouds of abstraction. They have been growing literary, so literary, in fact, that the time would seem to have arrived for the men of letters to return the compliment and become to the best of their ability philosophical.

The literary critic especially should be willing to meet the philosopher halfway, if it be true, as I have tried to show in this volume, that they are both confronted at present by the same central problem. For, to inquire whether the critic can judge, and if so by what standards, is only a form of the more general inquiry whether the philosopher can discover any unifying principle to oppose to mere flux and relativity. We are told by the new school that any attempt on the part of the intellect to unify life and impose upon it a scale of values is artificial, and that we must oppose to this artificial unity our vivid intuitions of change, of the infinite otherwiseness of things. Now, however little we may accept the whole of this thesis, we must grant that M. Bergson — and James, as it seems to me, even more than M. Bergson — has rendered a substantial service to philosophy in thus turning its attention to what Plato would have called the problem of the One and the Many. Most people, James admits, do not lose much sleep over this problem, yet he is right in thinking that all other philosophical problems are insignificant in comparison. If philosophy once gets firmly planted on this ground, it may recover a reality that it has scarcely possessed since the debates of Socrates and the sophists. Instead of the intricate fence with blunted foils to which the intellectualists have too often reduced it, we may once more see the flash of the naked blade.

In their dealings with the problem of the One and the Many, both M. Bergson and James have adopted, it would seem sufficiently plain, not the Socratic but the sophistical side of the argument. I have expressed my own conviction in the following pages that what is needed just now is not merely a reaction from scientific positivism (that we are getting already), but a reaction from naturalism itself. By this I mean that we should effect our escape from intellectualism not by sinking below it, after the fashion of the Bergsonians and pragmatists, but by rising above it, and this would involve in turn a use of the Socratic and Platonic method of definition. Instead of reducing the intellect to a purely utilitarian rôle, as M. Bergson does, we should employ it in multiplying sharp distinctions, and should then put these distinctions into the service of the character and will. If we are told that in order to get at reality we must abandon intellect for intuition, the obvious reply is that only by means of the intellect can we lay the proper foundations for a philosophy of intuition. In short, the word intuition itself is very much in need of being treated Socratically. If I have contributed even in a small degree to dissipate the dangerous sophistries that are accumulating so rapidly around this word in contemporary thought, I shall be satisfied. I have tried to show, especially in the essays on Joubert and Taine, that the term intuition is not simple but complex, that there are different orders of intuitions. Good sense itself, according to Dr. Johnson, is intuitive, and this is a kind of intuitiveness of which we stand in special need at the present crisis; for this word is not too strong to apply to a time when the philosophy of the flux is proclaimed so confidently and received with so much applause. This same naturalistic vertigo, we may remember, seized upon ancient Greek society at the very height of its achievement and marked the first downward step towards the abyss. "Too many of our modern philosophers in their search after the nature of things," says Plato in words that might have been written yesterday, "are always getting dizzy from constantly going round and round; and then . . . they think that there is nothing stable or permanent, but only flux and motion, and that the world is full of every sort of motion and change."

I have just said that to study the chief French critics of the nineteenth century is to get very close to the intellectual centre of the age. I am of the belief, however little I may have justified it by my practice, that this question of the One and the Many, on which all the other main aspects of our modern thought finally converge, may be studied to special advantage in connection with these critics. I have aimed, however, to estimate the work of each critic in itself and not to study it simply as part of an intellectual development. To this end I have made a very liberal use of quotation, on the principle laid down by Sainte-Beuve: *Avec des citations bien prises on trouverait dans chaque auteur son propre jugement.* In such a way one may stand aside and let the authors speak for themselves.

CAMBRIDGE, MASS.,
November 1, 1912.

CONTENTS

THE MASTERS OF MODERN FRENCH CRITICISM

I

MADAME DE STAEL

THE first year of the nineteenth century was appropriately marked by the publication of Madame de Staël's "Literature considered in its Relations to Social Institutions." This relationship between literature and society upon which the new century was to insist more than any previous century had been forced upon its notice by the very suddenness of its separation from the past. As Stendhal was to say later: "How could you expect a man who had been on the retreat from Moscow to care for literature written for the men who had taken off their hats at Fontenoy to the English column and said, 'Fire first, gentlemen'?" "Nothing in life should be stationary," wrote Madame de Staël in the "Germany," "and art is petrified when it no longer changes. Twenty years of revolution have given the imagination other needs than those it felt when the novels of Crébillon portrayed the love and society of the time."[1] Chateaubriand, at variance with Madame de Staël on so many other points, agreed with her that men's charac-

[1] *De l'Allemagne*, 2e Partie, c. xv.

ters had been profoundly transformed by the Revolution and that literature should reflect this transformation.

We should err, however, in supposing that the public in general at the beginning of the nineteenth century felt the need of changes in art and literature to express a changed society. The Empire as a whole was a period of artificiality and formalism. This would seem less strange if those who had learned nothing and forgotten nothing politically had alone shown zeal in maintaining the Old Régime in literature. On the contrary, the men who had innovated most rashly in other ways were often conspicuous for their literary conservatism. Men who had toppled over altars and beheaded a king were ready to kneel down superstitiously in the little Temple of Taste;[1] like Byron who, according to Goethe, showed no respect for any law human or divine except the law of the three unities. An occasional writer who felt a new spirit stirring vaguely within him, and set out to be original, only succeeded in becoming odd. Thus Népomucène Lemercier (Népomucène le Bizarre), after precipitating a bloody riot by the liberties he took with the unities and verbal decorum in his play "Christophe Colomb," afterwards declared in his "Cours de littérature," that a tragedy must fulfil precisely twenty-six rules[2] or conditions under penalty of ceasing to be.

The society of the Empire, made up as it was largely

[1] Cf. G. Merlet, *Tableau de la Littérature française, 1800–1815*, III, 21.

[2] *Cours analytique de littérature générale* (1817), I, 179. Comedy must observe twenty-two rules, epic twenty-three.

of parvenus and of persons whose education had been broken off abruptly by the Revolution, was almost naïvely willing to be schoolmastered. It wished to get on the easiest terms that tincture of humane literature that was deemed necessary not only to good taste but to good breeding. Hence no doubt the popularity during the first twenty or thirty years of the century of the "Lycée" of La Harpe, the last eminent critical authority of the Old Régime; for no one was better fitted than he to give a first general initiation into literary tradition. Sainte-Beuve calls the critics of the Empire the small change of Boileau — Boileau, conceived, of course, after the late neo-classical fashion, as the policeman of Parnassus, the vigilant guardian of literary orthodoxy. Sainte-Beuve points out that they had not only the limitations but the merits of the older type of critics: they were preëminently judicial. They felt themselves supported, moreover, in their judgments by a public opinion that had grown weary of the chaos and anarchy of the Revolution, and are even less important in themselves than as the mouthpieces of this opinion.[1]

Geoffroy, the representative critic of the period, was fitted by his past to play the pedagogue. He had been professor of "eloquence" at Paris before the Revolution and taught school in the village where he concealed himself during the Terror. Geoffroy, however, cannot be dismissed as a mere political and literary reactionary, though in a sense he was both. He makes frequent use of the historic method and is guided in his actual judg-

[1] See the whole article in *Causeries du Lundi*, I, 371 ff.

ments even more by vigorous good-sense than by a regard for formal requirements. At the age of fifty-eight, he created a new *genre*, the dramatic feuilleton, and for twelve years ruled the playwrights and actors of his time with a rod of iron. Like Jeffrey, with whom he has been compared, he belongs only partly to the old critical order by his method, but entirely to it by his temper, which was hard, imperious, and vituperative. According to an epigram, he died as a result of having sucked inadvertently the tip of his own pen.[1] His violence, like that of his opponents, is due to the same poisonous intrusion of politics into literature that one finds at about the same time in England. No wonder that a man who has to repel almost daily charges of venality and gluttony should in the long run become pugilistic. Quite apart from politics, however, Geoffroy believed in the virtues of *la critique amère ;* and something may as a matter of fact be said in behalf of a tonic bitterness in criticism. Unfortunately, he not only flourished the ferule too openly, but had against him the deeper currents of his time. He stood at most for a minor movement of concentration in an age which was in its underlying tendency expansive, and which, caring little for discipline, aspired towards a vast widening out of knowledge and sympathy. Of this underlying expansive tendency the true representative is Madame de Staël.

[1] "Nous venons de perdre Geoffroy.
—Il est mort ? —Ce soir, on l'inhume.
De quel mal ? —Je ne sais —Je le devine, moi ;
L'imprudent, par mégarde, aura sucé sa plume."

I

It has been said that the rôle of Madame de Staël was to understand and make others understand, that of Chateaubriand to feel and teach others to feel; which is only another way of saying that Chateaubriand is more intimately related to romanticism than Madame de Staël. That "unnatural amount of understanding" in Madame de Staël of which Schiller complained sets her off sharply from the romanticists and connects her with the eighteenth century. Her style is of that age; it lacks, however, the epigrammatic neatness of the eighteenth century before Rousseau, and though not always free from the sentimentality and declamation that the late eighteenth century had caught from Rousseau at his worst, it lacks the imaginative freshness and warmth of coloring of Rousseau at his best. It has its own merits as a medium for conveying ideas, but it is deficient in both the old art and the new poetry.

Madame de Staël belongs no less decisively to the Old Régime in preferring society to nature and solitude. Napoleon, in his ten years' duel with her, discovered that he could inflict sufficient torment simply by keeping her at a distance from Paris. She was especially impatient with those who suggested that she had a compensation for her enforced absence from the capital in the panorama of the Alps that unfolded itself before her at Coppet. She spent years in the presence of this panorama, as has been pointed out, without receiving from it the suggestion of a single image. However, her often quoted remark that she would travel five hundred leagues to meet a man of parts, but would not open her window to look at the Bay of Naples, gives a somewhat exaggerated idea of her indifference to nature.

In spite of her excess of understanding, her love of the drawing-room and her comparative coolness towards nature, Madame de Staël is nevertheless a disciple of Rousseau. We merely need to define carefully this discipleship. She might have said, though in a somewhat different sense from Rousseau, that "her heart and her head did not seem to belong to the same individual." Like Renan she was fond of attributing the conflict of which she was conscious in herself to a mixed heredity. "To be born a French woman," she says, "with a foreign character, with French taste and habits and the ideas and feelings of the North, is a contrast that wrecks one's life."[1] In the "Germany" Madame de Staël says that Rousseau introduced an alien element into French literature, an element that is Northern and Germanic. Now the element that Madame de Staël conceived to be common to Rousseau and herself and at the same time to distinguish the Germans, manifests itself especially in the power of "enthusiasm." She is, then, not only temperamentally an enthusiast, but also an enthusiast by the direct influence of Rousseau as well as by the Rousseauism that she received from Germany.

The more we study the literary revolution at the beginning of the nineteenth century, the more it becomes plain that everything hinges on the word enthusiasm. The romantic movement in its modern phase is even

[1] Letter to Friederike Brun, July 15, 1806.

more a renascence of enthusiasm than a renascence of wonder, or rather wonder itself is only one aspect of the new enthusiasm. The process by which the word enthusiasm itself changed in the course of the eighteenth century from a bad to a good meaning, by which the enthusiast and original genius supplanted the wit and man of the world, is one of the most important in literary history and can scarcely be traced too carefully.

Illuminating passages on the nature of the new enthusiasm and at the same time on Madame de Staël's relationship to Rousseau will be found in her very youthful "Letters on the Writings and Character of Jean-Jacques Rousseau." "Is it not in our youth," she exclaims in the preface to that work, "that we owe the most gratitude to Rousseau, to the man who succeeded in making a passion of virtue, who wished to convince by enthusiasm and made use of the good qualities and even the faults of youth to render himself its master." Elsewhere she says that "he invented nothing but set everything afire"[1]—even to the point it would appear of setting virtue afire. Virtue thus becomes an involuntary impulse, a "noble enthusiasm," a "movement which passes into the blood and sweeps you along irresistibly like the most imperious passions."[2] In other words, for Madame de Staël as for Rousseau, virtue is a mere process of emotional expansion, related to the region of impulse below the reason rather than to the region of insight above it. Rousseau and his followers introduce universal

[1] *De la Littérature*, 1e Partie, c. xx.

[2] *Discours préliminaire de la Littérature.*

confusion into morality, as Joubert says, by thus conceiving of virtue not as a bridle but as a spur. Of Madame de Staël in particular, he said that she had a native ethical gift which was corrupted by her notion of enthusiasm. "She took the fevers of the soul for its endowments, intoxication for a power, and our aberrations for a progress. The passions became in her eyes a species of dignity and glory."[1]

It would not, however, be entirely fair to Madame de Staël to see in her conception of morality a mere Rousseauistic intoxication. The two ruling passions of her life were hatred of Napoleon and love for her father, and as she grew older she showed herself more and more not merely the daughter but the disciple of Necker. Both her rationalism and her emotionalism were tempered by the traditional views of morality and religion of the Swiss protestant. In her political thinking again, both on her own account and as a follower of her father, she departed from Rousseau in putting her chief emphasis on liberty. In the very passage where she says that Rousseau invented nothing but set everything afire, she goes on to say that "the sentiment of equality which produces many more storms than the love of liberty, and which causes questions to arise of a quite different order, — the sentiment of equality in its greatness as well as in its pettiness stands out in every line of Rousseau's writings." Rousseau was nearer to the French in this respect than Madame de Staël. In making the love of liberty the mainspring of the Revolution, she was

[1] *Pensées*, 387 (édition Paul de Raynal, 1866).

under more illusions about the French character than Napoleon, who knew that the deeper craving of the French was for equality, even equality under a despot.

Rousseauistic enthusiasm remains after all the essential aspect of Madame de Staël's genius. She differs however from many of the posterity of Jean-Jacques in being intellectually as well as emotionally expansive. In so far as she desired only expansiveness and refused either an inner or an outer check, she was unbalanced and did not escape the Nemesis that pursues every form of lack of balance, especially, perhaps, lack of emotional balance. Yet it may be said in her behalf that the half-truths on which she insisted were the half-truths that the age needed to hear, and that the excess by which she erred was — in spite of the charges of masculinity brought against her by her contemporaries[1] — the excess of the feminine virtues. She really had the largeness and generosity of outlook that her theory required, and hers was above all a magnificently hospitable nature. The welcome that she extended at Coppet to visitors from the ends of Europe symbolizes fitly the breadth of her intellectual hospitality. She was cosmopolitan not only in the influences she received but in those she radiated. As Napoleon complained, she taught people to think to whom it would never otherwise have occurred to do so.

[1] Madame de Staël was supposed to have portrayed herself in the character of Delphine and at the same time to have satirized Talleyrand in the character of Madame de Vernon; whereupon Talleyrand remarked that he understood she had written a novel in which both he and she appeared disguised as women.

II

Any one who conceives of life as expansively as did Madame de Staël, comes inevitably to be interested less in form than in expression. The partisan of form is fastidious and exclusive, whether his sense of form rests on a living intuition or on the acceptance of certain traditional standards. Now Madame de Staël almost entirely lacked the living intuition of form and had repudiated the traditional standards. She was led by her interest in expression to exalt the variable element in literature, to see it not absolutely but relatively; above all, as we have seen, to look on it as the expression of society and therefore as changing with it. Saint-Evremond had opposed a keen sense of historical relativity to the overweening faith of the age of Louis XIV in the fixity and finality of its own standards. But Madame de Staël did not get her historical sense from Saint-Evremond, so far as she may be said to have had one at all at the time of writing her book on Literature; it is rather a development of what is already in germ in Rousseau. For Rousseau, unhistorical as he was in many respects, treated one of the literary forms, the drama, from the relative and expressionistic point of view. In the "Letter to D'Alembert" he maintains that the only possible kind of play is the problem play; furthermore that the dramatist is not free to choose his problem, but has it imposed upon him by the taste of his country and time.[1] Thus the

[1] "A Londres, un drame intéresse en faisant haïr les Français; à Tunis la belle passion serait la piraterie ; à Messine, une vengeance bien savoureuse ; à Goa, l'honneur de brûler les Juifs."

"Œdipus Rex" did not succeed because of its absolute human appeal, but because it expressed the taste of an Athenian audience of the fifth century B.C. If it were put on the stage to-day it would infallibly fall flat. Curiously enough Saint-Evremond made precisely the same use of the same illustration, and both Saint-Evremond and Rousseau would seem to have been convicted of error by recent successful revivals of the Œdipus as an acting play.

The use of the historical method in the book on "Literature" is much obscured by the utterly unhistorical conception of perfectibility, that faith in a mechanical and rectilinear advance of the human race which so many people still hold naïvely, imagining themselves to be evolutionists. Madame de Staël assumes the superiority of Roman over Greek philosophy simply because it comes later. She was at least led in this way to suspect something of value in those mediæval centuries which La Harpe had dismissed as mere "chaos and night."

We find in the "Literature," along with many other passages that anticipate at least faintly the "Germany," the first form of the celebrated distinction between the two literatures, that of the North and that of the South (she does not however as yet apply to the former the epithet romantic). She shows the limitations both of her taste and of her historic sense when, after deriving the southern or Græco-Roman tradition ultimately from Homer, she seeks for the headwaters of the northern literatures in Ossian! This love of Ossian was one of the few things she had in common with Napoleon. She relates that when Talleyrand presented Bonaparte to the Directorate on his return from Italy, he assured them that General Bonaparte "detested luxury and display, wretched ambitions of ordinary spirits, and that he loved the poetry of Ossian, especially because it detaches one from the earth." She adds that the earth would not have asked anything better than to have him detach himself from it.[1]

But let us come to the more mature expression of Madame de Staël's views. Her "Germany" bears the marks not only of her travels in Italy, Austria, and Germany during the ten years that had elapsed since the publication of the "Literature" but also of important personal influences. We are told that the proper rule to follow in accounting for the ideas of a woman is, *Cherchez l'homme;* and we cannot entirely neglect this rule even in the case of Madame de Staël, the most intellectual of modern women. Heine complained that throughout the "Germany" he could hear with disagreeable distinctness the falsetto voice of August Wilhelm Schlegel. It is not surprising that with such a guide she not only gave undue attention to certain German romantic writers, but inclined to romanticize Germany in general. She was especially indignant at a phrase of the letter in which Savary, Duke of Rovigo, announced to her the confiscation of the "Germany" and her banishment: "Your last work is not French." Yet in a sense Savary was right. The Germany that she paints

[1] *Considérations sur la Révolution française*, c. XXVI.

becomes (somewhat like the Germania of Tacitus) a sort of Arcadia, against which the French corruption "sticks more fiery off." The book brought up before Heine the image of a "passionate woman eddying about like a whirlwind through our tranquil Germany, exclaiming everywhere delightedly, 'O how sweet is the peace that I breathe here!' She had got overheated in France and came among us to cool off. The chaste breath of our poets was so comforting to her boiling and fiery heart. She looked upon our philosophers as so many different kinds of ices; she sipped Kant like a vanilla sherbet and Fichte like a pistachio cream. 'O what a charming coolness reigns in your woods!' she kept constantly exclaiming; 'what a ravishing odor of violets! How peacefully the canary-birds twitter in their little German nests! You are good and virtuous; you have n't as yet any idea of the moral depravity that prevails among us in France in the rue du Bac!'"

This legend of an idyllic Germany, a land of sentimental dreamers and philosophers who refused to interest themselves in anything less than the universe,[1] survived in France to some extent until the rude awakening of 1870. To this nation of noble enthusiasts Madame de Staël opposes the drily analytical French. It is at bottom the same contrast that Coleridge and Carlyle elaborated in England. The German is not, like the Frenchman, imprisoned in the uninspired understanding (*Verstand*), but dwells in the region of the imaginative and synthetic reason (*Vernunft*). The psychological ele-

[1] *De l'Allemagne*, 1e Partie, c. XVIII.

ments of the opposition thus worked up into a fine metaphysical distinction, are already manifest in the quarrel between Rousseau the enthusiast, and Voltaire the mocking analyst. We are simply witnessing the international triumph of Rousseau over Voltaire. The closing pages of the "Germany" in which she exalts enthusiasm as the distinctive German virtue and at the same time warns the French against the spirit of cold reasoning and calculation are, as she herself says, the summing up of her whole work.[1] They are also, we are told, the pages that give the best idea of her actual conversation.[2]

Madame de Staël is really arguing against a social order the ultimate refinements of which were necessary, as we have seen, for her own happiness. In her whole attack on French society, its artificiality and conventionalism and its abuse of ridicule, in her charge that the spirit of imitation had killed spontaneity and enthusiasm, she simply repeats, often less tellingly, the arguments of Rousseau. "It is unbelievable," says Rousseau of the French, "to what a degree everything is stiff, precise and calculated in what they call the rules of etiquette. . . . Even if this people of imitators were full of originals it would be impossible to discover the fact, for no man dares to be himself. *You must do as other people do;* that is the first maxim in the wisdom of the country. . . . You might suppose they were so many marionettes nailed to the same board or pulled by the same

[1] *De l'Allemagne*, 4e Partie, c. XI.
[2] Sainte-Beuve : *Chateaubriand*, II, 188.

wire."[1] "An aristocratic power," Madame de Staël complained in turn, "good form and elegance, had triumphed over energy, depth, feeling, wit itself."[2] It had pronounced "an ostracism against everything strong and individual. These proprieties, slight in appearance and despotic at bottom, dispose of the whole of life; they have by degrees undermined love, enthusiam, religion, everything save egotism, that irony cannot touch because it exposes itself to censure and not to ridicule."[3] A certain conception of decorum, a "certain factitious grandeur not made for the human heart," as Rousseau had put it, always stood in the way of naturalness. "In the pictures and bas-reliefs in which Louis XIV is painted," says Madame de Staël, "at one time as Jupiter, at another as Hercules, he is represented as naked or clothed simply in a lion skin, but always with his big wig on his head."[4]

This idea of decorum, as Rousseau had already pointed out, had been especially fatal to naturalness in the drama (*la scène moderne ne quitte plus son ennuyeuse dignité*). "We rarely escape," says Madame de Staël in turn, "from a certain conventional nature which gives the same coloring to ancient as to modern manners, to crime as to virtue, to murder as to gallantry."[5] The pathway of escape from this pale conventionality is a more thorough study of history. "The natural tendency of the age is towards historical tragedy." If she had said

[1] *Nouvelle Héloïse*, 2e Partie, lettre XVII.

[2] *De l'Allemagne*, 1e Partie, c. XI.

[3] *Ibid.*, 1e Partie, c. IX.

[4] *Ibid.*, 2e Partie, c. XXXI.

[5] *Ibid.*, 2e Partie, c. XV.

towards historical melodrama, she would very nearly have proved herself a prophetess.

The weapon with which society punishes those who depart from its notions of decorum and good taste is ridicule. "In France," says Madame de Staël, "the memory of social proprieties pursues talent even into its most intimate emotions, and the fear of ridicule is the sword of Damocles that no festival of the imagination can make it forget."[1] The whole error arises from confounding taste in the literary with taste in the society sense. Madame de Staël therefore makes her main attack on "good taste," and its tendency to be merely negative and restrictive. Taste in the literary sense should get beyond petty fault-finding, based on rules and formal requirements, and become generous and comprehensive and appreciative. Taste in poetry derives from nature and like it should be creative.[2] The principles of this taste are therefore entirely different from those that depend on social relations. She relates how she attended at Vienna the public course of A. W. Schlegel and was "dumbfounded at hearing a critic eloquent as an orator, who far from attacking faults — the eternal food of jealous mediocrity — merely sought to revive creative genius." "Next to genius what is most like it is the power to know it and admire it."[3]

This is the message that the chief romantic critics of France, England and Germany managed to get uttered in some form or other at the beginning of the nine-

[1] *De l'Allemagne*, 2e Partie, c. IX. [2] *Ibid.*, 2e Partie, c. XIV.
[3] *Ibid.*, 2e Partie, c. XXXI.

teenth century. "The rules," says Madame de Staël, "are only barriers to keep children from falling." These barriers are to be set aside and no new restrictive principle is to be imposed on either critic or creator, whose rôles indeed are very much confounded. Genius is to be purely effusive and the critic, instead of serving as a check on genius, is only to enter sympathetically and comprehensively into its effusions.

One might suppose that such an expansive view both of taste and of genius would not stop short of pure impressionism. Since there is no norm that can set bounds to the creative writer in the unfolding of his originality or to the comprehension and sympathy with which the critic enters into this originality, taste would seem bound to become entirely fluid. Germany is as a matter of fact praised as the land where there is no taste in the French sense, and where every man is free to follow his own impressions.[1] Criticism, if it does not judge, may at least reveal the individual, and in this respect Madame de Staël anticipates Sainte-Beuve. "Each character," she says, "is almost a new world for any one who knows how to observe with finesse, and I am not acquainted in the science of the human heart with any general idea completely applicable to particular cases."[2] Sainte-Beuve for his part had such a predilection for Madame de Staël that she has been called the heroine of the "Lundis."

[1] *De l'Allemagne*, 2e Partie, c. I. [2] *Ibid.*, 4e Partie, c. VI.

III

Though Madame de Staël is interested in differences rather than identities, the differences that interest her most after all are not so much those between individuals as those between nationalities. To the claims of the French and the classicist to possess a monopoly of good taste, what she really opposes are the claims of national taste. "It is national taste alone," she says, "that can decide about the drama. We must recognize that if foreigners conceive of the art of the theatre differently from us, it is not through ignorance or barbarism but in accordance with deep reflections that are worthy of consideration."[1] Few persons have been more preoccupied than she with questions of national psychology. In Corinne, for example, we have not merely the conflict and interplay of different characters, but of different civilizations; and as usual the French do not show to advantage in contrast with other nationalities. Napoleon himself is said to have written the article in the "Moniteur" in which Madame de Staël is attacked for having made of the amiable but hopelessly superficial Comte d'Erfeuil the typical Frenchman.

Her conception of the relation of nationalities to one another simply reproduces on a larger scale the Rousseauistic conception of the proper relation of individuals. Each nationality is to be spontaneous and original and self-assertive, and at the same time infinitely open and hospitable to other national originalities. Nationalism in short is to be tempered by cosmopolitanism, and

[1] *De l'Allemagne*, 2e Partie, c. xv.

both are to be but diverse aspects of Rousseauistic enthusiasm. The first law for nationalities as for individuals is not to imitate but to be themselves. Thus Madame de Staël is indifferent to the work of Wieland because it seems to her less a native German product than a reflection of French taste (*l'originalité nationale vaut mieux*).[1] Having, however, made sure of its own originality each nation is then to complete itself by foreign borrowings. For example, "in order that the superior men of France and Germany may attain to the highest degree of perfection, the Frenchman must be religious and the German somewhat worldly. Piety is opposed to the dissipation of spirit which is the fault and grace of the French nation; the knowledge of men and society would give the Germans in literature the taste and dexterity they lack."[2] "The nations should serve as guides to one another. . . . There is something very strange in the difference between one people and another: the climate, the aspect of nature, language, government, finally and above all the events of history,— a power even more extraordinary than all others, — contribute to these diversities, and no man, however superior he may be, can guess what is developed naturally in the mind of the man who lives on another soil and breathes another air. It is well then in every country to welcome foreign thoughts, for this kind of hospitality brings fortune to him who exercises it."[3]

Madame de Staël thus appears as the ideal cosmopol-

[1] *De l'Allemagne*, 2e Partie, c. IV.
[2] *Ibid.*, 2e Partie, c. I.
[3] *Ibid.*, 2e Partie, c. XXXI.

itan, as the person who has perhaps done more than anyone else to help forward the comparative study of literature as we now understand it. But is there not something utopian in the whole conception, is there any adequate counterpoise to the inordinate emphasis that is placed on the centrifugal elements of originality and self-expression? When individual or national differences are pushed beyond a certain point what comes into play is not sympathy but antipathy. Madame de Staël admits that her cosmopolitanism is only for the few. The ordinary Frenchman and German, for instance, remind her in their relationship to one another of the fable of La Fontaine in which the stork cannot eat off the plate or the fox out of the long-necked bottle. It is not sure that even the few will have sufficient comprehension and sympathy to overleap the invisible barriers that are set up by individual and national idiosyncrasy. We hear of the tact needed by Madame de Staël to keep in check the antipathies that were quivering just beneath the surface in the international élite she had gathered together at Coppet. Between Schlegel and Sismondi, for example, there existed what Sainte-Beuve calls *une haine de race.*

A still better test of the theory is the meeting of Madame de Staël with Goethe and Schiller at Weimar, perhaps the best instance on record of ideal cosmopolitan contact. Crabb Robinson, who was at Weimar at this time, insinuated to Madame de Staël that she did not understand Goethe's poetry; whereupon her black eyes flashed and she replied, "I understand everything that deserves to be understood." As for Goethe and Schiller, the letters they exchanged with one another during her visit do not make altogether agreeable reading. Schiller denied her any sense for what Germans call poetry, declared it a sin against the Holy Ghost to speak even one word according to her dialect, was overwhelmed by her volubility, and felt when she finally left as though he were just recovering from a severe illness. Goethe complains that she had no idea of duty and wished to settle in a five minutes' conversation the kind of questions that should only be debated in the depths of a man's conscience between himself and God. Both are agreed that she took her departure none too soon. Later, enlightened by the publication of the "Germany," Goethe dilates on the importance of a meeting that seemed at the time, he admits, a mere surface play of personal and national antipathies: "That work on Germany which owed its origin to such social conversations must be looked on as a mighty implement, whereby in the Chinese wall of antiquated prejudices that separated us from France, a broad gap was broken; so that across the Rhine and in consequence of this across the Channel, our neighbors at last took closer knowledge of us; and now the whole remote West is open to our influences." [1]

IV

Possibly the most important chapter in the "Germany" [2] is that in which Madame de Staël takes up again

[1] *Annals*, 1804. Carlyle has collected the passages from Goethe and Schiller that bear on Madame de Staël's visit to Weimar in an appendix to the second volume of his critical essays.

[2] 2e Partie, c. XI.

her distinction between the literature of the South and that of the North and definitely describes the two traditions as classic and romantic, thus giving international currency to the application that the Schlegels had made of these epithets to two distinct literary schools. Classic had always passed as the norm of perfection. But Madame de Staël refuses to discuss the relative superiority of classic and romantic taste. "It is enough to show," she says, turning determinist for the moment, "that this diversity of tastes derives not only from accidental causes, but also from the primitive sources of imagination and thought."[1] She here appears as a disciple of Herder and the other German primitivists who had themselves merely elaborated the primitivism of Rousseau on a national scale. In true Rousseauistic fashion we are to advance by looking backward, we are to progress by reverting to origins; only in this way can we escape from the artificial and the imitative and recover the spontaneous and the original. Our choice is not between classic poetry and romantic poetry, "but between the imitation of the one and the inspiration of the other." "The literature of the ancients is among the moderns a transplanted literature, romantic or chivalrous literature is indigenous among us and has been produced by our religion and our institutions." Writers who imitate the ancients have to conform to strict rules because they cannot consult their own nature and memories, all the religious and political circumstances that gave rise to the ancient masterpieces having changed. "Poems im-

[1] *De l'Allemagne*, 2e Partie, c. XI.

itative of the antique are rarely popular because they are not related at present to anything national." Since popularity is to be the test of poetry, we are to look in estimating its worth, not merely backward but downward. "French poetry being the most classic of all modern poetries is the only one which is not diffused among the people, whereas the stanzas of Tasso are sung by the gondoliers of Venice, and the Spanish and Portuguese of all classes know by heart the verses of Calderon and Camoens," etc.

The truth in passages of this kind is of course mixed up with the usual sophistries of the primitivist. The chief Rousseauist venom of the whole point of view is found in the elimination of the aristocratic and selective element from the standard of taste, and in the assumption that the proper judges of poetry are the illiterate. Emerson says that we descend to meet. This is no doubt true of certain kinds of meeting, of the kind that takes place at an afternoon tea, let us say; and Emerson probably did not mean much more than this. But the phrase may evidently have another and, from the humanistic point of view, far more sinister meaning. Instead of disciplining himself to some form of perfection set above his ordinary self, a man sinks down from the intellectual to the instinctive level, on the ground that he is thus widening his human sympathies. Thus Tolstoy, whose book on art is indeed the *reductio ad absurdum* of Rousseauism, rejects Sophocles and Shakespeare because of their failure to make an immediate emotional appeal to the Russian peasant.

Moreover Madame de Staël, to judge from her choice

of examples, seems to be in some confusion as to the nature of popular poetry. It is not clear that Tasso is more "popular" than Boileau, whom Madame de Staël attacks as the extreme type of classic artificiality. Boileau himself says that many of his lines became proverbs at their birth. They still remain proverbs, whereas the verses of Tasso are no longer sung by the gondoliers of Venice. In general to look for poetry at all among gondoliers and the like is, under existing conditions, at least, to chase an Arcadian dream. For at the very time that one side of our civilization is sentimentalizing about the primitive, another side of this same civilization is just as surely killing it. At the present rate the poetry of the people, poetry that is spontaneous in the Rousseauistic sense, will soon have given way all over the world to the yellow journal or the equivalent.

The special type of mediævalism worked out by the German romanticists and diffused by Madame de Staël, that is the mediævalism that would have the European nations break with the classical tradition and return each to its own infancy, had its own value as a revolt against formalism. But it tended to get rid of form along with formalism. Recent research has shown more and more clearly that, wherever in the East or West, we find what the French call *le grand art*, art that rises above the merely decorative and renders the more essential aspects of human nature itself, we are dealing with some survival of the great Greek tradition of form. The man who turns away from the masterpieces of this tradition to study the "Nibelungenlied," or the "Chanson de Roland," or the Irish Sagas is running the risk, even when he is not blinded by national enthusiasm, of impairing his sense of form.

Moreover mediævalism is not only likely to involve a loss of form, but a loss of ideas. No amount of talk about the men of the Middle Ages being of our own blood and religion will alter the essential fact that the main movement of the modern mind has been away from the mediæval point of view. If we are seeking, not for some tower of ivory into which we may retire from the present, but for men who had problems similar to our own, we shall find these men in certain periods of classical antiquity. The Frenchman of to-day is nearer to Horace in his outlook on life than to the author of the "Chanson de Roland." An instructor in government recently said to me that the most *modern* book on his subject was Aristotle's "Politics." This may prove that we are becoming pagans again, but we are not going to alter the fact by romantic dreaming.

To be sure, the mediæval primitivists, though they have rarely shone as men of ideas, have been in many cases not merely romantic dreamers, but also precise investigators, and in this way they have related themselves to one side of the modern spirit. I once asked a young American mediævalist what his chosen period actually meant for him. A rapt expression came into his eyes and he replied that for him the Middle Ages were all a beautiful dream. To judge, however, by what he actually published one would suppose rather that they were an unusually dry philological fact. And this is unfair to the Middle Ages. For if the romantic mediævalist by his delvings into the popular and the primitive has cut himself off in large measure from modern thought, he has also cut himself off, in at least an equal degree, from the thought of the Middle Ages. The works (mainly in Latin) in which this thought is to be found are not in the least popular or primitive or national, in Madame de Staël's sense,[1] but derive along manifold lines from Greece and Rome and Judæa.

This literature that expressed the mind of the Middle Ages was in the highest degree cosmopolitan, but cosmopolitan in the older and what may turn out to be the only genuine sense, — that is, it rested primarily on a common discipline and not on a common sympathy. Renan, who in his conception of the ideal relations between France and Germany, is perhaps the most distinguished of Madame de Staël's French followers, dreams of an international fraternity of savants, "an empyrean of pure ideas, a heaven in which there is neither Greek nor barbarian, neither German nor Latin." Saint Paul in the passage that Renan is here paraphrasing says that these and like distinctions disappear for those who have become "one in Christ." Now Christ, for Saint Paul, is evidently the living intuition of a law that is set above the ordinary self; by taking on the yoke of this law men are drawn together as to a common centre. Renan's notion that simply by collaborating in the expansion of scientific knowledge men can achieve the union that,

[1] In this sense Renan says that "le sentiment des nationalités n'a pas cent ans." (*Réforme intellectuelle*, 194.)

according to Saint Paul, is only to be achieved by spiritual concentration, may turn out to be utopian; and it is the fate of the utopist to suffer sudden and severe disillusions. Renan had his disillusion in 1870. He expected the new Christ to come from Germany, as some one has put it, and instead he got Bismarck. He was pained to see how fiercely German national sentiment blazed up in scholars whom he had regarded as being before all scientific internationalists, and how mercilessly they gloated over the downfall of France. On the other hand, many a Frenchman who had been indulging like Sully Prudhomme in humanitarian effusions, suddenly awoke in 1870 as from a dream and found that his love of mankind was as naught compared with his love of his own land.[1] "Let us suppress these unhealthy outbursts of national self-love," cries Renan. But in the name of what principle? In a crisis, the altruistic impulse either towards other individuals or towards other nations is likely to seem to most men pale and unsubstantial compared with the putting forth of personal or national power.

The modern cosmopolitan is to be blamed not for de-

[1] "'Mon compatriote, c'est l'homme!
Naguère ainsi je dispersais
Sur l'univers ce cœur français:
J'en suis maintenant économe.

. . . .

Ces tendresses, je les ramène
Etroitement sur mon pays,
Sur les hommes que j'ai trahis
Par amour de l'espèce humaine," etc.
(*Repentir.*)

veloping on a magnificent scale the virtues of expansion but for setting up these virtues as a substitute for the virtues of concentration. He would have us believe that every man can fly off on his own tangent, and then in some mysterious manner, known only to romantic psychology, become every other man's brother; and that the same process can be repeated on the national scale. There may after all be something in the traditional idea that in order to come together men need to take on the yoke of a common discipline. But the procedure of the Rousseauist is always to get rid of law or discipline on the ground that it is artificial or conventional, and to set up in its stead some enthusiasm or sympathy. Madame de Staël and the romanticists were strong in their attacks on formalism, but in discarding the idea of law itself along with the conventionalities in which it had got embedded they were almost incredibly weak. They are at least equally weak in the various sentimental sophistries and pseudo-mystical devices to which they resorted to prove to themselves and others that it is possible to have one's cake and eat it too, in other words, to have the virtues of centrality while in the very process of flying off from the centre.

As I have already said, there is something of this romantic sophistry in Madame de Staël's idea that a true cosmopolitanism may rest solely on the rounding out of national originality with international comprehension and sympathy. To stop at this stage is simply to dodge the more difficult half of the problem. It is excellent to be internationally comprehensive and sympathetic, but only as a preparation for being internationally selective. Few moments are more perilous for a country than the moment when it escapes from its narrow traditional discipline and becomes cosmopolitan. Unless some new discipline intervenes to temper the expansion, cosmopolitanism may be only another name for moral disintegration. Nations no less than individuals, as history tells us only too plainly, may descend to meet. Their contact with one another may result not in that ideal exchange of virtues of which Madame de Staël dreamed, but in an exchange of vices. A French traveller relates that on penetrating to a remote hill town in India he found on the mantel-piece of the only room for the use of Europeans in the local club "a collection of French books for exportation, all that frightful literature by which foreigners judge us." On somewhat the same principle the programme of the Moulin Rouge was recently posted about the streets of Paris in five languages. One touch of lubricity, as some one has put it, makes the whole world kin. A man may become cosmopolitan like young Grandet in Balzac, who travelled so much and saw so many standards of morality in different countries that he finally lost all standards himself and became a profligate. Madame de Staël was herself well aware of the danger of an indefinite widening out of one's horizons. "To see everything and understand everything," she says, "is a great cause of uncertainty."[1] *L'étendue même des conceptions nuit à la décision du caractère.*[2]

But what is the value of a breadth that has been

[1] *De l'Allemagne*, 1e Partie, c. II. [2] *Ibid.*, 4e Partie, c. X.

gained at the expense of judgment and lacks sufficient counterpoise in character? True cosmopolitanism, it would appear, like almost everything else that is worth having, is a mediation between extremes. We may have universal contact as at present, and an international confederacy of scientists, and plenty of persons who, in Rousseau's phrase, are ready "to embrace the whole of mankind in their benevolence," and yet we may fall short of being true cosmopolitans because there is still lacking the centripetal force, the allegiance to a common standard, that can alone prevail against the powers of individual and national self-assertion. "The pathway of modern culture," says Grillparzer, "leads from humanity, through nationality, to bestiality." Long before this final stage is reached there may be a sharp reaction from the half-truths of the Rousseauist.

V

The unit of Madame de Staël's thinking, it should be observed, is the nation and not the race. The nation as she conceives it, though she is not specially clear or consistent on this point, is not so much a mere product of environment as a sort of spiritual entity, a body of men united by common memories and achievements and aspiring to common ends. The idea of race is evidently much more naturalistic, and, as treated by many writers, has become almost zoölogical. No one would of course deny the importance of the racial factor, but the attempts that have been made to formulate it accurately have been curiously unsatisfactory. The endless theorizing that has gone on about race during the past century may indeed be seen in the retrospect to have been the happy hunting-ground of the pseudo-scientist. And this pseudo-science is often used to produce a sort of emotional intoxication that may take the form either of exultation at one's own superiority or else of contempt for the (supposedly) inferior breeds. It gives a man a fine expansive feeling to think that he is endowed with certain virtues simply because he has taken the trouble to be born a Celt or a Teuton or an Anglo-Saxon. What an exhilaration, for example, Fichte's audience must have felt when he told them that there was no special word for "character" in German because to be a German and to have character were synonymous. The Germans were an *Urvolk*, the elect not of God but of nature; and so character instead of having to be painfully acquired gushed up from the primordial depths of their being.[1]

Fichte speaks as a primitivist, and there is a clear connection between primitivism and modern determinism. Though Madame de Staël was also a primitivist, and although she felt the force of the deterministic argument as based especially, perhaps, on the influence of climate and of the historical "moment,"[2] she nevertheless shrank from accepting it. She admits that "no one can change the primitive data of his birth, his country, his age," etc.[3] Yet she is loath to admit that "circumstances create us

[1] "Charakter haben und deutsch sein ist ohne Zweifel gleichbedeutend, und die Sache hat in unsrer Sprache keinen besondern Namen, weil sie eben ohne alles unser Wissen und Besinnung aus unserm Sein unmittelbar hervorgehen soll" (*Reden an die deutsche Nation*, XII).

[2] Cf. p. 19 [3] *De l'Allemagne*, 4e Partie, c. v.

what we are." "If outer objects are the cause of everything that takes place in our soul, what independent thought would emancipate us from their influence? The fatality which descended from heaven filled the soul with a sacred terror, whereas that which binds us to the earth only degrades us."[1] This distinction between the psychological effects of the two types of fatality, that of Calvin, let us say, and that of Taine, would seem to be confirmed by the naturalistic novel and other developments in France and elsewhere during the second half of the nineteenth century.

The influence of Madame de Staël at home and abroad would require a separate study. Wherever this influence made itself felt, as in Italy for example,[2] it stimulated national sentiment, on the one hand, and on the other, undermined pseudo-classic formalism, especially in the drama. The French romanticists had rather a slender stock of ideas, but for such ideas as they had they drew largely on Madame de Staël. Hugo does not mention her in the "Préface de Cromwell," but the relationship between the "Germany" and this manifesto of romanticism can be easily established.

Madame de Staël's influence in both France and Italy is associated with that of another critic who was in some respects her disciple and who acted upon her in turn —

[1] *De l'Allemagne*, 3e Partie, c. I.

[2] This Italian influence is perhaps, however, overstated by Texte when he says of her visit to Italy: "Elle rencontra alors Confalonieri, apôtre de l'indépendance, et écrivit dans la *Biblioteca italiana* un article retentissant qui suscita le mouvement romantique italien" (Julleville's *Hist. de la Lit. fr.*, VII, 709–710).

Claude Fauriel, the friend and admirer of Manzoni. Perhaps no one did more than Fauriel for the establishment of the new scholarship in France at the beginning of the nineteenth century. Sainte-Beuve calls him the "secret initiator of most of the distinguished spirits of this time in literary method and criticism."[1] (I speak elsewhere of Fauriel's influence on Sainte-Beuve himself.) Fauriel covered a territory that would nowadays be divided among at least a score of specialists — Sanskrit, Provençal, early Italian, Basque, Celtic dialects, etc. He had a truly Rousseauistic passion for the primitive (we are told that among plants he preferred the mosses). The unconscious felicities of instinct appealed to him more than any form of deliberate art. In this sense we may say with Sainte-Beuve that he was the "most anti-academic mind by vocation that had ever appeared in France."[2] He was in fact a sort of French Herder, less enthusiastic and less enamored of general ideas, but with more scholarly precision. Yet though he was, as Sainte-Beuve estimates, twenty years ahead of his times, though he began most of the distinctively modern forms of investigation, he did not at any moment break abruptly with the past. He marks the gradual transition from the point of view of the eighteenth to that of the nineteenth century.[3]

[1] *Portraits contemporains*, IV, 127. [2] *Ibid.*, 232. [3] *Ibid.*, 178.

II

JOUBERT

If Madame de Staël is the best type of the Rousseauistic enthusiast at the beginning of the nineteenth century we have in Joubert the representative of a very different kind of enthusiasm, the enthusiasm that may be associated with Plato rather than with Rousseau. The sharpness of the contrast between the Platonist and the Rousseauist may be inferred from Joubert's very severe judgment on Madame de Staël which I have already quoted (p. 8). He writes in one of his letters that he had "avoided seeing her a thousand times and looked on her as a fatal and pernicious being."[1] Yet when she died and the news of her death had been received with general silence and indifference, in strange contrast to the tumult in which she had lived, one of those most sincerely moved was Joubert. "The clouding over of such a reputation," he writes, "really afflicted me, and when I saw that no one was willing to think of this poor woman, I began to think of her all by myself and to regret with inconsolable bitterness the misuse she had made of so much intellect, energy and goodness."[2]

[1] *Cor.*, 237. My references are to Paul de Raynal's edition in two volumes (4e éd., 1866). In the volume containing the *Pensées*, no numbers are used in the opening chapter ("L'auteur peint par lui-même"). The thoughts are arranged by subjects in the following numbered chapters, which are therefore called "Titres."

[2] *Ibid.*

So far as the general public was concerned Joubert himself lived in entire obscurity, more "enamored," in his own phrase, "of perfection than of glory." Yet he was singularly fortunate both in the friendships he enjoyed during his lifetime and the kind of reputation he has had since his death. His "Pensées" were presented to French readers by Chateaubriand and Sainte-Beuve, and to English readers by Matthew Arnold in one of the best critical essays ever written in English.[1] The literary "Pensées" show such a fine quality of critical insight that Joubert has come to be regarded as the critics' critic much as Spenser has been called the poets' poet. He has that gift of ornate conciseness which he himself declared to be the supreme beauty of style. It is not, however, his phrase that he polishes, he says, but his idea; "I wait until the drop of light that I need is formed and falls from my pen."[2] His ambition was so to express the exquisite as to give it general currency. Now it is not easy to imagine a continuous discourse made up entirely of the exquisite and we are not surprised when Joubert says he is unfitted for continuous discourse. "I lack intermediary ideas."[3] His saying that sages do not compose reminds one of Emerson's description of the sentences in his own essays as infinitely repellent particles.

The danger for a critic who aims solely at the exquisite or in his own phrase at "expressing the inexpress-

[1] I am assuming a familiarity with this essay on the part of the reader and have as a rule avoided translating the same *Pensées*.

[2] *Pensées*, p. 10.

[3] *Ibid.*, p. 8.

ible "[1] and who lacks intermediary ideas, is that he may become affected and obscure, and Joubert does not altogether avoid these penalties of oversubtlety. "To reach the regions of light," he says, "one must pass through the clouds."[2] Unfortunately Joubert does not always disengage himself from the clouds. But personally, I should not agree with those critics who prefer his "Letters" to the "Thoughts" because of their greater simplicity and naturalness. The "Letters," however, do reveal one essential side of Joubert far more completely than the "Thoughts." They are pervaded by a fine vein of whimsical humor, an habitual sportiveness, that suggests to Sainte-Beuve a comparison with Charles Lamb. It seemed to Joubert an important part of wisdom to distinguish the very few things that are to be taken seriously and then to take all other things playfully. *En tout il me faut quelque jeu.*[3] He is at the opposite pole from those "serious and gloomy spirits who have very futile doctrines"; a sentence that inevitably calls to mind many modern reformers.

Possibly the danger of a sort of transcendental *préciosité* in Joubert appears most clearly in some of his thoughts on religion. He recognizes the existence of matter only by courtesy. If the Creator withdrew his breath from the world, he says, it would "become what it was before time, a grain of flattened metal, an atom in the void, even less than this: a mere nothing."[4] Another sage of whom Joubert frequently reminds one,

[1] *Cor.*, 20. [2] Tit. I, XC. [3] *Cor.*, 119. [4] Tit. I, XIII.

does not feel that he can dispose of matter quite so lightly. "I can reason down or deny everything," says Emerson, "except this perpetual Belly: feed he must and will, and I cannot make him respectable." One is tempted to say that in both the literal and figurative sense, Joubert lacked body. He himself admitted the justness of Madame de Châtenay's remark that he seemed a pure spirit who had stumbled on a body by chance and made the best he could of it.

Though we can detect in Joubert something of the shrinking of the valetudinarian from the rough and tumble of life, we cannot insist too strongly that his spirituality is true spirituality and not the Rousseauistic imitation. The words that he traced almost with his dying hand really sum up the effort of his whole life: "22 March, 1824. The true, the beautiful, the just, the holy!" He is far removed from a man like Coleridge who retired from his actual obligations into a cloud of opium and German metaphysics. The contrast between Coleridge's speculations and his daily practice recalls Joubert's thought, "Religion is neither a theology nor a theosophy; it is more than all that: a discipline, a law, a yoke, an indissoluble engagement."[1] Though one of the frailest of invalids, Joubert never failed to meet the demands of life. He was justified in saying of himself, "Behind the strength of many men there is weakness, whereas behind my weakness there is strength; the weakness is in the instrument."[2] His fellow-citizens in the little town of Montignac where he

[1] Tit. I, LXII.
[2] *Pensées*, p. 8.

was born elected him justice of the peace and long preserved, we are told, the memory of his efficiency.

Sainte-Beuve does not seem to me to strike quite the right note of praise when he says that "once to have known one of these divine spirits (like Joubert) who seem the living definition of the phrase of the poet: *divinae particulam aurae*, is to be forever disgusted with all that is not fine, delicate, delectable; with all that is not perfume and pure essence; it is to prepare for oneself assuredly many annoyances and misfortunes."[1] This passage suggests too strongly that Joubert was too good for human nature's daily food, whereas he was one of the shrewdest and most practical of men. He even pushed too far his horror of the merely speculative when he said you can learn more of the art of government from a single page of Machiavelli's "Prince" than from the whole of Montesquieu's "Spirit of Laws."[2]

The danger of Joubert's avowed dislike for mere reality, *l'affreuse réalité*, as he calls it, is not so much a romantic retreat into the tower of ivory as an undue sympathy for certain conceptions of the noble style and the grand manner. He says in defending Corneille that we should rise above the trivialities of earth even if we have to mount on stilts.[3] His attitude towards the opposite school of art appears in his remark that the novels

[1] *Chateaubriand*, II, 138.

[2] As an example of his courage and good sense see his letter to Fontanes, then Grand Master of the University, in which he protests against the poor pay of teachers and professors (*Cor.* 217).

[3] Tit. XXIV, V, VII.

of Lesage "seem to have been written in a coffee-house by a player of dominoes just after leaving the theatre."[1]

Joubert's shrinking from *l'affreuse réalité* is also to be connected with the fact that he had lived through the Reign of Terror. "The Revolution," he says, "drove my spirit from the real world by making it too horrible for me."[2] "Revolutions are times when the poor man is not sure of his probity, the rich man of his fortune and the innocent man of his life."[3]

Joubert as a young man had come into contact with Diderot and had got the initiation into the new critical spirit that such a contact implies. But even without the Revolution Joubert would never have been a thorough-going modern. The ancients, he says, were appealed to by the magic of the past and not like the moderns by the magic of the future,[4] and he was in this respect a true ancient. The French are wont, rightly for the most part, to call their reactionaries "haters of things new" (*misonéistes*); but the epithet that should be applied to Joubert is the more gracious Greek, — "lover of things old" (φιλάρχαιος). "The great drawback of the new books," he says, "is that they keep us from reading the old ones."[5]

What the eighteenth century wanted, according to Joubert, was not religious liberty, but irreligious liberty.[6] It was for discarding as mere prejudice everything that did not make itself immediately intelligible either to

[1] Tit. XXXII. [2] *Pensées*, p. 4. [3] Tit. XVI, LIX.
[4] *Ibid.*, XVII, I. [5] Tit. XVIII, LVII. [6] *Ibid.*, XVIII, XIII.

reason or feeling. "My discoveries, and every one has his own," he says, "have brought me back to prejudices."[1] "Our reformers have said to experience: thou art a dotard, and to the past: thou art a child."[2] The other extreme towards which Joubert himself inclines is to impose the past too despotically on the present. Though he vivifies tradition with insight, more perhaps than any other French reactionary, he is nevertheless too resolutely traditional.[3] Such has been the revolutionary stress of the past hundred years that it has rarely failed to disturb the poise even of the most finely tempered spirits. Joubert tends to see only the benefits of order just as Emerson tends to see only the benefits of emancipation.

In the name of what he conceives to be order, he would be too ready to deliver society over to the Jesuits and fix it in a sort of hieratic immobility. He sees our main modern misfortune in what Emerson regards as our main modern gain. "Unhappy epochs," he exclaims, "when every man weighs everything by his own weight, and walks, as the Bible says, by the light of his own lamp";[4] when the broad communications that formerly existed with heaven are broken and every one has to build his private ladder.[5] Indeed the more leading-strings the better, if it be true, as he asserts, that "few are worthy of experience, most allow themselves to be corrupted by it."[6]

[1] *Pensées*, p. 4. [2] Tit. XVIII, XX.

[3] "Aux Grecs, et surtout aux Athéniens, le beau littéraire et civil; aux Romains, le beau moral et politique; aux Juifs, le beau religieux et domestique; aux autres peuples, l'imitation de ces trois-là" (Tit. XVII, XIII).

[4] Tit. XVIII, V. [5] *Ibid.*, XIV. [6] *Ibid.*, XVI, XIII.

Joubert is of course consistent in his severe handling of the two great leaders of eighteenth century thought, Voltaire and Rousseau. He can, to be sure, imagine good coming from a reformed Rousseau, but can conceive of no circumstances in which a Voltaire would be of any profit.[1] "Voltaire," he says, "would have read patiently thirty or forty folio volumes to find in them one little irreligious jest. That was his passion, his ambition, his mania."[2] Yet in the final analysis the irreligion of Voltaire is a less insidious danger than the pseudo-religion of Rousseau. "I speak to tender, to ardent, to lofty spirits, to spirits born with one of these distinctive characteristics of religion, and I say to them: Only J. J. Rousseau can detach you from religion and nothing but religion can cure you of J. J. Rousseau."[3]

If Joubert leans too much to the side of reaction in his politics and religion he preserves in the main a remarkable poise in his literary opinions. He was placed between an age that had been rational in a way to discredit the reason and an age that was going to be imaginative in a way to discredit the imagination. He protests against the excess of the past and utters a warning against the excess that was to come. Yet nothing would give a falser notion of Joubert's work than to look on it primarily as a warning or a protest, or upon his rôle as only negative and restrictive. For the French he is not merely the author of the "Pensées" but, along with Fontanes, the literary mentor of Chateaubriand.

[1] Tit. XXIV, XXXVIII. [2] *Ibid.*, XXV. [3] *Ibid.*, L.

Now of these two "guardian angels" of Chateaubriand, as Sainte-Beuve calls them, Joubert was the one who inspired and encouraged, whereas Fontanes was rather inclined to caution and hold back. In his attacks on formalism, in his plea for hospitality of mind and feeling, Joubert had his face turned towards the future. *Ayons le cœur et l'esprit hospitaliers* — this one phrase sums up about all that is legitimate in the new criticism.

The eighteenth century had wrought harm to poetry, partly by imposing a mechanical imitation, partly by the abuse of rationalism. Joubert is constantly vindicating the claims of the imagination against both the formalists and the rationalists. "Nothing that does not enrapture is poetry; the lyre is so to speak a winged instrument."[1] No view of life is sound that lacks imaginative wholeness. "Whatever we think, we must think with our whole selves, soul and body,"[2] and above all avoid one-sidedness. "Man is an immense being in some sort, who may exist partially but whose existence is delectable in proportion as it becomes full and complete."[3] It would not be easy to find an utterance more satisfying than this from the point of view of the humanist. Above all Joubert is severe upon the one-sided intellectualists (and here again his animus against the eighteenth century appears). Philosophers fall into unreality from "confounding what is spiritual with what is abstract."[4] He warns us to distrust words in philosophical books that "have not become generally current and are fit

[1] Tit. XXI, IX.
[2] *Ibid.*, IX, LII.
[3] *Ibid.*, V, LVII.
[4] *Ibid.*, XII, VI.

only to form a special dialect."[1] "How many people become abstract in order to appear profound! Most abstract terms are shadows concealing voids."[2] Philosophy should "have a Muse and not be a mere reasoning shop."[3]

Joubert, it should be added, was himself a man of wide philosophical reading. He was one of the first Frenchmen to make a thorough study of Kant, whom he read in the Latin translation — "a German Latin," he writes Madame de Beaumont, "as hard as pebbles." Getting at Kant's ideas is like cracking ostrich eggs with one's head and then most often finding nothing in them.[4] "A man," Joubert remarks, "may sprain his mind as well as his body," and he seems to have suffered a sort of intellectual sprain from reading this Latin translation of Kant. His final judgment on Kant is that he was intellectual where he should have been intuitive and so "missed the true measure of all things."[5]

Joubert, according to Chateaubriand, wanted his philosophy to be at the same time painting and poetry. A philosophical thought, as Joubert believed, when it got thoroughly matured lost its abstract rawness, as it were, and took on atmosphere, form, sound, light, color. Possibly his unwillingness to speak abstractly, even when abstraction is plainly indicated, is responsible for the somewhat over-luxuriant metaphor, the effect of *pré-*

[1] Tit. XII, XXV. [2] *Ibid.*, XII, XXXII. [3] *Ibid.*, VI. [4] *Cor.*, 62.

[5] He goes on to say that "la mesure de toutes choses est *l'immobile* pour le *mobile*, *l'infini* pour le *limité*, le *même* pour le *changeant*, *l'éternel* pour le *passager*," etc. (*Cor.*, p. 61). For his views of Kant see also *Pensées*, Tit. XXIV, XVII–XIX.

ciosité, that I have already noted in some of the "Thoughts." He seems very modern in his insistence that words should not be treated as mere algebraic signs after the fashion of the eighteenth century, that they should not be robbed, so to speak, of their aura of suggestiveness. He felt and encouraged the subtle emotional interplay and blending of the different arts that was to figure so largely in the romantic movement. "Beautiful verses," to quote one of his many utterances on this subject, "are exhaled like sounds and perfumes," [1] and this should seem good doctrine to a follower of Verlaine. "We should not portray objects," to cite another advanced saying, "but our feelings about objects"; [2] and this should satisfy even a post-impressionist.

But Joubert was careful to follow his own rule and never utter a truth without at the same time putting forth its complementary truth.[3] He did not, like so many moderns, go mad over the powers of suggestiveness. After speaking of *nous qui chantons avec des pensées et peignons avec des paroles*,[4] after saying that when "you understand a word perfectly, it becomes, as it were, transparent, you see its color and form, you feel its weight," etc., he admits that the main thing in a word is not its color or its music, but its meaning; and that when words are so chosen and arranged as to express the meaning most clearly, they are likely also to seem the most harmonious.[5] "What is wanted," he says, "is not merely the poetry of images but the poetry

[1] Tit. XXI, XXV. [2] *Ibid.*, XXIII, LXXVII. [3] *Ibid.*, XI, XVIII.
[4] *Ibid.*, XXII, LXXIV. [5] *Ibid.*, XXII, XXIX.

of ideas."[1] "When the image masks the object, and you make of the shadow a body, when expression gives such pleasure that you no longer tend to pass beyond, to penetrate to the meaning, when the figure in fine absorbs the whole of your attention, you are held up on the way and the road is taken for the goal, because a bad guide is conducting you."[2] This hits severely many of the French romanticists, Gautier certainly, and I should not hesitate to add, Hugo.

Unfortunately the French romanticists could scarcely have agreed with Joubert about the goal of poetry, for their enthusiasm was not like his, Platonic, but Rousseauistic, that is, they sought to escape from abstraction, not by rising above the ordinary intellectual level, but by sinking beneath it; and so the romantic movement turned in the main not to the legitimate revival of the imagination that Joubert desired, but to the glorification of an unchecked spontaneity. Joubert's actual use of the word enthusiasm might be made the subject of an interesting study. To what often goes by that name he applies some other word —*passion*, *verve*, *entrailles*, or the like. True enthusiasm in his sense is not associated with heat and movement as in Madame de Stael, but with light and serenity,[3] and might best be defined, says Sainte-Beuve, as "exalted peace." And so Joubert reserves the word for the great poets, the saints and the sages. He speaks, for example, of the enthusiasm of Virgil.

Perhaps the difference between the two types of en-

[1] Tit. XXI, XXIII. [2] *Ibid.*, XXII, CX. [3] *Ibid.*, XXIII, CVIII.

thusiasts, the Platonist and the Rousseauist, comes out most clearly in the use they would make of imaginative illusion. Joubert is nowhere more original than in his ideas about the rôle of illusion in life and art. Here if anywhere he justifies his boast that he is more Platonic than Plato (*Platone platonior*). He defends art and literature against Plato by arguments that are themselves highly Platonic. The artist should not be satisfied with copying the objects of sense, for in that case his works would fall under Plato's censure of being at two removes from reality, mere "shadows of a shadow world." He should, on the contrary, so use the objects of sense as to adumbrate a higher reality; so as to produce a cast, a hollow cast as it were, of a heavenly archetype.[1] Now this adumbration of a higher reality can only be achieved by the medium of imaginative illusion. By imaginative illusion communication may be established between the reality of sense and the reality of spirit. We may be made to "imagine souls by the means of bodies."[2] "Heaven, seeing that there were many truths which by our nature we could not know, and which it was to our interest, nevertheless, not to be ignorant of, took pity on us and granted us the faculty of imagining them."[3] We can perceive the truth in this sense

[1] Tit. XXI, II.

[2] Tit. XX, XLV. Joubert distinguishes sharply between *l'imagination*, an active and creative faculty, the sole intermediary between intellect and spirit, and possessed in a high degree only by the gifted individual; and *l'imaginative*, a sub-rational and passive faculty, that may manifest itself very strongly in children, timid people, etc. See Tit. III, XLVI–LII.

[3] *Cor.*, 85.

only through a veil of illusion, and it is the grace of the truth to be thus veiled.[1] This intimate blending of illusion and wisdom is the charm of life and of art.[2] "God deceives us perpetually and wishes us to be deceived; and when I say that he deceives us," Joubert adds, "I mean by illusions and not by frauds."[3] Illusion thus conceived becomes an integral part of reality,[4] and we must not strive to see anything in its nakedness; —*il ne faut rien voir tout nu.*[5]

There are evidently two extremes, that of Dean Swift, for example, who would tear all the veils from human nature and look on it without illusion, and that of Rousseau who would take the illusion and leave the reality (at least as Joubert would understand this word). In both cases the end was misanthropy. A comparison might indeed be made between Swift and Rousseau so as to illustrate in a curious way the maxim that extremes meet.

Joubert has remarks of extraordinary penetration not only on the right use of imaginative illusion, but on its misuse by the Rousseauists, on what one may call the false illusion of decadence. If Rousseau did not relate illusion to the reality of spirit, he did relate it in a way to the reality of sense; he used it to throw a sort of glamour over earthly impulse, especially the master impulse of sex.[6] In his attitude towards this master impulse, Joubert not only departs from Rousseau, but is one of the least Gallic of Frenchmen. "By chastity," he says,

[1] Tit. XI, XXXVI.

[2] Tit. IX, V. Cf. Tit. XX, X and Tit. XXIII, CXV.

[3] *Cor.*, 125. [4] Tit. XI, XXXIX. [5] Tit. XXI, XXI.

[6] I have treated this topic more fully in *The New Laokoon*, ch. V.

"the soul breathes a pure air in the most corrupt places, by continence it is strong whatever may be the state of the body; it is royal by its empire over the senses; it is fair by its light and peace."[1] Reason may suffice for ordinary virtues, according to Joubert, but religion alone can make us chaste.[2]

Bernardin de Saint-Pierre not only exalted passion *à la Rousseau*, says Joubert, but threw a pseudo-idealistic glamour over the whole of nature. The result is a sort of "ecstatic epicureanism, a gravely Anacreontic morality."[3] "There is in the style of Bernardin de Saint-Pierre a prism that wearies the eyes; when you have read him a long time you are charmed to see that verdure and trees are less highly colored in the country than in his writings. His harmonies make us love the dissonances that he banished from the world and that you find in it at every step. Nature, it is true, has its music; but luckily it is rare. If reality offered the melodies that these gentlemen find everywhere you would live in an ecstatic languor and die in a swoon."[4]

A question of some delicacy presents itself,—how did Joubert deal with the Rousseauism of Chateaubriand? "When my friends have only one eye," says Joubert, "I look at them in profile."[5] But it is plain that criticism did not lose its rights even in the case of his friends. "Chateaubriand," he says, "has given to the passions an innocence they do not have, or that they have only once. In 'Atala' the passions are covered

[1] Tit. V, CX. [2] *Ibid.*, CXII. [3] Tit. XXIV, LXVI.
[4] *Ibid.*, LXVII. [5] *Pensées*, p. 2.

with long white veils."[1] The letter that he wrote to Molé[2] about the character of Chateaubriand is a masterpiece of psychological analysis. In this letter Joubert anticipates some of the severest judgments of Sainte-Beuve, and at the same time contrives to seem not only amiable but affectionate. Joubert is not in the least a "beautiful soul" in the romantic sense with all the flabbiness that the phrase implies. We are asked to accept about everything nowadays on the ground that otherwise we shall show ourselves narrow and unsympathetic. "I love few pictures," Joubert replies, "few operas, few statues, few poems, and yet I am a great lover of the arts."

In other words, sympathy must be ideally combined with selection, which means in practice that expansion must be tempered by concentration, that vital impulse must be submitted to vital control. When Joubert was told that a great many passions are required in literature, "Yes," he replied, "a great many *restrained* passions."[3] I have already quoted his charge that Rousseau ruined morality by turning the conscience itself into a passion, by making it not a bridle but a spur; and Joubert adds that "taste is the literary conscience of the soul."[4] Now taste, like most other desirable things, is dualistic in its nature, is a mediation between extremes; but the selective and restrictive aspect of taste that Jou-

[1] *Pensées*, p. 393.

[2] *Cor.*, 106 ff. Sainte-Beuve says of this letter that "la psychologie de Chateaubriand y est coulée à fond." (*Chateaubriand*, II, 396); cf. also *Nouveaux Lundis*, III, 11.

[3] Tit. XXIII, CXXXI.

[4] *Ibid.*, XXIII, CXLVII.

bert emphasizes is not only the most important in itself, but it is the aspect which the moderns from Rousseau to Signor Croce have most persistently neglected and denied. We have seen that Madame de Staël tended to identify genius with taste, and to make both purely expansive. Joubert inclines rather to the extreme of concentration. "If there is a man," he writes, "tormented by the accursed ambition to put a whole book in a page, a whole page in a phrase, and that phrase in a word, it is I." [1] "The ancient critics said: *Plus offendit nimium quam parum.* We have almost inverted this maxim by bestowing praise on every form of abundance." [2] Joubert attacks repeatedly another closely related naturalistic vice, the worship of mere force or energy, the literary Napoleonism of which Sainte-Beuve accused Balzac. "Without delicacy," says Joubert, "there is no literature." [3] "To write well a man should have a natural facility and an acquired difficulty." [4] We are more familiar perhaps with the exact opposite, with the man who had little natural facility, but who has at least succeeded in acquiring the sterile abundance of the journalist. Joubert has not a trace of our modern megalomania. "What is exquisite is better than what is ample. Merchants revere big books, but readers love little ones," etc.[5] *Heureux est l'écrivain qui peut faire un beau petit livre.*[6]

Though Joubert was in a high degree judicial and selective, the standards by which he judged and selected

[1] *Pensées*, p. 8. [2] Tit. XVIII, LXXXVIII. [3] *Ibid.*, XXIII, XXIV.
[4] *Ibid.*, XLV. [5] *Ibid.*, XXIII, CCXX. [6] *Ibid.*, CCXXII.

were not formal, but intuitive. "Professional critics," he says, expressing his disdain for the formalists, "can distinguish and appreciate neither uncut diamonds nor gold in the bar. They are merchants and know in literature only the coins which have currency. Their criticism has balances and scales but neither crucible nor touchstone."[1] That was the difficulty with La Harpe; he knew the rules, but not the reason which is the rule of the rules, and which determines at once their limit and their extent. He knew the trade but not the art of criticism.[2]

Though he possessed the critical touchstone of which he speaks I am not setting up Joubert himself as infallible — that would be to accord him privileges too far beyond our common humanity. That he could be insufficiently on his guard against formalism even in poetry where he is usually most at home, is shown by his comparison of Milton with the Abbé Delille,[3] which is not only bad but almost monumental in its badness. Perhaps his blindness here is an instance of the potency of the *Zeitgeist* which he was one of the first to define adequately.[4]

Still his critical intuition puts him on his guard as a rule even against the *Zeitgeist*. Perhaps indeed Joubert may be most adequately defined in contradistinction to the formalist, as the intuitive critic. But in that case we shall need to define with some care the word intuition. The intellect is evidently dependent on intuition, as was

[1] Tit. XXIII, CXLV. [2] *Ibid.*, XXIV, LIV.

[3] *Cor.*, 251. It is only fair to add that Joubert did not read English.

[4] Tit. XVI, L.

pointed out long ago by Aristotle, for its knowledge both of what is below and what is above itself. We may therefore distinguish two main orders of intuitions corresponding closely to the two main types of enthusiasm we have already defined: on the one hand, the sensuous or æsthetic, and on the other, the spiritual, or as they are sometimes termed the intellectual, intuitions. Intuitions of the Many and intuitions of the One, we may also call them, making themselves felt respectively, to repeat a contrast I have already used, as vital impulse and vital control. We may speak, for instance, of the intuition of an Emerson; we may also apply the word to the æsthetic sensitiveness, the fine literary perception of a Charles Lamb. M. Lemaître says that Joubert was a *singulière et délicieuse créature*, but he does not make especially clear why Joubert was "singular" and "delicious." The reason, as it seems to me, is that he was intuitive in both of the main senses I have defined. Like Emerson he possessed "the gift of vision, the eye of the spirit, the instinct of penetration, prompt discernment; in fine, natural sagacity in discovering all that is spiritual."[1] Hazlitt says that Lamb tried old authors on his palate as epicures taste olives. So did Joubert. It would be almost needless to multiply examples of his literary perceptiveness.[2]

[1] Tit. III, XLIV.

[2] Chateaubriand has a simular combination of qualities in mind when he says more ambitiously that Joubert was a "Platon à cœur de La Fontaine." Joubert was, by the way, the first to point out that "Il y a, dans La Fontaine, une plénitude de poésie qu'on ne trouve nulle part dans les autres auteurs français" (Tit. XXIV, sect. V, XX)— an opinion since adopted by Sainte-Beuve, Amiel, and Matthew Arnold.

Moreover he never confuses, like so many mere æsthetes, the planes of being corresponding to the different orders of intuitions. Men have always been conscious of the contrast between the rational and the intuitive sides of human nature, a contrast that pervades the literature of the world as that between the head and the heart. But the word heart is evidently subject to the same ambiguity as the word intuition itself. When Pascal, for example, says that the "heart has reasons of which the reason knows nothing," he evidently refers to the super-sensuous or spiritual intuitions. When La Rochefoucauld, on the other hand, says that the "head is always the dupe of the heart," he evidently refers to the desires and impulses that rise like a cloud about the intellect from the sub-rational region of human nature. A comparative study might be made between Rousseau and Pascal in such a way as to show that, though both writers make everything hinge upon the heart, they attach to the word heart entirely different meanings because they use it to describe different orders of intuition.

These distinctions seem especially needed at present when the thinkers who have the attention of the world, thinkers like James and M. Bergson and Signor Croce, are all agreed at least in appealing from intellect to intuition. If Joubert has so little in common with these thinkers, it is plainly because they are intuitive only in the Rousseauistic sense, and not like him in the Platonic sense as well. James and M. Bergson do not, like Joubert, look on the One as a living intuition, but as an inert intellectual concept; and they would have us believe that we can escape from this intellectualism only by diving into the flux, — in other words by cultivating our intuitions of the Many. It is to be feared that Joubert would have said of this modern philosophy what he said of the philosophy of change in the form it had assumed in his own time: "I detest these horrible maxims as the ancient sages would have done."[1] He looked with suspicion on philosophies which, so far from throwing light on previous philosophies, simply contradict them;[2] and from this point of view, he would have looked with special suspicion on M. Bergson. For if M. Bergson's conception of reality be correct, most of the great philosophers of the past, beginning with Plato and Aristotle, have had, not merely a mistaken, but an absolutely inverted view of reality.

To say that Joubert is spiritually intuitive is to put him in the class of sages; a class, the representatives of which are recognizable through the infinitely diverse accidents of time and space by their agreement on essentials. It would, for example, be easy to collect a list of parallel passages from Joubert and Emerson. "When there is born in a nation," says Joubert, "an individual capable of producing a great thought, another one is born capable of understanding it and admiring it." Here is Emerson's favorite doctrine that "the hearing ear is always found close to the speaking tongue." The following thought, the equivalent of which might also be found in Emerson, we should be justified in calling Buddhistic,

[1] *Cor.*, 257. [2] Tit. XII, LIV.

especially if we remember that the very name Buddha means the Awakened: "How many people eat, drink and get married; buy, sell and build; make contracts and attend to their fortune; have friends and enemies, pleasures and pains; are born, grow up, live and die,—but asleep!"[1] Men tend to come together in proportion to their intuitions of the One; in other words the true unifying principle of mankind is found in the insight of its sages. We *ascend* to meet.

Possibly the contrast between the intuitiveness of Joubert and the sages and that of M. Bergson may be brought out most clearly by comparing their attitude towards time. Reality is a pure process of flux and change according to M. Bergson, and this change takes place in time; so that "time is the very stuff of which our lives are made."[2] We should strive to see things not *sub specie aeternitatis*, but *sub specie durationis*. Under how many forms, under what diverse conditions of time and space, would it be possible to find the opposite assertion! "The sage is delivered from time,"[3] says Buddha. "Happy is the soul in which time no longer courses!" says Michael Angelo. "Time," says Joubert, "measured here below by the succession of beings which are constantly changing and being renewed, is seen and felt, and reckoned and exists. Higher up there is no change or succession, or new or old, or yesterday or to-morrow."[4] (Elsewhere Joubert adds that there is time even in eternity, though not a terrestrial and earthly time which is

[1] Tit. VII, LXIII.

[2] *L'Evolution créatrice.*

[3] "Akappiyo." See *Sutta-Nipāta*, IV, 10.

[4] Tit. XIII, IV.

counted by the movement and succession of bodies.[1]) Emerson affirms in somewhat similar fashion of "the core of God's abysm": —

> "There Past, Present, Future, shoot
> Triple blossoms from one root."

And so we might lengthen indefinitely the list of those who have found their supreme reality, not like M. Bergson in time, but in transcending time.

If a man becomes a sage only by being spiritually intuitive, it is highly desirable, and indeed necessary, if he is to be a critic or creator of art and literature, that he should also be intuitive in the sense M. Bergson recommends. Perhaps, indeed, the wisest man is he who has both orders of intuitions and then mediates between them; who joins to his sense of unity a fine perception of the local, the individual, the transitory. Joubert's quality as a critic is revealed especially by the fact that he not only had standards but held them fluidly. His insistence on the fixed and the permanent is nearly always tempered by the sense of change and instability. "A man must provide himself," he says, in his highly metaphorical fashion, "with anchors and ballast, that is, with fixed and constant opinions, and then he should allow the banners to float free and the sails to swell; the mast alone should remain unshaken."[2] Again: "Truth in one's style is an indispensable virtue and sufficient to recommend a writer. If on every manner of subject we wished to write nowadays as people wrote in the time of

[1] Tit. VI. [2] Tit. IX, XLII.

Louis XIV we should have no truth in our style, for we no longer have the same humors, the same opinions, the same manners. . . . The more the *genre* in which you write is related to your character, to the manners of the age, the more your style should depart from that of writers who have been models only because they excelled in expressing in their works either the manners of their epoch or their own character. Good taste itself in this case allows you to depart from the best taste, for taste changes with manners, even good taste." Yet Joubert adds (and here, perhaps, the reactionary note appears), that there are *genres* that do not change. "I think that the sacred orator would always do well to write and think as Bossuet would have thought and written."[1] "The vogue of books," he writes in another passage, "depends on the taste of different centuries; even what is old is exposed to variations of fashion. Corneille and Racine, Virgil and Lucan, Seneca and Cicero, Tacitus and Livy, Aristotle and Plato, have had the palm only in turn. Nay more: in the same life, according to the ages, in the same year according to the seasons, and sometimes in the same day according to the hours, we prefer one book to another book, one style to another style, one intellect to another intellect."[2] "In literature and in established judgments on authors," says Joubert, in language that anticipates Anatole France, "there is more conventional opinion than truth. How many books, whose reputation is made, would fail to achieve this reputation if it had to be won again!"[3]

[1] Tit. XXII, LXXIII. [2] Tit. XXIII, CLXXVII. [3] Tit. XXIII, CLXXXIV.

Though Joubert is thus willing to concede a great deal to the element of relativity he is not ready to go to the point of seeing in literature merely an expression of society. "It is a hundred times better," he says, "to suit a work to the nature of the human spirit than to what is called the state of society. There is something unchanging in man; and that is why there are unchanging rules in the arts and in works of art, beauties which will always please or modes of expression that will give pleasure only for a short time."[1] *Il y a quelque chose d'immuable dans l'homme!* The writers who are themselves likely to endure are those who, like Joubert, really perceived this enduring something in man and aimed at it. "Heaven," as he says, "is for those who think about it." It is equally appropriate that the work of Madame de Staël, whose main interest was not in this essential aspect of literature, but in literature as the expression of society, that is, as the reflection of changing circumstances, should itself count less intrinsically than relatively and historically.

Joubert must of course rank below those who were truly creative, those who have left a definitive monument, who have had not only ideas but also, in his own phrase, the house in which to lodge them.[2] He spent so much time in meditating his own monument and in making sure of the materials that were to enter into it that when he had at last made sure, as he tells us, that

[1] Tit. XXIII, CCV.

[2] Mes idées ! c'est la maison pour les loger qui me coûte à bâtir (*Pensées*, p. 10).

he had found what he wanted, it was too late, it was time to die.[1] Yet in his own words, "a few memorable utterances are enough to make a great spirit illustrious. There are thoughts that contain the essence of a whole book."[2] His own reputation is likely to rest securely on a number of thoughts and utterances of this kind. The world cannot afford to forget him, unless indeed the gift of intuition, as I have tried to define it, should prove more common among critics in the future than it has been in the past.

[1] Tit. VII, LXXXIX.

[2] Tit. XXIII, CCXVII.

III

CHATEAUBRIAND

THE English writer with whom Chateaubriand is most often compared, with whom indeed he compares himself, is Byron. The influence of Byron in England, however, was slight as compared with his influence on the continent, whereas the influence of Chateaubriand, negligible outside of France, dominates the whole of modern French literature. "Chateaubriand," M. Faguet wrote some time ago, "is the greatest date in the literary history of France since the Pléiade. He ends a literary evolution of nearly three centuries and a new evolution taking its rise in him still endures and will long continue. . . . He is the man who renewed the French imagination."[1] Nowadays we should perhaps be more inclined to date the evolution of which M. Faguet speaks from Rousseau, and to look on Chateaubriand himself as merely the eldest son of Jean-Jacques.

The relationship to Rousseau is the common bond between Chateaubriand and Byron. They both exhibit differences from Rousseau due in large measure to an aristocratic rather than a plebeian origin. They also differ from one another in that Chateaubriand championed the Middle Ages, monarchy, and Catholicism, whereas Byron waged war on authority and tradition.

[1] *XIXe Siècle*, 71.

Yet their resemblance to each other and to their common literary ancestor is manifest in their solitary communings with nature, and in the way each is "possessed by the demon of his heart." In both men we have Rousseauism with an added touch of wildness and misanthropy. They both suffer like Rousseau from an unreconciled antinomy between thought and feeling ("My heart and my head do not seem to belong to the same individual"), and in both cases this opposition appears strikingly in their literary opinions.

"The taste of Chateaubriand," says M. Merlet, "was of a different school from his talent. He defended tradition by his doctrines, at the same time that he corrupted or renewed it by his example."[1] In much the same fashion Byron exalted Pope in theory while he was actually overthrowing the school of Pope by his practice. "I look upon this as the declining age of English poetry," he says in his letter to Bowles, and he goes on to express his shame that he himself had been one of the builders of the new Babel. He and his fellow romanticists were sailing splendidly it might be, but on the wrong tack. With Byron in this consciously critical vein we may compare Chateaubriand as he appears in a passage like the following: "Furthermore I am not like Rousseau an enthusiast over savages and, although I have perhaps as much ground to complain of society as this philosopher had to be satisfied with it, I do not think that *pure nature* is the most beautiful thing in the world. I have always found it very ugly, wherever I have had the op-

[1] *Tableau de la littérature française* (1800–1815), III, 157.

portunity to see it. Far from being of the opinion that the man who thinks is a *depraved animal*,[1] I believe it is thought that makes man. With this word *nature* universal havoc has been wrought. Let us paint nature, but selected nature (*la belle nature*). Art should not concern itself with the imitation of monsters." Chateaubriand has the assurance to write this in the preface to "Atala," a work in which he betrays on every page his passion for the primitive, and in which, so far from avoiding the monstrous in the name of *la belle nature*, he shows, as Sainte-Beuve points out, a special predilection for crocodiles!

Though according to his most recent critic, M. Lemaître, he had strange lacunæ in his own taste and put no serious check on his imagination, he had thoughts on taste and genius and the classic age that would be countersigned by Voltaire: "If genius brings forth, it is taste that preserves: without taste genius is only a sublime folly. Strange circumstance that this delicate tact should be still rarer than the creative gift! Intellect and genius are diffused rather evenly throughout the centuries; but there are in these centuries only certain nations, and in these nations only certain moments, in which taste is revealed in all its purity; before or afterwards everything offends by lack or excess."[2] He

[1] Contrast with this edifying profession of faith in reason the following: "On montre à Heidelberg un tonneau démesuré, Colisée en ruine des ivrognes; du moins aucun chrétien n'a perdu la vie dans cet amphithéâtre des Vespasiens du Rhin; *la raison, oui : ce n'est pas grande perte.*" (*Mém. d' Outre-Tombe*, 4 juin, 1833.)

[2] *Essai sur la lit. ang.*

stood for the clear-cut type (*la distinction des genres est née de la nature même*), and yet by his own style was encouraging one of the most fundamental of confusions, that between prose and poetry. He did more than any one else to popularize local color and at the same time pointed out its futility. "The genius of Racine borrows nothing from the cut of the clothes. . . . People imitate arm-chairs and velvet when they no longer know how to portray the character of the man seated on this velvet and in these arm-chairs."[1] René mocks at the malady of René. "Lord Byron," he says, "has founded a deplorable school. I presume that he has been as much afflicted at the Childe Harolds to whom he has given birth as I am at the Renés who are dreaming about me. If 'René' did not exist I should not write it again. If it were possible for me to destroy it I would destroy it. Renés in poetry and Renés in prose have sprung up in swarms. Nothing has been heard save disjointed phrases of lamentation. The only talk has been of winds and storms, of unknown words uttered to the clouds and to the night. No scribbler just out of school who has n't dreamed that he is the unhappiest of men, no sixteen-year-old stripling who has n't exhausted life and thought himself tormented by his genius, who in the abyss of his thoughts has n't given himself over to his vaguely aspiring passions," etc.[2]

Chateaubriand attributes to the classical influence of Fontanes[3] the fact that he had avoided the "roughness"

[1] *Essai sur la lit. ang.* [2] *Mém. d'Outre-Tombe.*

[3] *Essai sur la lit. ang.* Cf. Emile Deschamps: —

"Fontanes qui veillait, flambeau pur et brillant,
Comme un autre Boileau, près de Chateaubriand."

of his romantic followers. Much, however, of Chateaubriand's disparagement of Rousseau, on the one hand, and of the romanticists, on the other, is itself a romantic trait: he is so filled with the sense of his own uniqueness that he would acknowledge neither master nor disciples.

The contradiction between theory and practice is even more flagrant in Chateaubriand than in Byron. For Byron's laudation of the old literary order actually corresponds to something in his creative writing: he is creative in such poems as the "Vision of Judgment" as well as in the outgoings of his spirit to the mountains and the sea; he is in short a far less romantic personage than Chateaubriand. He shows himself less aloof from society than the Frenchman, even in his satire of it. Chateaubriand is thoroughly creative only when uttering his own nostalgia and nympholeptic longings, or when rendering suggestively the aspects of outer nature (these moods are of course often blended). There was, in Joubert's phrase, a "talisman" that clung to his fingers, and he used this gift of glamour, not for intellectual ends, but to enrich and deepen the life of the senses. "He is the man," says M. Lemaître, "who introduced into French the most music, the most images, the most perfumes, the most suave contacts, so to speak, and the most delights, and who wrote the most intoxicating phrases on voluptuousness and death." [1] On the creative side he has far less intellectual breadth than Byron, but is far superior to him as a critic. As soon as

[1] *Chateaubriand*, 342.

Byron reflected, says Goethe, he was a child; and then, too, he did not have at his side such "guardian angels" as Fontanes and Joubert. The point of view of the Letter to Bowles is on the whole pseudo-classic. Now Chateaubriand also had his pseudo-classical side which unfortunately overflows at times into what should have been his creative writing. He says in one of his romantic moods that he knew a Breton folk-song one line of which was worth more than all the twelve cantos of the "Henriade." Yet a large portion of his own "Martyrs" is at least as artificial as the "Henriade," and precisely in the same manner. He substitutes, in fact, a literary Christianity for a literary paganism, and in such a way as to justify Boileau's warning against the use of religious mysteries as vain literary ornaments. He has as implicit a faith in poetic "machines" as Father Le Bossu, and in few pseudo-epics is the creaking of the pullies with which this "machinery" is managed so painfully audible as in the "Martyrs."

But along with this pseudo-classicism Chateaubriand had a genuinely classical side, in other words a genuine perception of form. He would not have been capable like Byron of comparing Pope to a Greek temple. He can speak admirably on occasion of the "antique symmetry."[1] His protest against the sentimentality of the

[1] As, for example, in the following passage: "Les modernes sont en général plus savants, plus délicats, plus déliés, souvent même plus intéressants dans leurs compositions que les anciens ; mais ceux-ci sont plus simples, plus augustes, plus tragiques, plus abondants et surtout plus vrais que les modernes. Ils ont un goût plus sûr, une imagination plus noble : ils ne savent travailler que l'ensemble, et négligent les ornements ; un

eighteenth century has often been cited in illustration of his instinct for the grand manner: "It is a dangerous mistake, sanctioned, like so many other dangerous mistakes, by Voltaire, to suppose that the best works of imagination are those that draw most tears. One could name this or that melodrama, which no one would like to own having written, and which yet harrows the feelings far more than the 'Aeneid.' The true tears are those which are called forth by the *beauty* of poetry; there must be as much imagination in them as sorrow. They are the tears which come to our eyes when Priam says to Achilles: 'And I have endured, — the like whereof no soul on earth hath yet endured, — to carry to my lips the hand of him who slew my child'; or when Joseph cries out: 'I am Joseph your brother whom ye sold into Egypt.'"[1]

We have then in Chateaubriand a somewhat baffling interplay of classical, pseudo-classical, and romantic elements. The only element that counts, from the point of view of his influence even in criticism, is the romantic. What men received from him was a certain type of im-

berger qui se plaint, un vieillard qui raconte, un héros qui combat: voilà pour eux tout un poème, et l'on ne sait comment il arrive que ce poème, où il n'y a rien, est cependant mieux rempli que nos romans chargés d'incidents et de personnages. L'art d'écrire semble avoir suivi l'art de la peinture; la palette du poète moderne se couvre d'une variété infinie de teintes et de nuances; le poète antique compose ses tableaux avec les trois couleurs du Polygnote." (*Génie du Christianisme*, 2e Partie, livre II, c. II.)

[1] Preface to *Atala*. Cf. Arnold, *Essays in Criticism*, I, 277. Coleridge made a similar protest against the theatrical tearfulness of the eighteenth century. See *Lectures on Shakespeare* (Bohn), 124.

aginative and emotional stimulus, an initiation into the new passion and the new revery and the new suggestiveness. What they listened to was not his plea for selectiveness and "good taste," but his plea for sympathy and enthusiasm. His saying that the time had come "to substitute for the petty criticism of faults the great and fruitful criticism of beauties,"[1] a saying that only echoed Madame de Staël, was taken up by Hugo and became a favorite formula for that *critique admirative* so dear to the romanticist, the criticism that is æsthetic rather than judicial. Chateaubriand's own application of the æsthetic point of view in the "Génie du Christianisme" is above all a reaction from the eighteenth century; or it would be better to say a continuation of the quarrel of the eighteenth century of Rousseau with the eighteenth century of the *philosophes* and Voltaire. Rousseau himself may perhaps be most adequately defined as the great æsthete (using the word in its broadest sense, in its derivation from the Greek word feeling). The Savoyard Vicar proves God to his pupil by showing him the glories of the sunrise over the valley of the Po. The transition from this æsthetic deism to æsthetic Catholicism is evidently easy. In Chateaubriand the rays of the rising sun, in addition to falling upon a glorious landscape, also fall upon the consecrated wafer which Father Aubry was at that moment lifting in the air; whereupon the narrator exclaims,

[1] This is the form, in which the saying appears in the *Préface de Cromwell.* Chateaubriand's wording is slightly different. See his article on the *Annales littéraires* of Dussault, Feb., 1819.

"O charm of religion! O magnificence of the Christian cult!" The right title for the "Génie du Christianisme," as has been pointed out, would be the Beauties of Christianity. Chateaubriand would view everything æsthetically — even hell. Dante and Milton have shown that we might "possess hells as poetical as those of Homer and Virgil."[1]

Chateaubriand boasted that by this work he had definitively discredited the eighteenth century. "Why," he asks, "is this century so inferior to the seventeenth? For it is no longer time to dissimulate the fact; the writers of our age have in general been placed too high." (Sainte-Beuve was later to take this sentence as motto for his own book on Chateaubriand.) "If there is so much that is blameworthy in the works of Rousseau and Voltaire, what is to be said of the works of Raynal and Diderot?"[2] Chateaubriand's explanation of this inferiority is, of course, that the eighteenth century was irreligious, and irreligious because it was unimaginative, and unimaginative because it was over-analytical. "Cast your eyes on the generations that followed the age of Louis XIV. Where are those men with calm and majestic faces, with noble garb and bearing, with chastened speech . . . ? You look for them and no longer find them. Little obscure men move about like pigmies under the lofty porticos of the monuments of another age. On their hard features are stamped egotism and the contempt of God. They have lost both the nobility of garb and the purity of speech: you

[1] *G. du Christ.*, 2e Partie, livre IV, c. XIII.
[2] *G. du Christ.*, 3e Partie, livre IV, c. V.

would take them not for the sons but for the buffoons of the great race that went before them. The disciples of the new school wither the imagination with I know not what truth, which is not the veritable truth. . . . Modern writers make use of a narrow philosophy which divides and subdivides everything, makes precise measurement of feelings, submits the soul to calculation and reduces God and the universe to a passing modification of nothingness."[1] "The spirit of reasoning by destroying the imagination saps the foundations of the fine arts."[2] The sciences always bring on ages of irreligion, which are followed in close sequence by ages of destruction.[3]

These are themes the equivalent of which we can find developed in a thousand forms by French, German, and English romanticists at the beginning of the nineteenth century. Unfortunately, the fact that a person protests against analysis and appeals from intellect and analysis to the "imagination" or the "heart" or the "soul," or, like Madame de Staël to "enthusiasm," does not tell us all that it might regarding his ultimate point of view. Joubert uttered a similar protest against "the man who has become so anatomical that he has ceased to be a man and sees in the noblest and most touching gait only a play of muscles, like an organ manufacturer who should hear in the most beautiful music only the little clicks of the key-board."[4] But is the "soul" that Joubert opposes to this analytical excess the "soul"

[1] *G. du Christ.*, 3e Partie, livre IV, c. V.
[2] *Ibid.*, 3e Partie, livre I, c. VII.
[3] *Ibid.*, livre II, c. I, et II.
[4] Tit. XXIII, CLXXXVI.

opposed to it by the romanticist? That is the crucial question. The same ambiguity clings to the word "soul" as to the words "heart" and "intuition," which I discussed in the last chapter. The "soul" of Chateaubriand is plainly a Rousseauistic and not, like that of Joubert, a Platonic "soul." Formulæ of this kind must, of course, be applied with great caution to the mysterious unity of a living spirit — especially when the spirit is that of a man of genius like Chateaubriand. I for one should not deny him greatness of soul in any sense. Yet he is in the main intuitive of the Many and not of the One, and what he has to offer us therefore is not wisdom, but æsthetic perceptiveness.

Now æsthetic perceptiveness is in itself a precious thing, but to claim that because you are æsthetically perceptive you are therefore religious is to fall into the underlying romantic error, which may be defined as trying to make the things that are below the intellect do duty for those that are above it. "Incredulity," says Chateaubriand, "is the principal cause of the decadence of taste and genius." [1] We recognize here the central thesis of Ruskin. It is already a dangerous confusion to refer art and religion to a common source. A man may be truly religious without being in the least artistic, and conversely (though we should add that art and religion may and usually do interact in a thousand ways). The confusion becomes positively pernicious when the common ground on which both art and religion are made to rest is mere æstheticism. Sensible people feel a peculiar

[1] *G. du Christ*, 3e Partie, livre IV, c. V.

exasperation when romantic æsthetes like Rousseau and Ruskin and Chateaubriand set themselves up as religious teachers. They feel instinctively that something is wrong, even when unable to trace clearly the nature of the error. To lack true inwardness like Chateaubriand and at the same time to become the champion of religion is simply to substitute a pose for reality. "He never questions himself," says Joubert in the letter on Chateaubriand to which I have already referred, "unless it be to find out whether the exterior parts of his soul, I mean his taste and imagination, are content, whether his thought is harmoniously rounded and his phrases musical, whether his images are vivid, etc.; caring little whether it is all intrinsically good: that is his smallest concern."[1] And therefore we may say with Sainte-Beuve, that we are not in the year 1800 at the dawn of a great literary age, but merely of one of the most brilliant periods of decline.

Chateaubriand's slight regard for the truth of Christianity as compared with its æsthetic charm is one of the commonplaces of criticism. He has been charged with preferring beauty to truth, but it might be less misleading to say illusion to reality, since beauty after all is more than mere æstheticism. His aim, as he tells us, is less to convince our intellects than to enchant our imaginations. To the meagreness of the intellectual as compared with the æsthetic appeal of the "Génie du Christianisme" is due, no doubt, the fact that it has so largely ceased to interest. "But one half-pennyworth of bread," we are tempted to exclaim, as so often in roman-

[1] *Cor.*, 108–9.

tic writing, "to this intolerable deal of sack!" He finds a proof of original sin in the mode of locomotion of the serpent; the three Graces are used as an argument in favor of the Trinity; the celibacy of priests is backed up by the virginity of bees. He points out that "nature has not been as delicate as disbelievers . . . It has bestowed the form of the cross upon a whole family of flowers."[1] He proves the necessity of the Sabbath from the fact that "the ox cannot labor nine days in succession. On the seventh day his plaintive bellowings call for the repose ordained by the Creator."[2]

If we trace the influence of Chateaubriand we find at the beginning æsthetic and mediæval Christians, then æsthetic mediævalists, and finally æsthetes who are neither mediævalists nor Christians. The essential element from the start was the æstheticism. Though he failed to convert French writers as a class to Catholicism, even æsthetic Catholicism, he did lure them into the tower of ivory. He encouraged them to cultivate their sensorium and neglect their intellect. The heart and head of the century were thus put into opposition with each other. It is partly due to Chateaubriand that M. Faguet was enabled to write his studies of modern French writers in two series — the men of imagination in one series and the thinkers in another. It is a singular piece of good fortune for the Germans that their chief modern writer is not merely a great imaginative and emotional, but also a great intellectual, force. The contrast is striking in this respect between Goethe and Chateau-

[1] *G. du Christ.* 4e Partie, livre I, c. II. [2] *Ibid.*, c. IV.

briand; and still more striking between Goethe and Hugo.

Chateaubriand appears to far better advantage when he is dealing with Christianity not in itself, but in its relation to art and literature. Parts II and III of the "Génie du Christianisme" which treat of this relation, exhibit the somewhat baffling interplay I have already noted between classic, pseudo-classic, and romantic elements; and for this reason, no doubt, they have been somewhat variously judged, though on the whole more favorably than the other parts of the work. Sainte-Beuve seems especially conscious of the classic note.[1] He discovers in Chateaubriand a native instinct for literary excellence that has been fortified and enriched by humanistic memories; and so, though making sharp reservations as to the general thesis, he accords hearty praise to the details. "All that portion of the work," says Sainte-Beuve, "in which the author compares the natural characters in antiquity and among the moderns" (e.g. the comparison of husband and wife in Milton's Adam and Eve with the Ulysses and Penelope of Homer) . . . "abounds in delicate beauties and exquisite shadings: it is literary criticism in the grand manner." He goes on to say that "the best substance of classic French criticism should be sought in such pages." Scherer, on the contrary, though he admits that Chateaubriand rendered at times with a certain eloquence the impression produced on him by what he read, is conscious in the very comparisons singled out by Sainte-Beuve for

[1] *Chat. et son groupe littéraire,* I, 318 ff.

special praise of something set and formal and, in a word, pseudo-classic. They still lack the modern keenness of characterization. Chateaubriand for his part, who was of course the very last person to underestimate his own merits, observes in the "Mémoires d'Outre-Tombe": "The paragraphs in which I deal with the influence of our religion in our manner of seeing and painting . . . the chapters which I devote to investigating the new feelings introduced into the dramatic characters of antiquity, contain the germs of the new criticism."

In the comparisons of which he speaks Chateaubriand is served both by his classic taste and his romantic instinct. According as his mood is predominantly romantic or classical, he can oppose to pagan antiquity either the Middle Ages or the French seventeenth century, which was at once classical and Christian. Like other French reactionaries, including Joubert, he exalts Bossuet, "who loves to let fall from his lips those great words 'time' and 'death' which reëcho in the silent depths of eternity." It is but natural that the author of the "Martyrs" should show a special predilection for the two chief representatives of the Christian epic, Tasso and Milton. His thesis imposed upon him the somewhat difficult task of proving that the personages of Tasso, being at once Christian and mediæval, are more poetical than those of Homer. The combination in Milton of the grand manner with a Christian subject made a special appeal to Chateaubriand. Furthermore, we should not forget that he spent a number of the most formative years of his youth in England and that the English influence is very visible in him. A chief product of this influence was his translation of Milton and the somewhat rambling and superficial study of English literature which he wrote to accompany it. At times the intrusion into this study of the note of romantic egotism (as, for example, where he says: "Now that in our two countries monarchy is inclining towards its end, Milton and I no longer have any political quarrel with each other")[1] anticipates, though faintly, Hugo's extraordinary rhapsody on Shakespeare.

We have seen that Chateaubriand differed from Scherer and Sainte-Beuve in emphasizing especially the element of novelty in his own criticism. For example, he shows—"a thing that had not been at all understood previously—that with the same names and under somewhat similar outer forms the characters of Racine and Euripides express entirely different sentiments. Phædra in Racine is no longer a pagan but an erring Christian wife," etc. I believe that Chateaubriand puts us on the track here of his real influence as a critic. The lesson the new criticism took to heart was that it should penetrate beyond the mere form of a work of art to the soul.

But here again it is necessary to remember that the word "soul" is in itself ambiguous. Behind the mere outer form of a work of art there may be two "souls" (both only to be apprehended intuitively), a soul in virtue of which it has a general and representative value, and a soul in virtue of which it is unique. Both kinds

[1] Last paragraph of *Essai sur la lit. ang.*

of soul appear vitally fused in the work of art that is completely beautiful — one making itself felt as symmetry and repose, as inner form we may say, the other as individual life and expression. Stated Platonically the complete work of art suggests to us through the medium of the imagination the presence of the One in the Many. Now the soul that Chateaubriand instinctively seizes upon and renders is not the soul that makes for form and symmetry, but the soul that makes for expression (though he leans less one-sidedly towards expression than, for instance, Ruskin).

Moreover, he not only responds æsthetically to the present object and renders it in its uniqueness but he also has the gift, closely associated in its origins with romantic nostalgia, of journeying imaginatively in time and space, and then conveying vividly what is either temporally or spatially remote. For example, he does not give us an adequate idea of the Christianity of the period he has treated in his "Martyrs" — that would have required more insight into the permanent element in human nature than he possessed. He is, in fact, more at home with the paganism of the period, because behind his façade of æsthetic Catholicism, he himself lived more on the pagan than on the Christian level. What he does do at his best is to conjure up before our inner eye a vision of what was peculiar to the period, of its individual expression, of the precise picturesque details by which it differed from all other periods. This art of local color evidently concerns the historian at least as much as the literary critic; and Chateaubriand counts among the important initiators into the new historical spirit. The whole shifting of emphasis from the permanent to the local and transitory aspects of human nature is so well brought out in Augustin Thierry's account of Chateaubriand's influence upon him that I must quote from it in spite of its familiarity. Thierry, we should remember, though he prepared the way for Michelet and for the French romantic school of history in general, showed for his own part an almost Attic moderation in his use of the new picturesqueness.

Thierry, then, relates how in 1810 he read "Les Martyrs" in the vaulted class-room of the Collège de Blois while his fellow-students were off on a walk. He was especially moved by the narrative of Eudore, "that living history of the empire in its decline," and contrasted the style with that of his text-book: "Clovis, son of King Childeric, mounted the throne in 484 and strengthened by his victories the foundations of the French monarchy," etc. . . . "Nothing had given me any idea of those terrible Franks of M. de Chateaubriand, those Franks dressed in the spoils of bears, sea-calves, buffaloes, and wild boars; of that entrenched camp with its leather boats and its chariots drawn by great oxen; of that army drawn up in a triangle in which you could distinguish, in the midst of a forest of lances, only skins of wild beasts and half-naked bodies . . . The impression produced on me by the war-song of the Franks had in it something electrical. I left the place where I was seated and, walking up and down the room, I repeated aloud, making my feet ring out on the pavement: 'Pharamond! Pharamond! we have fought with the sword,' etc. . . . This moment of enthusiasm was perhaps decisive for my future vocation . . . This is my debt to the writer of genius who opens and dominates the new literary age. All those who in different directions are advancing along the pathways of this age have encountered him in the same way at the source of their studies, at their first inspiration; there is no one of them who might not fittingly say to him, as Dante said to Virgil:

'Tu duca, tu signore, e tu maestro.'"[1]

We thus see history ceasing to be abstract and colorless and becoming concrete and expressive; we see it getting rid of its old artificial unity and cultivating instead a sense of the variable in human nature — a sense that is not tempered by any new and vital perception of unity. Thierry possibly overstates Chateaubriand's influence upon himself and others. But it is evident that although Chateaubriand posed as a champion of the old order and the fixed standards it implied, by the actual force of his example he helped forward to an important extent the main movement of the century in both history and literary criticism from the absolute to the relative.

[1] Preface to *Récits des temps mérovingiens*.

IV

THE TRANSITION TO SAINTE-BEUVE

VILLEMAIN — COUSIN — NISARD

FRENCH criticism throughout the first half of the nineteenth century may be studied almost entirely in terms of the romantic movement. There is an extreme "right" of strict traditionalists opposed to an extreme "left" of literary radicals, a "centre" and a "left-centre" that welcome the more moderate innovations, etc. This critical alignment either for or against romanticism, which was more or less obscured during the second half of the century, is reappearing in our own days, except perhaps that there are fewer intermediary shades of opinion between extreme "right" and extreme "left." Nowadays those who are conservative in literature are at least superficially consistent in being religious and political conservatives as well; whereas in the earlier period there was a curious confusion in this matter that I have already touched on in speaking of the critics of the Empire. The political radicals were often the most "classical" in literature, whereas the romantic innovators were wont to pose, in the wake of Chateaubriand, as champions of the "throne and altar." It took Hugo, who began as a royalist and Christian of this type, several years to discover that romanticism is after all only "liberalism in literature."

The battle between the opposing literary factions was carried on by means of pamphlets, prefaces and articles in newspapers and reviews. Literary journalism has never been more flourishing in France than during the Restoration and the early days of the July Monarchy. "La Muse Française" (July, 1823, to July, 1824) was a typical organ of the romanticists in their early phase. It was very reactionary politically, admired the "Martyrs," and opposed, above all, the criticism of beauties, to the criticism of faults. At the opposite extreme was the politically liberal "Constitutionnel." Romanticist in this journal was synonymous with foreigner and reactionary, and at times with lunatic. "Romanticism," we read, "is not a subject of ridicule; it is a disease like somnambulism or epilepsy." A romanticist is a man who is beginning to lose his mind: "you must pity him, talk reason to him, bring him around gradually; you can't make of him the subject of a comedy, however, but at most of a medical thesis."[1] Beyond all doubt the most distinguished of these literary journals was the "Globe" (1824–1831), on which Goethe bestowed his admiration, noting especially the articles of the youthful Sainte-Beuve on Hugo. The "Globe" did as much as any journal of the time to help forward the new cosmopolitanism we have associated with Madame de Staël, and was especially active in behalf of Shakespeare.

To the strict traditionalists of this period the purity

[1] Quoted in Petit de Julleville, *Hist. de la langue et de la littérature française*, VII, 690.

and very integrity of the French language seemed to be menaced by a universal invasion of foreign influences. We read in one of the comic papers, as early as 1814, of the articles of a "romantic confederation." England and Germany are to be represented in this confederation by Madame de Staël and Benjamin Constant; Prussia, Russia, Austria, etc., by "le sieur" Schlegel; Italy and Spain by Sismondi and his "Literatures of the South." "The purpose of the confederation is to introduce into French, on the one hand, the obscurities of the languages of the North, and, on the other, the conceits and bombast of the south, and to continue the process until Frenchmen no longer understand one another."[1] Though a vast machinery was organized at this time for opening up a knowledge of foreign literatures, the romantic movement appears far more cosmopolitan than it really was. The hopes that the "Globe" and its editors inspired in Goethe were not fulfilled. Too many of the promising youths of this period were drafted into politics after the July Revolution. The romantic leaders were as a class rather innocent of foreign influences — indeed, of deep intellectual culture of any kind — unless we regard the influence of Rousseau and his French followers as a foreign intrusion into the pure French tradition. For even the two foreign influences that seem all-powerful at this time, those of Byron and Scott, do little more than affect the surface manifestations of the great main movement which comes down from Rousseau

[1] *Nain jaune*, 20 Dec., 1814; quoted in Maigron, *Le Roman historique à l'époque romantique*, 155.

and Chateaubriand. Byron helped forward the revolt against all kinds of authority, including literary authority; Scott coöperated powerfully with Chateaubriand in teaching the new art of travelling imaginatively in time and space. The fashion for local color and historical romance that was set by Scott has importance only as it testifies to something deeper, the tendency, namely, to see life and literature not absolutely but relatively and historically.

I

The advance towards a more historical and cosmopolitan point of view at this time was due, not merely to the diffusion of a knowledge of foreign literatures and to journals like the "Globe," but to the influence of three eminent professors. Perhaps the most stirring events in the politically dull days of the Restoration were the public lectures given by Villemain, Cousin, and Guizot. We hear of two thousand eager auditors at the courses of Cousin during the years 1828 to 1830. The originality of Cousin, Villemain, and Guizot was to infuse something of the new historical method into the domains respectively of philosophy, literary criticism, and history itself. Like the "Globe" with which they were more or less affiliated, and in which the lectures of Cousin and Villemain were published, all three lecturers were "left-centre" and continued Madame de Staël. Guizot carried into history the idea of integral and organic development; he did not isolate political history but related it to the other manifestations of the life and activity of a particular country and time.

Guizot, however, is very far from being a pure relativist. He was a leader of the "doctrinaires"; the admiration for parliamentary liberalism that had been inspired in Madame de Staël by the spectacle of England tended to harden in Guizot and the other doctrinaires into a political creed. He was too anxious to impose the discipline of this creed upon both past and present. In other words he had a philosophy of history, and the danger of a philosophy of history is always to force the infinite and living complexity of the facts into a somewhat arbitrary intellectual mould.

Cousin is distinctly inferior to Guizot in constructive power. The eclectic philosophy or "spiritualism" that he evolved is a somewhat indeterminate compound of religion and rationalism, alike unsatisfactory to the supernaturalist and the pure philosopher of nature. He made of it for many years, however, a very effective instrument of domination over French higher education. Cousin's real originality consists in having converted philosophy into the history of philosophy. He visited Germany, and in his interpretations of German thinkers, especially Hegel, to the French public, he continued the pioneer work of which Madame de Staël had set the example. He had, indeed, many of the instincts of the explorer and intellectual adventurer. This disposition became even more visible when later he turned from philosophy to literature — especially to the literature of the first part of the seventeenth century in France. He took possession of this new field with infinite zest, and established himself in it as a conqueror. He showed something of the gift of the actor in the way he identified himself imaginatively with the personages of the period, especially with the heroines of the Fronde. His very style with its seventeenth-century flavor is itself, in some degree, a histrionic impersonation, and can scarcely be said in any case to be the man. Cousin himself was impetuous and extreme, impatient of any outer check and unwilling to impose any check upon himself; and in this respect he was very far from the seventeenth century. By the gusto with which he dwelt on the charms of some of his heroines he exposed himself to various pleasantries. "He set out," said Sainte-Beuve, "to found a great system of philosophy—and fell in love with Madame de Longueville."[1] He not only showed a lover's partisanship, an unwillingness to admit any blemishes in the beloved object, but also a lover's jealousy. Sainte-Beuve relates how rudely he was "elbowed" by Cousin when he ventured to intrude on his preserve. Later Cousin's jealousy diminished, because, as he explained, "I love elsewhere."

The tendency to entrench one's self in a single field and then to allow one's comprehension of this field and sympathy for it to override one's judgment and sense of proportion are traits that we associate with the modern specialist. In fact we find in Cousin just that mixture of enthusiasm and insistence on the new and undiscovered fact, of romance and science in short, with which we are so familiar in our philological investigators. From this point of view Cousin's discovery of the original

[1] *Lundis*, VI, 166.

text of the "Pensées" of Pascal, and the presentation of his discovery to the Academy in 1843, mark an epoch. The discovery in itself was very much worth while, but the direction it gave to French scholarship and criticism inspired some disquietude in the humanistic observer. Critics sought in the wake of Cousin to shine not so much by their judgment and ideas and taste as by producing some unpublished fact or document from the archives of the seventeenth century or elsewhere. The Conrart papers, Sainte-Beuve complained, had become a mine of glory, and he added that Conrart's handwriting was extremely legible. Cousin, in short, did as much as any man of his time to inaugurate in France what has been termed the age of frenzied research, that *fureur de l'inédit* which Brunetière was to attack later, and which after all has been less disastrous to literary standards in France than in several other countries.

II

Villemain was without the faults and also to some degree without the virtues of the original investigator. His instinct was not so much to consider things in themselves as with a view to their oratorical effect. There are too many suggestions in his style of the flowers of the ancient rhetoric. He has even been accused of thinking first of a fine phrase and then of what he was going to put into it. He was less paradoxical than Cousin and had a surer taste in the traditional sense. His great merit indeed is to combine taste, as the word would have been understood by Voltaire and La Harpe, with the sense of historical relativity. Villemain's most effective lectures are those on the literature of the eighteenth century, and are an application to this period of the new cosmopolitan spirit. He undertakes to show the interrelationship during this period of French, English, and Italian civilizations, their "cross-fire upon one another," to use his own phrase, and at the same time the way eighteenth-century life thus studied in its totality finds its counterpart in certain literary forms. "What should have concerned Voltaire," he says, apropos of the "Henriade," "are not the rules imposed upon the epic, but the social conditions that allow it to arise."[1] Since literature is even more the outcome of social conditions than of individual choice, the edge is taken off one's censure. "Lesage," he says, "has been sharply criticised for having a prosaic habit of mind. What we see especially in this habit of mind is the mark of those last years of Louis XIV which melt together so perfectly with the first years of the Regency."[2] Villemain also relates the work to the author, as when he sees in the adventures of "Manon Lescaut" a reflection of the incidents of Prévost's own life.

The relationship established by Villemain between the work and the author, or between the work and the age, is, as compared with that of later adepts in the historical method, somewhat lax. The historical and critical elements seem at times to lie side by side and not, as in Sainte-Beuve, to interpenetrate.

[1] *Lit. au* XVIIIe *siècle*, I, 164. [2] *Ibid.*, I, 251.

III

Villemain, Guizot, and Cousin all three combine innovation with strongly conservative aud traditional elements; they are, as I have already said, "left-centre." The most distinguished representative of the extreme "right," that is, of literary conservatism during this period, is undoubtedly Désiré Nisard. The rôle played by Nisard in the first half of the century is somewhat similar to that played by Brunetière in our own day. The difference in the two men appears in Brunetière's complaint that he finds in Nisard "so little history, I mean so few dates, so few facts, so little biography." [1] In short, Nisard has less historic sense than Brunetière, less logical vigor, less science (and also less pseudo-science); he has, however, more native fineness of taste.

Nisard's reactionary spirit appears in the first place in the fact that he is neither a nationalist nor a cosmopolitan in Madame de Staël's sense. He protests against the "chimera of a purely national literature." [2] On the other hand, he says that "no nation can imitate foreign literatures successfully. In France, this imitation is deadly to the writer." [3] What is precious in literature must be not purely national, but universal and human; you are to escape however from national limitations, not by mere comprehension and sympathy, but by a definite discipline in the great humanistic and religious traditions, in what Nisard calls the twofold antiquity, classical and Christian. He looked on the new cosmopolitanism of comprehension and sympathy as a menace to

[1] *L'Evolution de la critique*, 212. [2] *Histoire*, I, 239. [3] *Ibid.*, 358.

some of the finest qualities in French literature. According to Goethe, as we have seen, Madame de Staël broke down the Chinese wall that separated Germany from France. Nisard would have been in favor of raising this wall again. The primary need is not knowledge but discipline. Now, to get discipline we must have a strong central authority and look with suspicion on all departures from the norm. The authority that Nisard sets up is a certain conception of the French spirit, which in its higher manifestations coincides, he would have us believe, with the human spirit itself. Departures from the French spirit or human spirit thus conceived are granted only grudgingly. Nisard is as unflinching as Brunetière in sacrificing the *sens propre* or individual sense to the *sens commun* or general sense. Other countries are "more favorable to liberty, which is full of perils and aberrations, than to discipline. . . . On the contrary, the French spirit is more inclined to discipline than to liberty. . . . The man of genius in France is he who says what everybody knows." [1] Nisard will not allow that the general sense as expressed in tradition could have erred. He is at the opposite pole from those modern scholars who are forever reversing the verdicts of the past, whitewashing what is traditionally black, and blackwashing what is traditionally white. In the case of Ronsard, for example, he says: "Boileau has spoken. All that is left is to give reasons in support of this judgment." [2] It goes without saying that the French spirit came to its perfect maturity, that is, coincided most fully with the

[1] *Histoire*, I, 14. [2] *Histoire*, I, 362.

human spirit, in the age of Louis XIV. Nisard adopts indeed in a somewhat extreme form the theory of the "classic age," before or after which everything errs, either by deficiency or excess. The French spirit itself can hardly be said to have come into existence at any particular time. It seems to exist out of time and space, in some scholastic heaven of its own, and from this altitude to smile down on any individual who has caught some of its lineaments. As Nisard says, the French spirit "recognized itself" in this individual. Now the French spirit could not recognize itself in the men of the Middle Ages who were still infantile, and so Nisard, like Brunetière, was disdainful of the Middle Ages. He finds, indeed, only intermittent gleams of the French spirit until he gets almost to the threshold of the seventeenth century. Having reached the seventeenth century he heaves a sigh of relief, and instals himself in it as in the centre of his subject. Of the four volumes of his "History" two are devoted to this period. In the seventeenth century itself he is partial to what is most authoritative and disciplinary. Light is thrown on his predilections by the actual number of pages he devotes to different authors. Montaigne receives thirty-two pages, Molière forty-four, La Fontaine thirty-seven: on the other hand, one hundred and twenty pages are devoted to Boileau, one hundred and thirty to Bossuet, and one hundred to Louis XIV himself!

In thus making everything in French literature converge on a single point or centre, Nisard is led to establish a sort of literary profit and loss account. All those works in which the French spirit recognizes itself are set down among the *gains*; those works, on the other hand, in which the pure lineaments of the French spirit are obscured and which prepare the descent from the luminous summits of the seventeenth century are reckoned among the *pertes*. "If it be true," he says, "that the perfection of the French spirit in the seventeenth century consisted in the inner union of the two antiquities, pagan and Christian, the day when this union is broken will see a decline in the French spirit, and the day of perfect works will have passed. What! decadence already? Let us avoid the word if you wish, but do not let us be blinded to the facts . . . Let us call by some other name the change that took place in French literature in the eighteenth century, provided it be not by the name of progress, provided the gains do not blind us to the losses." [1]

Nisard anticipates later reactionaries in his attack on Rousseau as the *fons et origo malorum*, as the man who did more than any one else to corrupt the integrity of the French spirit and prepare the triumph of the individual sense over the general sense as embodied in tradition. Rousseau carried the love of singularity so far, he says, that "he looked with more complacency on the evil that was his own than on the good he possessed in common with other people." [2] Yet this innovator who proceeds on the principle that everybody was wrong before him never writes better than when he agrees unwittingly with everybody and comes down from his proud

[1] *Histoire*, IV, 1. [2] *Histoire*, IV, 454.

reveries to the speech of experience and ordinary practice. Nisard treats Rousseau as the type of the utopist, the man who is more interested in reforming the world than in reforming himself. Now inasmuch as people of this kind were never more numerous than they are to-day, Nisard's psychological analysis of the utopist has by no means lost its piquancy. Apropos of the "Confessions," he says that Rousseau already sets here the example for later writers "who have made of their pride one of those Carthaginian idols to which they immolate everybody who is guilty of being born into the world at the same time as themselves."[1] He is, no doubt, here glancing at Hugo.

For Nisard's attitude towards the later romanticists we need to turn from the "History" to his miscellaneous essays, especially to those which he collected in his volume on the romantic school. For two or three years before the July Revolution he had himself had, as he tells us, a period of romantic aberration, during which he contributed laudatory articles on Hugo to the "Journal des Débats." "But classic good sense returned to me," he adds, "at the moment when I had corrupted my style sufficiently by affectation and subtlety to be encouraged and even enjoyed by several German writers."[2] He celebrated his return to classic good sense by publishing his "Manifeste contre la littérature facile," directed especially against the inferior forms of romanticism. A lively exchange of hostilities followed between him and Jules Janin in the "Revue de Paris." There is a strong po-

[1] *Histoire,* IV, 457. [2] *Essais sur l'Ecole rom.*, 166.

lemical intention, again, in his "Latin Poets of the Decadence." The value of what might have been a brilliant study of silver Latinity is impaired by the obvious desire to develop a parallel between the poets of decadent Rome and the poets of his own time. In the article "Victor Hugo en 1836," he proclaims that Hugo is lacking in "reason, taste, and critical sense," and that his "literary death is imminent and inevitable." He insinuates that his prose is better than his verse. Hugo is the type of the genius that does not mature. He has abundance without progress, and "in a body that is becoming stout an intellect that is growing lean." [1] Hugo's wrath at this article overflowed at intervals for the rest of his life. Thirty years later he wrote, "An ass that resembles M. Nisard is braying."

By his attacks on the imaginative unrestraint of Hugo and others Nisard laid himself open to the suspicion of being himself restrained in this respect because he did not have a great deal to restrain. His ideal norm reflects at times too clearly the limitations of his own temperament. The human spirit is not only identified with the French spirit but the French spirit often seems a projection of the spirit of Nisard. He is too ready to force the complex realities of French literature into the Procrustean bed of his logical definition, even at the risk of mutilation. The classic spirit thus conceived has about it something scholastic — something that justifies too much Taine's absurd identification of it with the spirit of abstract reasoning. The way in which Nisard

[1] *Essais sur l'Ecole rom.*, 280.

relates the abstract reasoning of Descartes to the classic spirit also encourages the same error.[1] Sainte-Beuve is really nearer classical good sense when he protests, "Critic, why have but a single pattern?"[2] when he opposes to the somewhat solemn image of the French spirit which Nisard sets up, Voltaire's saying that "we French are the whipped cream of Europe,"[3] and sees in Voltaire himself a Frenchman at least as representative as Bossuet.

Nisard can scarcely be said to have solved the difficult problem of being selective without being narrow and exclusive, of achieving a concentration that shall not at the same time seem a contraction. This problem is especially difficult in an age of great expansion like that in which he lived. It is hard to deny one's own time without appearing unduly negative, without appearing to be actuated, like so many French reactionaries, less by love of the past than by hatred of the present. "Criticism," says Nisard, "is the general and dominating faculty of the nineteenth century; . . . it is the soul of all works; it is mingled with all the *genres*."[4] But the criticism that dominates the nineteenth century is in many respects the exact opposite of what Nisard understood by the term, — it is primarily comprehensive and sympathetic and historical, and not, like Nisard's own criticism, primarily judicial. At a time when everybody was exalting the principle of sympathy, when Hugo

[1] Cf., however, what he says of Boileau: "La raison dans Boileau n'est pas la raison d'un géomètre," etc. (*Histoire*, II, 297).

[2] *Lundis*, XV, 211. [3] *Ibid.*, XI, 465. [4] *Histoire*, IV, 541.

affirmed that the only proper attitude to assume towards genius is "to admire like a brute," Nisard insisted that an author's enemies are more likely to be right about him than his admirers; that the worst condition for coming to a correct opinion about anything is to look on it with the "superstitious eye of love."[1] Nisard thus succeeds at times like Brunetière in seasoning his conservatism with paradox, in so defending the traditional general sense as to affront the general sense of his contemporaries.

The native fineness of Nisard's taste and judgment lends a positive value to many pages of his work quite apart from his system; and then, too, the work has in a high degree the virtues of its defects. Faulty though the system be, its consistent application gives to the "History," as a whole, something four-square and monumental. Sainte-Beuve cannot refrain from contrasting rather sadly from this point of view Nisard's performance with that of a contemporary with whom he was far more in sympathy, — J. J. Ampère, son of the naturalist. Ampère was highly accomplished in all the new historical and cosmopolitan virtues. His intellectual hospitality was all-embracing. He loved to pass rapidly from one country and language to another so as to enjoy sudden antitheses of thought and feeling, intellectual Turkish baths, as Sainte-Beuve puts it. He had more than obeyed the injunction of Madame de Staël (*il faut avoir l'esprit européen*) and extended his horizons even beyond Europe. Sainte-Beuve mentions as

[1] See *Histoire*, I, 370 and II, 26, etc.

an example of the "lofty dilettanteisms of the spirit" in which he indulged, that on one occasion he read a Chinese book amidst the ruins of Ephesus.[1] The history of French literature Ampère was planning would have had all kinds of advantages over that of Nisard, but it remained inferior in one important respect — it was never written. He never succeeded in coördinating his superabundant material, in imposing a synthesis upon it. He was deficient in that power of pulling himself together by which, according to Goethe, the master is first revealed, and which at all events is necessary if one is to get beyond "lofty dilettanteisms of the spirit," and achieve a monument.

One is tempted at times to ask whether modern criticism has not lost about as much on one side as it has gained on the other, whether its broadening out of knowledge and sympathy has not been offset by a decline in judgment. Modern critics, Sainte-Beuve complains, will talk marvellously about and around a subject but will not commit themselves to the point of saying, this is good; this is bad.[2] Villemain, for instance, lacked courage in backing up his instinctive good taste. He was too capable of dodging and evasion. For his contemporaries, especially, he was all flattery and compliance, dominated and fascinated by powerful natures like Hugo.[3] Cousin remarked to Sainte-Beuve that there was in Villemain a perpetual struggle between Interest and Vanity. "Yes," retorted Sainte-Beuve, "and it is usually Fear that tips the balance."[4] Of Cousin him-

[1] *N. Lundis*, XIII, 241.
[2] *Lundis*, I, 382.
[3] *Lundis*, VIII, 491.
[4] *Ibid.*, XI, 191.

self Sainte-Beuve says he was a great and eloquent spirit and a mediocre character.[1] Mediocrity of character has been known to coexist with high intellectual gifts before the nineteenth century. Yet Sainte-Beuve is right in insisting on that antinomy between an indefinite widening out of one's horizons and staunch convictions, which had already dawned on Madame de Staël. All the modern enrichments of criticism, Sainte-Beuve complains, do not take the place of the authority and sterling good sense of a Johnson.[2] We cannot help reflecting that Sainte-Beuve himself was not very Johnsonian in his power of imposing his authority. When accused of being too compliant towards Chateaubriand in his lifetime, he replied that he felt in writing about him at that time like the "cricket forced to chirp in the lion's maw."[3] Dr. Johnson in his dealings with authors had a way of making them feel that *they* and not he were in the lion's maw.

The whole problem, however, of the relationship between comprehension and sympathy, on the one hand, and judgment, on the other, is one that we can best study in Sainte-Beuve's own work. We have gained in this chapter some knowledge of the environment in which he spent his formative years. He was one of the most assiduous contributors to the "Globe," and followed the lectures of Guizot, Cousin, and Villemain.

[1] *Lundis*, XI, 472. [2] *Lundis*, XI, 490. [3] *Chateaubriand*, I, 18.

V

SAINTE-BEUVE (BEFORE 1848)

SAINTE-BEUVE's work is almost unique in the way it combines extent with richness and variety. Perhaps no other writer has written more than fifty volumes and repeated himself so little, or fallen so rarely, even towards the end, below his own best standard. Voltaire's volumes are still more numerous, but are filled with repetition, and often senile repetition at that. One way in which Sainte-Beuve avoided repeating himself was by renewing himself. He distinguishes no less than ten "literary campaigns and expeditions" in which he had engaged, "all of which," he adds, "need to be judged by themselves and as different wholes."[1] If we are dealing only with the more fundamental changes in point of view we can reduce these ten campaigns or periods of literary activity to three, as he himself has done elsewhere: first, his 'prentice years on the "Globe" and his career as a militant romanticist (1824–1831);[2] secondly, the seventeen years of his contributions to the "Revue des Deux Mondes" and other periodicals, a somewhat neutral type of criticism, more comprehensive and sympathetic than judicial (1831–1848); thirdly, the work of his full critical maturity beginning with the "Chateaubriand et son Groupe littéraire" and marked by a simpler style

[1] *Portraits lit.*, II, 526.

[2] Some would extend his career of militant romanticism to about 1834.

and more judicial attitude (1848–1869). The six volumes of "Port-Royal," which occupied him for more than twenty years, were begun in the second manner and finished in the third.

I

Perhaps these different stages in Sainte-Beuve's critical development may best be studied in their relation to certain large movements. We can follow in his work more interestingly perhaps than anywhere else, the interplay and conflict of the main intellectual currents of the nineteenth century. Those, indeed, who have written about Sainte-Beuve have often inclined to treat him from a point of view narrowly biographical, to seek to account on personal and often pettily personal grounds for his critical opinions. They have taken very much to heart his own advice to "eschew the academic bust" and to look on the seamy as well as on the right side of the tapestry. In this sense one may say he has been made the victim of his own method. But even Sainte-Beuve's affair with Hugo's wife, which has been such a delectable morsel for the ultra-biographical school, may be profitably subordinated to the larger question of his whole relationship to the romantic movement.

Adopting, then, the more intellectual, and I believe also the more equitable, method of approach, we have to consider first of all as reflected in the writings of Sainte-Beuve the great main struggle of the nineteenth century —that between tradition on the one hand, and the forces that may be summed up under the name of naturalism on the other. Now tradition is at least twofold. The term covers what Nisard would call *la double antiquité*, that is, both religious or Christian tradition and that classical or humanistic discipline which is often in accord, but also, at times, at war with Christianity. Naturalism, again, has its intellectual or analytical as well as its emotional aspects. These two main aspects of the movement reduce themselves virtually in the nineteenth century to science and Rousseauistic romanticism. We should add, however, that Sainte-Beuve was familiar, not merely through books, but by contact with its surviving representatives, with the older forms of the naturalistic revolt against tradition — that is, with both the sentimentalism and rationalism of the eighteenth century. He was intimate, for example, with his fellow-townsman, Daunou, who was at once an accomplished classicist and a thorough-going ideologist — terms that Taine confounds but that Sainte-Beuve is careful to keep separate.[1] He found in Daunou, as he tells us, the living embodiment of the older French literary tradition and at the same time was initiated by him into "the most advanced eighteenth century," which meant in practice into a very advanced form of philosophic materialism. He also came in contact with Fauriel in whom, as we have seen, we can trace the process by which the eighteenth-century point of view passes over into that of the nineteenth century. Fauriel's passion for origins assumes in Sainte-Beuve the form of interest in the origins or youth of the individual — "that ineffable moment," as he says, "from which everything dates."[2]

[1] See article on Daunou in *Portraits cont.*, IV. [2] *N. Lundis*, III, 25.

Sainte-Beuve was also initiated into the older social as well as the older literary tradition. We think of him during the last twenty years of his life as somewhat of a recluse, but before 1848 he frequented the best society of the time — the men and women who were in the true, as well as in the conventional, sense aristocratic. The Comte d'Haussonville who belonged to this society insinuates that Sainte-Beuve was himself no "gentleman." [1] It is of course true that in his origins and personal appearance as well as in many of his instincts Sainte-Beuve was intensely bourgeois. This is, no doubt, the sense of the legend that associates all the great adventures of his life with an umbrella. Thus we are told that throughout his pistol duel in the rain with M. Dubois, he insisted on holding up an umbrella, giving as his reason that he was resigned to being killed but not to catching cold. Still he acquired in the drawing-room of Madame Récamier and elsewhere a feeling for the graces and amenities of aristocratic society, for its urbanity and tact and measure, — all the old-world charm that has scarcely survived the rude contact with democracy. Indeed, through all of his middle period Sainte-Beuve had too much in mind as his ideal audience the women of these very refined circles, with the inevitable result that he inclined to *préciosité*. He admits that at this time he had become somewhat of a mannerist, or, in his own words, had got into the habit of "caressing and over-refining his thought." He thanks "necessity, that great

[1] Probably the least gentlemanly thing Sainte-Beuve ever did was to publish privately the *Livre d'Amour* in 1843.

muse which, at supreme moments, makes the dumb man speak and the stammerer articulate plainly," for having forced him to address a wider public, "to speak to everybody in the language of all."[1]

To the kind of knowledge that comes from living contact with literary and social tradition, Sainte-Beuve added the knowledge that may be gained by study. From his school-days he had been an excellent Latinist and kept adding throughout his life to his knowledge of Greek. Even during the last crowded years he found time to take lessons from a native Greek, M. Pantasidès, and to read through with him several times the "Iliad" and "Odyssey." "Immortal spirits of Rome and especially of Greece," he exclaims, "fortunate geniuses who have culled as though in a first harvest all the bloom and simple grace and natural grandeur of man, you in whom thought, wearied by modern civilization and our complex life, once more finds youth and strength, health and freshness, and all the unsophisticated treasures of manly maturity and heroic youth, great men, for us like gods and whom so few get close to and contemplate, do not disdain this study in which I receive you on festal occasions; doubtless others possess you more fully and interpret you more worthily; you are better known elsewhere, but nowhere are you more deeply loved."[2]

II

Sainte-Beuve's relation to Christian tradition and to religion in general is a delicate and important matter.

[1] *Portraits lit.*, III, 550. [2] *Port. cont.*, V, 467.

Here again he had the advantage of coming into contact with men who were living incarnations of Christianity, in both its Catholic and Protestant forms. For an initiation into the spirit of Protestantism and to some extent of Jansenism he was under a deep debt to the writings and personality of Alexandre Vinet. But before discussing further Sainte-Beuve's attitude towards Christianity or his capacity for definite belief at all, we may best quote his own account (written late in life) of the phases through which he passed in his early manhood: "No mind is more pliant than mine or more thoroughly broken in to every form of metamorphosis. I began frankly and crudely with the most advanced eighteenth century, with Tracy, Daunou, Lamarck, and physiology: that is my true substance. From there I passed through the doctrinaire and psychological school of the 'Globe,' but making my reservations and without becoming a follower. Thence I passed over to poetical romanticism and through the society of Victor Hugo, and seemed to melt into it. I traversed afterwards, or rather skirted, Saint-Simonism and almost immediately afterward the society of Lamennais, still very Catholic. In 1837 at Lausanne I skirted Calvinism and Methodism, and had to try to interest this community. In all these journeyings of the spirit I never abdicated my will and judgment save for a moment in the society of Hugo and by a sort of spell. I never pledged my belief, but I understood things and people so perfectly that I raised the greatest hopes in true believers who wished to convert me and believed me already one of them. My curiosity, my desire to see everything, to look on everything at close quarters, my extreme pleasure at finding the relative truth of everything, involved me in this series of experiments, which have been for me only a long course in moral physiology."[1]

Though Sainte-Beuve came to feel at a comparatively early period that it was his destiny "to be and remain outside of everything,"[2] he was not, I believe, as resigned to this lack of centre in his life as one might infer from this passage. Evidence on this point may be gathered from the letters he wrote for many years to the Abbé Eustache Barbe, who, before entering the priesthood, had been one of his fellow students at the Blériot Institute at Boulogne. The two youths had been wont to take long strolls together on the seashore and their talk, as Sainte-Beuve tells us, ran ordinarily on the most serious subjects and the eternal problems. The correspondence is continued in somewhat the same tone. "I suffer," he writes to Barbe, "from the absence of faith; of fixed purpose and pole; I have the sentiment of these things, but I lack the things themselves."[3] Later he adds, "My life is governed very much by chance; the flood is driving me on and my ship has no anchor."[4] Still later he tells Barbe that he escapes from eating his heart out only "by plunging up to his neck in study." "I am revealing to you the true secret of my condition."[5] "Work which is my great burden is also my great resource,"[6] he writes in one of his last letters to Barbe.

[1] *Port. lit.*, III, 545.
[2] Letter to Lerminier, 7 April, 1833.
[3] *Nouvelle Cor.*, 41 (1836).
[4] *Nouvelle Cor.*, 93 (1844).
[5] *Ibid.*, 110 (1846).
[6] *Ibid.*, 182 (1863).

His confession to the Protestant Vinet coincides closely with that to the Catholic Barbe. "I have passed into the state of a pure critical intelligence," he writes to him, "and look with saddened eye on the death of my heart." Later in the same letter he compares his intelligence to a "dead moon that bathes in its cold rays the cemetery of his heart."[1] In one of his detached thoughts he likens his soul, in a metaphor that seems to have suggested Arnold's "Dover Beach," to a sandy waste of shore from which the sea of faith has long since withdrawn.[2]

So much for serious Christianity in Sainte-Beuve. He lacked faith and a rule of life, but he adds, we must remember, that he had the sentiment of these things. In other words, although he was never really religious, he did pass through a spell of romantic religiosity. "I have followed in my return to religion," he writes to Barbe in 1830, "less the pathway of theology or even philosophy than that of art and poetry." In so far Sainte-Beuve is evidently a follower of Chateaubriand's. He is not, however, like Chateaubriand moved so much by the external poetry of Christianity, the æsthetic and imaginative charm of its rites and ceremonies, as by the poetry of its inner life. He defines Chateaubriand as an epicurean with a Catholic imagination. He might have defined himself, at least for a number of years, as an epicurean with a Jansenist sensibility. He repels Béranger's charge that he inclined "too much to religiosity, the mania of our epoch, and the very opposite, as I be-

[1] *Cor.*, I, 130. [2] *Port. lit.*, III, 540.

lieve, of religion." [1] Yet in a sense Béranger was right; it was in this mood that Sainte-Beuve composed the earlier part of "Port-Royal"; as the mood passed away, he came to regard the subject with cold detachment, as he himself tells us, or, as one of his secretaries maintains, with positive dislike.[2]

Even more questionable forms of religiosity appear in Sainte-Beuve. He speaks of "the six celestial months" (the six months of his affair with Madame Hugo), during which he composed his volume of religious verse, "Les Consolations." "My imagination," he says, speaking of his novel "Volupté," which was written about the same time, "has always been in the service of my sensibility. To write a novel is merely my way of being in love and saying so." Unfortunately, he might have made the same remark with equal truth of his religious poetry. It is an inextricable mixture of love and religion, the religion being so used as to throw a glamour over the earthly passion. This is what I have called elsewhere [3] pseudo-Platonism, and what in this case might be termed with equal propriety pseudo-Christianity. The spell upon Sainte-Beuve at this period, which led him to abdicate his will and become an active and militant romanticist, was not merely that of Madame Hugo, but, at the outset especially, that of Hugo as well. Sainte-Beuve was not one of those stern and masculine natures that have their centre in themselves. He was not, if we may borrow a phrase from the journal of the Goncourts, who are in

[1] *Port-Royal*, I, 550. [2] *Sainte-Beuve*, par Jules Levallois, 177.
[3] *The New Laokoon*, ch. v.

general among his least intelligent critics, a superior male (*un mâle supérieur*). He was richest naturally in the feminine virtues of comprehension and sympathy, and instinctively sought to attach himself to some cause or personality that should give him the sense of direction which he did not find in himself. He was an "Elisha always in quest of his Elijah." And so he attached himself for a time to Hugo, just as he was on the point of attaching himself a little later to Lamennais and others. It was a time when many tempting baits were set (new humanitarian religions and the like) for the intellectually unwary. But, though in Sainte-Beuve's own metaphor in regard to these new movements, he often nibbled at the cheese, he did not get caught in the trap. He did, however, as I have already said, carry on his quest with more real ardor and less as a cold-blooded experiment than would appear from his later accounts. His motto might have been: "Enthusiasm and repentance." Nor is his failure to fix himself to be ascribed entirely to his own instability; his successive disillusions in his search for an ideal were due in large measure to the fact that he was living in an age of pseudo-idealism, and that he had encountered so many pseudo-idealists. "If my readers of recent years," he says, "have noticed in me sentiments of distrust and habitual skepticism, they will never know what I have secretly had to suffer for having at the outset carried all my sincerity and tenderness of spirit into my political and literary relations."[1] What he saw on every hand was self-seeking that dis-

[1] *Port. Cont.*, III, 49.

guised itself under rose-colored clouds of fine sentiments. There was Cousin, the apostle of the true, the good, and the beautiful, who nevertheless put no serious check on his own instincts of domination; Villemain, so great a talent and so accomplished a wit, always professing generous, liberal, philanthropic, Christian sentiments, and yet "the most sordid soul, the most mischievous ape alive";[1] Hugo, in whom he had found only "the immense pride and infinite egoism of an existence that knows only itself";[2] Balzac, whom he had seen "exuding the intoxication with himself from every pore";[3] Chateaubriand, who posed part of the day as the author of the "Genius of Christianity" and then devoted the rest of the day to playing the elderly Don Juan.[4] No wonder he made it an essential side of his method to "eschew the academic bust," and to suspect that under the fairest semblances and the finest draperies assumed by the men of his time there was something hollow.

He had come to feel, after having been at least half a disciple of Lamennais, that even this leader was but a pseudo-idealist; that he was not a man with a rule of life, but a creature of impulse. Lamennais had shifted abruptly from one extreme point of view to another, "leapfrogging," as Sainte-Beuve puts it, over the heads of his moderate friends. "Know," he says to Lamennais (and it is easy to detect the plaintive personal note), "know that nothing is worse than to invite souls to

[1] *Cor.* I, 316.
[2] *Nouvelle Cor.*, 34.
[3] *Port-Royal*, I, 552.
[4] *Lundis*, II, 158.

believe and then to decamp without any warning and desert them. Nothing so inclines them to that skepticism which you still abhor although you no longer have anything definite to oppose to it. How many souls that were already learning to hope, souls whom you had got into your hold and were carrying with you in your pilgrim's wallet, are, now that the wallet has been cast away, left lying prostrate at the ditch-side." Of his eminent contemporaries in general, Sainte-Beuve said he "knew most of them too well for his own enthusiasm." "Having approached almost all of them from the point of view of admiration and praise I quickly went to the bottom and know unluckily the whole story of their secret vanity."[1] "I thought," he says, "when I entered Hugo's house that I was in the grot of a demi-god, but I found myself in the den of the Cyclops."[2] His own rôle in this house had been, as he puts it, to "throw a gauze over epicureanism," with a view to seducing a friend's wife; in other words, in a pseudo-idealistic age he had himself been a pseudo-idealist.

The study of the austere Port-Royalists, he tells us, had never taught him to rise superior to his own self-love.[3] This self-love had been wounded cruelly, especially perhaps by the comparative failure of his creative efforts in verse, above all of the "Pensées d'Août" (1837). And so he gradually comes round to the point of view of a writer who had also suffered severe youthful

[1] *Nouvelle Cor.*, 42. [2] *Sainte-Beuve*, par L. Séché, II, 65.
[3] *Port-Royal*, VI, 245.

disillusions — La Rochefoucauld. Like him, he inclines more and more to see in life, even in its most specious aspects, a universal triumph of the principle of self-love. After the shipwreck of the vessel freighted with his romantic hopes and aspirations, he resigned himself to take refuge on the raft of criticism,[1] and perfect himself, like La Rochefoucauld, in such wisdom as may lie in disenchantment. This break with his past is marked by the publication of the article on La Rochefoucauld in 1840, though the fading away of the romantic glamour had been fairly complete two or three years earlier. "This article on La Rochefoucauld," he writes in the last year of his life, "(if I may be allowed to call attention to the fact,) marks an important moment, a decisive date in my intellectual life. My early youth, from the moment I had begun to reflect, had been entirely devoted to philosophy and to a positivist philosophy in agreement with the studies of physiology and medicine for which I was preparing myself. But a grave moral affection, a great disorder of sensibility, had intervened about 1829, and had produced a real deviation in my ideas. My volume of verse, 'Les Consolations,' and other works that followed, notably 'Volupté' and the first volumes of 'Port-Royal,' bear sufficient witness to this restless and overwrought mood, which carried with it a considerable portion of mysticism. The study of La Rochefoucauld . . . marks the end of this crisis and the return of sounder views, in which years and reflection have only strengthened me."[2] It is, indeed, as we

[1] *Port. Cont.*, II, 486. [2] *Portraits de Femmes*, 321.

shall see still more clearly later, an essential part of Sainte-Beuve's method to trace out human self-love in all its myriad disguises. In his last article on La Rochefoucauld (1863), Sainte-Beuve speaks of the "subtilized and quintessentiated ego" he often detects even in utterances and points of view that seem most sublime and impersonal. Man, the everlasting prisoner of his self-love, "cuts and carves everything he encounters on his own pattern." He continues: "And I myself, first of all, I, who am writing this, if I force myself to love what I am not, or even the contrary of what I am, do it not through detachment from the ego; it is perhaps because I take pride in being nothing in particular, and like myself better apparently under this broken, fugitive and multiple form, than under any other. No, no, honest folk, La Rochefoucauld, rightly understood, is not so easy to refute as you suppose."[1]

Closely associated with his cult for La Rochefoucauld is his cult for La Bruyère, whose view of life coincides in so many ways with that of La Rochefoucauld, and who appealed to Sainte-Beuve furthermore by his consummate art in literary portrait-painting, or, as one might say, in the literary miniature. He remarks on the Countess of Albany's copy of La Bruyère with her marginal notes: "How I should like to have that copy before me and make a close study of it. Every sincere heart, every sincere intellect might thus jot down all his moral life on the margins of his La Bruyère. He has given the text, you have only to add the variants."[2]

[1] *N. Lundis*, v, 391. [2] *N. Lundis*, v, 427.

Elsewhere he advises us to have a copy of La Bruyère on the table at our bedside. Take a little of it at a time and frequently and he promises that the health of our minds will profit by the prescription.[1]

Both La Rochefoucauld and La Bruyère, it has been remarked, have a view of human nature very similar to that of Christianity, but with very little of the Christian hope. Pascal would have said that they had a right sense of man's wretchedness without grace, but an insufficient sense of the grandeur man may attain with the help of grace. Sainte-Beuve is entirely at one with La Rochefoucauld and La Bruyère in this respect. He can at least admire the Jansenists for their inexorable dealings with the ordinary facts of human nature. "Let those who cannot accept the remedies proposed by these mournful believers," he says of them, "respect them at least and pity them as fellow creatures for having felt so deeply on certain days the nothingness and wretchedness of human nature, that ocean of vices and pains, and its murmur, its fury, its eternal plaint."[2]

Sainte-Beuve remained to the end a "melancholy skeptic who is not sure of his own doubt." But from the outset he had been temperamentally with the naturalists rather than with the supernaturalists, and the naturalistic temper grew upon him. We are often reminded, by the forms it assumes, of the whole class of doubters known in the seventeenth century as the *libertins*. We can discover in Sainte-Beuve a direct relationship to several of these *libertins* besides La Rochefou-

[1] *Lundis*, II, 66. [2] *Port-Royal*, II, 115.

cauld. Pascal had noted this secession from Christianity in the name of nature, and in some of the most penetrating pages that have been written by any modern man he connects this naturalism with the naturalism of classical antiquity. Those moderns, he says, who try to live purely according to nature without the inner balance wheel of faith, fall inevitably, like all ancient naturalists, either into the extreme of stoic pride or into that of epicurean relaxation. He takes Montaigne as a type of the epicurean skeptic and in this sense the greatest of the *libertins*. Sainte-Beuve accepts substantially this conception of Montaigne in several of the most brilliant, though not perhaps soundest chapters of his "Port-Royal" (chapters written while he was still cultivating a Jansenist sensibility). We should associate with these chapters what he said towards the end of his life: "I have reached the same age as Bayle, Horace and Montaigne, my masters. I may die."[1] It is essential for a proper understanding of Sainte-Beuve to determine his relation to these three men, and first of all to Montaigne.

III

In his treatment of Montaigne Sainte-Beuve has not altogether avoided, I believe, a rather common error during the past century — that of confusing the planes of being. Three such planes may be distinguished — the religious, the humanistic, the naturalistic — though there are, of course, numerous intermediary stages, the rounds of the ladder, as it were, by which man may

[1] *Lundis*, XVI, 45.

mount or descend from one level to another of his being. On which of these planes does Montaigne live? We must grant Sainte-Beuve at once that he is not at home on the religious level. His view of life is not in the highest degree heroic, it is certainly not saintly. Like Sainte-Beuve himself, Montaigne idealizes youth. The temperamental bent is already visible at twenty, and Montaigne is loath to believe that this bent can be traversed and a new direction given a man by some miracle of grace or conversion. Montaigne, says Sainte-Beuve, has "no notion of that inverse moral and spiritual perfection, that growing maturity of the inner being under the withering outer envelope, that perpetual education for heaven, that second birth and immortal youth, . . . which makes the white-haired old man seem at times only in his first bloom for the eternal springtime; an illusion perhaps, and a last Utopia, but of the kind a Franklin himself cherished."[1]

If Montaigne is not at home on the religious level of human nature, we must grant Sainte-Beuve that he is very much at home on the naturalistic level. He has the expansiveness of the naturalist, his far-ranging intellectual and emotional curiosity, above all he has the naturalistic sense of flux and instability, the sense of all that is undulating and fugitive, and the closely-allied sense of infinite shades of difference even in things that seem identical. "*Distinguo,*" he declares, "is the most universal member of my logic." In these as in many other respects he is an epicurean naturalist, and Sainte-Beuve is no less plainly his disciple.

[1] *Port-Royal,* II, 430.

But what about the intermediary or humanistic level in Montaigne? One becomes humanistic in proportion as he grows aware of that law of order and measure and decorum that, according to Cicero, distinguishes man from other living creatures, and in proportion as he imposes the discipline of this law upon his ordinary or animal self; in proportion, that is, as he aims not merely to express his own idiosyncrasy, but to be a normal man. Now this humane preoccupation, so far from being absent from the work of Montaigne, is, I believe, at the very heart of it. Montaigne, says Sainte-Beuve, is pure nature. His ambition at all events was to be pure *human* nature. The vagabondage and egotism are more or less superficial. What we find under the surface is a fairly firm conviction based on the Greek, and especially the Latin, classics, as to what the true man should be; a conception which in the somewhat conventionalized form of the *honnête homme qui ne se pique de rien* — the gentleman and scholar who in the interest of his all-roundness is afraid of knowing any one thing too well — was to dominate the whole neo-classical period. Emerson puts us on the right track when he remarks that Montaigne rises to passion only when speaking of Socrates, and relates how in the cemetery of Père Lachaise, at Paris, he came upon the tomb of an Auguste Collignon, who died in 1830, and who, according to the inscription, "lived to do right and had formed himself to virtue on the essays of Montaigne."

Montaigne is misleading because unlike most people he affects not more but less certainty than he feels.

He obeys in part a humanistic motive in his very skepticism, which is a salutary protest against the "horrible mania of certainty" that had possessed the theological ages, and was still afflicting his own time.

In making of Montaigne a pure naturalist, Sainte-Beuve has fallen in too far with the tactics of Pascal and the Jansenists, who are for obliterating all the intermediary stages of purely human effort and virtue by which man may rise above the naturalistic level; who are, in short, for opposing a stark naturalism to a stark supernaturalism, so that man may have no resource save in their theological *deus ex machina*. That is why Jansenism, we may remark in passing, is an impracticable view of life. Sainte-Beuve makes of Montaigne a direct ancestor of Rousseau. "The fair foliage of his essays," he says, "is later to become a dense and dark and venomous forest, deadly to the Werthers and other dreamers who fall asleep in its shadow, . . . a tortuous abode of suicides, etc."[1] So far as the main direction of Montaigne is concerned, this is not only untrue but the exact opposite of the truth. Montaigne is moving towards the centre of human nature; the pure naturalists, whether sentimental or scientific, are moving away from the centre, no matter what pseudo-mystical devices they may employ to convince themselves and us of the contrary. What is the inevitable upshot of Montaigne? asks Sainte-Beuve. "'A little Jew, walking with measured tread,'[2] is going to tell us: . . . A great gloomy heaven,

[1] *Port-Royal*, II, 405.

[2] "Un petit Juif marchant à pas comptés." Voltaire's description of Spinoza.

a vast revolving universe, dumb and unfathomable, in which from time to time and in certain spots life makes its appearance, . . . in which man comes into being, glittering and dying with the thousand insects of the hour on this grassy islet floating in a marsh," etc. "All that is cheerful and flattering to the eye in Montaigne is merely there to curtain the abyss or, as he would have said, to turf the tomb."[1]

This is an eloquent assertion of the hopelessness and helplessness of a pure naturalism in dealing with ultimate problems. But so far as its relevancy to Montaigne is concerned, it is little more than rhetoric; it merely testifies to the success with which Sainte-Beuve during the time he was writing this part of "Port-Royal," had cultivated a Jansenist sensibility. The humanist certainly falls short of the saint, but he is just as certainly superior to the pure naturalist, whether stoic or epicurean, to any one, in short, who would reduce human nature and phenomenal nature to a common law.

IV

The same point may, perhaps, be made even more clearly by comparing Sainte-Beuve with another of the three men whom he claims as masters — Horace. There is a side of Horace that is more obviously and grossly epicurean than anything in Sainte-Beuve. Save for a mere fraction of his work, Sainte-Beuve is, in this respect, at the opposite pole from writers like Herrick, who boasted, as Catullus and Martial and other poets had

[1] *Port-Royal*, 442.

boasted before him, that though his muse was "jocund," his life was chaste. Yet in the final analysis Horace is more humanistic than Sainte-Beuve. He had been more deeply preoccupied with questions of conduct ever since his boyhood and those object lessons in morality he had received from his father. Through all his experimenting with stoical and epicurean tenets we can trace an ascending effort, a gradual ripening and mellowing, until in the most amiable and undogmatic fashion, and simply by the exercise of a keen good sense, he comes to assert that discipline which the human self and its law of measure impose on the ordinary self. "Dare to be wise," is the sum of his message. "A right beginning is more than half of the whole. Despise pleasures and bridle and chain the mind. If you do not command it, it will command you."[1] In one of his last poems he says that he is neglecting more and more the numbers and measures of Latin song for the numbers and measures of the true life. He is preoccupied, above all, with the problem whether he is becoming gentler and better with the progress of the years:

"Lenior et melior fis accedente senecta?"[2]

Religion goes higher than this; even the best poetry goes higher. Yet Horace's confidence in the power of the individual to perfect himself is plain. Let us quote by contrast a sentence of Sainte-Beuve: "Ripen! Ripen! as a man grows older, he rots in some places and hardens in others, but he does not ripen."[3] Sainte-Beuve's hu-

[1] *Epist.*, I, 2, 40–62. [2] *Ibid.*, II, 2, 211

[3] *Portraits cont.*, V, 461.

manism is not, like Horace's, a discipline and a rule of life; it is not active, erect, and militant, but has retired from the intellect and will to the sensibility, and so is more or less a matter of passive enjoyment. It bears about the same relation to genuine humanism that the æsthetic faith of Chateaubriand does to genuine Christianity. To be a humanist, even in this restricted sense, that is, to be one of the most exquisite of literary epicureans, still remains a rare distinction. And, after all, the humanistic façade to Sainte-Beuve's epicureanism is substantial compared to what we have seen in later writers — Walter Pater, for example. If Sainte-Beuve were defined as an æsthetic humanist, Pater would have to be defined at best as a humanistic æsthete.

The lapse from the religious or humanistic to the naturalistic level of being is, in almost a literal sense, decadent. The Rousseauistic romanticist usually dissimulates this lapse under a veil of pseudo-idealism. Of the presence of this false illusion of decadence in Sainte-Beuve's poetry and in "Volupté" I have already said something. His own contention was that he was trying to introduce a humbler and more domestic note into French verse, in imitation of Wordsworth and Crabbe. But he has little in common with these poets, who are themselves, save for the choice of lowly subjects, almost at opposite poles. Sainte-Beuve's poetry, however, especially "Joseph Delorme," does have a place in the history of the malady of the age, deriving as it does from Chateaubriand and pointing the way in its choice, not merely of the humble, but of the repulsive, subject to

Baudelaire. His muse, as he says, is not a brilliant odalisk, who dances with bared bosom, but a poor consumptive, devoted to the task of nursing an aged, blind and insane father. If at times she sings in order to charm away his delirious terror, she is interrupted in the midst of her song by a hacking cough. This consumptive muse would have inspired horror in Wordsworth, but very properly took under her protection "Les Fleurs du Mal." "You are right in saying," wrote Sainte-Beuve to Baudelaire, "that my poetry had much in common with yours. I had tasted of the same bitter fruit, full of ashes in the end."[1]

We not only find in Sainte-Beuve the false illusion of decadence, we also find in him — and this is far more important for our present purpose — its false disillusion. Wisdom, for Sainte-Beuve, is not a positive insight, the final reward of the struggle for self-mastery, but something cold and negative. To make clear this conception of wisdom, we shall need to treat from the point of view of ideas the aspect of Sainte-Beuve's life that has so often been treated from the point of view of gossip; or rather we should apply his own method to him, and let him speak for himself in this matter. We should, so far as possible, dip the elements of our judgment of him, as he phrases it, "out of his own inkwell." "In my youth," he says, speaking in the person of Amaury (the hero of "Volupté"), "my philosophy came to me especially through voluptuousness, through the use of pleasures." Most philosophers, he goes on to say, do their

[1] *Cor.*, I, 360 (1865).

meditating in the plenitude of life and at the height of illusion. He, on the contrary, did his "in the pale light of the morrow that follows pleasures, in that weariness of which Lucretius speaks, and which reveals the bottom of things. I saw constantly the seamy side and the end of everything, the nothingness which I already felt and the foretaste of which is not without melancholy delights." His mind, when he did his observing, "was in a state of slightly icy limpidity, and with the minimum of illusion."[1] Sainte-Beuve asserted more than once in his own name this strange doctrine that the truest vision of life is to be had "in the cold gray dawn of the morning after." "I have had my weaknesses," he writes magnificently, "the weaknesses that in King Solomon inspired disgust with everything and satiety of life."[2] "Like Solomon and Epicurus," he says elsewhere, "I have penetrated into philosophy through pleasure. That is better than to reach it through logic like Hegel or Spinoza."[3] If philosophy is to be attained in this way, it must coincide with a general lack of convictions, for, as Sainte-Beuve remarks elsewhere, voluptuousness is a great dissolvent of the inner life. "The principle of certainty in us is undermined by it in the long run."[4]

The truth is, Sainte-Beuve's emotional, like his intellectual, life was almost entirely unchecked and expansive. Now the master motive of a life that expands freely in this way is curiosity; and Sainte-Beuve's curiosity, both

[1] *Lundis*, XVI, 43.

[2] Cf. "Il ressentait cet incurable dégoût de toutes choses qui est particulier à ceux qui ont abusé des sources de la vie." (*Portraits Cont.*, V, 464.)

[3] *Port. lit.*, III, 543.

[4] *Proudhon*, 102.

intellectual and emotional, was enormous. There exists in most men, he says, a poet who dies young.[1] This poet never died completely in Sainte-Beuve, but appears to the end in his extremely metaphorical and at times even flowery style. On the other hand, we feel even during the most romantic period of his youth that there existed in him alongside the poet an insatiably curious critic. It is even truer, perhaps, that he is a critic in his poetry than that he is a poet in his criticism. "Did Conrad," he asks in one of his poems, "know Latin better than Jouy? Did he use up fewer pens than Suard? Did Doctor Guy Patin have more than ten thousand volumes?"[2]

V

The particular kind of curiosity that appears in this passage suggests the affinity between Sainte-Beuve and Bayle, the last in date of the three men he mentions as his masters. "It is incredible how much Bayle there is in Sainte-Beuve,"[3] says M. Faguet. And Sainte-Beuve's kinship to Bayle is even more apparent than that to Horace and Montaigne. Bayle was converted in his youth from Protestantism to Catholicism and then back

[1] *Port. lit.*, I, 415.

[2] See the whole poem *Mes Livres* (*Joseph Delorme*). *A La Rime*, perhaps the best of his poems, is at least semi-critical. Several of his happiest critical phrases are found in the poems, e.g.: —

"Lamartine ignorant, qui ne sait que son âme"

and

"Vigny, plus secret,
Comme en sa *tour d'ivoire*, avant midi, rentrait."

(Both from the poetical epistle "*A M. Villemain.*")

[3] *Politiques et moralistes*, III, 208.

again to Protestantism, and lost all his fire of faith in these changes of creed. He finally became a libertine, though only in the seventeenth-century sense, and not, like Sainte-Beuve, in the nineteenth-century sense as well. We should note, however, regarding his emotional curiosity (not to speak of the rumor that he made love to Madame Jurieu), the somewhat morbid predilection for certain kinds of anecdotes that is familiar to all readers of the Dictionary. Bayle's intellectual curiosity is at all events unbounded. "There are minds," says Sainte-Beuve, "the vocation of which is to know simply for the sake of knowing; minds which the passion of Faust possesses, and which do not refer back their acquisitions and efforts to the supreme and perfect goal capable of rectifying them."[1]

Sainte-Beuve was, like Bayle, insatiably curious even about the trivial ("Did Conrad use up fewer pens than Suard?"). Faguet says that Bayle must have gossiped over his evening meal with his housekeeper. He goes rather far, however, when he adds that his books, like those of Sainte-Beuve, frequently savor of the servants' hall and a bit of the pantry.[2] Like Bayle, Sainte-Beuve is more likely to fall into the gossipy and familiar vein in his notes than in his main text (as he says, one feels more at home on the ground floor than in the grand apartments upstairs). Like Bayle, too, he has a way of insinuating into his notes some of his boldest statements, and like Bayle's, his method, especially before 1848, is at times feline and perfidious. He undermines by subtle

[1] *Port-Royal*, II, 160. [2] *XVIIIe Siècle*, 23.

indirections what he is appearing to praise. "God save me from being eulogized by you," said one of the Goncourts to him at a Magny dinner.

We are dwelling, however, on the smaller side of the likeness between the two men. What Bayle stands for in the history of thought is the idea of tolerance, and it is on this side, after all, that we are to seek for the important relationship between him and Sainte-Beuve. No Frenchman of the nineteenth century was more afraid than Sainte-Beuve of that narrowing of the mind that comes from preconceived ideas or party spirit. "To the deuce with all fetishes," he said, "of whatever wood they are manufactured." Sainte-Beuve was in this respect a true disciple of Bayle and not like so many of his followers in the eighteenth century and since, who have managed to be fanatical in their very preaching of tolerance. Sainte-Beuve relates how one day M. Franck of the Collège de France was giving an address on tolerance. Some one present ventured to show disagreement, whereupon he was slapped by the person seated next to him, and finally thrown out of the hall by an audience that had grown enthusiastic over tolerance![1] Sainte-Beuve adds that intolerance is the French fault *par excellence*, and this is, of course, due to the tendency of the Frenchman to carry to an excess his virtue of logicality, and then to put emotion into the service of his logic. Sainte-Beuve was acutely conscious of the difference between the workings of his own mind in this respect and that of most

[1] *N. Lundis*, IX, 197.

Frenchmen. He deals with life and literature with a maximum of good sense and a minimum of mere logical exclusiveness, and this is of course a trait that appeals strongly to the English and American reader. The student of heredity might attach some weight to the fact that he had English blood.

We must, however, show care in defining the particular type of tolerance displayed by Sainte-Beuve and Bayle. The highest type, as Sainte-Beuve himself says, is the tolerance that is allied, not with the contempt for everything, but with a profound faith in something.[1] The tolerance of Sainte-Beuve and Bayle can scarcely be said to be of this latter type, but rather of the skeptical and epicurean variety that is so widespread in the world to-day. They enter with an admirable breadth of comprehensive sympathy into all the modes of being, but when it comes to drawing conclusions are pure Pyrrhonists. "Who am I," says Sainte-Beuve, "to decide in the name of absolute truth?"[2] He sets aside every preference of his own and merely tries to establish the two extreme poles without inclining in favor of either, and thus to give to thought its full and free play.[3] The only rôle that befits him, he says again, "is to balance over against one another the diverse and changing aspects of incomprehensible reality."[4]

Sainte-Beuve took this somewhat neutral view of criticism more particularly in what I have termed his middle period. From this point of view, the article he wrote

[1] *N. Lundis*, IX, 199.
[2] *Port-Royal*, III, 409.
[3] *Port-Royal*, II, 155.
[4] *Ibid.*, III, 423.

in 1835 on "Bayle and the Critical Spirit" is almost autobiographical. The extent to which he reduced the critic's rôle at this time to mere comprehension and sympathy may also be seen in a "thought" like the following: "The critical spirit is by nature facile, insinuating, mobile and comprehensive. It is a great and limpid stream which winds and bends its way about the works and monuments of poetry, as about so many rocks, fortresses, vine-clad hills and leafy valleys that border its shores. While each one of these objects remains fixed in the landscape and cares little for the other, while the feudal tower disdains the valley, and the valley knows nothing of the hillside, the stream goes from one to the other, bathes them without doing them violence, embraces them in its living waters, *comprehends* them, reflects them, and when the traveller is curious to know and visit these varied spots, it takes him in a boat, carries him smoothly along, and unfolds to him in succession all the changing spectacle of its course."[1] M. Lemaître took this passage as motto for his impressionistic "Contemporains." Perhaps it fits the dilettante[2] even more than the impressionist, for the impressionist, in lieu of fixed principles, has at least sharp temperamental exclusions, whereas the critic, as Sainte-Beuve defines him at this time, neither excludes nor concludes. The critic is a sort of gypsy or vagrant in the intellectual world, without settled abode of his own, that is, without any central and dominating point of view; or to use another of Sainte-Beuve's com-

[1] *Joseph Delorme*, Pensée XVII. Cf. also *Portraits Cont.*, II, 512.
[2] As the term is defined in the chapter on Renan (p. 279).

parisons, is like an actor who assumes every evening a new rôle.

This conception of the critic could scarcely satisfy Sainte-Beuve permanently, nor could he fail to feel the differences as well as the similarities between Bayle and himself. Bayle's curiosity is not only omnivorous, but indiscriminate. He gives, as has been pointed out, ten times more space in his "Dictionary" to D'Assoucy than to Dante. Aristotle or Peckins, as M. Faguet puts it, is all the same to him. His attitude towards the literature of his own time is essentially journalistic. "The last book I see," he writes, "is the one I prefer to all others." He is equally interested, for example, in the "Phèdre" of Racine and that of Pradon.[1] Now Sainte-Beuve was not only literary to his finger-tips, but as he got away from the special atmosphere of the romantic movement, he became more and more classical. One may say, indeed, that with increasing age his hold upon the Christian tradition lessened and that upon the humanistic tradition grew stronger. Furthermore, as he matured and got more confidence in himself, he felt it was not enough for the critic to be comprehensive and sympathetic, he must also be judicial. "I have played the part of an advocate long enough," he exclaims, "let me now play that of judge."[2] As a result of thus feeling the need of being more judicial at the same time that he was becoming more classical in temper, he was led to honor Boileau, a critic who was in the highest degree judicial along traditional lines, and almost at the

[1] *Port. lit.*, I, 382. [2] *Ibid.*, III, 550.

opposite pole of criticism to Bayle. He had always, he tells us, lived in imagination with Boileau, but in his attitude towards him he went through several phases. There is first the brisk romantic attack of 1829,[1] then the partial palinode of 1843,[2] and finally the full tribute of admiration and praise in the article of 1852.[3]

We may also trace in Sainte-Beuve an interesting relationship to Goethe. Some of his earlier references are very superficial, as, for example, when he contrasts the spiritual elevation of Pascal with the lack of it in Goethe and Talleyrand![4] Later he makes ample reparation. He pronounces Goethe the greatest of critics,[5] and when he is looking for a high critical impartiality to oppose to the excess of partisanship he found in his French contemporaries, he thinks of Goethe even more than of Bayle. "O immense lake, vast and calm mirror of Goethe, where art thou?"[6] he exclaims. Sainte-Beuve was himself in this respect the most Goethean of Frenchmen. When an admiring correspondent compared him to Goethe, however, he replied: "He naturally lived on the summits, whereas I have been a dweller in the valley."[7] The difference is really even more fundamental. The final impression one carries away from Sainte-Beuve is that of a man who has suffered an inner defeat; from Goethe, that of a man who has fought and conquered. Sainte-Beuve, during his later period, was at all events very much at one with Goethe in aiming to

[1] *Port. lit.*, I, 3 ff.
[2] *Ibid.*, 23 ff.
[3] *Lundis*, VI, 494 ff.
[4] *Port-Royal*, III, 356.
[5] *Lundis*, XI, 505.
[6] *Lundis*, XV, 368.
[7] *Cor.*, II, 3.

be both a humanist and a naturalist; to unite the most comprehensive sympathy for the modern movement with the cult of literary tradition.

Perhaps the best way to understand Sainte-Beuve's critical activity during his last twenty years is to study in him this interplay and at times conflict of naturalism and humanism. I have been trying in this chapter to relate him in his naturalism to the "libertines" of the seventeenth century and to the epicureans of all ages. But to grasp his critical method, it is needful to go more fully than hitherto into certain forms of naturalism that belong especially to the nineteenth century.

VI

SAINTE-BEUVE (AFTER 1848)

In his loss of romantic illusions Sainte-Beuve anticipated by only a few years the course of the century itself. The culmination of political romanticism in the Revolution of 1848 was followed by sudden and violent disenchantment. The fairest millennial visions had collapsed at the first contact with reality. The "idealists" had had an abrupt descent from the clouds, and lay bruised and bleeding upon the earth. What really goes with the naturalistic view of life is imperialism. Those who would set up as idealists and at the same time live on the naturalistic level simply hasten the triumph of the opposite cause to that they are preaching. Thus the men of '48 proclaimed an "evangelical" republic, and the paroxysm of hideous anarchy that ensued prepared the way for the *coup d'état* of 1851, and the advent of the densest materialism the world had seen since the Roman decadence. This is the true romantic irony — far more poignant than what usually goes by that name. Sainte-Beuve says that the example of Napoleon had done much to corrupt the nineteenth century and encourage the cult of mere force even in literature. But Napoleon himself is only the ironical reply of the Nature of Things to the Utopias of the French Revolution. It was scarcely due to Napoleon that Sainte-Beuve himself showed traces of the imperialistic temper, — an undue partiality at times for the prevailing faction. When any sweeping is going on, it is well, as the French saying has it, to be on the side of the broom handle. I believe that there were more honorable motives for the promptness with which Sainte-Beuve accepted the Second Empire. Still it was unfortunate that in his article "Les Regrets,"[1] he should have given even the appearance of insulting the vanquished and rejoicing over their discomfiture.

I

From the bankruptcy of romantic idealism most men of the mid-nineteenth century drew the inference that all idealism is vain. It was time, they reasoned, to cease dreaming and face the facts. Man himself they would treat as a fact, subject to the same laws as other phenomena. In striking contrast to the wreckage of romantic hopes that littered the earth was the structure of solid achievement that the scientists were gradually raising by patient submission to the facts. In science man might recover part of that faith in himself that had just been so seriously shaken. Now the age in taking this trend was in a sense following the line of Sainte-Beuve's own development. He had also become a positivist in his own way. He had taken as his seal the English word Truth, by which he meant of course relative and contingent truth, the establishing of the facts. "If I had a motto," he said, "it would be the *true*, the true alone. And as for the good and the beautiful they might come off as

[1] *Lundis*, I, 397 ff.

best they could."[1] In his passion for authenticity, in his almost morbid fear of being duped, he would not only get at the truth, but as the French put it, at the true truth, which is sometimes very different from the mere truth. Though his attitude towards literature is not primarily scientific, he satisfied the strictest scientific standards in his scrupulosity as to facts. The gracefulness of the superstructure in his essays is equalled by the solidity of the foundations. "You would have had to know Sainte-Beuve," says Scherer, "to realize the almost morbid importance that he attached to the spelling of a proper name, to a bit of information, to a date. He wished to see everything with his own eyes, to verify everything."[2]

On the purely naturalistic side, therefore, Sainte-Beuve felt very much at home in the new age. He saw a generation of younger men coming up with Taine and Renan at their head, who were in many respects his own disciples and by whom he was influenced in turn. He did not seem, like Lamartine and others, a forlorn survivor into an uncongenial epoch, but was stimulated to do some of his best work. Here again, however, we must make some important distinctions. It is difficult to make too many distinctions in writing of Sainte-Beuve. He remained the skeptic to the end, "holding no form of creed but contemplating all"; convinced with Bayle, that the only hope is in a moderate and reasonable human nature, and at the same time that human nature never can be moderate and reasonable; convinced above

[1] *Cor.*, II, 41. [2] *Etudes*, IV, 107.

all with La Rochefoucauld that human nature can never be disinterested. But man it would appear is an incurably religious animal. If deprived of other objects of worship he will fall to worshipping himself. And this is what those who were influenced by Bayle in the eighteenth century actually did. This idolatry of humanity and its future progress is almost universal among our modern naturalists and separates them from those seventeenth-century "libertines" with whom I have been comparing Sainte-Beuve.

What was Sainte-Beuve's own attitude towards the idea of progress, and in general towards the great Goddess Humanity before whose image we are all prostrated so devoutly to-day? Here again we must distinguish. There are evidently two main classes of humanitarians, not to speak of the blendings of the two types, and the sub-varieties of each. First there are the humanitarians who believe that mankind as a whole is going to be regenerated by the triumph, in some manner or other, either evolutionary or revolutionary, of the principle of fraternity or social pity over self-love. In the second place there are the humanitarians who believe that mankind is to be regenerated through science. The disciple of La Rochefoucauld who had been unable to feel the religious hope in the salvation of the individual, was not likely to fall in with the hope of the sentimental humanitarian in the salvation of the race. I do not mean to accuse Sainte-Beuve of heartlessness. He speaks, indeed, as we have seen, of the "death" of his heart, and so far as the religious intuitions are concerned, I believe that this is true. But though one of the most irritable, Sainte-Beuve was also one of the kindliest of men,—even more capable of sympathy perhaps for the poor and the humble than for men of his own class. "The heart of Joseph Delorme," we read in the Life prefixed to the Poems, "was divided between an unbounded love for the suffering portion of humanity and an implacable hatred for the powerful of this world." Joseph Delorme, in short, embodied in himself both the rebellion and the social pity of the Rousseauist, and something of Delorme survived in Sainte-Beuve to the end. Though unable to acquiesce in the humanitarian creed he had a good deal of the humanitarian temper as appears in the volume he devoted to the agitator Proudhon.

One who, like Sainte-Beuve, saw barbarism always trembling just beneath the surface of human nature, is at best, however, a doubtful recruit for either scientific or sentimental humanitarians. "He who has not witnessed," he says, "an army of brave men in complete rout, or a political assembly that supposed itself sensible thrown into a frenzy by some passionate speech, does not know to what point it remains true that man at bottom is only an animal and a child. O eternal childhood of the human heart!"[1] No wonder he looked doubtfully on man's attempt to set up his own image for worship in the sanctuary left vacant by *la grande absence de Dieu.* In the course of one of the finest tributes that have ever been paid to Molière (the greatest of all the seventeenth century "libertines"), Sainte-Beuve writes that "to love

[1] *Port. lit.*, III, 549.

Molière is to make sure of not falling into a smug and limitless admiration for a humanity that idolizes itself, and forgets of what stuff it is made and that it is always, try as it may, only puny human nature."[1] Perhaps it is not well to become quite so expert as Sainte-Beuve in the art of detecting self-seeking. He comments as follows on one of the most disenchanted thoughts of Marcus Aurelius: "And so Marcus Aurelius drank his chalice, too, but he drank it in silence. He did not cry out like that cynical revolutionist:[2] 'I've had my fill of men' (*Je suis soûl des hommes*), but he thought it. Cicero too said it in his manner. This feeling of nausea at men often came upon him and there was a moment when everything appeared odious to him except death. Cæsar towards the end no longer took the trouble to defend his life. He seemed to say: 'Let them take it, if they want it.' We arrive at this same feeling of disgust by all paths. It is enough to have lived a long time and to have had too close dealings with the human species." It is to be feared that any one who has come to feel in that way will not be able to profit by John Morley's advice and satisfy his religious sense by communing with Humanity in its past, present, and future.

Yet, after all, Sainte-Beuve's nearest approach to a definite belief is his belief in scientific progress. "If we go beyond the ephemeral triflings," he says, "of present literature, which cumber up the front of the stage and obstruct one's gaze, there is in this age a great and powerful movement in every direction, in every science.

[1] *N. Lundis*, v, 278. [2] Danton.

Our nineteenth century in contradistinction to the eighteenth is not dogmatic, it seems to avoid giving its opinion, it is in no haste to conclude. There are even little superficial reactions which it seems to favor by fearing to oppose them. But patience! At every point men are at work — in physics, chemistry, zoölogy, botany, in all branches of natural history, in historical and philosophical criticism, in oriental studies, in archæology, everything is being gradually transformed, and the day when the century takes the trouble to draw its conclusions, you will see that it is at a hundred leagues, a thousand leagues, from its point of departure. The vessel is in the open sea. The knots are reeled off without being counted. The day when men take their bearings they will be amazed at the distance they have covered."[1] This sounds encouraging, though it does not tell us *where* we are going, but merely that we are on the way. Sainte-Beuve quotes with approval the saying of Pascal that "the inventions of men increase from age to age, but that the goodness and badness of the world remain in general the same," and adds that he should like to see this saying used as epigraph for all our grandiose theories of progress.[2]

I have already spoken of the interplay and conflict of the humanistic and naturalistic elements in Sainte-Beuve's later writing. It is perhaps the main form in him of the opposition between thought and feeling (for his humanism is largely a matter of feeling) that so permeates our modern period. One must of course not

[1] *Port. lit.*, III, 549. [2] *Port-Royal*, II, 261.

be over hasty in setting down as a contradiction what is one of Sainte-Beuve's most admirable traits — his readiness to observe impartially and record all the facts without attempting to reduce them to some premature system. Still the contradiction exists. If as a scientific naturalist he believed in progress (with the serious reservation we have just seen), as a humanist he believed in decadence. That is precisely the significance of the volume on Chateaubriand — the first in which he deliberately sets out to be a judicial critic. He makes a humanistic survey of Chateaubriand and concludes that he is the first great writer of the decadence, the writer who transferred the capital of French prose from Rome to Byzantium. Like Voltaire or Nisard, he accepts the theory of the classic age and asserts that his own time is already on the descending curve. "I believe to my great regret," he says, "(and I held out against the belief as long as I could) that literature is on the highroad to corruption."[1] This stand implied, of course, an open rupture with much of his own literary past and his associates in it. In his attitude towards the romanticists, especially the romantic poets — Hugo, Lamartine, Vigny, etc. — Sainte-Beuve is supposed to have been influenced by the jealousy of the unsuccessful creator for those whose creations have succeeded. But there is a larger aspect even to what seem the most personal of his feuds and animosities. He was only too capable of rancor, but he has in turn suffered more than most men from rancor in others. The reason he himself has very clearly stated:

[1] *Chateaubriand*, I, 102.

"Parties and sects have a deadly grudge against any one who, having passed through them, has refused to bind himself to them irrevocably. I have given no one the right to say 'He is one of us.' I have certainly had my vices and weaknesses, but it is for what is good in me, for my love of integrity and truth and my independence of judgment, that I have irritated so many people in my life and aroused so much wrath."[1] Thus the romanticists and their partisans have borne Sainte-Beuve a deadly grudge and have sought to explain on personal grounds opinions that contain a serious judgment. Like Goethe, Sainte-Beuve as he grew older sided more and more with the Olympians against the Titans. It is as a humanist that he protests against the violence and excess of Hugo's romanticism, against the violence and excess of the naturalism of Balzac. Later, under the compliments he lavishes on his friend and admirer, Taine, one can distinguish the same note of protest against the dehumanizing tendencies of an excessive naturalism. "In spite of everything," he writes to a correspondent in explanation of his small esteem for Balzac, "I have continued of the classic school, that of Horace and the singer of Windsor Forest."[2] Yet nothing sounder and juster has been written on Balzac than Sainte-Beuve's article of 1850,[3] only a few years after Balzac's outrageous diatribe against him in the "Revue parisienne" (1840).

Sainte-Beuve will never, I believe, rank with Boileau in the sureness of his judgments on contemporaries.

[1] *Lundis*, XVI, 44. [2] *Nouvelle Cor.*, 235. [3] *Lundis*, II, 413 ff.

Yet as the nineteenth century, with its own special atmosphere, recedes into the distance, these judgments are likely to be increasingly accepted. Indeed Frenchmen are already coming around to them now that they are beginning to react against the romantic and naturalistic movements. The "Chateaubriand" which called forth the most opposition and which suffers from an unmistakable bitterness of tone, is not only one of the most interesting of Sainte-Beuve's works, but may also turn out to be one of the most judicious. In his recent book on the same subject, M. Lemaître has done little more than reaffirm Sainte-Beuve, the only difference being that as he unveils depth upon depth of romantic egotism in Chateaubriand, he keeps repeating that, with all his faults, "we love him still."

II

Sainte-Beuve lived in an age when it was especially difficult to adjust the claims of the real and the ideal in art. His perfect tact and measure and good sense can always be counted on to put him on his guard against everything that is extreme and one-sided, whether it claims to be ideal or naturalistic. He was impatient of those who set up as idealists, but were in reality only romantic dreamers, as well as of those who set up as idealists and were in reality only pseudo-classic formalists. "O ye friends of the ideal," he writes with special reference to these latter, "I am not going to quarrel with you. I grant that there is an ideal; but grant too that there is a true and a false one, and if ever you come across an ideal or something that calls itself such, cold, monotonous, sad, colorless under its appearance of nobility, hazy, stiff, insipid, not brilliant and various like marble, but white like plaster, not full of warmth and power as in the flourishing days of Greece when warm torrents of purple blood throbbed through the veins of demi-gods and heroes, . . . but pale, bloodless, ascetic as in Lent, denying itself the sources of fruitful inspiration, living on pure abstractions, rheumatic from head to foot, soaked and saturated with ennui, oh, make no mistake, that is the very ideal that has so long cast a chill over the French muses, and would be capable of chilling them again, that is the ideal to avoid."[1] In general he attacks those who try to confine beauty to some one type and produce ever paler and paler copies of it.[2] To be sure he would not have the writer, he says, display the point of the scalpel "still dripping with blood and pus, but then again, let not thorough-going anatomy and physiology be disregarded and absent under your folds and draperies; let us be conscious of genuine flesh and blood even under your silk and lace."[3]

Sainte-Beuve's own aim, as he says, was to introduce into criticism a certain charm and along with it more reality than had been put into it previously, in a word, poetry and a certain amount of physiology.[4] It is easy, indeed, to discern the *disjecta membra* of the romantic poet in his critical writing. He has in particular a strange knack for dissimulating his probing and dis-

[1] *N. Lundis*, I, 13. [2] *Ibid.*, 14. [3] *Ibid.*, V, 37. [4] *Port. lit.*, III, 546.

secting under the flowers of metaphor. But if he did not fall into the naturalistic excess we must ascribe the fact less to his poetry, which is a romantic survival, than to his humanistic tact. He shrank back instinctively from anything that was violent and narrow and sectarian; and naturalism as held by the men of the Second Empire was often all three. He was placed in a somewhat delicate situation because many of these men were his friends and in part his disciples. But even at the risk of having his motives misinterpreted he spoke out. The malignant gossip of the Goncourts is due in part to the sheer inability of the brothers to grasp the ideas that Taine, Renan, Sainte-Beuve, and others exchanged at the Magny dinners, in part to resentment at the reservations Sainte-Beuve had made in regard to their own particular form of naturalism. He criticises in a similar spirit Flaubert's "Salammbô." "Let us never be in literature," he says, "among those who are called in this novel 'the eaters of unclean things.'" This over-refinement and perversion of taste seemed to him to mark the end of a literary school. He finds it impossible to belong to this school. "I will love you individually," he says to Flaubert and his other ultra-naturalistic friends, "but I shall never be of your sect."[1] He rebelled especially against the penchant of the sectarian naturalists for what has been called aggressive unpleasantness. "At the risk of losing what credit I may still have with many of my contemporaries," he writes, "and among them some who are very dear to me, I confess

[1] *N. Lundis*, IV, 91.

in matters of taste to a great weakness: I like what is agreeable."[1] His simple remark in a letter to Zola that the verb "wallow" (*vautrer*)[2] occurs too frequently in his novels is worth pages of ordinary criticism.

Sainte-Beuve also made a humanistic protest against the dangers and excesses of scientific naturalism. Science is interested primarily not in the man who has assimilated the riches of tradition and is harmoniously developed and wise in himself, but in the man who can contribute definitely to the great cause of progress, which means practically in the specialist, the man who has fixed with enthusiasm and tenacity on some particular field, at whatever risk of narrowing his horizons. Both the romantic and scientific sides of the naturalistic movement converge upon the idea of originality. We have already seen that the dangers of this modern conception of originality were visible to Sainte-Beuve in Cousin and his school. "Let us encourage," he says, "all laborious investigation, but let us give in everything the first place to talent, meditation, judgment, reason, taste." "It seems," he complains, anticipating Brunetière and his "Fureur de l'Inédit," "that to edit an old book already published, or to print some insignificant scrap for the first time, is nowadays a more serious claim to esteem than to have a style and ideas."[3]

None appeared to Sainte-Beuve (again anticipating Brunetière) more in need of moderating the fury of their research by a knowledge of the humanistic tradition than the mediævalists. The resemblance between Sainte-

[1] *N. Lundis*, x, 403. [2] *Cor.*, II, 315. [3] *N. Lundis*, v, 372.

Beuve and Goethe is here obvious. "True and incomparable beauty," says Sainte-Beuve, "has shone forth in its perfect exemplars only once or perhaps twice under the sun. There are, to be sure, beauties of different sorts and degrees. The manifestations of human life and the human spirit are infinite. Let us welcome them all; yet let those of us who have seen or glimpsed true beauty never forget it. Let us preserve faithfully within us its lofty and delicate image, if it were only that we might not lavish its name on every occasion and forever profane it, as I see being done by estimable investigators who are deeply versed in mediæval documents (*qui ont beaucoup paperassé sur le Moyen-Age*), and who have no knowledge of anything else."[1] "Many of these mediævalists," he says again, referring especially to Paulin Paris, "do not possess in themselves all the necessary terms of comparison."[2] They fall into aberrations of taste that "would be impossible for any one who has read Sophocles in the original text."[3]

In speaking at one moment as a humanist and at another as a naturalist Sainte-Beuve is not, I must repeat, necessarily inconsistent. Yet the opposition between the two sides of his nature, between the scientific investigator, and the æsthetic humanist, is at times unmistakable. To whom, for example is the conflict between head and heart not palpable in a passage like the following? "Where is the time when you could read a book even though you yourself were an author and a professional without so many complications. . . . The time when you

[1] *N. Lundis*, III, 378. [2] *Ibid.*, 384. [3] *Ibid.*, 396.

read ancients and moderns, reclining upon your couch, like Horace during the dog-days, or stretched out on your sofa like Gray, saying to yourself that you had something better than the joys of Paradise or Olympus; the time when you could read strolling around in the shade, like that respectable Hollander, who said he could not imagine any greater happiness here below at the age of fifty than to walk slowly through a fair countryside, book in hand, closing it at intervals without desire or passion, sunk in meditation; the time when like the 'Reader' of Meissonier in your solitary room on a Sunday afternoon near the open window overshadowed with honeysuckle, you read a unique and cherished book? What has become of this happy age? How very different things are to-day when you are always on pin-points in reading, and have constantly to be on your guard and interrogate yourself unceasingly, and ask whether it is the right text, whether there is n't some corruption, whether the author you are enjoying has n't taken it from somewhere else, whether he has copied reality or invented, whether he is really original and how, whether he was true to his nature, his race, etc. . . . and a thousand other questions which spoil pleasure, engender doubt, make you scratch your forehead, force you to climb up to the highest shelves of your library, to pull about all your books, to consult and make excerpts, finally to become once more a laborer and a workman instead of a voluptuary and delicate amateur who was breathing the spirit of things and taking of them only what he needed for his pleasure and delight. Epicureanism of taste, forever lost I fear; henceforth impossible at least for all critics; last religion even of those who had no other; last honor and virtue of a Hamilton and a Petronius, how I understand and regret you in the very act of opposing and abjuring you!"[1]

The various virtues of the critic, including the richness and depth of literary sensibility that appear in this passage, are so happily mingled in Sainte-Beuve that no one, I presume, would wish him different. Yet the passage also makes plain why he has been influential as a naturalist rather than as a humanist — quite apart from the fact that in his naturalism he fell in with the main current of his time. A humanism that hopes to act upon the world cannot afford to recline even with Horace and Gray. It must take hold on the character and will and not be simply epicurean. If humanism is merely an epicureanism of taste it is not only sure to be lost but the loss will not be altogether irreparable. Sainte-Beuve was very much preoccupied with the quarrel of ancients and moderns. His belief as to the final outcome may be inferred from the following: "Sooner or later I fear, the ancients with Homer at their head will lose the battle, or at least half the battle. Let us endeavor for the honor of the flag, we who are defending the retreat, that it may be as late as possible, and that innovation in literature, that innovation in part so legitimate, may nevertheless not put tradition utterly to rout."[2]

[1] *N. Lundis*, IX, 86–87. [2] *Ibid.*, V, 323.

III

In spite of this flourish of military metaphor we are not to look here for the militant side of Sainte-Beuve. He put forth a man's effort, only it was in the service of naturalism. "I have but one pleasure left," he writes, "I analyze, botanize; I am a naturalist of minds. What I should like to establish is the natural history of literature."[1] The method that Sainte-Beuve here outlines, so far from being humanistic, is in many respects antagonistic to humanism. In order to make this clear we shall need to study his method in some detail, especially as set forth in the second article on Chateaubriand in the third volume of the "Nouveaux Lundis." He wrote the article partly in reply to the question that had been raised whether he had any method. He justified the somewhat uncoördinated aspect of his essays by saying that he was simply preparing sound monographs for some future generalizer. The science of criticism in his hands is in the same state as botany before Jussieu or comparative anatomy before Cuvier: but on the basis of all this detailed observation it may be possible to discover some day the great natural divisions corresponding to the families of minds. "These true and natural families of minds are not so numerous. . . . It is just as in botany for plants, in zoölogy for the animal species. . . . One individual carefully observed is referred quickly to the species of which you knew only in a general way, and throws light on it."[2]

[1] *Port. lit.*, III, 546. [2] *Port-Royal*, I, 55.

One is inevitably led at this point to apply Sainte-Beuve's method to himself and ask what was the attitude of the *primitive* Sainte-Beuve towards this whole question, or at any rate of Sainte-Beuve before that moment in the century when any one who wished to be taken seriously had to make his peace with Science.

The phrase I have just quoted, "One individual carefully observed," puts us on the right track to the answer. Sainte-Beuve is interested before everything else in the living individual. A marvellous psychological finesse in seizing and rendering the living individual — this I believe to have been his primordial gift. Behind the book he sees the man and in the man himself what is most vital, personal, characteristic, in a word, expressive. He would lay siege to his ultimate idiosyncrasy. He is an incomparable literary portrait-painter, or it might be more correct to say, in view of the infinite multiplication of fine strokes, a literary miniaturist. The best way to "judge and penetrate writers is to listen to them long and carefully; just let them unfold themselves freely, without hurrying them, they will tell you everything about themselves, they will come and paint their images upon your mind."[1] (This passage also makes clear why Sainte-Beuve has been called a lay confessor.) When a writer has thus posed before you for a certain time, says Sainte-Beuve, there is mingled little by little with the vague abstract and general type which the first glance had taken in, an individual reality; and "when at last you seize the familiar trick, the telltale smile,

[1] *Chateaubriand*, I, 161.

the indefinable wrinkle, the secret line of pain that is hidden in vain under the already scanty hair, at that moment analysis disappears in creation, the portrait speaks and lives, you have found the man."[1] Sainte-Beuve was only twenty-seven when he wrote these lines. Indeed some of the contortion of his earlier manner is to be ascribed to this almost desperate pursuit of the final degree of expressiveness. "I confess," he says, "that in my efforts to get a true likeness, to render the finer shadings of every physiognomy, I may at times have been far-fetched and over subtle."[2] In thus making expressiveness his aim he realized that he was embarking in a sense on an impossible quest. "Can you ever flatter yourself that you know a soul?" — "the inexpressible monad," as he calls it elsewhere. When you seem to have reached something final it turns out to be expressive of something still more remote. Human nature is an endless series of false bottoms.

In this striving for the expressive, Sainte-Beuve is at the very heart of the nineteenth century. Beauty of form seemed to him the prerogative of the ancients. Interest, curiosity, the faithful and various rendering of everything that goes on under our eyes without any preoccupation with the ideal,[3] he looked upon as belonging rather to the moderns. He is not interested, however, primarily in expressiveness on the larger scale — in literature, for example, as an expression of society. He always keeps as close as possible to the individual. Unlike Taine, he loves to particularize rather than to

[1] *Port. lit.*, I, 239. [2] *Port. cont.*, I, 274. [3] *N. Lundis*, III, 409.

generalize, to deal with men singly rather than in "zones or layers," to feel life in its infinite complexity rather than impose upon it logical formulæ. He says that he is "habituated and inclined by nature to study especially individuals."[1] He takes a group like that of the Jansenists in the seventeenth century who at this distance are lost in a gray uniformity, and multiplies his fine shadings and delicate discriminations, until each figure of the group stands out distinctly. "To particularize Nicole," he says, "is the greatest service one can render him."[2] A greater particularizer in this sense than Sainte-Beuve never lived. When he has finished with M. de Saci he is justified in saying that we have got so close to him that we seem almost to hear him chatting.[3] Du Guet, again, "has his *nuance* which distinguishes him from M. Singlin, from M. de Saci."[4] On reading all these particulars, he says, "you feel as if you yourself belonged to this same society."[5]

An enormous knowledge of the facts, a marvellous psychological finesse and in addition a sort of divination, are needed thus to reanimate the past. In Sainte-Beuve, if anywhere, is found the triumph of that historical second-sight on which the nineteenth century prided itself. Sainte-Beuve was aided in his art of mediating between the past and the present by the "moment": he lived at a time when it was still possible to receive a living initiation into tradition, that is to say, to see the past as it saw itself, which means in practice to live in a

[1] *N. Lundis*, IX, 180. [2] *Port-Royal*, IV, 411. [3] *Ibid*

[4] *Port-Royal*, V, 132. [5] *Ibid.*, 512.

world of absolute values; it was already possible, on the other hand, to detach one's self from the past and to see it relatively and phenomenally. This art of mediating between the past and the present is becoming more difficult for us to-day. We tend to see the past only relatively; this relativism is further complicated by the dogma of Progress. This dogma is so successful in putting blinders on the human spirit not only because it is a dogma, but a dogma founded upon the flux. For example, the writer of a recent book hurries through the palace of Versailles and decides that people who had such a defective system of plumbing and sanitation could hardly have been worth while. He evidently had no sense for the greatness man may attain with a system of plumbing different from his own, or indeed without any plumbing at all.

Let us repeat that Sainte-Beuve's own hold on tradition and the sense of unity that goes with it was mainly æsthetic, and therefore comparatively ineffective. He had no intuition of unity and was rightly skeptical of any attempt to impose a mere logical unity upon the facts, and so was left without adequate counterpoise to his perception of the Many. Everything, including literary reputation, seemed to him subject to the same instability. He took as motto for his "Portraits Contemporains" the sentence of Sénac de Meilhan: "We are mobile and judge mobile beings." "Every day I change," he writes: "the years follow the years; my tastes of a former season are no longer my tastes of to-day; my friendships themselves wither up and are renewed. Before the final death of the mobile being that bears my name, how many men have already died within me!—You think that I am speaking of myself personally, reader: but reflect a moment and see if the same is not true of you."[1] He sees everything gradually growing out of everything else and notes the almost imperceptible differences that mark the transition from one stage to another of this growth. Man, according to Emerson, is a bundle of roots, and a knot of relations. No one ever surpassed Sainte-Beuve in following out the finest filaments of these relationships. However ineffective he may have been as a humanist, as a relativist he has been enormously influential. He has indeed been correctly defined in his influence as a great doctor of relativity. M. France, for example, writes of M. Lemaître, "He has even more than Sainte-Beuve, from whom we are all sprung, the sense of the relative."[2]

It should appear from the foregoing in what sense Sainte-Beuve was from the outset and instinctively a *naturaliste des esprits*. His later endeavor in obedience to the spirit of the age to organize this instinctive naturalism into a definite method led him to the verge of pseudo-science; but even here he is usually saved at the last moment by his native tact and prudence from taking the final step and looking on the living individual, especially the superior individual, as a mere link in the chain of phenomena; just as in "Port-Royal" there is a point where he pauses and refuses to apply his naturalistic dissection to the ultimate raptures of religion.

[1] *Port. lit.*, III, 544. [2] *Vie lit.*, I, 9.

"Doubtless," he says, "you will never be able to proceed for man exactly as for animals and plants. . . . He has what is called *liberty*."[1] Of some of his utterances one would be inclined to say, that though not pseudo-scientific in themselves, they encourage others to pseudo-science.

IV

But before discussing this point further let us take up in detail certain features of Saint-Beuve's method, illustrating his theory so far as possible from his actual practice. The first connection he establishes in his network of relativity is that between a work and its author; between the author in turn and his family, race, and age; and then between the age and the preceding age, and so on in widening circles. In thus seeking to account for a literary product in terms of natural causes, he keeps as close as possible, as I have said, to the specific and immediate, and is comparatively unconcerned with those more general causes, race and climate and the like, that are made so much of by Taine. He does not deny the importance of the racial factor, but says that this deep root is usually concealed. He admits that sooner or later the theory of climate and environment imposes itself. "As is the scene so are the actors. The ancients had the broad general perception of this relationship: it is for the moderns to work out the precise and detailed proof."[2] He protests, however, that this bond between localities and their inhabitants is being forced and exaggerated even to the breaking point.[3]

[1] *N. Lundis*, III, 17. [2] *Ibid.*, IX, 323. [3] *Ibid.*, XIII, 218.

He is more at home in tracing the way in which one age is related to the previous age and grows inevitably out of it, inasmuch as this relationship is more literary and more readily studied in terms of the individual. He discovers, for example, in the fine and ingenious, but somewhat manneristic turn of Du Guet's style something that smacks already of the eighteenth century.[1] "We have learned how to distinguish," he says, "wherein the style of the first period of Louis XIV differs from the average style of the middle of the reign, and wherein this reign at its end has already its manner bordering on that of the eighteenth century. Pascal, Retz, and La Rochefoucauld do not write like La Bruyère, and the exquisite and just language that Madame de Maintenon in her old age teaches to the Duc du Maine is not to be confused with any other *nuance* in the language of the same time."[2]

In virtue of the same historical sense, you come to perceive how the age of Louis XIV itself developed from the preceding age. You come to feel that the age of Louis XIV was not an *accident* (. . . as an acquaintance of mine once said) but rather the result and natural fruit of a continuous culture and development.[3] In the same way you come to feel that the great writer is no more an accident than the great age. "After men like Saint-Cyran and Le Maître and Saci, when we come to Pascal we are ready to see more clearly the proportions; . . . to measure the glorious side of genius, without granting more than neces-

[1] *Port-Royal*, VI, 21. [2] *Lundis*, V, 173. [3] *N. Lundis*, VI, 364.

sary to this glory. . . . In a word, we are well and duly prepared."[1]

Almost any subject when thus studied relatively, that is, as the outgrowth of something else, ramifies in every direction. "If you live in a subject a short time," he says, "you are, as it were, in a city filled with friends. You can scarcely take a step in the main street without being instantly accosted right and left and invited to enter."[2] "Port-Royal" thus became not simply a history of Jansenism, but in at least an equal degree a history of French literature and society in the seventeenth century. In Sainte-Beuve's own phrase, it is simply a method for "traversing the epoch."[3]

If Sainte-Beuve likes to trace by individual examples the process by which one age passes over into another, by which as he would say the spiritual climate (*le climat des esprits*) changes, he gets still closer to biography, and is therefore still more at home, in studying the relationship between the individual and his epoch. The old criticism, as he says, was especially weak in this respect; for example, the defective historical sense of La Harpe appears in the fact that he tries to represent the creative genius of Corneille as independent of circumstances.[4] Sainte-Beuve insists for his part that it was possible for Corneille to create "Polyeucte" only because there was "something about him (whether he knew it or not) that equalled and reproduced the same miracles."[5] Racine again put into his work all the poetry properly so-called that the polite society of the time could receive.[6] Of

[1] *Port-Royal*, II, 376. [2] *Ibid.*, I, 412. [3] *Ibid.*, I, 146.
[4] *Ibid.*, I, 119. [5] *Ibid.*, I, 115. [6] *Ibid.*, VI, 128.

Balzac he says that his feeling for unity and the things of the spirit marked him a contemporary of Richelieu.[1] Saint-Evremond, "the firm-souled epicurean," acquired his insight into great historical characters as a result of his own experiences in the Fronde.[2] "That powerful spirit," he says of Arnauld, "remained more than half plunged in the general prejudices and zones of illusion prevailing in his time; his horizons were bounded on every hand."[3] The work even of so great an innovator as Chateaubriand is conditioned in the same way. Sainte-Beuve points out the analogy between the death of Atala and a group in marble by Canova.[4]

It is, however, with what we may term the purely biographical relationships that we reach the heart of Sainte-Beuve's method. First of all there is the connection between the book and its author. In what M. Guizot offers him, he says, as a general solution of the problem of life, — a philosophy and theology, — he sees a distinct and special type of man determined by his temperament and past.[5] Since the work is thus expressive of the man, the important point is to know the man; and to know a man, in other words something else than a pure spirit, we cannot go to work in too many different ways. We must approach him in the first place from the point of view of heredity, we must strive to discover what he owes to his ancestry and his parents, above all to his mother (great men nearly always have distinguished mothers), and how

[1] *Port-Royal*, I, 115.

[2] *N. Lundis*, III, 227. Saint-Evremond is another of the seventeenth-century "libertines" with whom Sainte-Beuve felt an inner kinship.

[3] *Port-Royal*, V, 313. [4] *Chateaubriand*, I, 257. [5] *N. Lundis*, IX, 109.

he resembles his sisters (the sister of the great man sometimes has a distinction superior to that of the great man himself); finally we must study him in his brothers and children. Nature frequently does the analyzing for us and traits are often easier to seize as they appear thus separately in them than when blended in the eminent person himself.[1]

We can thus follow Sainte-Beuve as he weaves about the individual the meshes of the new fatality. For necessity, as Pater remarks, "has ceased to be for the moderns a sort of mythological personage without us, with whom we can do warfare: it is a magic web woven through and through us, like that magnetic system of which modern science speaks, penetrating us with a network subtler than our subtlest nerves, yet bearing in it the central forces of the world." Not only does a man's work reflect his temperament, but this temperamental self is constantly changing. We must learn to see these successive and fatal transformations of the individual from youth to old age, and their relationship to his work, and for this another world of *nuances* is needed. I have already noted Sainte-Beuve's predilection for the first flush of youth, and that this is the form the cult of the primitive assumes in him. Man is most fully in possession of his faculties at the age of thirty-five. And then as we follow still further the fatal curve we come to the moment of decline when the very excess of the virtue becomes a fault, when some writers grow rigid and dry and wither, and others let themselves go,

[1] *N. Lundis*, III, 18 ff.

when still others harden or become heavy, and when some grow sour; when the smile becomes a wrinkle.[1] The painter, Horace Vernet, has Sainte-Beuve's approval because he went through all the stages of a noble career: "Like all complete organizations he had in succession the fruits of each season. The moment of his greatest merit coincides with the hour of his maturity and his old age did not lack serious thoughts."[2] "There comes an inevitable hour when everything grows dark within us and about us. Long before the arrival of this moment and in the midst of our last spells of sunshine, a sudden presentiment heralds it at times and the gayest, the most prone to laughter, find themselves growing pensive."[3] Evidently a successful attempt to maintain one's faculties and spirits at their best level in old age would have seemed to Sainte-Beuve a sort of affront to the Goddess Natura.

We must, however, deal with a man in a still more intimate and personal way. We must ask ourselves questions that at first sight seem most foreign to the nature of his writings. For example, "What were his religious opinions? How was he affected by the spectacle of nature? How did he behave in the matter of women? in the matter of money? Was he rich or poor? What was his hygiene and daily mode of life? Finally, what was his vice or weakness? Every man has one."[4] This theory of the essential vice, we may note in passing, Sainte-Beuve probably took from La Rochefou-

[1] *N. Lundis*, III, 26–27.
[2] *Ibid.*, V, 62.
[3] *Ibid.*, 122.
[4] *Ibid.*, III, 28.

cauld.[1] It was also an important part of Sainte-Beuve's method to get at the fault of the master by studying its exaggeration in the disciples. He is ready to carry even to the foot of the altar and beyond what he calls his "intimate perscrutation of talents."[2] "When you have to do with a woman," he says, "even with a model of saintliness, two or three inevitable questions present themselves: Was she pretty? Did she ever fall in love? What was the determining motive of her conversion?"[3]

The perils of the pursuit of *la vérité vraie* when pushed to this point are manifest. The "grand" curiosity (*la grande curiosité*), in the name of which Sainte-Beuve would pursue his inquiries, may very easily degenerate into curiosity of the petty and even the prurient type. "I have observed," says Addison ironically, "that a reader seldom peruses a book with pleasure until he knows whether the writer of it be a black or fair man," etc. This universal human instinct flourished as never before in the nineteenth century, when instead of having any check put upon it, it received a sort of scientific sanction. "Our century," says Sainte-Beuve, "loves these intimate details. It never can get too many of them."[4] Yet it has been said that when a man falls into his anecdotage it is all over with him, and the same may be true of criticism. We can follow Sainte-Beuve's own method here and study the master's fault as exaggerated in the disciples. Critics less discreet and

[1] "Il n'y a guère de personnes qui dans le premier penchant de l'âge ne fassent connaître par où leur corps et leur esprit doivent défaillir."

[2] *N. Lundis*, VI, 419. [3] *Ibid.*, I, 213. [4] *Ibid.*, XII, 215.

tactful than he have indulged in a veritable orgy of biographical and autobiographical indiscretions. Under pretext of explaining the author's work all the decencies of his private life have been violated; in Peacock's phrase, "he has been dished up like a savory omelette to gratify the appetite of the reading rabble for gossip."

Sainte-Beuve has spoken with fitting contempt of the more trivial forms of curiosity, but he cannot himself be held to have been entirely free from them. Are we helped for instance, in judging the writing of Charles Magnin by a knowledge of the fact that every evening about nine he used to see his grandmother safely to bed?[1] Is much light thrown on Nicole's spiritual nature by knowing how often he shaved or that his wig was frequently on awry?[2] Nicole would have a right to exclaim with the Reverend Dr. Folliott, "What business have the public with my nose and wig?" Sainte-Beuve is not above commenting on Michaud's finger nails (*il les avait fort noirs, les ongles*),[3] and used occasionally, we are told, to invite in to dinner the cook of Dr. Véron so that he might gossip with her about the great personages of the Second Empire.[4]

Unless we go into details of this kind, Sainte-Beuve would tell us, we are likely to have some Olympian simulacrum palmed off on us as the actual person. He would have us perfect ourselves in what, according to Chamfort, is the greatest of all arts, the art of not being taken in. Strange things, for example, went on under the smooth

[1] *N. Lundis*, v, 456.
[2] *Port-Royal*, IV, 598.
[3] *Lundis*, XI, 486.
[4] See *Nouvelle Cor.*, 226.

surface of the somewhat Jesuitical decorum of the seventeenth century. Where should we be if we had not a Saint-Simon to warn us against this false nobility and under the solemn and conventional poses to show us the real man?[1] Sainte-Beuve often reminds one of Thackeray, especially in this instinct for uncovering shams. "Queen Anne," says Thackeray, "was only a hot red-faced woman not in the least resembling that statue of her which turns its stone back on Saint Paul's," etc. Louis XIV, again, "was a hero for a book if you like, or for a brass statue or a painted ceiling — a god in Roman shape, but what more than a man for Madame de Maintenon, or the barber who shaved him or Monsieur Fagon, his surgeon?" If we are to get at the real man, we must, it would seem, see him through the eyes of his barber, or his surgeon, or possibly his cook. It has been said of Sainte-Beuve as of Voltaire that he had a grudge against all pedestals. He would do for his time what Saint-Simon did for his and put posterity on its guard. He excels in what one may term the disenchanting anecdote. He relates, for example, how one day he was with Chateaubriand at Madame Récamier's when Lamartine came in. "Jocelyn" had just appeared and Madame Récamier began to praise the book eagerly to Lamartine, who entered with naïve fatuity into this praise of himself. But Chateaubriand when called upon by Madame Récamier to bear witness also, did not utter a word; he simply took his scarf and held it between his teeth according to his wont when determined not to speak. Scarcely,

[1] *N. Lundis*, x, 268.

however, had Lamartine left the room when Chateaubriand burst out all at once, as if he were alone, and exclaimed, "The great ninny!" (*le grand dadais*). "I was there," adds Sainte-Beuve, "and I heard it."[1] After a few anecdotes of this kind we are in no danger of seeing either Chateaubriand or Lamartine on pedestals.

V

Any process of idealization not only seemed to Sainte-Beuve unreal in itself, but it interfered with the virtue, that, as I have already said, he was chiefly seeking in common with his century — expressiveness. However far he fell short of the antique symmetry, he could at least render life in all its infinite variety, and did so with extraordinary success. No writer is more vital. He is at once the best read and the least bookish of critics. The actual men of the past rise before us, not precisely in their habits as they lived, but, what is more to the purpose, each in his inner psychological truth. To read Sainte-Beuve is to enlarge one's knowledge, not merely of literature but of life. Indeed, the somewhat paradoxical charge may be brought against his criticism that it is not sufficiently literary. He says of himself, it is true, that he was one of those who had the religion of letters, and so indeed he had — in about the sense, to quote his own phrase, that a Hamilton or a Petronius had it. I do not believe that the religion of letters, or even a sound defence of literary tradition, is, in the long run, compatible with Sainte-Beuve's philo-

[1] *Chateaubriand*, II, 389–90.

sophy of life. His own performance we must repeat is unique. But we have a right to judge it not only in itself, but in its tendency and influence, in its relation to the laws of its *genre*. Now thus considered criticism in Sainte-Beuve is plainly moving away from its own centre towards something else; it is ceasing to be literary and becoming historical and biographical and scientific. It illustrates strikingly in its own fashion the drift of the nineteenth century away from the pure type, the *genre tranché*, towards a general mingling and confusion of the *genres*. We are scarcely conscious of any change when Sainte-Beuve passes, as he does especially in the later volumes of the "Nouveaux Lundis," from writers to generals or statesmen.

Yet history and biography and science are at best preparations for literary criticism, preparations that are always relevant to be sure, but likely to be less relevant in direct ratio to the distinction of the man who is being criticized. The greater the man, for example, the more baffling he is likely to be to students of heredity. The higher forms of human excellence, says Dante, are rarely subject to heredity; and this God wills in order that we may know that they come from him alone. The truth Dante thus puts theologically is, I believe, a matter of observation so far as the past is concerned. As for the future it is not yet clear that our schemes of eugenics are going to outwit God. The genius of Keats is precisely that part of him that cannot be explained by the fact that he was the son of the keeper of a London livery stable. In this sense we may say with Emerson that "great geniuses have the shortest biographies." "Can any biography," he says, "shed light on the localities into which the 'Midsummer Night's Dream' admits me? Did Shakespeare confide to any notary or parish recorder, sacristan, or surrogate, in Stratford, the genesis of that delicate creation? The forest of Arden, the nimble air of Scone Castle, the moonlight of Portia's villa, 'the antres vast and desarts idle' of Othello's captivity,— where is the third cousin, or grand-nephew, the chancellor's file of accounts, or private letter, that has kept one word of those transcendent secrets? In fine, in this drama, as in all great works of art . . . the Genius draws up the ladder after him, when the creative age goes up to heaven, and gives way to a new age, which sees the works and asks in vain for a history."

Sainte-Beuve was of course too shrewd to make of genius merely a product, to claim that it can be dealt with merely in terms of heredity and environment. "Very great individuals," he says, "are independent of a group"[1] (*Les très grands individus se passent de groupe*).[2] They become a centre themselves and people gather about them. Ordinary talents are imprisoned in their time, he says, following Goethe; when they have given back to their time what they have received from it, they are poor. But the true genius does not depend on borrowed waters, he is an ever-flowing fountain. Sainte-Beuve

[1] "Group" as used by Sainte-Beuve is applied to individuals born about the same time and brought more or less into contact with one another. It is not to be confounded with a "natural family of minds," the members of which may be widely scattered in time and space.

[2] *N. Lundis*, III, 23.

pointed out with masterly precision the weakness of the naturalistic method when pushed to its last extremity by Taine. He had, at all events, in a high degree the sense of the uniqueness and inexpressibleness of the human monad. There are no equivalents, he insists, in matters of taste. Suppose one great talent less, suppose the magic mirror of a single true poet shattered in the cradle at its birth, there will never be another that will be exactly the same or that will take the place of it.[1] As some one puts it, one trembles to think that Shakespeare and Cervantes were subject to the measles at the same time.

Yet Sainte-Beuve has his own naturalistic method and cannot refrain from a certain satisfaction when an author and his work are less unique and so more capable of being explained. "In truth," he says, "M. Coulmann pleases me in his 'Mémoires' by his very lack of all originality. He is the honorable and facile expression of the environment in which he lives; he registers its temperature for us with a good deal of precision, without the admixture or resistance of too individual a character."[2] We here begin to see how Sainte-Beuve, without being pseudo-scientific himself, yet points the way to pseudo-science. This passage is a sort of first adumbration of the pseudo-scientific theory of the normal man. "Normally," says Sainte-Beuve, "fifteen years constitute a literary career."[3] His own career ran to just three times this length, and he ended in better form than he began. He was also comparatively cheerful at the end, whereas at the beginning he was lugubrious. That first

[1] *N. Lundis,* VIII, 86. [2] *Ibid.*, IX, 141. [3] *Ibid.*, III, 27.

bloom of youth that he in general found so enchanting, was in his own case a *fleur du mal*. How are we to account by Sainte-Beuve's method for the fact that Tennyson wrote some of his best lyrics ("Crossing the Bar," for example) when above seventy, that Titian painted some of his best pictures when above eighty, that Sophocles wrote one of his best plays, the "Œdipus at Colonus," when above ninety? Yes, we are told, but these men are exceptions. The obvious reply is that men have a rank in literature only by being exceptional and that in order to have high rank they must be supremely exceptional. Thereupon the pseudo-scientist, who sees the human spirit escaping him, takes the step that Sainte-Beuve does not himself take, and identifies the exceptional with the morbid and the pathological. The man who is not normal as he understands the term, that is, who is not studiously commonplace and above all unimaginative, he sets down as a distinguished degenerate. Few things are likely to seem more repulsive in the retrospect than the dealings of pseudo-science in the second half of the nineteenth century with the man of genius. There is something in the spirit of man that looks down upon and mocks these attempts of the scientific intellect to confine it in formulæ, of the lower element to impose itself dogmatically on the higher. We should admit, however, that the emotional side of the modern movement has coöperated here as elsewhere with the scientific side and produced in confirmation of the thesis a long series of eccentric and pathological geniuses from Rousseau down.

The whole confusion as to the nature of genius has

arisen from a neglect of Plato's simple distinction between the two kinds of madness — "the one produced by human infirmity, the other by a divine release from the ordinary ways of men." To feel a writer's "madness" in the Platonic sense is to feel his sheer elevation. Man, says Emerson, is great only by the supernatural; and this coincides with the definition Longinus gives of the sublime.[1] Both writers, it scarcely seems necessary to add, mean by the supernatural not the thaumaturgical, but what is above the ordinary intellect. Now Sainte-Beuve had comparatively little of the Longinian or Emersonian sense of the sublime. He asserted that this lack was more or less a racial trait. In his criticism as in his poetry he was, in his own phrase, for stopping half-way up the hill. Criticism, one may add, as he conceives it, is a sort of half creation (like that of an actor creating a rôle), and he has been accused, as various actors have been, of preferring a rôle in which his own creative power would not be too much overshadowed by that of his author.

Whatever the cause, he is plainly more concerned in arriving at horizontality, if I may be allowed the word, than in determining altitudes. There is an element of truth in the saying that in his pages all men are six feet tall. He exercises his incomparable gift for psychological biography with at least as much complacency on second-rate as on first-rate writers. He obeys too far at times the injunction *ne despicias minores*. One angel, we are told, differs from another angel in glory. His

[1] *On the Sublime*, c. XXXVI.

effort at times would seem rather to show how one minor author differs from another minor author in insignificance. I have already dwelt on his gift for discovering even in the smallest writer his shade of originality. Like a modern pragmatist he escapes from the formulæ of the intellectualist by his lively intuitions of the Many, and not like a Platonist by his intuitions of the One. He is therefore less excellent in showing wherein a man is great than wherein he is individual. He did not undertake, however, to topple over the pedestals of any of the supreme figures of literature (with the very doubtful exception of Chateaubriand), but is inclined at times to pass these figures by. He is more at home, it has been said, with the Greek Anthology than with Æschylus. There is an evident opposition between his naturalistic temper and the Longinian or Emersonian doctrine that man is great only by the supernatural. The general result of his method is on the contrary, as he expresses it, to "desupernaturalize" genius.

VI

I have reserved for more detailed treatment at this point the side of Sainte-Beuve's method that tends most clearly to desupernaturalize genius, but also shows how his naturalism was happily tempered even in its extreme applications by his humanism. The doctrine I refer to, if one may use so dogmatic a word in speaking of Sainte-Beuve, is that of the master faculty along with the closely allied theories of natural sympathies and antipathies and of the "natural families of intellects."

The more general hypothesis as to natural families of intellects may be dismissed very briefly for the reason that Sainte-Beuve himself makes only slight use of it. If worked out with any rigor, it would almost inevitably run into pseudo-science. If we note certain recurring types in human history, the type of the great dominator like Richelieu or Bonaparte, for example, are we to trace their common passion for domination to the fact that they were conformed organically, and one is tempted to say zoölogically, in the same way? Sainte-Beuve even speaks in one passage of a *natural* family of mystics.[1] In such classifications he does not seem to have avoided entirely that dangerous juggling with the words "nature" and "natural" that so permeates our modern thought. There evidently intervenes here a force that is peculiar to human nature, the instinct of conscious imitation even of the distant past. If one of the mystics Sainte-Beuve mentions had lived on an island in the South Sea, and had never heard of Saint Augustine or of Christianity in general, would he have become a mystic by the fatal unfolding of some inner organ or faculty?

That men are born with certain leanings and are drawn to men who have leanings like their own and repelled by those whose leanings are too different, is not in itself a pseudo-scientific theory, but a fact, a fact indeed so patent that men observed it long ago and devised their own explanations. Some knowledge of this past theory is an aid to the understanding of the theory in its modern phases. Sainte-Beuve himself frequently

[1] *Port-Royal*, IV, 322.

refers to Pope and his utterances on the ruling passion; it may be helpful to go for a moment even behind Pope.

The older explanations are usually associated with the theory of the humors which comes down from classical antiquity. A man's temperament was supposed to arise from the proportion in which the four elements were mingled in him: —

> "Hot, Cold, Moist and Dry, four champions fierce,
> Strive here for mastery."

The element that prevailed over the others determined his humor. Men of similar humors naturally attracted, those of opposite complexions naturally repelled, one another. Ben Jonson's familiar definition of a humor also defines excellently the ruling passion: —

> "When some one peculiar quality
> Doth so possess a man, that it doth draw
> All his affects, his spirits and his powers
> In their confluxions all to run one way,
> This may be truly said to be a humor."

The humors in their attractions and repulsions were also accounted for astrologically. Men were differently constellated. According to the ruling planet their dispositions were jovial, mercurial, saturnine, etc.

In the course of the seventeenth and early eighteenth centuries, the theory of humors passes over into that of the ruling passion. We can follow in the process a gradual yielding of the religious or the humanistic to the naturalistic view of life. From this point of view Pope's "Epistle to Cobham" marks an epoch. The frequency with which Sainte-Beuve refers to Pope is perhaps due in part to his satisfaction at finding a humanistic authority for a conception that in its extreme form is subversive of both humanism and religion. The confusion in Pope's own mind between the two opposing views of life is evident. At one moment he tells us that the ruling passion is the "mind's disease," at another he proclaims, like a disciple of Rousseau,

> "The surest virtues thus from passions shoot,
> Wild nature's vigor working at the root."

Dr. Johnson at any rate is not open to the charge of inconsistency in his defence of the religious view of life. More than any man of his time, perhaps, he saw the full implication of the theory of the ruling passion and never missed an opportunity to attack Pope for espousing it. "This doctrine," he says, "is in itself pernicious as well as false." "True genius is a mind of large general powers accidentally determined to some particular direction." "I am persuaded that had Sir Isaac Newton applied to poetry he would have made a very fine epic poem. I could as easily apply to law as to tragic poetry." To this last assertion we assent with a smile. In his indignation at those who would make mind mechanical, Johnson plainly overleapt himself, and flew in the face of facts of common observation.

Even more fatal to Johnson's campaign against the ruling passion was the fact that it ran counter to the main currents of the time. With the advent of the romantic theory of spontaneity, the idea that a man has only to follow his original genius, in other words, his ruling impulse, received a tremendous impetus. Lamb and Hazlitt, to mention two representative romantic critics in England, simply revel in fatal temperamental leanings and the sympathies and antipathies that they imply. "The dilatory man," says Hazlitt, "never becomes punctual. Resolution is no avail. . . . Can you talk or argue a man out of his humor? . . . The disease is in the blood," etc. He believes in the fatality not only of individual but of national humors. "Who shall make the French respectable?" he asks, "or the English amiable?" Lamb is prone rather to dwell on inevitable attractions and repulsions. He declares that he himself is "the veriest thrall to sympathies, apathies, antipathies." He had been trying all his life to like Scotchmen and had been obliged to desist from the experiment in despair. His mind was in its constitution essentially anti-Caledonian. He can believe the story of two persons meeting (who never saw one another before in their lives) and instantly fighting. He quotes with approval a story from Haywood's "Hierarchie of Angels," of a Spaniard who attempted to assassinate a King Ferdinand of Spain, and being put to the rack could give no other reason for the deed but an inveterate antipathy which he had taken to the first sight of the king.

> "The cause which to that act compelled him
> Was, he ne'er loved him since he first beheld him."

The form in which Thackeray holds the doctrine is even closer to Sainte-Beuve. "We like or dislike each other," says Thackeray, "as folks like or dislike the odor of certain flowers, or the taste of certain dishes or wines, or certain books. We can't tell why; but as a general rule, all the reasons in the world will not make us love Doctor Fell, and as sure as we dislike him, we may be sure that he dislikes us." Thackeray would have us believe that an antipathy of this kind existed between Fielding and Richardson. "Fielding could n't do otherwise," he says, "than laugh at the puny cockney bookseller, pouring out endless volumes of sentimental twaddle, and hold him up to scorn as a mollcoddle and a milksop. *His* genius had been nursed on sack-posset, and not on dishes of tea. *His* muse had sung the loudest in tavern choruses, had seen the daylight streaming in over thousands of emptied bowls, and reeled home to chambers on the shoulders of the watchman. Richardson's goddess was attended by old maids and dowagers, and fed on muffins and bohea. 'Milksop!' roars Harry Fielding, clattering at the timid shop-shutters. 'Wretch! Monster! Mohock!' shrieks the sentimental author of 'Pamela'; and all the ladies of his court cackle out an affrighted chorus."

The theory of the humors, then, and their inevitable attractions and repulsions came to Sainte-Beuve as a part of the naturalistic inheritance. First, as to the attractions and repulsions, we may note a parallel here as elsewhere between Sainte-Beuve and Goethe, who is nevertheless no fatalist. "If we survey the history of the past," says Goethe, "we shall everywhere encounter personalities with some of whom we could agree and with others of whom we should certainly find ourselves quarreling ere long." We are told to love our neighbor as ourself. If he belongs to a different natural family, replies Sainte-Beuve, so far from loving him, we are forced to hate him. *Que voulez-vous?* It is in our blood and temperament. After his wont, however, he confines the theory to the individual. He does not, like other naturalistic theorists, evoke those terrific visions of whole races and nationalities impelled to mutual slaughter by a sort of zoölogical necessity, the outcome of almost imperceptible differences in their cranial measurements. In its application to the individual, however, there are few theories that he employs more frequently. How, for instance, are you going to force Boileau to enjoy Quinault, or Fontenelle to have much regard for Boileau, or Joseph de Maistre to love Voltaire?[1] Montaigne and Malebranche belonged to different natural families and were mutually antipathetic;[2] so were Nisard and Ampère,[3] Schlegel and Sismondi,[4] Molé and Alfred de Vigny,[5] Collé and J.-J. Rousseau,[6] Boileau and Perrault,[7] etc. Emerson called Poe the "jingle man." That simply shows, Sainte-Beuve would have said, that Poe and Emerson were natural antipathies. "What God hath put asunder," as Emerson himself phrases it, "let no man join together." Of how many meetings might one say what De Quincey says of the meeting of Wordsworth and the precise, calculating, unpoetical M. Simon; "They met, they saw, they *interdespised*." "As is well known," says Sainte-Beuve, "there is no-

[1] *N. Lundis*, I, 300. [2] *Port-Royal*, V, 391. [3] *N. Lundis*, XIII, 236.
[4] *Ibid.*, VI, 45. [5] *N. Lundis*, VI, 438. [6] *Ibid.*, VII, 376.
[7] *Ibid.*, I, 300.

thing more acrimonious in its way than the hatreds of librarians; that is to say, of people who see one another daily, who are seated almost opposite one another, who detest each other from one table to another and who spend their lives in accumulating contrary fluids."[1] Librarians are thus put on a level with electric jars. Does not Sainte-Beuve often make the whole process too instinctive? An agreement or conflict of interests may run counter to these temperamental fatalities and rise superior to them. If the English and Germans are now glowering at each other across the Channel, it is less because they are naturally antipathetic than because they conflict in their interests and ambitions. A century ago when they had similar interests and ambitions, they sank their natural antipathies (assuming that any such exist). A change or shifting of belief again draws a man towards many persons by whom he was formerly repelled. Renan, for example, when young, attacked Béranger and his epicurean philosophy. Sainte-Beuve declared that Béranger and Renan were natural antipathies, but as Renan himself grew more epicurean with advancing years, he came to praise in Béranger the very traits he had formerly blamed.[2]

VII

But let us come to Sainte-Beuve's ideas about the master faculty itself of which the theory of sympathies and antipathies is after all only one aspect. As a disciple of La Rochefoucauld Sainte-Beuve believed that

[1] *N. Lundis*, v, 452. [2] Cf. p. 288.

a man is always governed in the last analysis by his self-love. Now what is most intimate in a man's self is the master impulse that has been implanted in him by nature. A main form of self-love is therefore the passion for self-expression, for the unrestrained play of this master impulse. This is the secret mainspring that explains everything else. A man may restrain to some extent his minor impulses, but not his master impulse — *le jeu de la faculté première* is beyond his control. Sainte-Beuve generalized in part from his own experience with the pseudo-idealists of the romantic movement. "I do not believe in the freedom of the will," he wrote to Cousin, "because I do not believe that it is in your power to put a check on your main appetite."[1] Temperament understood in this sense is, as Emerson says, "unconsumable even in the fires of religion." "It puts all divinity to rout." Sainte-Beuve takes an almost malicious pleasure in showing the survival of the ego in its essential impulse even after religious conversion. Converts are no friends of mine, said Goethe. Sainte-Beuve might have said the same, and this because conversions are "upsets of nature,"[2] denials of the law of temperament. *On a beau être saint, on a son petit amour-propre.*[3] "The mark of the natural vocation still persists under the cross."[4] Each Port-Royalist still preserves after conversion distinct traits of his temperament and nature. Pascal even when converted retains his passion for geometry (though flattering himself that

[1] *Cor.*, I, 118.
[2] *Port-Royal*, I, 401.
[3] *Port-Royal*, II, 284.
[4] *Ibid.*, IV, 335.

he despises it). Racine in his nights of repentance was haunted by some passionate tragedy, by the figure of some Monime in tears, and before he could reduce the guilty vision to silence, he composed melodious lines, whole scenes perhaps, that were heard by himself alone.[1]

But a rare and special gift like that of Racine is itself susceptible of a religious explanation. Talent, Sainte-Beuve admits, is at the origin a gratuitous gift, a sort of undeserved predestination, in a word a *grace*, in all the rigor of the Jansenist and Augustinian sense, quite apart from a man's will and works. You thus find "deep down in the gifted individual one of those mysteries which show to what a point psychological observation alone encounters in other terms the same problems as theology."[2] Still it makes a difference whether one deals with these problems in a religious or naturalistic temper. "There is no lack of people," he says, "who are scandalized every time that they thus find set forth without any concealment the doctrine of divine grace. But have these same persons ever reflected on that strange fatality which sets its deep and distinct mark upon us even from our birth and childhood? Either these persons are religious or they are not. If they are *not* religious, I can understand perfectly that they fall back on the physiological explanation of race, temperament, etc. If on the other hand they do think themselves religious, to what doctrine will they have recourse which does not enter into that of divine grace?" (We may note in passing that Sainte-Beuve neglects a

[1] *Port-Royal*, III, 315. [2] *Ibid.*, I, 116.

third hypothesis, that embodied in the Oriental doctrine of karma). "But after all most minds are neither religious nor the contrary. They float around in the intermediary space and shrink from the consequences: they remain at the halfway house in everything — this is what is called common sense, that is to say, the average degree of illusion." [1]

In the battle that is thus engaged, as he phrases it, between the Christian and naturalistic moralists [2] he plainly inclines towards the latter. Speaking of Malebranche he says, "I hope I may be allowed a comparison which would make solemn philosophers frown if there were any left, but which would make Montaigne smile. Malebranche discovered one day his talent for metaphysics on reading Descartes's treatise on 'Man,' just as Garat, the singer, discovered one day his voice when still a child and on coming out of a performance of the 'Armide' of Gluck. The latter, the singer, disappeared for more than a day. His family searched for him; his father, worried, had the streets of the city scoured in every direction. One of his brothers, going to the further end of the garden, found open an old store-room that was usually closed. He enters there, and finds to his great amazement the young Garat. 'What's the matter? What are you doing here?' 'Silence,' said the boy, 'sit down and listen.' And he began to sing to him the opera of 'Armide' which he knew by heart without having learned it, and which he had been constantly repeating like a nightingale for twenty-

[1] *Port-Royal*, III, 491. [2] *Ibid.*, VI, 107.

four hours past. Divine singer, and almost divine metaphysician, your themes and your music differ, but it is from nature that you both proceed."

We have heard of the poets who lisped in numbers, for the numbers came. Sainte-Beuve is very fond in general of studying this first awakening of a vocation.[1] M. Le Tourneux, for example, was born a preacher. When he was still a child at Rouen, people used to amuse themselves after church by setting him up on an arm-chair and getting him to preach over again the sermon they had just heard.[2] As often conceived by Sainte-Beuve the master faculty is plainly organic. Thus he says of Horace Vernet that "on both his father's and mother's side everything had contributed to make of him a man of the brush, — involuntarily and irresistibly a painter; his hand, delicate, slender, long and elegant, was born with all the special aptitudes, ready formed and fitted to paint as the foot of the Arab horse is to run."[3] Here again we are reminded of Thackeray. "'I never can desire,' says Mrs. Warrington, 'that my son and the grandson of the Marquis of Esmond should be a fiddler.' 'Should be a fiddlestick, my dear,' the old colonel answered. '. . . Suppose George loves music? You can no more stop him than you can order a rose not to smell sweet, or a bird not to sing.' 'A bird! a bird sings from nature; George did not come into the world with a fiddle in his hand,' says Mrs. Warrington with a toss of her head." I confess that my sympathies in this dialogue are with Mrs. Warrington.

[1] *Port-Royal*, IV, 8. [2] *Ibid.*, V, 210. [3] *N. Lundis*, V, 43.

At other times the master faculty appears to Sainte-Beuve in its early manifestations as a sort of dæmonic power, almost independent of the conscious self and riding it irresistibly. "His vocation gets the upper hand," he says of Molière, and the "demon rages within him never to cease again. . . . The theatre needed him, and he needed the theatre."[1] Racine again was ready to attack even his saintly masters of Port-Royal when he found them in the way of his passion. "Woe to those, whoever they may be, that you thus encounter across the path of your master passion when it is in haste to find an outlet. They make a mistake. Later when this poetical passion is satisfied and about exhausted, Racine will return to them and make them honorable amends. That will be easy for him, the favorite passion, the young, greedy, hungry and irritated passion no longer being there between them and him."[2]

Just as Sainte-Beuve likes to show that the secret mainspring of every man is operative in him even before the awakening of reason, so he likes to show, very much in the fashion of Pope, that it survives reason and sets its seal on his dying breath: "The miser up to the last moment refuses to say 'I give.' If you whisper in the ear of the geometrician in his death agony, 'What is the square of twelve?' he will answer as though you had pressed the spring of a machine, 'One hundred and forty-four.' The poet is infatuated with immortality and thinks of his verses. The hero sees once more in his delirium his military trophies and his comrades in the

[1] *N. Lundis*, v, 270. [2] *Ibid.*, vi, 98.

clouds. The writer dies correcting proof. . . . Paillet asked to have his lawyer's gown for a shroud. A jockey, knocked over in a race, and rolling half dead upon the track, still moved his fingers, muttering, 'My whip.' In Balzac the Baron Hulot, in his dotage, says to his cook to seduce her, 'Agathe, you will be a baroness'; and he will live long enough to keep his promise. Every man dies in his own element."[1]

The last words of Piron, says Sainte-Beuve, must have been a diatribe against Voltaire. Sainte-Beuve's treatment of Piron illustrates, indeed, his view of the master faculty in its extreme form and so is worth dwelling on for a moment. Piron's ruling impulse was to make epigrams. He was an admirable automaton, according to Sainte-Beuve, set up by nature to launch sallies and epigrams.[2] "Whether it was the Almighty, a friend, a relative, anybody in fact, when a bright saying came to the tip of his tongue he did not hold it back. Some one has said: La Fontaine grew fables, Tallemant bore anecdotes, Petrarch distilled sonnets, Piron *sneezed* epigrams. Sneeze was Piron's own word. Well, you can't hold back a sneeze."[3] Piron not only made epigrams throughout his life, he arranged to keep on making them after his death. "Voltaire, as long as I lived," he wrote, "hardly ventured to attack me. But I know him. The rogue is cowardly enough to insult me after I am gone, as he did my illustrious fellow-countryman, Crébillon. I have foreseen his kindly intentions. Amongst my manuscripts is a little box containing a hundred and fifty epigrams in

[1] *N. Lundis*, VIII, 128. [2] *Ibid.*, VII, 463. [3] *Ibid.*, 400.

his honor. If, when I am no more, he breathes the slightest word against me, I direct my literary heir to send every week one of these epigrams to Ferney. This little supply thus husbanded will cheer up for three years the solitude of the respectable old gentleman dwelling in that canton."[1]

We are reminded of Victor Hugo and his ruling passion for making antitheses. He kept on making them all his life, his dying utterance was an antithesis (*c'est le combat du jour et de la nuit*), and he arranged for an antithetical funeral. He was buried in the midst of almost unheard-of pomp and ceremony, but according to his own directions in a paupers' hearse. We find in Hugo not merely the practice but the theory of the master faculty. The genius, he would have us believe, is the man who cannot control himself. As regards his inspiration the great poet is like Mazeppa bound and helpless on the back of the courser that is bearing him headlong over the steppes.[2] Of Shakespeare in particular, Hugo says that he was "badly bridled on purpose by God, so that he might go soaring with free sweep of the wing through the infinite." One cannot help reflecting that this is also Taine's view of Shakespeare — except of course, that Taine does not put romantic unrestraint

[1] *N. Lundis*, VII, 463.

[2] "Ainsi, lorsqu'un mortel, sur qui son dieu s'étale,
S'est vu lier vivant sur ta croupe fatale,
Génie, ardent coursier,
En vain il lutte, hélas ! tu bondis, tu l'emportes,
Hors du monde réel, dont tu brises les portes
Avec tes pieds d'acier !"

(*Les Orientales.*)

under the immediate patronage of God. True human spontaneity is shown, not in following, but in resisting impulse. By exalting the opposite type of spontaneity — the triumph of the unconscious and instinctive over the conscious and rational self — the Rousseauist plays directly into the hands of the determinist, another example of the perpetual irony that besets this form of romanticism. Taine bases on Michelet, one of the most spontaneous of all writers in the Rousseauistic sense, his assertion that "the human spirit is constructed as mathematically as a watch." Indeed, no subject perhaps illustrates more clearly than this of the master faculty, the way in which science and Rousseauistic romanticism have coöperated during the last century in the dehumanizing of man.

VIII

Taine was largely influenced in his theory of the master faculty by Balzac who more perhaps than any other great creative writer of the century takes the deterministic view. Characters not only appear in the pages of Balzac as the product of a highly complex environment, but each one of his main characters tends to be the logical working out of a ruling passion. We have already seen that Sainte-Beuve himself cites one of the characters of Balzac in support of the master faculty. Yet right here we are to note that he diverges sharply from Balzac and those who, like him, are for carrying through the theory to the end. Theoretically Sainte-Beuve leaves us no choice, if we would avoid superficiality, between a purely naturalistic or else a purely theological attitude towards the master faculty. But in practice he refuses to be impaled on the horns of his own dilemma; he prefers to remain in the "average degree of illusion known as common sense," or rather what gets the better of him is the humanistic dislike of extremes, naturalistic or other. If as a naturalist he believes in the master faculty, as a humanist he demands the balanced faculty, the faculty that is kept under control and tempered by its opposite. He attacks Balzac and the disciples of Balzac on this very point.[1] He is ready enough to grant that a Piron was a mere machine for making epigrams, but not that the great writers of the world have been nothing more than sublime automatons and monomaniacs of genius. He had a naturalistic distrust of the power of the individual to put a check upon himself, and believed at the same time that art requires restraint. Here is in part the secret of the high regard he had during his later years for a critic like Boileau, who was a visible principle of authority and supplied the writers of his time with the curb they might not have found in themselves. Sainte-Beuve's judgment on Boileau is worth quoting, both from this point of view and as the homage of the greatest modern French critic to the chief representative of the older school of criticism: "Let us salute and acknowledge to-day the noble and mighty harmony of the *grand siècle*. Without Boileau, and without Louis XIV, who recognized Boileau as his Superintendent of Par-

[1] *N. Lundis*, x, 262.

nassus, what would have happened? Would even the most talented have produced in the same degree what forms their surest heritage of glory? Racine, I fear, would have written more plays like 'Bérénice'; La Fontaine fewer 'Fables' and more 'Contes'; Molière himself would have run to 'Scapins,' and might not have attained to the austere eminence of 'Le Misanthrope.' In a word, each of these fair geniuses would have abounded in his natural defects. Boileau, that is to say, the common sense of the poet-critic authorized and confirmed by that of a great king, constrained them and kept them, by the respect for his presence, to their better and graver tasks. And do you know what, in our days, has failed our poets, so strong at their beginning in native ability, so filled with promise and happy inspiration? There failed them a Boileau and an enlightened monarch, the twain supporting and consecrating each other. So it is these men of talent, seeing themselves in an age of anarchy and without discipline, have not hesitated to behave accordingly; they have behaved, to be perfectly frank, not like exalted geniuses, or even like men, but like schoolboys out of school. We have seen the result."

Sainte-Beuve is at his best in his insistence on the necessity of a balance of virtues in true greatness. The contrast is striking between his gentle and humane Shakespeare and the Shakespeare of Taine, who is an unchained force of nature, "the most immoderate of all violators of language." In the following passage taken from his address on "Tradition in Literature"[1]

[1] *Lundis,* xv, 356 ff.

Sainte-Beuve appears in his happiest vein as a humanist: "But great men of letters have appeared, you will say, quite outside of the classical tradition. Name them. I know only one such who is indeed very great, Shakespeare: and are you very sure that he is entirely outside the tradition? Had n't he read Plutarch and Montaigne, those copious repertories, or rather those reserve hives of antiquity, in which so much honey has been stored? Admirable poet and doubtless the most natural since Homer, though in so different a way. . . . Oh, it is not to you that I need to say that this man so thoroughly human was not a savage or of disordered mind, and that we must not confuse him because at times he was over-energetic or over-subtle — because he fell into the rudeness or excess of refinement of his time — with the eccentric and the madmen full of themselves, drunk with their own nature and their own works, drunk with their own wine. If we saw him appear of a sudden and enter in person, I imagine him to myself as noble and humane of aspect, having nothing of the bull, the wild boar, or even of the lion; bearing on his countenance, like Molière, the noblest features of the species and those which speak most immediately to the mind and soul. I imagine him moderate, sensible of speech, and most often (through pity or indulgence) smiling and gentle. For he too has created beings of ravishing purity and gentleness, and he dwells in the very centre of human nature. Is it not in him that we must seek the most expressive phrase to render gentleness itself — 'the milk of human kindness' — that quality which I always require energetic talents to mingle with their strength so that they may not fall into harshness and brutal offensiveness, just as I require of talents who incline too much to gentleness that there be mingled with them a little of what Pliny and Lucian called bitterness, the salt and seasoning of strength: for it is thus that talents become complete: and Shakespeare in his way, and save for the faults of his age, was complete. Be reassured, gentlemen, great men of every kind, and especially I will say those who are great in the order of the intellect, are never madmen or barbarians. If any writer appears to us in his behavior and in all his personality violent, unreasonable, offensive to good sense, and the most natural proprieties, he may have talent (for talent, a great talent, is compatible with many faults), but be sure that he is not a writer of the first quality and the first mark in humanity. Homer at times nods; Corneille in conversation is heavy and nods; La Fontaine nods; they have fits of forgetfulness and absent-mindedness. But the greatest of men are never extravagant, ridiculous, grotesque, pretentious, boastful, cynical, constantly violating decorum. As for me, however much I may allow for the individual varieties and peculiarities of human nature, I will never imagine to myself the revered choir of the five or six great men of letters and creative geniuses of whom humanity boasts and who after all can be only the five or six first gentlemen of the world, as a mere gang or pack of men beside themselves, as monomaniacs each one rushing headlong for his prey. No, tradition tells us this, and the consciousness of our own civilized nature tells us so even more plainly, reason always must preside, and does preside at last even among these favorites and elect of the imagination." [1]

Sainte-Beuve thus manages to get both the truth and the counter-truth uttered on the subject of the master faculty, but with some sacrifice of coherency. In this respect he is like Emerson who says that there is "no adaptation or universal applicability in men but each has his special talent. . . . We do what we must and call it by the best names we can"; and then goes on to declare elsewhere that "the differences in men are not organic." Emerson's incoherency, however, is due to a certain looseness and lack of mental grip in linking a genuine faith in human liberty with the observed facts. The incoherency of Sainte-Beuve, who had a tremendous grip on the facts, is due rather to a final absence of definite conviction, though he had a strong leaning as we have seen towards the materialistic side. After reviewing the various beliefs, naturalistic and theological, on the freedom of the will, he concludes as follows: "How many contrasts and oppositions! Before this sea of human opinions as on the brink of an ocean I wonder at the ebb and flow. Who will tell me the law of it all?" [2]

His skepticism, I believe, goes deeper than the various efforts of his time to unify reality merely through the intellect or the emotions. He saw all that was implied in the weakening of traditional standards in litera-

[1] *Lundis*, xv, 366 ff. [2] *Port-Royal*, I, 409.

ture and religion, he saw the approach of the "great confusion";[1] at the same time he was too clear-sighted really to warm up to the new religions that were offered as substitutes for the disciplines of the past. The underlying method in all these nineteenth-century attempts at religion — whether it be the religion of Passion, or the religion of Beauty, or the religion of Science, or the religion of Humanity — is always the same: to take some element of human nature that is immensely important, indeed, but still secondary, and then try to exalt it to the supreme and central place. We must realize the completeness of Sainte-Beuve's detachment from every form of faith, new or old, if we are to penetrate to the last desolate depth of his inner life (*jusqu'au fond désolé du gouffre intérieur*). "The only unity I am ambitious of," he writes, "is that of comprehending everything."[2] But mere comprehension is not in itself a principle of unity at all, but rather of dispersion. In aiming at nothing beyond comprehension, Sainte-Beuve was destined to become, as some one called him, the Wandering Jew of the intellectual world. It is not unnatural that he should have suffered from the "absence of fixed pole and centre," and sought an escape from the "void that mined his breast" in unremitting toil.

The world, as the Latin adage has it, wishes to be deceived (*Vult mundus decipi*). On the negative side, therefore, the function of the critic is to keep mankind, so far as possible and in spite of its natural proclivity, from being devoured by charlatans. Sainte-Beuve pos-

[1] *Port. lit.*, III, 550. [2] *Port-Royal*, III, 589.

sessed in an eminent degree the wisdom of disillusion needful for the performance of this task. Few men have practised with more success the art of not being taken in; and this in an age, as he himself points out, of false religions, that is of false unifications of life and so of charlatanry.[1] "My Lucretian view of criticism," he says, "is not gay, but it is better than the worship of idols."

But though comparatively free from the illusions of his time, he had in the fullest measure its virtues. He is likely to be looked on more and more, in M. France's phrase, as the universal doctor, the Saint Thomas Aquinas of the nineteenth century; not as the greatest man of the century, but possibly as the most representative, the one who embodied most completely its aspiration towards horizontality, its magnificent widening out of knowledge and sympathy, and, some would add, its lack of adequate central aim. That so shrewd an observer as Sainte-Beuve could find no firm anchorage for the spirit in the movements peculiar to this century may in the long run turn out to be not to his discredit, but to the discredit of the century. It may become apparent that something was omitted in the whole nineteenth century view of life and that this something is the keystone of the arch.

[1] "Ce dix-neuvième siècle, qui sera réputé en grande partie le siècle du charlatanisme littéraire, humanitaire, éclectique, néocatholique," etc. (*N. Lundis*, v, 253).

VII

SCHERER

PERHAPS what first strikes one about Scherer is the contrast between his solid merit as a critic and his lack of popularity in France either during his life or since. No volume of his critical studies ever went into a second edition, and some of the volumes are already out of print. He was not even a member of the Academy, though more in sympathy with its aims than almost any other important writer of the day. The natural inference is that he was in certain respects out of touch with his time and environment. Scherer himself took pleasure in recalling that he was born in Paris on the Boulevard des Italiens; but he was far from being a typical Parisian or even a typical Frenchman. In the first place, he was not predisposed to the French point of view by his ancestry. His father was of German-Swiss origin. His grandfather on his mother's side was English, his grandmother Dutch. He lived in England some time as a youth and thus acquired a perfect command of English as well as developed his hereditary leaning towards England, a leaning that appears most clearly, perhaps, in his love of liberty in contrast with the French passion for equality. Later he resided for several years at Strasburg, and became deeply versed in German literature and scholarship, especially in the "higher criticism." He also had a thorough knowledge of Italian. He was, in short, probably the most accomplished cosmopolitan of his time, admirable in his power to combine general ideas with broad and accurate information.

But if he was at least half a native in England and Germany, he was half a foreigner in Paris. The difference between his outlook and that of a Frenchman, of which one is so conscious, is a matter of religion even more perhaps than of heredity. It is as important to remember in his case that he was an emancipated clergyman as it is in the case of Renan that he had studied for the Catholic priesthood. We might apply in part to Scherer himself what he says of Alexandre Vinet, who influenced him so deeply: "The French language is Catholic, like the French nation, like French literature, and one may inquire whether a Protestant, in whatever circumstances he may be placed, ever loses entirely in his thoughts and manner of writing the stamp of his origin."[1] One can feel in Scherer's style, as Sainte-Beuve says you can in that of Vinet, a certain theological chill. It is indeed natural that a man who was a professional theologian to the age of forty-five should, even after giving up theology, have retained a severe moral reserve. It is equally inevitable that literary Paris should have looked on him in some degree as an outsider. There is a certain symbolic value in the account the Goncourts give of the way he held himself aloof at the Magny dinners (*Scherer, épouvanté et regardant la table du haut de son pince-nez*).[2] On one occasion,

[1] *Etudes*, I, 281. Cf. also *ibid.*, 279.
[2] *Journal des Goncourts*, 22 June, 1863.

the Goncourts relate, as the guests were preparing to depart, Gautier went up to Scherer, the mutest person in the company, and said to him, "Come now, I hope you will improve the first opportunity to compromise yourself; for we are all compromising ourselves and it is not fair that you should remain among us as a cold observer."[1]

Scherer had the instincts not merely of a Protestant but of a puritan. He came out, for example, as a heretic in his article on Molière ("Une hérésie littéraire"), and his reason for protesting against the established orthodoxy was that Molière falls too far short of purity in his diction.[2] Scherer protests against those who were corrupting the purity of French speech in his own time, with a warmth that would no doubt have reminded Molière himself of Alceste: "A superficial culture which has lost the sentiment of the right use of terms, and a need of over-refinement which wishes to innovate at any price, such are the principal agents in the corruption of this magnificent language, which three centuries of great writers had brought to a degree of incomparable perfection. . . . I read recently in a newspaper that '*un crime venait de s'accomplir dans des conditions d'atrocité inouïe.*' Can you imagine, my dear friend, the mental state of a man who can write such a phrase! To come to such a pass must he not have been pretty completely abandoned by both gods and men! And has n't everybody the right to exclaim in the speech of Voltaire that

[1] *Ibid.*, 20 July, 1863.

[2] See Brunetière's reply, *La langue de Molière* (*Etudes critiques*, VII, 85 ff).

there are not enough floutings, not enough foolscaps, not enough pillories in France for such rascallions." [1]

I

Some of the very traits in Scherer, however, that are unrepresentative of the narrower environment make him representative in a larger way. "Scherer," says M. Gréard, "belongs to the small number of those who will bear witness before posterity to the crises that human thought traversed in the nineteenth century." [2] If Scherer's life is thus typical, it is because it exhibits with special acuteness the central conflict of the century between science and faith. He had begun by granting nothing to the new critical spirit, by a belief in the literal inspiration of the Bible, and ended by granting the new spirit everything. The creed he had held absolutely came, with his acceptance of the historical method, to seem purely relative; what he had taken to have outer reality appeared a mere emanation of the mind, not, in short, objective but subjective. It was not surprising that Scherer regarded this distinction between objective and subjective as having been of more moment to the world than the discovery of America.[3]

Scherer's use of this and similar distinctions suggests his obligations to German thought. As a matter of fact he was one of those who did the most to make certain aspects of this thought known in France during the second half of the century. His article on Hegel in the "Revue des Deux Mondes" in 1861, which marked

[1] *Etudes*, v, 379. [2] *Edmond Scherer*, 4. [3] *Etudes*, VIII, p. xii.

his emergence as a critic, was probably the most influential he ever wrote. The essential idea which he took from Hegel and other Germans was that of development. "The universe," he says in the preface to his first volume of literary essays, "is only the eternal flux of things; and the same holds of the true, the good and the beautiful as of the rest: they do not exist, they are made; they are less the purpose or goal towards which humanity tends than the mobile resultant of the efforts of all men and all centuries." "Hegel," he wrote in the article of 1861, "has taught us the respect and intelligence of the facts. Through him we know that what is has the right to be. . . . Hence a powerful method of study and criticism. . . . We no longer make the world over in our image; on the contrary, we allow ourselves to be modified and fashioned by it. . . . In the eyes of the modern savant everything is true, everything is well in its place; the place of every truth constitutes its truth. The structure of the old world rested on faith in the absolute. Religion, ethics, literature, everything bore the stamp of this notion. Men knew only two causes — that of God and the Devil; two camps among men, the good and the wicked; two places in eternity, the right and the left of the judge. Error was all on one side; truth all on the other. Nowadays nothing is any longer for us either truth or error; we no longer know religion, but religions; not morality, but manners; not principles, but facts. What a marvellous understanding of the past we have in consequence! How it lives again before our eyes! The affiliations of peoples, the advance of civilizations, the character of different times, the genius of languages, the sense of mythologies, the inspiration of national poetries, the essence of religions, are so many revelations due to modern science. . . . As is our science so is our æsthetic. It prefers to contemplate and study rather than judge. . . . It has given up the barren method which consists in opposing one form of beauty to another, in preferring, in excluding. It bears with everything. It is vast as the world, tolerant as nature. . . . It is of the very essence of things that a truth is complete only in so far as its contrary is introduced into it; that one assertion is no truer than an opposite assertion and always ends in a contradiction, to rise afterwards to a higher conciliation; that the present fact has only a fugitive reality; a reality that consists in its disappearance as well as in its appearance, a reality that is produced to be denied as soon as affirmed. It is therefore not enough to say: everything is only relative; we must add: everything is only relation. The true is not true in itself; there is no definitive truth. . . . The only equitable and useful judgment you can pass upon systems, is the judgment they pronounce upon themselves by their transformations," etc.

It would, in short, be hard to imagine a more thorough relativist than Scherer. Truth and reality for him are entirely implicated in the flux. They are not anterior to the facts but are the progressive outcome of them. This extremely pluralistic view of truth associated him with a certain type of scientific positivist in his own time and would to-day associate him with the pragmatists. If he had lived in the Middle Ages he would have been a strict nominalist. No one devoted keener logic than he to proving that life is not logical, that all attempts to unify it intellectually are vain. The absolute in this sense is a metaphysical illusion. The attempt of the mind to set up a theory of itself is equally illusory. It is as though a man should look out of a window in order to see himself pass by in the street.

One form of the metaphysical illusion, as it seemed to him, was the proneness to erect certain words into a sort of absolute, and to render them mystical homage. He assailed this illusion not only in its past forms, but in the forms it was assuming in his own day (and here we have an additional ground for his unpopularity). In the preface to the eighth volume of his "Etudes," sometimes called his literary testament, he makes an attack of this kind on the word Humanity. He sees in this word merely "one of those abstractions which meet our incurable needs for mysticism." We have a family and city and friends and kin, but that does not suffice; we widen out the relationship which is already unsubstantial, until we embrace the whole *genus homo*, which we proceed to personify, speaking of it only with emotion and raising hymns in its honor. "We shed ink upon the altars of this personification, — ink and sometimes blood. . . . In the great shipwreck of belief, we have carried over to this conception all our needs of faith and love. Nay more, it was Comte himself, the founder of positivism, who undertook to make of Humanity an object of worship. We have rid the world of theology and metaphysics and yet remain the sport of a word." As he looks over the races of the world, Scherer is led to ask irreverently whether the Goddess Humanity does not often have a strange resemblance to a monkey. "It is possibly very wrong of me that I am thus constituted. I am fundamentally a nominalist. Humanity means nothing for me. Where do you see this humanity? Where do you find it? Even among men and women I meet, how many are there that I feel no need to know more intimately! I cannot wonder enough at the power of abstraction of people who in the overflow of their sympathies forget the ugly, the stupid and the vulgar, and leave out of account the vicious, the vile and the atrocious. You would n't shake hands with this man: nevertheless, he 's a brother. You send him to jail, you cut off his head: always brother!"

Scherer would escape from the mesh of illusion in which we are imprisoned by the word. He would get rid of all illusions and gaze on the truth in its nakedness. "It seems to me," he says in his Literary Testament, "as I look back upon my life that I have simply experienced a certain passion for getting at the bottom of things (*voir les choses dans leur fond*)." But perhaps the attempt to get at the bottom of things in this sense, that is, to see them stripped of all their veils of illusion, is itself an intellectualist error. Illusion, as Joubert says profoundly, is an integral part of reality. If you leave out illusion, you see the fact or "law" in a hard isolation and not in its mysterious interconnection with the whole. In this way you arrive at the false disillusion of the decadent who sees not only in the outer world, but in himself, nothing but phenomena and phenomenal relationships, who has no countervailing intuition of the One to oppose to his perception of the Many. The highest wisdom, according to Scherer, is illusion that knows itself illusion; and he would have us believe that there is a strange and horrible joy in thus recognizing the final inanity of all.[1] But we have the testimony of Gréard that Scherer never seemed so sad as when celebrating the joys of disenchantment.[2]

Scherer reminds us almost inevitably here of Amiel, and he is only consistent in proclaiming the deep wisdom and sublime poetry of Amiel's speculations about illusion and disillusion, Maya and the Great Wheel—all that portion of the "Journal Intime" that Arnold so shrewdly set down as pathological. Scherer, however, was at one with Arnold as to the practical unprofitableness of such speculations. He regarded as highly beneficent the instincts that keep man from looking too fixedly at insoluble problems. "We must," he says, "avoid coming to too close quarters with life. It is a slender crust over which you must walk without bearing down too hard. Hit your heel into it and you make a hole in which you will disappear. True philosophy has never consisted in probing all problems, but often on the contrary in eluding them. We are skirting the abyss: beware of vertigo." Scherer did instinctively what Arnold regretted Amiel did not do: he escaped the vertigo of the abyss by turning literary critic.

[1] *Etudes*, VII, 36. [2] *Edmond Scherer*, 155.

II

Scherer may indeed be regarded as a middle term between Amiel and Arnold.[1] All three men were preoccupied in a somewhat similar way with the religious problem. All three had suffered from the noblest form of the malady of the age, the feeling of emptiness that ensues upon the loss of faith, the desolateness of the man who is suspended between two worlds, — one dead, the other powerless to be born. Though Scherer did not, like Amiel, suffer a paralysis of the will as the result of this divided allegiance, he exhibits its ravages in other ways at least as acutely. At twenty, as he tells us, he had undergone conversion, he had caught a glimpse of "that ideal of a pure and holy life which, when it has once appeared, takes possession of all the powers of one's being." And then supervened the scientific conception which reduces everything to natural history. "In spite of its protest, religion is comprised, like everything else, in the knowledge of nature. That is the point I reached at forty."[2] Arnold had not conceded so much to faith at twenty as did Scherer, and conceded far less to science at forty. He would not,

[1] I speak later of Arnold's tribute to Scherer. He must in turn have felt satisfaction when he read passages like the following: "C'est un repos d'ouvrir les livres (de M. Arnold) lorsqu'on vient de lire ceux des grands maniéristes dont s'enorgueillit si à tort la littérature de nos voisins : Carlyle au jargon conscient, voulu, calculé; Ruskin et ses affectations de profondeur, sa laborieuse recherche d'expression, toutes ces poses étudiées d'un charlatanisme qu'on regrette de voir allié parfois à un mérite réel, et qui constituent un péché contre le vrai sérieux et le grand goût." (*Etudes*, VII, 5.)

[2] *Etudes*, IX, 221.

like Scherer, have lumped together as subjective everything that did not conform to the standards of scientific truth; he would not, for example, have granted that the Sermon on the Mount is subjective in the same sense as Lamartine's poetry. To Scherer's contention that religion *rentre comme tout le reste dans la connaissance de la nature*, he would have replied: —

> "Man hath all which nature hath, but more,
> And in that *more* lie all his hopes of good."

Arnold's view of life, in short, was not entirely stoical, but at least partly humanistic. He was inferior to Scherer in logical vigor and breadth of knowledge, but superior to him in instinctive good sense. Then, too, he was consoled, as Scherer was not, by visitations of the Muse. There were moments when, in his own phrase, he breathed immortal air, though he never mounts, as Tennyson does at times, to the purely religious intuitions. Scherer moved freely in the moral world, Joubert would have said, "but not in that other world that is above it." One is therefore led to surmise that his earlier faith was a mixture of theology and romantic religiosity. It is indeed as important in his case to study the relationship to Lamartine as it is in the case of Arnold to study the relationship to Senancour. Scherer looks on Lamartine as a true idealist; which means in practice that he confuses religion with romantic longing. He contrasts this idealism with the flat-footed and prosaic spirit of his contemporaries and yet concludes that his contemporaries are right after all. The faith in the invisible and the infinite was merely an incident in the romantic youth of the world, with its ignorance and its illusion, but also with its victorious charm. But the world has matured and bid adieu to its youthful dreams. The net result of the effort of its prime will be an increasing comfort with an increasing vulgarity.[1]

Romantic disillusion thus played an enormous rôle in Scherer's conversion to scientific positivism. We have seen that Sainte-Beuve's attempt to rest religious faith on treacherous romantic foundations had ended in a somewhat similar disillusion. It was appropriate therefore that Scherer should have chosen Sainte-Beuve as his master when he broke definitely with his theological past, and that Sainte-Beuve should have been the first to proclaim Scherer's intellectual distinction. Scherer not only had a genuine cult for Sainte-Beuve (he always worked with his bust before him), but he was in some respects, more than Taine and others who had a similar cult, a genuine disciple. Like Sainte-Beuve he had the thoroughness and accuracy that we associate with the best type of investigator, but, like Sainte-Beuve and unlike many modern scholars, he loved letters for their own sake and not merely as a *corpus vile* for investigation. Sainte-Beuve seemed to him a vanishing type, one of the last of the humanists (*soyons les derniers des délicats*, as Sainte-Beuve himself had said). "And now we must take leave of him," Scherer wrote immediately after Sainte-Beuve's death, "take leave of this lucid intelligence, this marvellous writer, this charming talker, this indulgent friend. . . . Happy if the melancholy antici-

[1] *Etudes*, IX, 287.

pations natural at such a moment do not come true. Happy if the death of a man who has occupied so great a place in our literature is not at the same time the end of a literary epoch; if delicacy and taste, deprived to-day of their last representative, are not destined to disappear with him: if the royalty of letters is not destined like other royalties to give place to general mediocrity and violent procedures. I frequently had the impression that Sainte-Beuve himself, towards the end, felt that he was a stranger in the midst of the new tendencies; and it is inevitable, perhaps, when you lose a man like him, to imagine that everything is ended when everything is only being transformed."[1]

In a sense Scherer's literary criticism, though it has a strong moral and philosophical tinge, is truer to the type than Sainte-Beuve's; it does not, like his, melt almost insensibly into biography and history and science. Moreover Scherer resembled Arnold rather than Sainte-Beuve, in being interested in the general more than in the particular. The difference in temper between Sainte-Beuve and Scherer is, of course, striking. "What he has not as a critic," says Arnold of Scherer, "is Sainte-Beuve's elasticity and cheerfulness. He has not that gaiety, that radiancy, as of a man discharging with delight the very office to which he was born, which in the 'Causeries' make Sainte-Beuve's touch so felicitous, his sentences so crisp, his effect so charming." Scherer is less light-hearted as a critic than Arnold himself, who has even been accused at times of jauntiness. The reason is

[1] *Etudes*, IV, 111.

perhaps that Arnold had found an outlet for his romantic disillusion in his poetry. Sainte-Beuve had not only effected a similar purgation of the malady of the age in his own verse, but there were other reasons why he found the process of adjustment to the new order less painful than did Scherer. Sainte-Beuve was afflicted as a humanist and *honnête homme*, by certain modern developments, but did not retain, after the loss of his romantic religiosity, an undue moral severity (quite the contrary). Furthermore he had in him a strong plebeian element that, in spite of his radical distrust of human nature, inclined him at times towards the humanitarian hope. Scherer was not merely a stern moralist, but temperamentally an aristocrat, who drew back with a proud patrician gesture (*potius mori quam fœdari*) from that growing democratic commonness in which intellectually he acquiesced.

III

This clash between the head and the heart which appears so often in Scherer and so poignantly, is precisely what gives to his life that representative value of which M. Gréard speaks. At one moment Scherer exults over the doctrine of relativity, at another he exclaims, "No, I am not made for an epoch of universal transformation like ours; my sympathies are with the past; and yet I feel that there is in human affairs a certain declivity that you cannot reascend. And so I see myself carried away by my intellectual convictions towards a future that inspires in me neither interest nor confidence." People were naturally disconcerted when they saw Scherer stand forth intellectually as a modern of moderns and at the same time turn away in disdain from everything distinctively modern. Most men have given their allegiance to the new order not by a process of cool reasoning, but by an act of faith. Scherer, however, showed the same "sad lucidity of soul" in dealing with the new faith that he had shown in dealing with the old. We have already seen how he disposes of the word Humanity; he is no less merciless in exposing the illusions that have clustered round the word Progress. So far from making a religion of progress, so far from believing that the world is moving towards "some far-off divine event," he believes rather, as we have seen, that it is moving towards general mediocrity, with an increase of material comfort for the masses. Industrial and scientific progress he grants is possible, since each new invention or discovery becomes the point of departure for further conquests. The error begins when we transfer what is true of the practical and positive order to the world of moral values; when we suppose that society increases in uprightness, equity, moderation, modesty, delicacy of feeling by a necessary evolution and an automatic development. And this error comes in turn from another which is the confusion of comfort with happiness, whereas comfort is at most but one of the conditions of happiness. Happiness is, above all, a state of the soul, so that you may be happy with few enjoyments, and miserable in the lap of luxury. Rightly understood, therefore, progress can assure the happiness of no one, still less promise that of mankind. Progress may even work counter to happiness which is a product of wisdom, and wisdom in turn presupposes an intellectual culture more refined than is compatible in all appearances with the levelling process of democracy.[1]

Democracy, as Scherer uses the term, means of course not the love of a well-ordered liberty, but what it has meant practically in modern France, the passion for equality. We can possibly, as I have pointed out, see the working of heredity in his own estimate of the relative value of freedom and equality. He saw an ironical contrast between the efforts that had been made to bring about democracy of the French type and the resultant dead level of platitude. "So be it. The world at this rate will resemble some day the plain of Saint-Denis. And to think how many outcries and writings it will have cost, how much ink and blood, enthusiasm and sacrifices, to realize this ideal!" The future of humanity, he surmises, will be something like a bee-hive or ant-hill, — regularity, uniformity, platitudinous happiness, life less everything that makes life worth while.[2] European society seems to him destined to push on in the pathway of narrow and superficial logic until this logic is shattered against the very nature of things, against the inequalities of strength and worth that distinguish men, against the instincts and needs that create private property, against the necessity that is imposed upon society to organize itself in order to live, and to this

[1] *Etudes*, VIII, pp. viii–ix. [2] *Etudes*, V, 317.

end to accept the necessary subordinations.[1] Republican France with its dreams of equality is more Catholic than it imagines since it is still engaged in the quest of the absolute. It has concentrated upon a chimera all the powers of idealism that formerly found expression in religion.[2] "Our generation is pursuing a mirage vainer than that of the desert, absolute equality and universal felicity."[3] "Let us not forget that the masses are idealistic. They refuse to recognize the most thoroughly established facts when they themselves are the victims of them. They are accustomed in the simplicity of their political ignorance to consider institutions as capable of remedying everything, human nature as capable of adjusting itself to all experiments. There has thus grown up little by little a social situation singularly critical."[4]

Since the masses are necessarily idealistic, the only hope would seem to be to oppose to the chimeras of the pseudo-idealists a true idealism. All Scherer himself has to oppose to these chimeras is a cold disillusion.

IV

With such a view of democracy, Scherer, so far from believing in progress, evidently inclined to the opposite belief. Towards the end especially he was haunted by the idea of decadence. He was prone to bestow almost exaggerated praise upon writers who, in the midst of the growing commonness, still displayed delicacy and

[1] *Etudes*, x, 240. [2] *Ibid.*, 55.
[3] *Ibid.*, 19. [4] *Ibid.*, 274.

reserve, even if these qualities were not accompanied by sufficient strength — writers, for example like Doudan, Fromentin, Montégut, Weiss. He cites the enormities of Zola as an example of the influence of the mob on literary standards, and as we have already seen, discovers a similar symptom in what is known nowadays as *la crise du français*. "It is possible," he says, "that all these pollutions are only a passing effect of the trend towards equality, of a levelling process that has submerged only for a time the delicacy of men's minds and the polish of their manners."[1] "But if this were not so, if democracy really meant the abolishment of what used to be called the scholar and gentleman (*honnête homme*) one would have reason to ask what can result from an art without decency and a society without shame." "Former literatures that perished yielded in part to the shock of barbarians. Is that the fate in store for us, and will democracy play the rôle of the barbarians?"[2] He expresses a doubt whether French literature can long maintain itself in such an extreme of debauchery and imbecility.

Scherer protests as a humanist against this cheapening and lowering of literature, but his humanism, like that of Sainte-Beuve or that of any one whose own philosophy does not rise above the naturalistic level, is too much a matter of taste and not enough a matter of standards and discipline. "Taste," he says, "is toil that conceals itself, and we applaud only ostentatious artifice. It is delicacy, and we worship strength. It is meas-

[1] *Etudes*, x, 330. [2] *Etudes*, ix, 347.

ure, and we prostrate ourselves before everything that is unmeasured. Formerly the pencil was never light enough, now it gouges a hole through the paper. Expression is no longer addressed to the spirit, but to the senses. The greatest writer is the one who has at his disposition the widest and most daring vocabulary. M. Zola speaks like a man convinced that he has the public with him; nay, more, like a man who is convinced that he is inaugurating a new art. Unhappily I am not far from thinking so too. I expressed a belief when Sainte-Beuve died that something was ending with him. That something was literature in the old sense, the preoccupation with what is noble and elevated, fine and delicate, the quest for truth in thought, and measure in expression; in short, what has been called hitherto literary taste and the art of writing. All that appeared to me deeply compromised, and I confess that what has taken place since has not contributed to make me change my opinion. Literature is in a way to disappear, or if you prefer, to be transformed. Language is changing visibly. There is still orthography in books and newspapers because there are still compositors to put it there, but there is no longer any grammar. As for the choice of subjects, people prefer violent ones and get what they desire. Highly spiced dishes are needed to awaken the coarse senses of the masses, the jaded palates of the over-refined, the intellectual apathy of all; and numerous writers are found to provide the necessary stimulants. All this is proclaimed progress, the literature of the future. As to the future, that is possible; I know nothing about it. But progress? That is precisely the point at issue."[1]

Scherer sums up his worst apprehensions in the phrase: *Nous allons à l' américanisme.*[2] Certain of the perversions against which he directs his diatribes have plainly very little to do with democratic commonness, the baleful process of Americanization. There is surely a difference between the lack of distinction that may fairly be associated with a certain type of democracy and the perversions of over-refinement, though both presuppose a breaking down of the standards of the *honnête homme*. The perversions of over-refinement should be connected rather with the general literary development of the century, especially with the romantic movement. Scherer's attitude towards the romantic movement needs rather careful defining. He himself, as I have tried to show, is closely related to one side of this movement, to the elegiac and emotional side that appears, for example, in the poetry of Lamartine. But there is another side of the movement that is not primarily elegiac and emotional, but pictorial and descriptive, a side, according to Scherer, entirely different from the other. We may grant him that the two sides are distinct but not that they are radically separated. At any rate his sympathy for romantic writers diminished in exact proportion as they ceased to express that infinite longing of the heart that he associated with religion, and as they became pictorial. He has only disapproval for the more advanced forms of romantic word painting, that would have language overstep its natural

[1] *Etudes*, VII, 194–95. [2] *Ibid.*, IV, 22.

boundaries even at the risk of being emptied of its intellectual content. Description seemed to him to overtop thought in Hugo, and he grants him at best perfunctory praise. For Gautier, who approaches still closer to descriptive virtuosity, he has a disdain that he does not attempt to conceal. Of all writers that ever lived Gautier was "the most foreign to any lofty conception of art as well as to any virile use of the pen." [1] How can one fail to be struck, says Scherer, at the place description has taken in contemporary letters! "When you hear a page in a book praised, or you are told of a newcomer that he has talent, you may be sure in advance that this kind of virtuosity is meant. The manifest reason is that a writer may be brainless and yet endowed with the eye that sees forms and the hand that reproduces them." [2]

Scherer, however, reserves his supreme contempt for the writers who not only reduce literature to the quest of sensation but of morbid sensation at that. Now among the writers of this kind who connect the older romanticism with the so-called decadent movement, Baudelaire is probably the chief. Baudelaire, and the cult of Baudelaire, seem to Scherer to sum up everything in the age that tended towards degeneracy. Whenever he touches on this topic he becomes vitriolic. "Baudelaire," he says, "gave me the feeling of decadence, and revealed to me the nature of it. I had always supposed it was an empty word by which old men condemned works foreign to their habits. I had said to myself that everything is

[1] *Etudes*, VIII, pp. xxi-xxii. [2] *Ibid.*, pp. xix-xx.

relative; that every period has its language and literature; that this language and literature are good by the very fact that they express the thoughts of men at a moment in the life of society. But no, there is in the human spirit an old age as well as a youth; there is senility after virility, a moment when the intelligence weakens, speech grows thick and forms become distorted; a time when instead of being beautiful, supple, and strong, one becomes ugly, driveling and impotent. To question this fact you would have to begin by abolishing the distinction between beauty and ugliness. It is true that is just what the Baudelaires are busy doing." "When once in the arts you begin to pursue sensation, you want sensation at any price. After beauty, ugliness; after the shapely, the misshapen. If we can't charm you, we can make you shudder. . . . The same thing happens as with drunkards, who in order to excite their jaded palates gulp down raw spirits; as with the Marquis de Sade, who seasoned voluptuousness with cruelty. And there is no reason why all this should end. The terrible once exhausted, you arrive at the disgusting. You paint unclean objects. You linger over them; you wallow in them. But this rottenness itself grows rotten. This decomposition engenders a fouler decomposition, until finally there remains an indescribable something that no longer has a name in any language—and that is Baudelaire." [1] He concludes, that "Baudelaire is a sign not merely of decadence in literature, but of a general lowering in intelligence. What is grave, as a

[1] *Etudes*, IV, 284.

matter of fact, is not that a man has been found to write four volumes like his, but that such a man should have a reputation and admirers and even disciples; that we should take him seriously; that I myself should be busied in writing an article about him." [1]

One is inclined to smile when, after such passages, Scherer says that he cannot understand those who would discuss literary preferences or who proceed by predilections and aversions.[2] It is true that in this matter of critical standards he appeals at times from the philosophy of the flux, in part to common sense and in part to tradition. He is willing to admit "neither an æsthetic absolute nor the equal competency of all judges. Neither so high nor so low; neither the ideals of Plato nor the anarchy of individual feelings. Now that the absolute has escaped us we are not to suppose that everything becomes arbitrary. Good judges have at all times admired certain masterpieces and there are corruptions that no society or literature can tolerate under penalty of ceasing to be." [3]

If Scherer is not so flexible and comprehensive as Sainte-Beuve, if, as has been charged, he frequently shows bias and partiality, the fault lies less in the excess of his philosophy and logic than in his moral severity, a severity that often has a somewhat Alceste flavor. In other words, in spite of his disavowals he is more or less subject to temperamental predilections and aversions. Both as a humanist and relativist he is on his guard against the extreme and the sectarian, against

[1] *Etudes*, IV, 289. [2] *Ibid.*, X, 334; V, 66, etc. [3] *Ibid.*, X, 329.

holding any view too absolutely. He protests repeatedly against the logical exclusiveness and intolerance to which the French mind has always been prone and which seemed to him especially common in his own time. He complains of his "rôle of isolation in this age of universal fanaticism. The whole of literature is divided nowadays into sects, each one of which writes on its banner: Out of our ranks, no salvation. The romanticists are as exclusive as the realists, the Parnassians as narrow as the romanticists. I sometimes wonder what has become of the scholar and gentleman, in the seventeenth-century sense, who, according to La Rochefoucauld, does not pride himself on anything."[1] There may still be half a dozen persons left, he estimates, strangers to the horrible mania of certainty that you encounter everywhere in our time, who are not so fierce in their likes and dislikes, sensitive to force but still more to perfection, and not feeling themselves obliged to despise Racine because they admire Shakespeare, or Shakespeare because Racine charms them. "What scorn M. Zola would feel for one of these men if he chanced to meet him. And yet let him make no mistake, it is men of this kind who in the long run will be his judges."[2]

V

Scherer's natural severity appears not merely in his attitude towards Zola or Baudelaire, but in his treatment of the most illustrious names. No critic is farther from a flabby appreciativeness. We read with curiosity his

[1] *Etudes*, VII, 171. [2] *Ibid.*, 172.

essays on some of the great reputations to see what is going to survive of them after they have undergone the scrutiny of one so naturally austere and so free from merely conventional admirations. Arnold has made familiar to English readers two essays of this kind, those on Milton and Goethe. The essay on Goethe sprang, like the essay on Molière, from the Protestant side of Scherer's nature, from his inability to acquiesce passively in any orthodoxy as such. He saw in the German cult of Goethe a proof of the assertion that man cannot get along without an authority into the hands of which he may abdicate his judgment. "The Germans have long since exhausted the keenness of their criticism on God the Father and God the Son. They have left nothing standing of the infallibility of the church,"[1] but they have got even, he goes on to say, by their blind worship of Goethe. "The biographers have traced all his steps, collected all his conversations, chronicled all his loves, written the lives of all the persons who had any relation with him, and they are determined not to stop before they have established what the great man was doing at every moment of his existence. For the works of Goethe, of course, still more pains are taken to be complete. His slightest quatrains, his slightest notes are hunted down; his apothecary bills are printed; the parings of his nails and the hairs of his beard are collected."[2] The real merits of Goethe have been exaggerated by the superstitious admiration of a "nation that did not have any literature before him and

[1] *Etudes*, VIII, 52. [2] *Ibid.*, 53.

has not had much since."[1] Such a sentence must have been peculiarly exasperating to the German reader and perhaps Scherer was not altogether sorry that it should be. We feel at times in the essay the smart of the Franco-Prussian War. Yet he ends by exalting Goethe as the representative modern man. He not only proclaims his international importance, but gives the right reasons for it.

The mixture of intellectual keenness and moral severity in Scherer is equally apparent in what he says of the other great figure of the modern age, Napoleon. He admits that Napoleon had all the secondary virtues. "He was no less admirable as an organizer than as a soldier. He was economical, laborious, possessed of the most diverse aptitudes. He had the knowledge of men and the art of making use of them. He has not been surpassed as a negotiator. He knew how to profit by a success; how to intimidate, dissimulate, circumvent. No one, in a word, ever carried further the purely intellectual faculties. But this marvellous intelligence only made more sensible in Napoleon the absence of true creative genius. When you try to render an account to yourself of what he wanted after all, of what he did, of what he left behind him, you find nothing; he had no general guiding idea, he acted without purpose, he lived at random; he moved feverishly in the void. He saved France, but only to allow it to fall lower than it was before. . . . He engaged in that barbarous and insensate thing, war for the sake of war. He undertook conquests after the

[1] *Etudes*, VI, 350.

fashion of the ancient despots of the Orient. He dreamed of the empire of Charlemagne, perhaps that of Alexander. That keen glance which penetrated the secrets of diplomacy, which foresaw with superhuman sagacity all the movements of a campaign, did not see what the meanest clerk in the foreign office might have told him — that he was headed for the abyss. Napoleon ventured to believe in the duration of his empire. He flattered himself that he should transmit it to his son; or rather he believed nothing, thought nothing. He advanced at random, from victory to victory, from conquest to conquest, after the fashion of the gambler who at every throw of the dice doubles his stake, being no longer able to dispense with the excitement of the camp, forgetting in his sublime and mad diversions that the life, the honor of nations, the safety of his country were involved. Napoleon is of all men the one who exhibits most clearly the two extremes of grandeur and littleness. He is genius in the service of madness." [1] Note that Scherer's repulsion for Napoleon was mainly a moral repulsion. "He is one of those southern natures," he says, "in whom the moral man is simply absent. That is why he is at once so great and so small, so astonishing and so vulgar."

"Does not criticism," asks Scherer, "consist above all in comprehending?" [2] No, one might reply, but in judging. It should be evident by this time, however, that no one ever needed less than Scherer to be reminded of the critic's judicial function; that he is remarkable,

[1] *Etudes*, I, 141–142. [2] *Etudes*, I, 322.

on the contrary, for the intrepidity and severity of his judgments. Some might even see in his readiness "to deal damnation round the land," a survival of his theological past. This disaccord between his instinct and theory is flagrant. For if, as he says, duty is phenomenal [1] and morality relative,[2] like everything else, on what basis outside of those temperamental aversions and predilections that he disavows will he justify his severity? He is more preoccupied, again, with the whole question of decadence than befits a philosopher of the flux. Renan is, perhaps, a truer relativist when he says that "decadence is a word that must be definitively banished from the philosophy of history." [3]

The intimate contradiction in Scherer's being comes out in what he says of Darwin as it had come out in his earlier dealings with Hegel. "When you have once acquired," he says, "a scientific way of thinking, it no longer occurs to you to ask why the universe is what it is. The fact is accepted in its sovereignty. . . . There is no real but the real, and Darwin is its prophet. That is the declivity down which the human reason is slipping at this moment at the risk of leaving on the way many of the things that have constituted its strength and joy." [4] It is an eloquent testimony to the force of naturalism in the nineteenth century that a man who so craved fixed standards as Scherer, should yet have bowed his neck beneath its yoke in spite of the rebellion of his heart, and admitted that the only reality is change.

[1] *Etudes*, x, 125. [2] *Etudes*, vi, 209.
[3] *Avenir de la science*, 73. [4] *Etudes*, vi, 124.

Naturalism pushed to this point always involves some confusion of the planes of being, some subordination of what is higher in man to what is lower, and on the theoretic side, some measure of that metaphysical illusion against which he was so on his guard. He is, however, far less sectarian in his naturalism than his fellow stoic, Taine. His literary criticism is not compromised by any excess of scientific zeal, and this should count in its favor in the long run. There is too much stoical bleakness about it, too much sheer disillusion, for it ever to win the popularity that it missed during Scherer's life. But the serious student will continue to consult it, not only because of the light it throws on certain spiritual crises of the nineteenth century, but for its rare combination of accurate and cosmopolitan information with austere sincerity, vigorous handling of ideas, judicial courage, and "a passion for getting at the bottom of things."

VIII

TAINE

Taine, who had a positive dislike for Scherer, was at one with him in the heartiness of his homage to Sainte-Beuve. We may judge, however, from Taine's article on Sainte-Beuve that the book he had planned on the same subject would, if he had lived to write it, have given a somewhat distorted image of the master. This article recalls Sainte-Beuve's theory of literary reputation which is itself only another application of his favorite theory of *amour-propre*. When a man survives in the memory of others, according to Sainte-Beuve, they do not see and admire him as he really was; they merely see and admire themselves in him. Viewed from Taine's special angle, Sainte-Beuve appears chiefly as a precursor of Taine. All Taine claims to have done is to have coördinated and systematized the scientific method that is everywhere latent in the "Lundis." Seeing in him above all the naturalist, Taine pronounces him one of the five or six chief servants of the human spirit in the nineteenth century. Taine's eagerness to pass as the continuer of Sainte-Beuve is in curious contrast to Sainte-Beuve's own anxiety to mark the points wherein he and Taine diverge.

I

The differences between the two men are, as a matter of fact, much more striking than the similarities. Sainte-

Beuve, as I have said, is above all a particularizer. He is open to the charge of being excessively prudent intellectually, of not coming out into the open often enough with the bold and direct affirmation. Taine, on the other hand, pushes his passion for generalization to the point of temerity. He not only loves to think, as he tells us, but to "think quickly." It is to be feared that he thought far too quickly on many subjects, and then clung too tenaciously to his first conclusions. Perhaps he might have been less tenacious if he had been more discursive and less logical in his thinking. But he possessed in the highest degree that gift for abstract reasoning which is so closely related to the mathematical gift that Pascal termed it *l'esprit de géométrie*. Indeed Pascal's famous distinction between *l'esprit de géométrie* and *l'esprit de finesse* constantly occurs to one in comparing Sainte-Beuve and Taine. No critic ever surpassed Sainte-Beuve in the *esprit de finesse*, the art of rendering life in its infinite complexity, without preconceived system, *sans tant de méthode*, as he phrases it. It is with books as with grapes; you lose the finest flavors that may be extracted from them if you subject them to too severe a pressure.[1] Taine, on the contrary, is for squeezing out the very last drop of what seems to him general truth from anything that has once gone into his critical winepress.

Before becoming a recluse Sainte-Beuve had had a many-sided contact with the world. "As for me," he writes in one of his earlier letters, "I go into society and I observe."[2] Taine began too much as Sainte-Beuve

[1] *Chateaubriand*, I, 234. [2] *Correspondance inédite*, 224.

ended. Sainte-Beuve himself was struck by a loss of balance in the youth of the generation to which Taine belonged. Many of the youths of this generation might have said of themselves with Renan, that they suffered from a sort of encephalitis. We may indeed define the malady that afflicted these representative young men of the middle of the century, as a frenzied intellectualism. The congestion of all the powers of the personality in the brain is apparent in Taine in a very literal sense. When only a boy he had leeches applied to his head at the time of the general examinations. His intellectual high-pressure was so continuous in later life that he was subject to periods of complete prostration, in one case lasting for two years.

To see life so purely from the angle of the intellect is to have an extreme and one-sided view. But Taine did not shrink back instinctively from the extreme and one-sided. Psychologically no more important question can be asked about a man than whether he is a mediator or an extremist. The contrast between Taine and Sainte-Beuve is in this particular especially striking. We have already seen this contrast in Taine's cult of the master faculty without any humanistic counterpoise. He revels in a rampant naturalism. The violence and excess of Balzac, which so repels Sainte-Beuve, exercises upon Taine a positive fascination. The Essay on Balzac was perhaps more influential as a naturalistic manifesto than the "Préface de Cromwell" had been as a manifesto of romanticism. Balzac, according to Taine, is a type of the enormously expansive personality, so exuberant and forceful that he is incapable of self-control. The same exuberant force is found in his creations. You would not care to encounter such characters in real life, but in literature they are admirable. If you were walking in the country you would rather meet a lamb than a lion, but if the lion is behind bars he is more interesting than the lamb. Art is the equivalent of the bars. Artists should therefore exhibit to us wild beasts as a relief from the platitude of everyday prose. This Balzac does to perfection. We are not interested in his men and women as such. "They are merely the pedestals of a statue which is their master passion."[1] This passion has eaten up their humanity. Hulot is not a man but a temperament. The master impulse develops in Philippe Bridau until there is "no longer anything human left in his nature" — nothing but "the inhuman and sinister glitter of a bronze statue."[2] Grandet is impressive because his passion has come to such a pass that "it has cut off in him the very root of humanity and pity."[3] Like Shakespeare, Balzac paints monomaniacs of every species. Taine notes with satisfaction that one of his short stories contains no fewer than seven monomaniacs.

A writer in the London "Spectator" remarked recently that Bernard Shaw lacks the sense of the human. It is evident from the passages I have quoted that Taine suffered from a similar lack. In his "English Literature" he sets Madame Marneffe (the very character that inspired a special aversion in Sainte-Beuve) above Becky Sharp, apparently because Becky Sharp still remains a

[1] *Essais de critique*, etc., 147. [2] *Ibid.*, 138. [3] *Ibid.*, 144.

human being, albeit a very perverse one. Madame Marneffe, on the other hand, is the inevitable outcome of her environment and temperament and so is not amenable to ordinary human or moral standards. "She is perfect in her kind, like a dangerous and splendid horse that you admire and fear at the same time."[1]

Taine's lack of sense of the human has played him some evil turns, especially, it would seem, in his treatment of the Renaissance. The Renaissance was an age of great naturalistic expansion, but also in important respects a humanistic age. All Taine sees in the period is the "complete and violent expansion of nature."[2] As for the art and literature of the time it is an unusually well-stocked menagerie; there is a refreshing absence of tame domestic animals, and wild beasts a-plenty. "We can hear through the plays, as through the history of the time, their savage growling; the sixteenth century is like a den of lions." The dehumanizing of Shakespeare that he had begun in the Essay on Balzac he completes in the "English Literature." He cannot find epithets enough to describe the immeasurable unrestraint of human nature as it appears in Shakespeare and the other dramatists of his time. We see in all these dramatists "genuine and primitive man beside himself, aflame, the slave of his animal impulses, and the plaything of his dreams, entirely given up to the present moment, compacted of lusts, contradictions and follies; who, with outbursts and quivers, with cries of voluptuousness and anguish, rolls consciously and deliberately down the

[1] *Lit. ang.*, v, 122. [2] *Ibid.*, II, 1.

steep slopes and jagged points of his precipice."[1] If Shakespeare had written a psychology he would have said that man is a "nervous machine governed by temperament, disposed to hallucinations, carried away by unbridled passions, essentially unreasonable, a mixture of animal and poet, having feeling as his virtue, imagination as mainspring and guide, and conducted at random by the most highly determined and complex circumstances to pain, crime, madness and death."[2]

In Taine's somewhat decadent cult for energy, even when displayed in madness and crime, we can trace in him as in various other respects the influence of Stendhal. In fact we might establish the wideness of the gap between Taine and Sainte-Beuve, not merely by comparing them directly, but by studying the respective influences upon them. Most of the men who exercised a major influence upon Taine either did not act upon Sainte-Beuve at all, or were positively antipathetic to him. The authors that Taine affected during his formative years were those who made either intellectually or emotionally for a pure naturalism. His special partiality for Balzac and Stendhal is perhaps to be explained by the fact that they combined both the intellectual and emotional aspects of the movement. They had the cult of pure spontaneity in the Rousseauistic sense, along with the scientific and deterministic explanation of it. One should also note Taine's predilection for Alfred de Musset (especially in the poems of passion) and Michelet, possibly the two romantic writers who let themselves go most furi-

[1] *Lit. ang.*, II, 48.
[2] *Ibid.*, II, 259.

ously. The closing pages of the "English Literature," in which Taine exalts Alfred de Musset above Tennyson on the ground of his superior spontaneity, are almost too familiar to mention.

On the scientific side Taine's naturalism is indebted to England and Germany as well as France. He is under important obligations to Stuart Mill (who himself reflects in some measure the influence of Comte) and in general to the minutely experimental and utilitarian school of Englishmen, the school that would confine itself to facts, and their interrelationships. "Little facts," Taine declares in a celebrated sentence, "carefully chosen, important, significant, abundantly circumstanced and minutely noted, such is to-day the substance of all knowledge."[1] But after all he craved a more ample theory. He wished to pass, as he could not in this English thinking, "from the accidental to the necessary, from the relative to the absolute, from appearance to truth."[2] And for this intellectual absolute he turned to Germany. The reading of Hegel's "Logic" was one of the great events of his youth. He describes it as "the monster I spent six months digesting at Nevers."[3] As to the way these English and German elements combined in his thinking, we may let Taine speak for himself. After saying that "experiment and abstraction constitute between them all the resources of the human spirit," he adds: "One directs practice; the other, speculation. The first leads one to look on nature as a body of facts, the second as a system of laws; em-

[1] *Intelligence*, I, 4. [2] *Lit. ang.*, V, 410. [3] *Vie et cor.*, II, 30.

ployed by itself, the first is English ; employed by itself, the second is German." He goes on to say that France may profitably undertake the task of mediating between the two schools. "We broadened out English ideas in the eighteenth century ; we may in the nineteenth-century give precision to the ideas of Germany. Our business is to temper, correct and complete the two spirits by each other, to fuse them into one, to express them in a style that everybody understands and thus give them universal currency."[1]

Taine got from Hegel and the Germans the idea of development, especially the development according to fixed laws, of great bodies of men — in other words, a philosophy of history. Sainte-Beuve had small liking for this attempt as it appears, for example, in a writer like Guizot, to impose an intellectual order upon the facts of the past. We can never, he says, slash too deeply into any possible philosophy of history. He is distrustful of systematic general views, of "those trumpet blasts," as he calls them, "which coördinate the facts, line them up instantly, and make them march in good order as though under a banner."[2] Now Taine is attracted by the very side of Guizot that seemed so doubtful to Sainte-Beuve. His philosophy of history is not the same as Guizot's, but he believes in a philosophy of history, and is indeed less interested in art and literature for their own sakes, than as aids towards such a philosophy. Moreover, in his way of reaching his results he shows himself more akin to Guizot than to the Germans. We

[1] *Lit. ang.*, v, 416. [2] *N. Lundis*, vi, 79.

should be justified by Taine's own method in seeking to explain as a racial proclivity the special type of logicality that we find in his mind as well as in Guizot's.

II

We might indeed accept Taine's method more readily if it applied to every one as well as it does to himself. He may be studied more than most men as a product of race, environment and, above all, historical moment; and we can see in him, more clearly than in most men, how these various factors combined to determine the nature and exercise of his master faculty. M. Saisset, one of Taine's teachers at the Normal School, writes a very eulogistic note on his pupil, but adds: "His principal fault is an excessive taste for abstraction." A year earlier M. Vacherot, another of his teachers, wrote in the course of a similar note: "He is over-fond of formulæ to which he too frequently sacrifices reality, without suspecting the fact, to be sure, for he is perfectly sincere."[1] Taine's dominant trait, here so happily characterized, is also the dominant trait of the French as compared with other peoples. This passion for pure logicality manifests itself in the scholastic philosophy, manifests itself in Descartes, who attacked scholasticism, manifests itself in Taine, who assailed the excess of *raison raisonnante* in the political Cartesians of the eighteenth century. Taine sees a survival of the old Scandinavian sea-rover in young Englishmen who hunt bear in the Rocky Mountains or elephants in South

[1] *Vie et cor.*, I, 123.

Africa. We have at least as good ground for seeing the survival of a primordial racial impulse in his own love of formulæ.

The two other main elements in Taine's work, which may be defined as the love of little facts and the love of local color, are subordinated to his love of formulæ. He has pages of word-painting worthy of Gautier, but we suddenly discover that the word-painting is not for its own sake, as it would be with Gautier, but is in the service of a demonstration. He accumulates little facts again in enormous numbers, but the formula presides over their selection. We should add with M. Vacherot that this choice is unconscious, for Taine, after all, had a mind of admirable probity. But with this proviso we may say of Taine, as Aristotle said of the Pythagoreans, that where there was "any slight misfit between the logic and the facts some gentle pressure would be applied" to bring the facts into accord with the system; or we may apply to Taine what Dr. Johnson asserted with less justice of Hurd: that he "is one of a set of men who account for everything systematically; for instance, it has been a fashion to wear scarlet breeches; these men would tell you that, according to causes and effects, no other wear could at that time have been chosen." In much this way, Taine undertakes to prove that in an ascetic period such as certain moments of the Middle Ages, it was, according to causes and effects, impossible for any individual to have and, above all, to express a cheerful view of life.

Taine's constant pursuit, then, of the master trait,

whether of a race or an epoch or an individual, is in reality the pursuit of the master formula. "The difficulty for me in an investigation," he writes, "is to find some characteristic and dominant trait from which everything may be deduced geometrically, in a word to have the formula of the thing. It seems to me that the formula of Livy is as follows: an orator who becomes an historian." And so Taine proceeds to write a book on Livy, in which the Roman historian and his works in all their complexity are forced into this logical mould. For the ruling passion with Taine is not, as it is with Sainte-Beuve, one passion among other and more or less independent passions, but "like Aaron's serpent, swallows up the rest," or rather it commands them by a sort of mathematical and mechanical necessity. Taine puts this interdependence of faculties under the patronage of science, under the name of the law of mutual dependencies.[1] "Just as in an animal the instincts, teeth, limbs, bony framework, muscular apparatus are bound together in such wise that a variation in one of them determines in each of the others a corresponding variation, and just as a skilled naturalist can, from a few fragments, reconstruct by reasoning almost the whole body,"[2] even so an historian who knew one part of a civilization might half predict the other parts. You can thus find the common formula of phenomena apparently as distinct as a flower-bed at Versailles, a philosophic and theologic reasoning of Malebranche, a precept of versification by

[1] See especially preface to *Essais de critique et d'histoire.*

[2] *Lit. ang.*, Int., I, p. vi.

Boileau, a law of Colbert on mortgages, a courtier's compliment at Marly, a sentence of Bossuet on the divine omnipotence. They are simply different ways in which the "ideal and general man" of that age expressed his dominant faculty.[1]

Taine's emphasis on the master faculty is due not merely to his love of the master formula, but as I have already pointed out, in speaking of his relation to Balzac, to his love of an unchecked spontaneity. In studying the forms that his love of Rousseauistic spontaneity assumes we can once more apply his own method to himself, and trace in him the effect of environment, especially of early environment. "I was born," he says, "in the forest of Arden and I love it; and yet I have of it only childish memories. But the river, the meadow, the woods, one has seen in his first walks, leave in the depths of the soul an impression that the rest of life completes and does not disturb. Everything that you imagine later takes its rise there; it even seems that everything is there, and that the full day can never equal the dawn."[2] Throughout his life Taine's imagination was haunted by the woods, and at Paris he often suffered a veritable nostalgia for them, and in general for the forms of outer nature. He has been called a poet-logician. But perhaps more is needed to make a poet than a gift for rendering vividly the forms of outer nature. His style does, however, combine to a singular extent logic with local color. It is at once and to an almost paradoxical degree ana-

[1] *Essais de critique et d'histoire*, pp. xiv–xv.
[2] *Derniers Essais*, etc., 43.

lytical and pictorial, abstract and impressionistic. In a curious self-examination that was found among his papers, he raises the question whether the secret warfare between these two elements in his style was not responsible for the fatigue he felt in composing.[1] Perhaps it is due to the final predominance of analysis in his mind that he falls short in his descriptive passages of the highest effects of the word-painter: he does not give us so much complete vision as intense segments of vision.

To the predominance of analysis is also due the fact that the total effect of Taine's style is not, in spite of the profuse imagery, one of imaginative freedom. One suspects that if, in Johnson's phrase, he was for making mind mechanical, it was because his own mind was somewhat mechanical. His style lacks inner give and elasticity. It reflects a materialistic age in that it conveys the impression of sheer power rather than of grace and measure. Scherer says that he can never read Taine without thinking of "those gigantic steam trip-hammers that strike repeated and noisy blows. Under this constant impact the steel is bent and fashioned. Everything gives you the feeling of force. But you must add that you are stunned by so much noise and that, after all, this style, which has the solidity and glitter of metal, has also at times something of its heaviness and hardness."[2]

One of Taine's unfulfilled projects was to write, as a companion volume to his treatise on the "Intelligence," a treatise on the "Will"; but we may be sure he would have identified the will with energy. "Our mind is con-

[1] *Vie et cor.*, II, 261. [2] *Etudes*, VI, 135.

structed as mathematically as a watch," he says in the essay on Michelet. "The movement which the mainspring (that is, the master faculty) communicates to the parts of the mechanism escapes the control of our will because *it is our will itself.*" In other words, he has no belief in that other form of spontaneity, that inner check that may restrain the *élan vital* and direct it to some human end. He worships vital impulse as much as M. Bergson, only he would subordinate it strictly (and herein of course he differs from M. Bergson) to mechanical law. He has endless comparisons to suggest how inevitably human faculties unfold and how little they are a matter of individual choice and volition. At one time he compares man to the lower animals; his only aim as an historian, he says, is to be a student of moral zoölogy.[1] "You may," he says again, "consider man as an animal of superior species who produces philosophies and poems about as silkworms produce their cocoons and bees their cells."[2] He is going to study the transformation of France by the French Revolution as he would the "metamorphosis of an insect."[3]

But normally he inclines to a form of spontaneity even more inevitable and instinctive than that of the insect — that, namely, of the plant. Sainte-Beuve had described himself in one of his naturalistic moods, as a botanist of the human spirit.[4] Taine takes up this metaphor and applies it with a persistency and literalness that would never have occurred to Sainte-Beuve. Both

[1] *Origines, La Révolution,* III, Préface.

[2] *La Fontaine,* Préface.

[3] *Origines, Ancien régime,* Préface.

[4] See p. 145.

as a scientific and as a sentimental naturalist (whose memory was haunted by the forest of Arden) he found his account in his unending comparisons of human beings to trees and plants. The word for which he has the greatest predilection is probably sap (*sève*). What most delights him is the vigorous rising of the sap in the human vegetation. Like Stendhal he admires Italy because it is there that the human plant grows most luxuriantly. We are going to see in his pages the whole genius of Shakespeare "unfold before us like a flower." He does not feel that he is lowering Shakespeare by thus comparing him to a plant. We could not ask anything better than to be like trees. "These great trees make you great; they are happy and calm heroes; you become so by contagion on seeing them. You feel like crying out to them: You are beautiful and powerful oaks, you are strong, you enjoy your force and your luxuriant foliage."[1]

This aspiration towards a sort of vegetative felicity is thoroughly Rousseauistic. It must indeed be clear by this time how closely one whole side of Taine is related to romanticism. To understand this relationship we shall have to study the influence of the moment and thus complete our application of his own method to himself. We need to interpret his work with reference to the open and avowed materialism of the Second Empire, just as we need to interpret Sainte-Beuve's earlier work with reference to the pseudo-idealism of 1830. I have already pointed out that this pseudo-idealism met utter discom-

[1] *Thomas Graindorge*, 253.

fiture in 1848. It had become clear that the real world at all events would have none of it. And so Taine gave over the real world to the dominion of the literal fact, and set out to rear on this foundation the new cult of science. At the same time, however, that he is a scientific positivist, he is a disillusioned romanticist, and his whole work is pervaded by the bitter flavor of this disillusion, — by the sense of the ironical contradiction between the desires of the heart and the actual. Nature, for Taine and the men of his time, was no longer the kind mother that she had been for Wordsworth and Lamartine (*la nature est là qui t'invite et qui t'aime*), but a collection of inexorable laws. The most definite personification of nature in Taine is the following, taken, to be sure, from his most cynical book, the "Life and Opinions of Thomas Graindorge": "Towards the end of his life Louis XI had a collection of young pigs that he had dressed up as nobles, bourgeois and canons. They had been cudgelled into obedience, and danced in this equipage before him. The unknown lady, called Nature, does the same; probably she is a humorist; only, when by dint of hard lashings she has got us to fill our rôles and has laughed abundantly at our grimaces, she sends us to the pork-butcher and the salting-tub."[1]

The romanticists not only believed in the goodness of nature, but in the natural goodness of man even though he is commonly perverted by society. "Man," says Taine, on the contrary, "has canine teeth like the dog and fox, and like the dog and fox he buried them at the begin-

[1] *Thomas Graindorge*, pp. ix–x.

ning in the flesh of his fellows. His descendants slaughtered one another with stone knives for a bit of raw fish." The equivalent still goes on under the surface of our modern conventions.[1] Life was never so hideous, he says of one period of the Renaissance, and this hideousness is the truth. Thus Taine's head finds its truth and reality in an order that is abhorrent to his heart. The instinct of the heart is to escape from such a reality into a *pays des chimères*. This is what he calls creating for yourself an alibi: One such alibi, as we have already seen, is to lose yourself in æsthetic contemplation of the forms of outer nature. Another way of creating an alibi is to study history. "Through this gate you enter into revery. All opium is unhealthy; it is prudent to take it only in small doses and from time to time. Since Werther and René we have taken too much of it, and are taking it in heavier doses every day; consequently the malady of the age has been aggravated, and in music, painting and politics a number of symptoms prove that the derangement of reason, imagination, sensibility and nerves is on the increase. Among all the drugs that give us at our will factitious absence and forgetfulness, history is, I believe, the least dangerous."[2] A third way of creating an alibi is by music. *Jouez du Beethoven.* The whole point of view may be defined as positivism mitigated by romantic revery.

[1] *Thomas Graindorge*, 267. [2] *Derniers essais*, etc., 226.

III

Taine recognized that he and his contemporaries could never hope for more than a half recovery from the malady of the age, which was a part of their legacy from the preceding generation. "We shall attain to truth," he says, "but not to calm. All that we can cure at this moment is our intelligence; we have no hold on our feelings."[1] But he hoped that in their descendants this warfare between head and heart might cease, and that they would give themselves up without qualms or regrets to scientific positivism. It was in fact as a scientific positivist that Taine was enormously influential on the men of his own and the following generation. Before carrying further, therefore, our study of his attitude towards nature and human nature, we shall need to consider more carefully certain aspects of this positivism. Taine himself has taken pains in one of his essays to define it and show in what respects it is hostile to the old idealism: "Its first rule in the search for truth is to reject all extraneous authority, to yield only to direct evidence, to wish to touch and to see, to have faith in testimony only after examination, discussion and verification; its greatest aversion is for affirmations without proof, which it calls prejudices, and for unquestioning belief which it calls credulity"; it opposes reason to faith, nature to revelation, experiment and induction to *a priori* formulæ. The struggle between these rival views of life, which has been in progress since the Re-

[1] *Lit. ang.*, IV, 423.

naissance, is what has been called the warfare of science and religion.

To Descartes rather than to Bacon belongs the honor of having brought the natural sciences into entire accord with the modern spirit. He reduced the phenomenal world to a mere problem of space and movement; he substituted quantities and mathematical measurements for the discussion of qualities; he banished from science the speculations about entities, essences, occult properties and final causes which had encumbered the philosophy of the schools. Descartes, however, still remained in great measure mediæval in his psychology, conceiving as he did of the soul as living quite apart from the body, having its seat in the pineal gland, in much the same way, to quote a recent writer, "as the hermit crab resides in its borrowed shell." The constant tendency since Descartes has been to deny man this superiority of essence over the rest of creation, and to assimilate him more and more, body and soul, to the lower animals. Molière, in "Les Femmes Savantes," is one of the first to protest against the mechanical separation of the soul from the body, for which the *précieuses* sought a sanction in Descartes: —

> "Oui, mon corps est moi-même,"

and

> "Mon âme et mon corps marchent de compagnie," etc.

The last step is taken by Taine when he affirms that the soul is a natural product, and should therefore be treated by the same methods as other natural phenomena. In psychology as in the other sciences we must refrain from all consideration of qualities and absolute values, and confine ourselves to observation and exact measurements. "Science draws near at last and draws near to man; it has passed the visible and palpable world of stars, plants and stones to which men had disdainfully confined it; it is laying hold upon the soul, having at its disposal all the keen and exact instruments of which three hundred years of experiment have proved the precision and measured the scope."[1]

This one thought — the application of scientific method to the soul — runs through all the writings of Taine, and gives them their extraordinary unity. He has ranged through ancient and modern history, literature and art, in search of illustrations for this his main thesis. A book or picture interests him chiefly as a "sign" or "document" giving evidence of some phase of the human spirit in the past. This general character visible in a work of art is due, not to the free choice of the artist, but to the fact that he acted under the impulse of a "master faculty"; and the nature of this "master faculty" is determined in turn by the artist's "race" and heredity, the climate and "environment" which have made his race what it is, and by the "moment" in the historical development of his race at which his life has happened to fall. Under this accumulation of outer influences the free agency of the individual tends entirely to disappear. For it would not be possible to prove that "vice and virtue are products like sugar and vitriol,"[2] if a single act of the individual will

[1] *Lit. ang.*, IV, 423. [2] *Lit. ang.*, I, p. XV.

intervened to break the chain of natural causes and thus baffle all the previsions of the analyst. This determinism or scientific fatalism, though nowhere expressly formulated by Taine, is a necessary corollary of his doctrine.

Taine is also led logically by his method to deny the existence of the soul in the sense of a permanent ego behind the flux of phenomena. Thus understood, the soul is only the last and most troublesome of the mediæval "entities" of which the positivist is trying to purge science. The ego in the eyes of Taine is only a resultant — the point of convergence of certain natural forces, with no reality apart from these forces, or from what he calls the "succession of its events."[1] "Beings, whether physical or moral," seen from this point of view, resemble "an infinite number of rockets . . . forever and unceasingly rising and falling in the blackness of the void."[2] Man, thus bereft of all principle of superiority over nature, is tossed helplessly in the vast ebb and flow of natural forces: —

> "O we poor orphans of nothing — alone on that lonely shore
> Born of the brainless nature who knew not that which she bore!"

In a celebrated image,[3] Taine compares the position of the human family in the midst of the blind and indifferent powers of nature to that of a lot of field-mice exposed to the tramplings of a herd of elephants; and he concludes that "the best fruit of our science is cold resignation which, pacifying and preparing the spirit,

[1] La file de ses évènements. — *Préface de l'Intelligence*, 9.

[2] *Ibid.*, 11.

[3] *Vie et opinions de Thomas Graindorge*, 265.

reduces suffering to bodily pain."[1] Bourget[2] has traced the relation between this philosophy of Taine and the pessimism and discouragement so rife in France during the last generation. All the nobler aspirations of man, all his notions of conduct, had clustered around the old-time conception of the soul, and of the struggle between a higher and lower self. The weakening of the traditional belief has been followed by such an unsettling of all fixed standards, by such intellectual and moral chaos, that we are inclined to ask whether the modern man has not lost in force of will and character more than an equivalent of what he has gained in scientific knowledge of life. Do we not miss in Goethe himself, that high-priest of the modern spirit, a certain elevation and purity, such as we find, for example, in Pascal, one of the last great representatives of the mediæval idealism? The triumph of naturalism has been followed by a serious falling-off, for the moment at least, in the more purely spiritual activities of man. Taine refused to recognize himself in M. Sixte, the philosopher in Bourget's "Disciple," whose deterministic doctrines impelled Robert Greslou to crime.[3] He resented still more strongly the claims of writers like Zola to be his disciples. Yet there is a real relation between the doctrines of Taine and those of Zola and the other promoters of what has been termed *la littérature brutale* — the literature which exalts the power of the animal passions, proclaims the tyranny of temperament, and seeks the determining fac-

[1] *Vie et opinions de Thomas Graindorge*, 266.

[2] *Essais de psychologie contemporaine*, 233 ff.

[3] *Vie et cor.*, IV, 287 ff.

tors of conduct in the blood and nerves. Taine himself in his "English Literature" has multiplied epithets describing the irresistible pressure of natural causes upon man. "What we call nature is this brood of secret impulses, often maleficent, generally vulgar, always blind, which tremble and fret within us, ill-covered by the cloak of decency and reason under which we try to disguise them; we think we lead them and they lead us; we think our actions our own, they are theirs."[1] This fatality of instinct makes even the romantic fatality of passion look respectable.

If Taine took so brutal a view of life it was not because he himself was brutal, but because he was, on the contrary, one of the gentlest of men. Life is likely to seem especially ferocious to the man who stands aside from action and becomes extremely sensitive and intellectual without at the same time developing in himself, as Pascal did, for example, the sense of a principle of superiority in man to the monstrous, blind forces of nature. Taine would not indeed admit that he was a pessimist, or an optimist, either, for that matter. He looked upon both attitudes towards life as unscientific. He disclaimed on the same ground any moral responsibility for the practical consequences of his thinking. He asserted, especially at the beginning of his career, the doctrine of science for the sake of science.[2] He was also ready to affirm the doctrine of art for art's sake. The older he grew the more anxious he became to justify art and science, if not morally, at least socially. A

[1] *Lit. ang.*, IV, 130. [2] *Philosophes classiques*, 36-37.

pure naturalist may, according to Pascal's great generalization, be either a stoic or an epicurean. Taine is one of the best examples in recent times of pure stoicism. In enumerating the main influences upon him I failed to mention that his favorite author was Marcus Aurelius. "Our positive science," he says, "has penetrated more deeply into the details of the laws that rule the world, but save for differences of language it culminates in this total view"[1] (that is, the view of Marcus Aurelius). And he writes in a letter towards the end of his life, "Marcus Aurelius is the gospel of those of us who have passed through philosophy and the sciences; he says to people of our cultivation what Jesus says to the common people."[2] This, I take it, is a good example of the stoic pride. In some respects it is farther from true wisdom than the epicurean relaxation.

Taine was at all events a worthy disciple. It is difficult to make a long study of him and not esteem him personally, however one may withhold this esteem from his philosophy. Marcus Aurelius was as much filled as one of our modern humanitarians with the zeal for service, and in this respect Taine came more and more to resemble his master. He had begun by saying that the scientific critic neither blames nor praises, but merely takes cognizance of and explains; and we have already seen to what kind of human fauna he accorded his æsthetic approval. "Criticism," he says, "does like botany, which studies with equal interest at one moment the orange tree, at another the pine; at one moment the

[1] *Nouveaux essais*, etc., 316. [2] *Vie et cor.*, IV, 274.

laurel, and at another the birch; it is itself a sort of botany applied not to plants but to the works of man." But in his "Philosophy of Art" (1865–69) he strives to value and classify as well as take cognizance and explain. It is not necessary to dwell at length on his efforts in these volumes to arrive at a standard of judgment; first, because these efforts have been comparatively uninfluential; secondly, because he does not succeed after all in transcending naturalism — in other words, the phenomenal and the relative. Perhaps the chief point he makes is that we may judge of a work of art by its degree of beneficence, that is by its social utility. We may say that some books and works of art are noxious weeds, whereas others are to be esteemed by their fruits. This is a standard that on the whole works against his early romantic admirations; and so we may note a growing severity for the romanticists, especially in his essays on George Sand and Edouard Bertin. If he had lived to write the last volume of the "Origines" we may infer from the memoranda he left behind him that his treatment of the school of 1830 (including Alfred de Musset) would have been scathing.[1] Taine puts this development in his point of view under the patronage of Goethe, "the great promoter," as he calls him, "of all our contemporary culture." But Goethe was not simply a great naturalist; he was also a humanist. He felt intuitively that side of man which is on a different level from the animal or plant. So far as his intuitions are concerned, Taine seems to me never to have risen above the botanical or zoölogical levels.

[1] *Vie et cor.*, III, 309 f.

IV

I have just spoken of the "Origines." The shock of the war of 1870 and the Commune, which so undermined the seriousness of Renan, had just the opposite effect on Taine. He became more austerely serious than ever, and in undertaking his great historical work he was moved by a passionate desire to serve his country and warn it against the abyss towards which it seemed to him to be hastening. The indignation that quivers in his style contrasts strangely with his promise to study the Revolution with the coolness of a naturalist observing "the metamorphosis of an insect," and in general with the attitude of the determinist who looks on vice and virtue as products like vitriol and sugar. His passion animates his logic and his logic imposes upon him in turn the choice and arrangement he makes of his immense accumulation of little facts. He manages so to select these little facts as to add gloom even to the Reign of Terror. Views of the Revolution may be held very different from those of Taine, but it is hardly likely that what one may term the legend of the Revolution will ever recover from the sombre and concentrated energy of his attack. It will not be easy for the Hugos and Michelets of the future to grow rhapsodic over the "giants of '93." One may say that the whole work converges on his psychological analysis of the Jacobin. Taine's violent logic is never so effective as when thus used to attack men who are themselves violently logical.

The weakest part of his argument is the attempt to

show that the excess of abstract reasoning for which he assails the Jacobins is a direct outcome of the classic spirit. He has been misled in an extraordinary way in assuming that the pseudo-classic veneer one finds in a Robespierre, for example, has any relation to the reality of classicism. Boileau, says Taine, was the ancestor of Robespierre.[1] Now the authentic ancestor of Boileau was Horace, so that Horace is thus held indirectly responsible for the Reign of Terror! Taine has lost sight of the simple distinction implied in John Adams's saying that man is a reasoning, but not a reasonable, animal. This saying is manifestly true of the Jacobins, but if applied to a true classicist would have to be exactly reversed. Reason, though somewhat more abstract in Boileau than in Horace, still means the intuitive good sense that is opposed to everything fantastic and extreme (including the extreme of logic). Boileau himself was remarkably intuitive in this sense, but somewhat weak, especially for a Frenchman, in logic. Taine's identification of Jacobinism with the classic spirit is therefore, as M. Faguet says, about the most complete blunder ever made both in the interpretation of texts as well as in literary history.

The presence in man of an intuitive good sense peculiarly his own, and warning him against violence and excess, Taine simply denied. To say that he was conscious of no such balance wheel in man is only to repeat in another form my assertion that he lacked the sense of the human. "Properly speaking," he had written in

[1] *Vie et cor.*, III, 268.

his "English Literature," "man is mad as the body is sick by nature. Reason as well as health is in us only a momentary success and a happy accident."[1] He was confirmed in this blackly naturalistic view of man by his study of the Revolution. He came to feel with Coleridge that human nature is not a goddess in petticoats, but a devil in a strait-waistcoat. In that case why not return to the régime of the strait-waistcoat? Since man is not capable of an inner check, why not seek to recover the outer checks, the traditional restraints, religious and political? But Taine would not, like others who have followed a similar course of reasoning, abdicate his pride of science and become a reactionary.

On the contrary, the first volume of the "Origines" (in some respects his masterpiece) is an attack on the old order that alienated the true reactionaries. He set out to show that the abuses of the Monarchy produced inevitably the abuses of the Revolution, and the abuses of the Revolution those of the Empire. He thus offended in turn all parties — monarchical, radical, Napoleonic. He not only had to face this general disappoval, but suffered also in one of his cherished friendships, that with the Princesse Mathilde, who broke with him abruptly on the publication of his portrait of Napoleon. The final impression one has of Taine is that of an increasing moral solitude.

In cutting himself off from so much human sympathy, he did not even have the consolation of believing in the efficacy of the enormous task to which he had devoted

[1] *Lit. ang.*, II, 158.

twenty years of toil. "I probably made a mistake twenty years ago," he writes towards the end, "in undertaking this series of investigations; they are darkening my old age, and I feel more and more that from the practical point of view they will be useless; an enormous and swift current is carrying us away; of what avail is it to write a memoir on its depth and swiftness?"[1] He had schooled himself too thoroughly to see in history, not the action of individuals, but of certain collective causes against which the individual is well-nigh powerless. We are always hearing in his philosophy of the way the outward acts upon the inward, but rarely of the way the inward acts upon the outward.

He evidently failed to respect sufficiently the mystery of personality in thus making of it only the meeting-place and playground of outer influences. Sainte-Beuve, as we have seen, anxious though he was to write "l'histoire *naturelle* des esprits," showed greater prudence when he confessed: "We shall doubtless never be able to treat man in exactly the same way as plants or animals."[2] The contrary supposition has found fitting expression in a certain school of experimental psychology. Emerson perceived this drift towards scientific materialism and raised a cry of warning: "I see not, if one be once caught in this trap of so-called sciences, any escape for the man from the links of the chain of physical necessity. Given such an embryo, such a history must follow. On this platform one lives in a sty of sensualism, and would soon come to suicide. But it is impos-

[1] *Vie et cor.*, IV, 338. [2] *N. Lundis*, III, 16.

sible that the creative power should exclude itself. Into every intelligence there is a door which is never closed, through which the creator passes. The intellect, seeker of absolute truth, or the heart, lover of absolute good, intervenes for our succor, and at one whisper of these high powers we awake from ineffectual struggles with this nightmare. We hurl it into its own hell, and cannot again contract ourselves to so base a state."[1] We may add that in the most commonplace personality there is a fraction, however infinitesimal, which eludes all attempts at analysis; and this indefinable fraction, this residuum of pure and abstract liberty, not to be expressed in terms of time and space, increases in strict ratio to the man's originality. What is true of the individual applies equally to a race or historic period. The bushmen of Australia fall more readily into the categories of Taine than the Greeks of the age of Pericles. There is something in the best work of this age that is set above all the changing circumstances of time and place, and still appeals to a kindred element in us. But Taine is more concerned with differences than with identities. He has in this respect pushed to an extreme the method of Madame de Staël. In works like his "English Notes," he undertakes to define the English national type in its ultimate differences from other national types much after her fashion in "Corinne" and the "Germany." In the "La Fontaine," again, he tends to see in the poet the expression of certain French racial traits and of French society in the seventeenth century rather than the uni-

[1] Essay on Experience.

versal human appeal. To treat a writer in this way is to run the risk of losing sight of what gives him rank and importance in literature. A writer, to have high literary standing, must combine in himself two things, neither of which is primarily an expression of his race and time. In the first place he must be unique. In the second place we must feel mysteriously interwoven with his uniqueness the presence of our common humanity. Great writers therefore refuse to be imprisoned in their environment. They radiate even more than they receive influences. In this sense it has been said of the man of genius that he is a monarch who creates his subjects, and so is a contemporary of the future.

It is but natural that Taine should have failed most signally in his "English Literature" in trying to apply his method to the supreme originality of Shakespeare. We may object to his attempt to confine the genius of Shakespeare in a formula as he would a chemical gas, even though we may not, like Matthew Arnold, see in Shakespeare one who "out-tops knowledge," even as a mountain, which

> "Making the heaven of heavens his dwelling-place
> Spares but the cloudy border of his base
> To the foil'd searching of mortality."

In fact, what most strikes one about Taine's method as applied to great writers is its extraordinary irrelevancy. We may imagine twin brothers, one with a superior literary gift, the other a mediocrity. The same influences of race, environment and moment have acted upon them. They ought according to the theory to have the same master faculty. There is plainly an unbridgeable gap here between causes that are collective and general and a cause like the master faculty that is in the highest degree individual. As applied to the great Corneille, Taine's method, it has been said, explains everything that he had in common with his brother Thomas, that is, everything that might, without great loss, have remained unexplained. All this historical setting and background was originally intended to bear to literary criticism about the relationship that the frame does to the picture; but in Taine and his school, as has been pointed out, the frame tends to take the place of the picture. Scherer remarks with his usual severity that in the "Philosophy of Greek Art" Taine gives us two hundred pages of elegant and ingenious description of Greece and Greek life, but "take away six lines from the beginning, and the volume of M. Taine will be found to contain not a word of art and not a word of philosophy."[1]

To use art and literature merely as a "sign" or "document" to explain a society or epoch, instead of using the history of the society as an aid to the understanding of its art and literature, is in itself a radical confusion of the *genres*. The difficulty would have been at least partly remedied if Taine had, for example, called his work on English literature by some such title as "English Society as Reflected in its Literature." For if he does not always do justice to individual writers, he often does succeed admirably in marking the main characteristics of an epoch, in following out the great streams of tend-

[1] *Etudes*, IV, 267.

ency, in noting interactions and interdependencies. His logic and intellectual vigor not only show to advantage here, but are precious as correcting a lack of these virtues in ourselves. A hundred English and American readers have probably received a wholesome stimulus from the "English Literature" for one who has been unduly affected by its pseudo-scientific bias. And then, too, if we are to judge Taine equitably, we must make another most important reservation. It is true that his method from a purely literary point of view is one of the worst ever devised, but it is likewise true that he is often a great critic not because of this method, but in spite of it. He looked on himself as being above all a psychologist; so far as he means by this that he applies science to the human soul, he is only too often pseudo-psychological. We simply have a harsh application of the *esprit de géométrie* to values that elude it. But very often, too, he forgets his system and becomes psychological in the same sense as Sainte-Beuve, that is, he shows the gift for psychological portraiture which the French have been cultivating for centuries and in which they have attained an extraordinary perfection. But even when he is psychological in this very legitimate sense we are occasionally brought up with a jerk, and reminded unpleasantly that we are tethered to a system.

V

The era of scientific positivism, of which Taine is a chief representative, appears at present to be drawing to a close. The forms in which it embodied itself are coming to seem too dogmatic to the scientists themselves. "I believe that absolute, concatenated, geometrical science is possible,"[1] wrote Taine as a young man. If he had lived in the Middle Ages he would no doubt have believed that absolute and geometrical religion exists. Both the theologian and the dogmatic scientist are victims of the metaphysical illusion. Taine not only believed that both nature and human nature can be brought under a common law, but that ultimately they may be brought under a common formula. The single gigantic scientific Formula of which he has a glimpse at the apex of his pyramid of generalizations is the nearest equivalent in his work to the theologian's vision of God. "This creative formula . . . fills time and space and remains above time and space. It is not comprised in them and they derive from it. All life is one of its moments, all being is one of its forms; and the series of objects descend from it in accordance with indestructible necessities, bound together by the divine links of its golden chain. The indifferent, the immobile, the eternal, the all-powerful — no name exhausts it; and when its calm and sublime face is unveiled, there is no human spirit which does not bow, stricken with admiration and horror. At the same moment our spirit is uplifted; we forget our mortality and pettiness; we enjoy sympathetically the infinitude of our thought and participate in its grandeur."[2]

In spirit this is worthy of Marcus Aurelius and the other stoics at their best; in substance it is an extreme example of the metaphysical illusion. Formulæ are

[1] *Vie et cor.*, I, 47. [2] *Phil. classiques*, 370–76.

excellent and necessary in dealing with both the human and the natural law, but must always be provisional, because both laws lay hold upon the infinite. That is why, as Emerson says, truth is "so unbottleable and unbarrelable a commodity." We need therefore to piece out our formulæ with our intuitions; intuitions of the Many if we are dealing with the natural order; intuitions of the One if we are dealing with man's peculiar domain. Wisdom for the humanist, as I have already said, does not lie in putting too exclusive an emphasis on either order of intuitions, but in mediating between the two orders, between vital impulse (*élan vital*) and vital control (*frein vital*).

To each order of intuitions corresponds its own type of spontaneity. The attempt of Taine and the determinists to imprison both nature and human nature in their formulæ is a denial of both types of spontaneity. As appears from a passage I have quoted from Emerson (p. 246) we may escape from this nightmare of intellectualism by an appeal to our intuition of the One. But rather than consent to have the activity of their own spirits reduced to a "problem of mechanics,"[1] to the grinding of cogs and the creaking of pulleys, men are ready to follow those who appeal from intellectualism to the intuitions of the Many; though in itself this appeal can result only in a decadent naturalism. To the exaltation of this type of spontaneity is due the vogue of a long series of philosophers from Rousseau to M. Bergson. Man is no longer with Bergson, as with Taine, a "living

[1] *Lit. ang.*, I, p. xxxii.

geometry," whose formula may be worked out mathematically and whose future may be predicted from his present, in such a way as to eliminate time as an effective factor. This, says M. Bergson, is to impose mechanism upon organism, the geometric upon the vital order.[1] For the organic, "time is the very stuff of reality,"[2] accompanied as it is by a "constant gushing-forth of novelties," unpredictable from the platform of intellect. In fact we can get a glimpse of reality, says M. Bergson, giving a new form to the Rousseauistic strife between head and heart, only by twisting ourselves about and "intuiting" the creative flux.[3] Instead of inviting us, like Plato, to use our intellectual distinctions as rounds in the ladder that leads to the intuition of the One, he would have us turn our backs on our intellects in order that we may peer down into the vast swirling depths of the evolutionary process. He does not recognize the potentiality in man of a spontaneity that resists the flux and imposes upon it a human purpose. M. Bergson sees no escape from the frenzied intellectualism of Taine and his contemporaries save in an equally frenzied romanticism; and herein of course he agrees with James and the pragmatists. We may note in passing that James not only defends the romantic attitude directly, but strives to discredit the word classical by adopting Taine's misapprehension of it, and making it synonymous with the scholastic and dryly rational.[4] As a matter of fact the intellectualism of Taine is much nearer to being clas-

[1] *L'Evolution créatrice*, 247. [2] *Ibid.*, 4. [3] *Ibid.*, 175.

[4] See article by James in *The Nation* (New York), March 31, 1910.

sical as he and James misunderstand the word than is the intuitive good sense of a Horace, let us say, or a Boileau.

VI

Our impatience at the exaggerated determinism of Taine and his disciples should be tempered by the reflection that it was perhaps only a necessary recoil from an equal exaggeration in the opposite direction. Mediæval religion tended to isolate man altogether from nature and from his fellows, to raise him above time and space, and to regard him as entirely dependent upon divine grace and his own free will. The saint strove to attain perfection by the repression of all the natural instincts. The extravagances of the romances of chivalry which Cervantes satirized, are only another expression of this cult of the heroic personality in defiance of all the limitations of the real. Taine, on the contrary, has devoted extraordinary powers of analysis to showing the manifold ways in which the individual will is limited and conditioned by natural law, and to demonstrating how "every living thing is held in the iron grasp of necessity."[1] He also undertakes to prove that man is circumscribed in his institutions no less than in his individuality by this natural necessity; these too are historical products, largely related to their surroundings, and to be modified, if at all, only by slow process of evolution. He is, therefore, perfectly logical in his attack upon the French Revolution; for at bottom the revolutionary spirit is only a transformation of the old idealism and its mis-

[1] *Lit. ang.*, v, 411.

application to politics. The Jacobin, like the mediæval doctor, substitutes an ideal entity for living, breathing men, lets formulæ come between himself and direct contact with reality, and believes of human institutions as his mediæval predecessor had believed of individuals, that they may be made over with reference to an abstract model by a mere fiat of the will.

Naturalism has thus worked a far-reaching transformation in all departments of thought by its twofold instrument of historical sympathy and scientific analysis. In literary criticism, for instance, it will hardly be possible after Sainte-Beuve and Taine to return to the point of view of an older type of critic — to treat a book as though it had "fallen like a meteorite from the sky,"[1] and judge it by comparison with an æsthetic code, itself constructed on *a priori* grounds like a mediæval creed. In general, as a result of the labors of the naturalists, it will not be easy for men to neglect as they once did the element of change and relativity. They are not likely to revert to the crude dualism, the mechanical opposition of soul and body, the ascetic distrust of nature that marked the mediæval period. In short, the great naturalistic movement which extends from the first thinkers of the Renaissance to Taine will be seen in the retrospect to have been a necessary reaction against the excesses of the idealism of the past, a necessary preparation for a saner idealism in the future.

Taine's work will always be highly significant in the history of this movement, highly expressive of the "mo-

[1] Flaubert, *Correspondance*, III, 196.

ment" at which it probably culminated. He had in the fullest measure the "spirit of his own time," to borrow Voltaire's distinction; it is less certain that he combined it with that "spirit which passes to the remotest posterity." It is already apparent at all events that his criticism is not going to wear so well as that of Sainte-Beuve.

IX

RENAN[1]

RENAN says that his purpose in his "Souvenirs" is not so much to narrate the incidents of his youth as to trace his intellectual origins and "transmit to others his theory of the world."[2] The intellectual life he has thus recorded, extraordinarily rich in itself, derives an added interest from the fact that it is so largely representative of his age. He speaks in one of his essays of *la pensée délicate, fuyante, insaisissable du xixe siècle.*[3] These are the very epithets that best describe his own thought. He is a Proteus, whom no one has yet succeeded in binding. It would be possible to do justice to him, says Sainte-Beuve, only in a Platonic dialogue; but who, he adds, could be found to write it?[4] If Renan is thus subtle and many-sided, it is because he embodies so perfectly the spirit of modern criticism. The first step in understanding him is to have clearly in mind the difference between this new critical ideal and the old. The critic's business as once conceived was to judge with reference to a definite standard and then to enforce his decisions by his personal weight and authority. The nature of

[1] Most of this chapter is reprinted from the introduction to my edition of the *Souvenirs d'enfance et de jeunesse*, with the kind permission of D. C. Heath & Co.

[2] *Souvenirs*, p. iii. [3] *Dialogues philosophiques*, 299.

[4] *Nouvelle correspondance*, 175.

the reaction against this conception is summed up in a phrase of Carlyle's: "We must see before we begin to oversee." Flexibility of intelligence and breadth of sympathy come more and more to take the place of authority and judgment as the chief virtues of the critic. Mere judging — "the blaming of this or the praising of that," says Renan, "is the mark of a narrow method."[1] If the weakness of the old criticism was its narrowness and dogmatism, the danger of the new is that in its endeavor to embrace the world in a universal sympathy, it should forget the task of judging altogether. Renan would rest his criticism on the "excluding of all exclusiveness,"[2] on an intellectual hospitality so vast as to find room for all the contradictory aspects of reality. "Formerly," he says, "every man had a system; he lived and died by it; now we pass successively through all systems, or, better still, understand them all at once."[3] No one was ever more penetrated by the teaching of the Hegelian logic, that a truth, to become true, needs to be completed by its contrary. At first glance he would seem to be a new kind of skeptic, who, instead of doubting everything, affirms everything — which is, of course, only an indirect way of denying the absolute truth of anything. Yet we could fall into no more serious error than to suppose that Renan is a real skeptic. "Woe to the man," he exclaims, "who does not contradict himself at least once a day."[4] But there are some points on which he never

[1] *Avenir de la science*, 199. [2] *Avenir de la science*, 66.

[3] *Dialogues phil.*, p. ix.

[4] *Etude sur l'Ecclésiaste*, 24. Renan ascribes this sentiment to the Hebrew writer, but in such a way as to make it his own.

contradicts himself, however much they may be overlaid in his later writings by irony and paradox. We can come at these essential affirmations more readily if we turn to that remarkable work of his youth, "L'Avenir de la science," recollecting that though written in 1848 it did not appear until 1890, with a preface in which Renan avers that at bottom he has not changed in the interval. In the peculiar fervor of the cult it renders to science, the book marks a moment, not in the life of Renan merely, but of the century. We have but to listen to the dithyrambic tones in which he speaks of science to see that he has turned away from the faith of his childhood only to become the priest of another altar: "Science, then, is a religion; science alone in the future will make creeds; science can alone solve for man the everlasting problems the solution of which his nature imperiously demands."[1] After humanity has been scientifically organized, science will proceed to "organize God."[2]

I

Renan has evidently carried over to science all the mental habits of Catholicism. As Sainte-Beuve remarks, "In France we shall remain Catholics long after we have ceased to be Christians."[3] Renan, indeed, may be best defined as a scientist and positivist with a Catholic imagination. For instance, he arrives at the conception of scientific dogma,[4] of an infallible scientific papacy,[5] of a scientific hell and inquisition,[6] of resurrection and

[1] *Avenir de la science*, 108.
[2] *Ibid.*, 37.
[3] *Nouvelle correspondance*, 123.
[4] *Avenir de la science*, 344 and 442.
[5] *Dialogues phil.*, 112.
[6] *Dialogues phil.*, 113 and 120.

immortality through science,[1] of scientific martyrs.[2] When scientific progress is at stake, he is even ready to resort to the Jesuitical doctrine that the end justifies the means. "Let us learn not to be severe with those who have employed a little trickery and what is usually known as *corruption*, if they really have as their object the greater good of humanity."[3] He promises us that if we imitate him we may hope to be, like himself, sanctified through science: "If all were as cultivated as I, all would be, like me, happily incapable of wrongdoing. Then it would be true to say: ye are gods and sons of the Most High."[4]

Renan thus has a special gift for surrounding science with an atmosphere of religious emotion. Like Lucretius of old, he lends to analysis an imaginative splendor that it does not in itself possess. In this way, he attracts many who would have been repelled by a hard and dry positivism. They can have in reading him the pleasant illusion that, after all, they are making no serious sacrifice in substituting science for religion. "God, Providence, soul," says Renan, "good old words, a bit clumsy, but expressive and respectable, which science will interpret in a sense ever more refined, but will never replace to advantage."[5] In other words, all the terms of the old idealism are to be retained, but by a system of subtle equivocation they are to receive new meanings. Thus a great deal is said about the "soul,"

[1] *Dialogues phil.*, 134–35.
[2] *Ibid.*, 129.
[3] *Avenir de la science*, 351.
[4] *Ibid.*, 476.
[5] *Avenir de la science*, 476, and *Etudes d'hist. rel.*, 419.

but, as used by Renan, it has come to be a sort of function of the brain. "Those will understand me who have once breathed the air of the other world and tasted the nectar of the ideal."[1] When this is taken in connection with the whole passage where it occurs, we discover that "tasting the nectar of the ideal" does not signify much more than reading a certain number of German monographs. Men, he tells us, are immortal, — that is, "in their works," or "in the memory of those who have loved them," or "in the memory of God."[2] Elsewhere we learn that by God he means merely the "category of the ideal." By a further attenuation, the ideal has ceased to be the immediate personal perception of a spiritual order superior to the phenomenal world — of idealism in this sense there is more in one sentence of Emerson than in scores of pages of Renan. It is simply the faith in scientific progress reinforced, as we have seen, in his own case, by a religious sensibility of unusual depth and richness. His creed, as he himself formulates it, is "the cult of the ideal, the negation of the supernatural, the experimental search for truth."[3] In spite of the first article of this creed, Renan is like other positivists in his extreme distrust of the unaided insight or intuition of the individual. We should note how careful he is to rest his revolt from Catholicism, not on the testimony of the reason or the conscience, but on the outer fact.[4]

The belief was once held, and in France with a firmer

[1] *Avenir de la science*, 56.
[2] *Dialogues phil.*, 139.
[3] *Dialogues phil.*, 1.
[4] See *Souvenirs*, 250 and 297 f.

assurance than elsewhere, that truth might be attained by abstract reasoning. In Malebranche's dialogue, Théodore and Ariste shut themselves up in their room with drawn curtains so as to consult more effectually the inner oracle, and then start out from this luminous proposition: *Le néant n'a point de propriétés.* Renan, for his part, will be satisfied with nothing less than the entire overthrow of apriorism and metaphysical assumption. He regards "the slightest bit of scientific research" as more to the purpose than "fifty years of metaphysical meditation."[1] To be sure, every man has a right to his philosophy, but this philosophy is only his personal dream of the infinite, and has no objective value apart from the scientific data it happens to contain.[2] Superficial readers of Renan are disconcerted when they learn that nothing he had done gave him so much satisfaction as his "Corpus Inscriptionum Semiticarum,"[3] the most aridly erudite of all his works, the one into which he has put the least of himself, according to ordinary standards. But what, Renan might reply, is a mere dream of the infinite, however artistically expressed, compared with the honor of contributing even a single brick to that edifice of positive knowledge which is being reared by science, and is destined to take the place of the air-palaces of the metaphysicians?

Renan is careful, then, to found his study of man not on introspection, but on the positive evidence of

[1] *Avenir de la science*, 163. [2] *Dialogues phil.*, 240, etc.

[3] A bit of paper found in Renan's desk after his death had written upon it: "De tout ce que j'ai fait, c'est le *Corpus* que j'aime le mieux."

history and language. "There is no science of the individual soul."[1] This one phrase contains the denial of the old religion and psychology; but he offers to substitute for this traditional idea of human nature a definite image of humanity as it is revealed in its past. "The only science of a being in a constant state of development is its history."[2] History, therefore, rises at once into immense importance as the means by which man is to arrive at the necessary truths about his own nature.

II

Renan himself was so admirably endowed for historical study that in thus exalting it he may be suspected of viewing life too exclusively from the angle of his own special faculty. "All the misfortunes of men," says the dancing-master in Molière, "all the fatal reverses that fill the world's annals, the blunders of statesmen and the shortcomings of great captains arise from not knowing how to dance." We cannot, however, easily overrate the importance of the revolution that took place early in the last century in the manner of understanding history. Renan himself was one of the first to see in this new historical sense the chief acquisition and distinctive originality of the nineteenth century.[3] "History," says Sainte-Beuve, "that general taste and aptitude of our age, falls heir, in effect, to all the other branches of human culture."[4] A few believers in direct vision, like Emerson, protested:

[1] *Dialogues phil.*, 265.

[2] *Avenir de la science*, 132.

[3] *Essais de morale et de critique*, 104.

[4] *N. lundis*, I, 103.

"Our age is retrospective. It builds the sepulchres of the fathers. It writes biographies, histories, and criticisms." But in this matter Emerson's voice was that of one crying in the wilderness. The fascination of what he calls "masquerading in the faded wardrobe of the past" has made itself felt more and more, until it has come, in such forms as the historical novel, to appeal to the veriest Philistine.

In itself, this imaginative and sympathetic understanding of the past was worth acquiring, even at the cost of some one-sidedness. The old-fashioned historian had an entirely inadequate notion of the variable element in human nature. He had before him in writing a sort of image of man in the abstract which he supposed to hold good for all particular men "from China to Peru"; he used very similar terms in speaking of Louis XIV and a king of the Merovingian dynasty, and judged them in the main by the same standard. A historian like Renan, on the contrary, uses all his art in bringing out the differences that separate men in time and space. He has little to say about man in general, but he makes us feel the ways in which an Athenian of the time of the Antonines had ceased to resemble an Athenian of the age of Pericles, how the mental attitude of a Greek differed from that of a Jew, in what respects an inhabitant of Rome was unlike an inhabitant of Antioch. "The essence of criticism," he tells us, "is the ability to enter into modes of life different from our own."[1] In this definition he favors

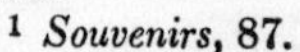

[1] *Souvenirs*, 87.

once more his own talent, which excels in nothing so much as in seizing and rendering the finest shades of thought and feeling, in making the most subtle distinctions. He has in a high degree what he himself calls "the direct intuition of the sentiments and passions of the past."[1] For this gift of historical divination there is needed, in addition to exact scholarship, a perfect blending of those feminine powers of comprehension and sympathy to which Goethe has paid tribute at the end of the second Faust. Renan himself is fond of insisting on this feminine side of his nature. "I have been reared by women and priests. In this fact lies the explanation both of my virtues and my faults. . . . In my manner of feeling I am three-fourths a woman."[2] Elsewhere he ascribes this predominance of feminine traits to the entire Celtic race, and especially to his own branch of it.[3]

With his native aptitude for noting minute changes, Renan was peculiarly fitted to receive the new theories of evolution. The German scholarship and speculation, which he did so much to make known in France, are permeated by this idea of gradual growth and development. The old psychology had studied man from the static point of view; in the philosophy of Renan, even God evolves. For him, the great modern achievement is to "have substituted the category of becoming for the category of being, the conception of the relative

[1] *Essais de morale et de critique*, 110.
[2] *Feuilles détachées*, pp. xxx–xxxi. Cf. also *Souvenirs*, 113 f.
[3] *Essais de morale et de critique*, 385.

Bergson

for the conception of the absolute, movement for immobility."[1] One who has found, like Renan, how much may be explained by the historical method, is tempted to use it to explain everything. He is curiously loath to grant that a work of art, for example, may be valuable by virtue of its universal human truth, and not simply as the mirror of a particular type of man or civilization. "It is not Homer who is beautiful," he says, "but Homeric life, the phase in the existence of humanity described by Homer." "If the Ossianic hymns of Macpherson were authentic, we should have to place them alongside of Homer; as soon as it is proved that they are by a poet of the eighteenth century, they have only a very trifling value."[2] Renan's historical finesse does not compare favorably here with the vigorous good sense of Dr. Johnson, who remarks characteristically of Ossian: "Sir, a man might write such stuff forever if he would only *abandon* his mind to it."

It would be possible to multiply passages from Renan to show that his attitude towards literature is not primarily literary but historical or philological. He confesses that he valued literature for a time only to please Sainte-Beuve, who had had a great deal of influence upon him.[3] No worse heresy from the point of view of the lover of letters was ever uttered than when Renan said that "literary history is destined to take the place in great part of the direct reading of the works of the human spirit";[4] or when he declared that he would "ex-

[1] *Averroès*, p. ii.
[2] *Ibid.*, 190 f.
[3] *Souvenirs*, 354.
[4] *Avenir de la science*, 226.

change all the beautiful prose of Livy for some of the documents that he had before his eyes in writing his history."[1]

III

It was Renan's ambition, however, to be something more than a mere historian and philologist. It should be remembered that the second article of his creed is the negation of the supernatural, "that strange disease," as he describes it elsewhere, "that to the shame of civilization has not yet disappeared from humanity."[2] All his early training had turned him towards the study of religion. After his conversion from Catholicism to science, there was superadded the desire to apply his new faith, to prove that the positive methods of history and philology are adequate to explain what has always been held to be wholly beyond them. Religion assumes that there is a realm of mystery into which the ordinary reason is unable to enter. There can be no real triumph for the rationalist until this main assumption of religion is attacked and discredited. It was with all this in mind that Renan wrote when a very young man: "The most important book of the nineteenth century should have as its title 'A Critical History of the Origins of Christianity.'"[3] Renan devoted over thirty years of his own life to the accomplishment of this great task. The result is embodied in the seven volumes of his "Origines du Christianisme," and the five complementary volumes of his "Histoire du peuple d'Israël." These works, though

[1] *Essais de morale et de critique*, 36. [2] *Ibid.*, 48.
[3] *Avenir de la science*, 279.

not perhaps the most important of the century, are, at all events, the most considerable that have appeared in France for one or two generations.

It is quite beyond the scope of the present study to discuss in detail Renan's treatment of the grave questions that necessarily confront a historian of Christianity. The method of this treatment is evidently borrowed from Germany. He has pressed the French talent for expression into the service of German research, and thrown into general circulation ideas that had previously been the property of a few specialists. German scholars, however, had left to scriptural exegesis at least a semblance of special privilege. Renan's work is significant by the very boldness with which he abolishes the distinction between sacred and profane learning, and puts the narratives of the Old and New Testaments on precisely the same footing as those of Livy and Herodotus. The Bible, instead of being absolutely inspired and all of a piece, thus becomes purely human and historical and bears the impress of all the changing circumstances of time and place. The book of Ecclesiastes was once thought to be the word of God; Renan sees in it only the "philosophy of a disillusioned old bachelor."[1]

It is usual to contrast this historical method of Renan with the irreligion of the eighteenth century, founded entirely on reasoning and often as intolerant in temper as the dogma it attacked. This temper is well exemplified by Voltaire's warfare upon the supernatural, especially by the famous watchword of his crusade upon Catholi-

[1] *Dialogues phil.*, 27.

cism, *Ecrasez l'infâme*. The militant atheism of former times was, as has often been remarked, a sort of inverted faith. "There is no God, and Harriet Martineau is his prophet." We can accept the contrast between Renan and this type of disbeliever, provided we remember that Renan's philosophy also carried with it no small share of dogmatic rationalism, and something, too, of the mocking irreverence that in France, at all events, nearly always accompanies it. This element comes to the surface more and more as he grows older. There are even moments when he deserves the epithet his enemies have given him, — that of an "unctuous Voltaire." This flippancy in dealing with religious matters is often amusing enough in itself, but one would have preferred to see a man like Renan follow the counsel of the ancient sage and "not speculate about the highest things in lightness of heart."

We cannot be too careful to distinguish these different elements in a nature as complex as Renan's. He has some points in common with Voltaire, and still more with the critics of Germany. On the other hand, he resembles by his sentimental cult for Christianity a Catholic apologist like Chateaubriand. It was to this last trait that he owed much of his power to influence his own generation. For religion, even after it has lost all effective hold on the reason and character, still lingers in the sensibility. When it has ceased to appeal to us as truth, it continues to appeal to us as beauty. As Renan puts it, "We are offended by the dogmas of Catholicism and delighted by its old churches."[1] We

[1] *Dialogues phil.*, 328.

are thrilled with emotion by mediæval architecture, by the poetry of Christian rites and ceremonies, by the odor of incense, or, like Renan himself, by the Canticles to the Virgin.[1] This mood may be termed religiosity, and is not to be confused with real religion, with which it has no necessary connection.

Renan, then, came at the precise moment when men were most divided between this sentimental yearning towards the past and their intellectual acceptance of the new order. The heart refused to acquiesce in the conclusions of the head. This struggle between the head and the heart was especially common towards the middle of the century, so much so that, according to Sainte-Beuve, it had become a fashionable pose.[2]

> "Ma raison révoltée
> Essaie en vain de croire et mon cœur de douter."[3]

The religious sentiment had still been strong enough in the case of Chateaubriand and a considerable number of his contemporaries to carry with it the reluctant reason. But fifty years later the balance had turned in favor of the modern spirit, and many men were preparing to bid the religious forms of the past a tender and regretful farewell. Renan is their spokesman when he says that "the belief we have had should never be a bond. We have paid our debt to it when we have carefully wrapped it in the purple shroud in which slumber the gods that are dead."[4] He sets out then in his

[1] *Souvenirs*, 65. [2] *N. lundis*, v, 14.
[3] Alfred de Musset, *L'Espoir en Dieu*. See also for the same mood parts of Musset's *Rolla*. [4] *Souvenirs*, 72.

"Origines" to weave the shroud of Christianity, and to give it — so far as it implies faith in the supernatural — a sympathetic and respectful burial. We have already spoken of the faculty that specially fitted him for this enterprise. No one knew better than he how to gild positivism with religiosity and throw around the operations of the scientific intellect a vague aroma of the infinite. *Il donne aux hommes de sa génération ce qu'ils désirent, des bonbons qui sentent l'infini.*[1] Religion that has thus taken refuge in the sensibility becomes largely a matter of literary and artistic enjoyment. This is evidently so in the case of Chateaubriand, and it is not difficult to detect in Renan the same epicurean flavor. He tells us that he has a "keen relish"[2] for the character of the founder of Christianity. He speaks in another passage of "savoring the delights of the religious sentiment."[3] Perhaps nothing so offends the serious reader of the "Vie de Jésus" as Renan's assumption that the highest praise he can give Jesus is to say that he satisfies the æsthetic sense. He multiplies in speaking of him such adjectives as *doux*, *beau*, *exquis*, *charmant*, *ravissant*, *délicieux*.

But we have just seen that this religiosity, however little it may be to our liking, was exactly suited to the taste of a large contemporary public. It was the timeliness of the "Vie de Jésus," even more than its intrinsic merit, that won for it its extraordinary success,

[1] Doudan, *Lettres*, IV, 143. The whole passage on Renan and his time is worth reading.

[2] *Souvenirs*, 312.

[3] *Avenir de la science*, 248.

and made of its publication, as Scherer has said, "one of the events of the century." [1] Sixty thousand copies of the work were called for in the first five months, and it was soon translated into many languages. The orthodox, Protestants as well as Catholics, saw in it, in spite of the outward forms of respect in which it clothed itself, the most insidious and deadly attack that religion had yet sustained, and within a year or two of its appearance hundreds of books, pamphlets and magazine articles had been poured forth in reply.[2] The Bishop of Marseilles had the church bells tolled every afternoon at three against Renan, the Antichrist; Pope Pius IX called him the "European blasphemer." In some cases polemic was reinforced by calumny. Thus it was reported that the wealthy Jew, M. de Rothschild, had paid Renan a bribe of a million francs for writing his attack on Christianity.[3]

Without venturing into this dangerous region of theological controversy, we can see at this distance that Renan is not at his best in the "Vie de Jésus." Some would go even further, and say, in the words of Fleury, that "any one who thinks he can improve on the Gospel narrative does not understand it." Renan chiefly excels in rendering, by his art of delicate shadings, the element of relativity in the records of the past; whereas Jesus, as Arnold expresses it, "is, in the jargon of modern philosophy, an *absolute;* we cannot explain,

[1] *Etudes sur la littérature contemporaine*, VIII, 108.

[2] For a partial list see Milsand, *Bibliographie des publications relatives au livre de M. Renan, Vie de Jésus* (1864).

[3] *Feuilles détachées*, p. xxii.

cannot get behind him and above him, cannot command him." The historical method is most serviceable when it is brought to bear on a work like the Apocalypse, or on an event like the persecution of Nero. But it is not what is needed to make us feel the sheer spiritual elevation of Jesus. It fails as conspicuously as it does when applied by Taine, in his "English Literature," to the eminent personality of Shakespeare. Neither Jesus, nor Shakespeare, it would seem, is to be accounted for by any theory of environment, or by the convergent effect of any number of "influences."

Renan's age resembled our own in that it was extraordinarily strong in its sense of what the individual owes to society, and extraordinarily weak in its sense of what he owes to himself; and so, in obedience to the time-spirit, Renan reduces the mission of Jesus, so far as possible, to sentimental and humanitarian effusions. The masculine religion of the will is almost entirely sacrificed in his narrative to the feminine religion of the heart. But, as Sainte-Beuve remarks, two great families of Christians may be distinguished from the first — on the one hand the "gentle and the tender," and on the other the "resolute and the strong." [1] The traits that were thus separated in the followers were united in the founder. As a result of Renan's failure to recognize this fact, there is a real incoherency in his picture of Jesus. It is not made clear to us how the "delicate and amiable moralist" of Galilee becomes the "sombre giant of the last days."

[1] *Port-Royal*, I, 217.

Renan can scarcely conceal his dislike for Saint Paul, whose interest is evidently centred in the spiritual life of the individual, and who cannot, by any device of historical interpretation, be made into a humanitarian. He calls him the second founder of Christianity, but he has little sympathy for the distinctive features of the Pauline religion, its haunting sense of sin and the stress it lays on the struggle between a lower and a higher self, between a law of the flesh and a law of the spirit. "Wretched man that I am!" exclaims Saint Paul, "who shall deliver me from the body of this death?" Renan, for his part, likes to remind us that he is the fellow countryman of the Breton Pelagius, who taught, in opposition to the orthodox church fathers, the natural goodness of human nature. A Christian (in the old-fashioned sense of the term) would see in all this a proof that Renan was lacking in some of the essentials of the inner life. It is, at all events, a curious example of his determination to view everything from the narrow angle of philology. "I confess," he says, "that the dogma of original sin is the one for which I have least relish. There is no other dogma that rests like it on a needle's point. The story of the sin of Adam is in only one of the two versions which alternate with one another in making up the book of Genesis. If the Elohistic version alone had come down to us, there would be no original sin. The Jehovistic story of the fall . . . was never noticed by the ancient people of Israel. Paul first drew from it the frightful dogma which for centuries has filled humanity with gloom and terror."[1]

[1] *Feuilles détachées*, 375–76.

Renan's positivism is also well illustrated by his attitude towards miracles. He is nowhere so dogmatic as in the confidence with which he decides what is "natural" and what is "supernatural," and rejects forthwith everything that cannot be properly tested in the laboratory of M. Berthelot. As though, with our infinitesimal fragment of experience, we really knew whether the ordinary "law" may not be at times superseded and held in abeyance by a higher "law"! In the "Vie de Jésus" he occasionally resorts to the theory of pious fraud. Much scandal was caused by his suggestion that Lazarus deliberately planned and acted out the scene of his coming to life with a view to increasing Christ's fame as a thaumaturgist. Elsewhere he inclines rather to see in the miraculous the distortion of some natural incident. For example, the story of the Pentecost and the tongues of fire probably had its origin in the lightning flashes of a violent thunderstorm.[1] Paul, overcome by heat and fatigue, was suffering from cerebral congestion, accompanied by an attack of ophthalmia, and so imagined that he met Jesus on the road to Damascus.[2] The doctrine of the resurrection — one, as Renan says, in which the whole future of Christianity was involved — grew out of a hallucination of Mary Magdalene,[3] etc.

Positivist though he is in all these ways, Renan still retains in his thought many traces of the romanticism he was so careful to banish from his style. Hence an occasional lack of objectivity and inability to get away from himself, a tendency to honor the historical person-

[1] *Les Apôtres*, 62. [2] *Ibid.*, 180 ff. [3] *Ibid.*, 8 ff.

ages whom he admires by ascribing to them his own qualities. He has put many of his own traits into his portraits of Jesus and Marcus Aurelius. He himself inclines more and more to ironical detachment, and is unwilling to think that Jesus could have been denied the same superiority. "Jesus had in the highest degree what we regard as the essential virtue of a distinguished person — I mean the gift of smiling at his own work, of rising superior to it, of not allowing himself to be haunted by it."[1] Renan pursues his romantic dream through the outer circumstance and sometimes subordinates the outer circumstance to it. In his unsuccessful electoral campaign of 1869, only a year before the Franco-Prussian War, he advised a reduction of the army. A real statesman would have sacrificed his humanitarian vision of peace, in case he happened to have one, to the actual danger of war which was already patent to a careful observer. The Celtic race, according to Renan, has ever tended to "take its dreams for realities." "The essential element of the poetical life of the Celt is *adventure*, that is to say, the pursuit of the unknown, the unending quest after the ever-fleeting object of desire."[2] Renan himself has found a relation between these racial traits and his own romanticism and love of intellectual adventure. He arrives at few certainties in his studies on religion, but he makes up for these gaps in our positive information by a surprising fertility in hypothesis. There is something stimulating in the very freedom with which he handles ideas

[1] *L'Antéchrist*, 102. [2] *Essais de morale et de critique*, 386.

and events, or, as some might say, in his lack of intellectual prudence and sobriety. A person intellectually prudent can only marvel at the boldness with which Renan and Taine launch forth into some subject like Buddhism[1] — vast, obscure, imperfectly known as yet even to the specialist — and reduce it all to a few generalizations as fallacious often as they are plausible. "Nature," says Emerson, "resents generalizing, and insults the philosopher in every moment with a million of fresh particulars." Renan, who has made popular so many ideas on race psychology, especially on the psychology of the Semite, asserts, among other things, that the "desert is monotheistic." Yet the "particulars" that tend to disprove this statement were collected during his own lifetime and embodied in the "Corpus" of which he himself was the founder.

It is instructive to compare Renan's method with that of a real skeptic like Sainte-Beuve, to note Sainte-Beuve's care to select a subject that involves no leap into unknown places, and then the invincible caution with which he advances, exploring every foot of the way. To hear Renan speak of Saint Paul one would imagine that he had known him personally. This "ugly little Jew," as he informs us, "was short of stature, thickset, and bent. He had a small, bald head, oddly set on heavy shoulders. His pale face was almost overgrown by a thick beard; he had an aquiline nose, keen eyes, black eyebrows that met over the forehead."[2]

[1] Renan's essay on Buddhism is contained in his *Nouvelles études d'histoire religieuse*; that of Taine in his *Nouveaux essais de critique et d'histoire*.

[2] *Souvenirs*, 66, and *Les Apôtres*, 170.

Sainte-Beuve had seen Chateaubriand for a number of years in the drawing-room of Madame Récamier, yet he devotes a special appendix of his work on Chateaubriand to discussing the color of his eyes, and then only to arrive at the melancholy conclusion that we must be resigned to say of Chateaubriand's eyes as of the color of Mary Stuart's hair and so many other things: *Que sais-je?*[1]

But we must not linger so long on these doubtful aspects of Renan's genius as to forget the ways in which he is really eminent. Future historians of Christianity may arrive at conclusions entirely different from his regarding those events in its records that transcend ordinary human experience. They may avoid some of the faults that come from his romanticism and abuse of conjecture. But we can be sure that no student of the Bible will be taken seriously hereafter who is without the sense of historical development; and for imparting this historical sense, Renan is, as we have seen, an incomparable master.

IV

Renan was so ardent a believer in evolution that it is only fair to apply to him his own method, and inquire in what way he himself evolved. He describes himself in his autobiography as a "bundle of contradictions."[2] One of the contradictions which he possibly had in his mind is that between the end of his life and its beginning. Some allusions have already been made to the

[1] *Chateaubriand et son groupe littéraire*, II, 404. [2] *Souvenirs*, 73.

character of this change. Renan had always been abundantly provided with the cheerfulness that is one of the marks of a rich and resourceful nature; but this cheerfulness is something quite distinct from the ironical "gayety" of his old age, in such striking contrast with the serious, almost solemn tone of a youthful work like "L'Avenir de la science." In one of the articles of this early period he makes an indignant attack on Béranger for his cult of the *Dieu des bonnes gens*, the easy-going divinity who smiles indulgently on the failings of Gallic human nature.[1] At about the same time, he refers to gayety as that "strange forgetfulness of the human lot";[2] and so we are surprised when he announces to us some twenty years later that, after all, this "ancient Gallic gayety is perhaps the profoundest of philosophies." In a public address, he exhorts his hearers to "teach all nations to laugh in French. It is the sanest and most philosophical thing in the world. French comic songs are good too. I once said hard things about the *Dieu des bonnes gens; mon Dieu*, how mistaken I was. . . . Did not someone say that God took more pleasure in the oaths of a French soldier than in the prayers of the ministers of certain Puritan sects? We enter by gayety into the deepest views of Providence."[3]

Renan's own account of this change is simple enough: he was of mixed descent, and the light, mocking Gascon had got the better of the serious Breton in his nature.[4]

[1] See *Questions contemporaines*, 461 ff.

[2] *Essais de morale et de critique*, 383.

[3] *Feuilles détachées*, 263–264.

[4] *Souvenirs*, 141.

We might, however, miss much of the significance of his life if we took this explanation too seriously. We should rather remember that Renan is a man over whose whole being the intellect reigned supreme, and then ask ourselves what is the philosophy that goes with this predominance of intellect. "The first dangerous symptom I report," says Emerson, "is the levity of intellect, as if it were fatal to earnestness to know much. Knowledge is the knowing that we cannot know. . . . How respectable is earnestness on every platform! But intellect kills it." Renan begins by regarding the intellect with religious earnestness, by making it the source of all certainty, and is then slowly but surely forced by the logical working-out of his own premises into the attitude that Emerson describes. In 1890 he still thinks as in 1848 that science is our one serious concern; but what a falling-off there is in what he hopes even from science! He no longer claims that science can take the place of religion, and admits that "it preserves us from error rather than gives us the truth."[1] Towards the very end, he says in words that seem an echo of Emerson: "We do not know— that is all that can be said definitely about what is beyond the finite. Let us deny nothing, let us affirm nothing, let us hope."[2] "Let us know how to wait; possibly there is nothing at the end; or who can tell whether the truth is not sad? Let us not be in such haste to discover it."[3] "Everything is possible, even God."[4]

[1] *Avenir de la science*, p. xix.
[2] *Feuilles détachées*, p. xvii.
[3] *Feuilles détachées*, p. x.
[4] *Ibid.*, 416.

This later development of Renan is, then, the natural result of the exaggerated emphasis he put from the outset on intellect, of his attempt to exalt the intellect into a position that belongs only to the character and will. For whatever importance we may attach to Knowledge, we must say to her at last in the words of Tennyson: —

> "Let her know her place:
> She is the second, not the first."

Renan's cult for knowledge is in part a survival of the Catholic craving for an outer authority. For the authority of the church he substitutes the authority of the scientific fact. He wishes to keep the ideal, but he is unwilling to rest it on the bold affirmation of a principle in man superior to phenomenal nature, and so he is forced to find in the outer facts a coherency and orderly sequence that he is forbidden by his philosophy to seek in himself. In other words, his only resource against skepticism is a philosophy of history.[1] All the outer facts, the manifold happenings of the past, that seem so chaotic and unrelated to a skeptic like Sainte-Beuve, are, he would have us believe, "moving inly to one far-set goal"; this goal is, of course, the triumph of the scientific reason. The "primitive" and instinctive ages have now been succeeded by an age of conscious reflection and analysis, and above this Renan can imagine no more exalted state. He does not admit that beyond the spontaneity of instinct and the analytical

[1] Some of the elements of this philosophy of history are borrowed from Hegel, others (especially the theory of the primitive) from Herder.

activity of the intellect there may lie the higher spontaneity of the soul. He bravely accepts all the consequences of his own logic, and foresees a time when such forms of the "spontaneous" as art and poetry and even morality in the ordinary sense will have disappeared, and science will be all in all.[1] At times he finds it hard to avoid a patronizing tone in speaking of religion, since, after all, he is viewing this "spontaneous" creation from the superior platform of analysis.

How far can the facts be made to conform to any such theory? History, if studied strictly from the standpoint of personal righteousness and the reaction of this individual conduct on the common welfare, has perhaps a stern morality of its own. A person who studies history in this way will not necessarily conclude with Renan, from the success of the English, that egotism is alone rewarded in the actual world,[2] nor will he see in the failure of the Revolution of 1848 a proof that the ideal is incompatible with the real.[3] But, if we are to judge from Renan's experience, it is not easy to have an intimate knowledge of the past, and then adjust this knowledge to any scheme for the progressive regeneration of mankind as a whole. Then, too, the facts during Renan's own lifetime seemed to take a perverse pleasure in running counter to his theories. He confesses he never recovered from the pessimism inspired in him by the events of 1851 and 1870.[4] Finally he gives over altogether the attempt to read the ideal into the real;

[1] *Dialogues phil.*, 83 f. [2] *Souvenirs*, 124. [3] *Ibid.*, 122.
[4] *Ibid.*, 124, and *Dialogues phil.*, p. xviii (note).

instead of dissimulating the immorality of history, he exaggerates it. "Things are getting back to their normal state," says Metius, the aristocrat, towards the end of the "Prêtre de Némi." "The world is going to repose in its natural bed, which is crime. Absurd illusion of these meddlesome fanatics who think it possible to get on without violence, to govern by reason, to treat the people as a reasonable being. The world lives by successful crimes."

But what could be graver than such an admission for one who like Renan has no refuge from the outer fact — who does not found his philosophy on the validity of the inner sense? Religion, the former sanction for the moral life, Renan has dissolved by his analysis; the outer fact in which he hopes to find a new sanction fails him in turn, and so the moral sense is left suspended in the void. "Let us make up our mind to it," says M. Séailles, "the facts will not decide for us, nothing will free us from initiative and from responsibility for our own ideas. The intellectual life of Renan is an experiment made for the benefit of all; it teaches us where logic leads a sincere mind, which, determined to follow the truth to the very end, looks for it in the sole testimony of facts."[1] If he is still virtuous, Renan tells us, it is because the direction given to his life by faith persists when faith itself has disappeared.[2] "We are like those animals whose brains have been taken out by physiologists and who continue none the less certain functions by sheer force of habit. But these instinctive

[1] *Ernest Renan*, 341. [2] *Souvenirs*, 12.

movements will grow weaker in time. . . . We are living on the shadow of a shadow; what are people going to live on after us?"[1] Everything thus tends to assume in the intelligence of Renan the form of an acute antithesis — reason and sentiment,[2] the classic and the romantic,[3] the real and the ideal,[4] science and morality. He is unable to fuse together and reconcile these contradictory terms in the light of a higher insight. Instead of choosing between opposite and equally plausible conclusions, he sets "the different lobes of his brain to dialoguing"[5] about them. Such a state, if prolonged, would lead to a paralysis of the will. "The dead planets are perhaps those in which criticism has triumphed over the ruses of Nature; I sometimes fancy that, if everybody attained to our philosophy, the world would stop."[6]

We must not, however, take all this too literally. Renan still had enough faith in scientific progress to sustain him through years of austere labor and devotion to duty. Only this faith has ceased to be, he tells us, anything more than a purely personal preference. The facts lend themselves about as readily to the opposite hypothesis. For aught we know some deception is being practised upon us by "God" and nature. Indeed, the world may be only a huge farce, the work of a "jovial Demiurge."[7] Nevertheless, let us remain steadfast in virtue, but let us show at the same time by our

[1] *Dialogues phil.*, p. xix ; see also *Souvenirs*, 343.
[2] See *Souvenirs*, 57 ff. (Prière sur l'Acropole).
[3] *Ibid.*
[4] *Ibid.*, 122.
[5] *Dialogues phil.*, p. viii.
[6] *Dialogues phil.*, 43 f.
[7] *Drames phil.*, 359.

gayety and ironical detachment that we do not take Nature any more seriously than she takes us. In this way, even if life should turn out to have no meaning, we shall not have been entirely mistaken.[1] Renan declares in his "Avenir de la science" that if he ever ceased to believe in science he would "either commit suicide or turn epicurean."[2] His faith in science, without disappearing, had been shaken, and so, with his love of combining opposites, he sets out to be at one and the same time scientific stoic and epicurean. He had long recognized that the morals of Epicurus are alone suited to the masses. Only those partake of the "ideal" who advance the cause of science, — a privilege evidently reserved for an intellectual *élite*. To the common people he leaves what Wordwsorth calls "the primary felicities of love and wine." He is opposed to temperance societies that would deny the lower classes such legitimate satisfactions as drunkenness. He only asks that this drunkenness "be gentle, amiable, accompanied by moral sentiments (!)."[3]

There are times when these epicurean consolations do not come amiss even to the scientific sage. It was in some such mood that Renan wrote his "Drames philosophiques." In reading a production like "L'Abbesse de Jouarre," in which the most chastened language is used to express ideas that are the contrary of chaste, we are tempted to exclaim: *Purissima impuritas!* Many of these faults of taste would doubtless

[1] The foregoing argument is condensed from *Feuilles détachées*, 394 ff.

[2] *Avenir de la science*, 411. [3] *Feuilles détachées*, 384.

have been avoided if Renan had continued to receive the counsel and guidance of his sister Henriette. But it was largely because of these very faults that he became during the closing years of his life one of the most popular men in France. He was often seen in fashionable drawing-rooms, and was in constant demand for public addresses, dinners, and receptions. "France," as he expresses it, "likes one to flatter her and to share her faults."[1]

V

We are naturally led in discussing this epicurean side of Renan to speak also of the "dilettanteism" with which his name is so often associated. Here again we have only to follow out the consequences of his first assumption that knowledge is an absolute and self-sufficient good which does not need to be made tributary to anything higher than itself. Renan sanctifies his intellect by putting it into the service of science, and starts out to be "sacredly curious of everything."[2] If he was still in many ways a Catholic, nothing proves more conclusively that he had ceased to be a Christian than this exaltation of curiosity as the highest power of our nature.[3] He himself says that "Jesus and his disciples had quite neglected that part of the human spirit which craves for knowledge."[4] The Christian tendency has been to run into the opposite extreme, to attach an en-

[1] *Questions contemporaines*, 66; see also *Souvenirs*, 352–53.

[2] *Avenir de la science*, 157.

[3] "La science restera toujours la satisfaction du plus haut désir de notre nature, la curiosité," etc. (*Avenir de la science*, p. xix).

[4] *L'Eglise chrétienne*, 142.

tirely bad sense to the word curiosity,[1] and to see in all intellectual activity only a form of the *libido sciendi*, one of the three lusts by which man is assailed. We are told that the teachers of Port-Royal dismissed a boy from their school because he showed too great an intellectual eagerness.[2] Bishop Wilson, expressing the moderate Christian view, remarks, "An eager desire for knowledge ought to be governed and restrained, being as dangerous and sinful as any other inordinate appetite, even as those that are confessedly sensual."

Renan, for his part, can imagine no limit either to the pleasures or the profits of curiosity. Even paradise, he thinks, must be tiresome — made up in large part, as it is said to be, of pious old ladies — unless, indeed, it should be enlivened by trips of observation from planet to planet.[3] We cannot but sympathize with him when he wonders that Amiel, instead of giving himself up to the joys of scientific curiosity, should prefer to write a *journal intime* of sixteen thousand manuscript pages, filled with morbid brooding and introspection. "My friend, M. Berthelot, would have enough to keep him busy for hundreds of consecutive lives, without ever writing about himself. I compute that I should need five hundred years to complete my Semitic studies, as I have planned them, and if my interest in them grew less, I should learn Chinese."[4]

[1] See Pascal, *Pensées*, art. II, 6: "Curiosité n'est que vanité," etc. Cf. also Tertullian, *De praescr. hær.*, c. 7: "Nobis curiositate opus non est post Jesum Christum, nec inquisitione post evangelium."

[2] See Sainte-Beuve, *Port-Royal*, III, 495.

[3] *Feuilles détachées*, p. xvi.

[4] *Ibid.*, 359.

Curiosity, in fact, is so satisfying that even if the services it is supposed to render in bringing about a scientific millenium should prove illusory, it would still be a sufficient reward in itself. "Whatever system we adopt regarding the universe and human life it cannot be denied that they appeal keenly to our curiosity. . . . We can abuse the world as much as we like, we shall not keep it from being the strangest and most absorbing of spectacles,"[1] etc. "Philosophical curiosity thus becomes the noblest and surest use of thought. Even though all the rest were vain, it seems that curiosity would not be so; and even if it, too, were vanity, it would in any case have been the most delightful way of passing one's existence."[2] We have in such utterances the germs of dilettanteism. If we go back to the original Italian meaning, the dilettante is one who pursues a thing without any ulterior end, and solely for his own delight (*diletto*). In this particular case, the "delight" is in exercising curiosity for its own sake, in taking the world purely as a spectacle. In short, the dilettante is an intellectual voluptuary, one who uses the mind as a means of delicate enjoyment. The intelligence, released from all restraint, rejoices in its own ubiquity, and passes rapidly from negative to affirmative, proving that all points of view are plausible and that none is certain. Dilettanteism, as Bourget defines it, "is a disposition of mind at once intelligent and voluptuous, that inclines us towards the different forms of life, one after the other,

[1] *Essais de morale et de critique*, 330.
[2] *Ibid.*, 330 f.

and leads us to lend ourselves to all these forms without giving ourselves to any."[1]

We must not, however, fall into the error of the frivolous Parisian public, and see in Renan only the epicurean and dilettante. He retained to the end, and in the midst of all his uncertainties, much of his first faith in science. This at once puts a wide gap between him and most of his disciples. He still looked upon the scientist and philologist as privileged persons, whose pursuits surpass in seriousness all others. M. Anatole France, on the contrary, is at pains to make us feel that the occupations of his aged savant, M. Sylvestre Bonnard, do not differ in real seriousness from those of M. Trépof, the collector of match-boxes. Renan thinks it would be worth while for a thousand laborious investigators to spend their lives in following out the local forms of a single legend, that of the Wandering Jew, for example.[2] But one who sees in literature and erudition only refined forms of pleasure is logical in putting them on a level with other kinds of self-indulgence. "Those who read a great many books," says M. Anatole France, "are like eaters of hashish. . . . Books are the opium of the West. A day will come when we shall all be librarians, and that will be the end. . . . Fifty volumes a day are published in Paris alone without counting newspapers. It is a monstrous orgy. We are going to come out of it mad. The fate of man is to fall successively into contrary excesses. In the Middle Ages ignorance engendered fear. There were mental diseases then with which we are now un-

[1] *Essais de psychologie contemporaine*, 59. [2] *Avenir de la science*, 224.

familiar. At present we are hastening by study to general paralysis."[1]

We need not spend much time on these disciples of Renan. The faith in science had diminished, even in the master; it is still further attenuated in the followers. "What is perfectly plain," says M. Anatole France, "is that our confidence in science, which used to be so strong, is more than half lost. . . . Even M. Ernest Renan, our master, who believed and hoped in science more than any one else, confesses that there was some illusion in thinking that modern society could be entirely founded on rationalism and experiment."[2] But with the loss of this faith in scientific progress, the last safeguard against skepticism tends to disappear, and the world resolves itself into a flux of meaningless phenomena. For M. France holds with Renan that philosophy, apart from phenomena, is only one's personal dream of the infinite, a mere romance of the individual sensibility. Man is thus deprived of all standard of certainty, either within or without himself. He is doomed to a hopeless subjectivity, and might as well give over the attempt to get beyond the prison walls of his own personality.[3] Being is entirely swallowed up in becoming. These modern adepts of the "flowing" philosophy have come to resemble the ancient sophist[4] who banished from his conversation all use of the verb *to be.*

> "There is no rest, no calm, no pause,
> Nor good nor ill, nor light nor shade,

[1] *La Vie littéraire,* I, pp. viii–ix.
[2] *Ibid.,* IV, 43.
[3] *Ibid.,* I, p. iv.
[4] Lycophron, a disciple of Gorgias.

Nor essence nor eternal laws:
For nothing is, but all is made."

The intellect and sensibility, no longer consecrated to the service of science or of anything else higher than themselves, are put to purely epicurean uses. As a result we had some years ago M. Maurice Barrès and the philosophers of the "me" (*moiistes*), who "cultivated their *ego* ardently," and converted it into a mosaic of refined sensations.[1]

Renanism has thus come to be synonymous with some of the most subtle forms of intellectual corruption the world has yet known. But it would be quite unprofitable to dwell any longer on these dangers of dilettanteism. The failings of Renan are the very last to which men of our own race are liable. We can be counted on to avoid his over-emphasis on thinking as compared with doing. The natural impulse of the Anglo-Saxon is rather to rush into action without any adequate notion of what he is acting for, and then congratulate himself on leading the strenuous life. The very excess of Renan may serve as a corrective of what is correspondingly deficient in ourselves. Our ordinary estimate of an author needs to be thus completed by the standards of that ideal cosmopolitanism which Goethe taught and illustrated so admirably in his own life. For it is hardly worth while to spend so much time on foreign literatures if they cannot be used to round out what is narrow and counteract what is inadequate in

[1] For the more recent and very different point of view of M. Barrès, see p. 368.

our national culture. If Renan himself was in such despair at the falling-out between France and Germany, it was because he believed that French thought and German thought cannot work to advantage separately, that one is needed to correct the other.[1] The intellectual sensitiveness and critical finesse, the delight in the free play of ideas, and the large hospitality of mind that characterize men like Renan and Sainte-Beuve, are not qualities that from present appearances we run any risk of overdeveloping. It would hardly be going too far to say of Renan and Sainte-Beuve, quite apart from the question of their absolute rank, that they are, of all French writers of the nineteenth century, the ones likely to prove of most value to English and American readers.

VI

There is one more way in which Renan may become our teacher. Any study of him would be singularly incomplete that failed to do justice to his greatness as an artist. He owes his preëminent place in recent literature even less, perhaps, to his importance as a thinker than to the perfection of his literary workmanship — to a finish of form that is rare in French prose, and still rarer in English. "More than any other writer of the century," says M. Faguet, "he has *charm*, the indefinable something that envelops and finally takes possession of us. Certain pages of the 'Souvenirs d'enfance' — for example, the 'Prayer on the Acropolis' — are among the finest that have been written in French."[2]

[1] See *La Réforme int. et mor.*, 124.

[2] *Histoire de la littérature française*, II, 401.

The high quality of this charm is attested by the very fact that it eludes all analysis. The highest art should be thus free from any trick or mannerism that can be caught or imitated. As Joubert remarks: "We do not like in the arts to see whence our impressions arise. The Naiad should hide her urn; the Nile should conceal his sources."

In short, Renan has accomplished the rare feat of having a style without being a stylist. He tells us that he was "always the least literary of men."[1] This utterance has in it something of the unjust disdain of the philologist for the man of imagination, but it is intended even more as a protest against the too deliberate straining after literary effect that Renan found in so many of his contemporaries. He cannot conceal his impatience at those who are men of letters before being men, at the æsthete who busies himself with the means of expression before making sure that he has anything to express. When asked by a reporter of the "Figaro" for his opinion of the Symbolists and other literary schools that were making such a stir at Paris a few years ago, he replied: *Ce sont des enfants qui se sucent le pouce.*[2] Renan, in fact, was inclined to see in this too consciously literary attitude towards life, the great malady of his time: "*Morbus litterarius!* The distinctive feature of this disease is that we love things not so much for themselves as for the literary effect they produce. We come to see the world through a sort of

[1] *Souvenirs*, 354.

[2] Huret, *Enquête sur l'évolution littéraire*, 422.

theatrical illusion. . . . The glare of the footlights spoils us for the light of day."[1] Literature seemed to him to have been invaded by that instinct for posing and stage effect to which, in its lower forms, the French give the name of *cabotinage*. It would not be easy to exaggerate this element in French character, especially since Rousseau and the romanticists. *Natio comœda est*. Some one said of Chateaubriand that he would like to occupy a hermit's cell — on a stage. Of late things in France have come to such a pass that duels are fought in the presence of press representatives and amateur photographers. The strange maladies that Renan saw flourishing around him under the name of art and literature furnished him many hints for the picture he has drawn in his "Antéchrist" of Nero — the imperial *cabotin* — and Roman society of the decadence. Nero, he tells us, was a "conscientious romanticist," the first to discover that art and literature are the only things in life to be taken seriously, and therefore an authentic ancestor of the school of *l'art pour l'art*.

Renan, in his anxiety to avoid these errors of æstheticism,[2] was even ready to proscribe all systematic teaching of rhetoric and composition as tending to instil into the young the dangerous heresy that expression has a value independent of what is expressed.[3] He early discovered,

[1] *Feuilles détachées*, 232.

[2] We should recollect that Renan avoids these errors in the form and not in the substance of his writings. Reference has already been made to his moral æstheticism. Cf. also passages like *Souvenirs*, 115, where he asserts that beauty is to be preferred to virtue.

[3] *Souvenirs*, 253 f.; see also 220.

he says, that "romanticism of form is an error,"[1] and so he remained faithful to the classic tradition of French prose, to that ancient school of literary good breeding which saw in a quiet and unobtrusive style a virtue akin to quietness and unobtrusiveness of dress. There is a strict analogy between the legendary red waistcoat of Théophile Gautier and Gautier's style. Renan was so apprehensive of falling into these excesses of the picturesque that he spent a whole year, as he informs us, in "toning down" the style of the "Vie de Jésus."[2] This respect for the traditional standards of French prose in the very midst of the romantic revolt, he owed in part to his own native good taste, and still more, perhaps, to the influence of his sister Henriette. "She it was who convinced me that it is possible to say everything in the simple and correct style of the classic authors and that new expressions and violent images always come either from pretentiousness or ignorance of our real riches."[3] "Ah! do not say," he adds elsewhere, "that they achieved nothing, those obscure wits of the seventeenth century, whose lives were spent in passing judgment upon words and weighing syllables. They achieved a masterpiece — the French language. They rendered an inappreciable service to the human spirit by creating the Dictionary, by preserving us from that undefined liberty which is fatal to languages. . . . A man has really attained to his full maturity of mind only when he has come to see

[1] *Souvenirs*, 89. [2] *Ibid.*, 355.

[3] *Ma Sœur Henriette*, 35 f. Other persons who exercised a happy influence on Renan's style were Augustin Thierry (see *Souvenirs*, 371), and M. de Sacy of the *Journal des Débats* (see *Feuilles détachées*, 135).

that the Dictionary of the Academy contains all that is needed for the expression of every thought, however delicate or novel or refined it may be."[1] To grasp the full significance of the conservative, and even timid, attitude that Renan here assumes towards his native tongue, we have only to contrast it with the attitude of a literary *sans-culotte* like Victor Hugo, who boasts that he has dealt like a Robespierre with the French vocabulary and "put a red liberty cap on the old Dictionary."

In spite of the precept and example of Hugo and most of the men of letters of his time, Renan persisted to the end in thinking that sobriety and restraint and regard for traditional good taste are literary virtues. As a result, his style is so uniformly perfect that it rarely if ever falls short, save in so far as it images the shortcomings of his character and philosophy. The masculine elements do not predominate in his character, and his style is therefore without the virile ring that we find in the prose of a Pascal. There is not enough in his philosophy to exalt him above himself, so that his pages do not often have the communicative warmth that can come only from a vital conviction. If, instead of trying his work by these severe standards, we compare it with other recent achievement in France or elsewhere, we can hardly fail to recognize its rare distinction. Our total judgment of Renan may be summed up by saying that, though he is a great intelligence, he has few of the qualities of a great philosopher, but

[1] *Essais de morale et de critique,* 341 f.

many of the qualities of a great historian, and nearly all the qualities of a great artist. He is a consummate master of prose style in a language that easily surpasses in the general excellence of its prose all other modern literatures.

X

BRUNETIÈRE

Few men have ever crowded more intense activity into a life of fifty-seven years than Brunetière and there are few more striking examples of what may be achieved by a frail physique when sustained by an indomitable will. After having in his youth been refused admission as a student to the *Ecole Normale*, he finally entered as a teacher into that inner citadel of French higher education. He became member of the Academy in 1893, and almost at the same time, after long service in a subaltern post, editor-in-chief of the "Revue des Deux Mondes." His trip to America early in 1897 was only one of his many appearances as orator and lecturer. He published on an average at least a volume a year during the thirty years or more of his activity as a critic, yet died before finishing the History of French Classicism which promised to be his monument: *Pendent opera interrupta.* The completed portions of this work are suggestive of a greater mellowness, or at least of some toning-down of the logical asperity of his style. The study of Montaigne, which is one of the last things he did, is also one of the best, a remarkable achievement for a man in the final stages of a wasting disease. Montaigne, a notable embodiment of the *esprit de finesse*, has rarely if ever been better judged than by

Brunetière, an embodiment of the *esprit de géométrie;* for one can scarcely admit, as M. de Vogüé contends in his commemorative article in the "Revue des Deux Mondes," that there was a perfect balance in Brunetière's mind between the two elements defined by Pascal. His real kinship in the sixteenth century is not with Montaigne, but with that master logician, John Calvin. There is the same lack of delicacy, amenity, charm; but one should add of Brunetière's style, as he himself says of Calvin's, that "its severity has after all its own nobility, and its very angularity and tension its own special majesty."[1]

I

Calvin is the first eminent example of the *esprit de géométrie* in French prose, but the same turn for dialectic is visible in the earlier scholastics who wrote in Latin. Like Taine, Brunetière makes us feel how much scholasticism still lingers in the land of its origin. Though both tried to apply the methods of inductive science, they remained scholastic in their passion for vast structures of general ideas conceived with geometric symmetry and with reference less to the observed facts than to a logical requirement of the mind; they are scholastic by their use, as well as by their abuse, of dialectic, by their proneness to mistake ratiocination for reason. This passion for logical consistency has been from the start the chief merit of the French mind, or, when indulged in at the expense of the facts and common sense, its most serious failing. The French

[1] *Hist. de la lit. fr. classique*, 1e Partie, 218.

readiness on occasion to oppose ratiocination to plain evidence reminds one of M. Jourdain and the skill in fence that enabled him to kill a man *par raison démonstrative*. Perhaps the most irritating example in the case of Brunetière is the attitude he assumed during the Dreyfus affair. Yet in a general way Brunetière's logic shows more respect for the facts than Taine's. Facts that enter Taine's mind are like rays of light passing through a bit of Iceland spar, — they are refracted and polarized along the lines of his theory. There is less real science in Brunetière than in Taine and also less pseudo-science, or at least the pseudo-science is less intimately interwoven with his treatment of literature; it does not, like Taine's determinism, impose upon him a method that is not only unliterary but positively anti-literary. In spite of his attempt at literary Darwinism, to be noted later, Brunetière is not a scientist, but a logician with a brilliant oratorical gift and a keen sense of historical development.

The sense of historical development is the main point of contact between Brunetière and Sainte-Beuve, and this point of contact only emphasizes their differences. Sainte-Beuve, who was supremely endowed, as I have said, with the *esprit de finesse*, had almost as great a passion for the particular as Brunetière had for the general. He aims, as he puts it, to *particularize* everything, and when he generalizes it would seem that he does so only under protest. No man was ever more on his guard against the deceit that lurks in universals, Yet if, in Emerson's phrase, "nature resents generalizing," what is highest in human nature resents the lack of it. We are justified in demanding a compromise between the multiplicity of the facts and the craving for unity. The epigraph of Brunetière's "Evolution de la poésie lyrique" was evidently directed against the method of Sainte-Beuve: "Whenever we are trying to get at the meaning of a complex phenomenon, it is useless if not dangerous to go too minutely into details." The volume on Balzac written by Brunetière shortly before his death is almost bare of details about Balzac's life; this too is a protest against the tendency of the modern school to substitute biographical small-talk for the serious business of criticism.

Brunetière is admirable as an historian of ideas when his logic is tempered by a sufficient knowledge of the facts, as is the case for nearly the whole of French literature from the latter part of the sixteenth century[1] to the present day. Throughout this whole field his erudition is immense and is aided by a marvellous memory. He is at his best in tracing main currents of ideas — in such articles, for example, as the one on the "Formation of the Idea of Progress." This is a kind of writing which is thoroughly worth while in itself, and of which we have only too little in English. Brunetière, however, knew virtually nothing at first hand about Greek, very little about the Middle Ages, and not enough of other modern literatures besides French. He

[1] For Brunetière's imperfect knowledge of the early sixteenth century in France, especially in its relations to Italy, see article by M. Henri Hauvette, in *Revue critique* (8 juillet, 1905, 14 ff).

is capable of saying that Lessing[1] wished to rid Germany of Greek and Latin, that Burns *and Shelley*[2] were at the opposite extreme of the social scale from Byron, and that Plato "argues like a sophist and thinks like a child."[3] We may suspect that a man who pronounces such a judgment on Plato is not a trustworthy witness to some of the higher things of the imagination. For the critic who is himself unimaginative lacks the "fit key," as Chapman expresses it, "with poesy to open poesy." Brunetière lived for neither the senses nor the imagination, but solely for ideas. One might say of him, reversing Gautier's familiar remark, that he was a man for whom the visible world did *not* exist. "He was possibly," says M. de Vogüé, "the only great man of letters of the nineteenth century for whom Rousseau had never lived, nor Rousseau's eldest son, Chateaubriand, and who did not have in his blood a single drop of their delicious poisons." We may admit the truth of this assertion, if not for Brunetière's temperament, at least for his style. He is in curious contrast in this respect to Taine, who had according to M. Lemaître, a "violent and carnal imagination," and who at any rate indulges in almost a superabundance of picturesque details.

If Taine mixes his logic with local color, Brunetière's logic is militant and oratorical. The title of some of his last volumes, "Discours de Combat," would be equally appropriate for his collected works. He is fond of saying of the great French writers of the seventeenth

[1] *Etudes critiques*, VI, 225. [2] *Ibid.*, 234. [3] *Discours de combat*, 90.

century that they had a "spoken style" — that they did not "see themselves write," but "heard themselves talk." This remark holds good of his own style, which always has the movement of the spoken word without having anything of the ease of conversation. The arguments are clamped and mortised together by logical connectives, and pushed forward in menacing array, in a manner that suggests the advance of Roman legionaries with interlocked shields. He has been called the inventor of militant criticism. He reminds one of the old saying about the father of logic: *Quaerit Aristoteles pugnam.* "A man would not feel himself alive," Brunetière remarks in the course of a plea for Christianity (!), "if he did not have adversaries."[1] In default of a real adversary he frequently addresses himself to an imaginary one. His rude and imperious temper has been likened to the testiness of the neo-classical Aristarch, a Boileau or a Dr. Johnson. But, unlike Brunetière, these men had an underlying geniality that saved them, even when most severe, from seeming atrabilious.

Sainte-Beuve, as we have seen, said of modern critics that they abounded in all the critical virtues except the essential virtues of authority and judgment; that what they had gained in brilliancy and versatility they often seemed to have lost in weight and impressiveness. It is the distinction of Brunetière to have avoided the reproach of Sainte-Beuve and to have given back to the word "critic" something of its former meaning. He had convictions and insisted on judging with reference to

[1] *Discours de combat*, 2e série, 166.

them at a time when convictions, at least among the educated classes, had almost completely gone out of fashion. He possessed something of the power that usually belongs to those who have convictions to impose themselves on those who have none. He persisted in the somewhat antiquated notion that books exist primarily to express ideas, whereas most people nowadays turn to books, not for ideas, but for entertainment or at best for elegant æsthetic sensation. He made himself the champion of the classical tradition and proclaimed the supremacy of reason at an epoch when art was given over to every form of morbid subjectivity. He was stern and ascetic in a period of easy-going self-indulgence. He produced work marked by eminently masculine qualities at a time when literature had fallen to a great extent under the influence of women. He restricted his style so far as possible to the syntax and vocabulary of Bossuet in an age that saw the publication of the sonnets of Mallarmé and the Journal of the Goncourts.

Renan urges us not to get ruffled, but "to suffer the destinies of the planet to be fulfilled; our outcries will be of no use, our ill-humor would be quite out of place."[1] This comfortable philosophy is the exact opposite of Brunetière's. He liked to quote Comte's saying that humanity is composed of more dead than living. He so championed the opinions of this dead majority as to come into conflict with nearly all the main tendencies of his own age. A modern Siger of Brabant, he took it

[1] *Souvenirs*, p. xx.

upon himself to syllogize truths unpalatable to most of his countrymen. He defended the general sense of mankind in such a way as to isolate himself from his contemporaries. "It is a sort of joy," he remarks, "for a man to stand apart in the midst of an indifferent or hostile society, living in it and belonging to it, but judging it." Of this austere joy Brunetière must have had his fill, especially if, as his friends claim, he was very far from being steeled to the inevitable reprisals. Possibly his sympathy for Alfred de Vigny was due, not only to a common pessimism, but to the fact that, like Vigny, he concealed a great sensitiveness under outer coldness and reserve. A stoic, born into a somewhat neurasthenic age, Brunetière looked on it as his special mission to attack every form of epicurean relaxation. There was, then, an almost necessary conflict between him, the least Gallic of Frenchmen, and contemporaries whom he describes as "epicureans of the decadence"; between himself and M. France, whom he deemed to be no better than a literary voluptuary; between himself and Renan, who seemed to him bent on turning the intellect itself into a means of refined enjoyment.

The history of Brunetière's work as a critic is, to a great extent, the history of his polemics. Three of these polemics in particular deserve attention. At the very beginning of his career as a writer in the "Revue des Deux Mondes" he singled out Zola and the naturalists for his attacks, and continued these attacks in a running fire of articles extending over a period of twelve years. Later on, he proclaimed that modern science was bankrupt,[1] that it had failed to keep its promises, and he thus became involved in a war of pamphlets with Berthelot and other advocates of purely experimental methods. And finally, for a number of years he never lost an opportunity to assail M. Jules Lemaître and M. Anatole France and the partisans of impressionistic criticism.

II

The volume in which Brunetière collected the earlier articles of his first critical campaign ("Le Roman naturaliste," 1883) was the first weighty protest against the naturalistic doctrine that had held unquestioned sway since "Madame Bovary" and Taine's essay on Balzac. He took special pains to demolish the scientific pretensions of Zola and his followers, especially the cult of the "human document." The collection of notes and minute observations of the passing show of life, he says, renewing a favorite distinction of Goethe's, can at most give the actual, but not the real, which it is the aim of art to render. Applied to the past the method is equally futile. Edmond de Goncourt had not succeeded in disengaging a true history from the "thirty thousand pamphlets and two thousand newspapers"[2] that according to his own statement he had read in preparation for his book on the eighteenth century. Stripped

[1] The phrase "faillite de la science" occurs in the article in the *Revue des Deux Mondes* (1 janvier, 1895), written after his return from the Vatican. M. Berthelot replied in the *Revue de Paris* (1 février, 1895).

[2] *Le Roman naturaliste*, 296.

of its veneer of pseudo-science, its piling up of notes of life literally observed, naturalism, so far from being a reaction against romanticism, is in many respects its logical continuation. The temperament of Zola reproduces on a lower plane the temperament of Hugo; the romantic dream has merely changed into a nightmare. "M. Zola reconstructs nature and adjusts it to the exigencies of his own hallucinations,"[1] says Brunetière. He substitutes audaciously for reality "the obscene or grotesque visions of his overheated imagination."[2] Brunetière points out the relationship between Flaubert and Chateaubriand. The "impressionism" of the Goncourts, which he defines as a systematic confusion of the art of painting with the art of writing,[3] is also plainly of romantic origin.

Naturalism, indeed, is already in germ in the "Confessions" of Rousseau; and so Brunetière was consistent in taking a distinctly hostile attitude towards the whole literature which issued from Rousseau. He was one of the first to point out what he called the essentially "lyrical" character of the great romantic writers: and by this he meant their complete self-absorption, their unwillingness to occupy themselves with anything except their own emotions, their imperviousness to ideas. At the distance of nearly a century, the attempt of Chateaubriand to stem the current of modern thought, and to react in the name of religion towards the Middle Ages, is seen to have resulted, not in the maintenance of a Christian ideal in literature, but in the isolation of literature from

[1] *Le Roman naturaliste*, 350. [2] *Ibid.*, 348. [3] *Ibid.*, 94.

life. It had been the ambition of André Chénier to effect a reconciliation between the artistic imagination and modern science, but the writers who followed the lead of Chateaubriand took a certain pride in remaining ignorant of the intellectual and scientific aspirations of their age. The penalty they paid was an increasing incapacity for ideas. Chateaubriand himself was concerned more with the images and the musical cadences of his periods than with their intellectual content. Resolutely silencing in himself any velleity he may have had to think, and bidding defiance to the *bourgeois*, Gautier gave himself up exclusively to the search for rare and refined æsthetic sensation. As time went on the means employed by the different schools to arrive at a titillation of the æsthetic faculty became increasingly complex and incomprehensible to the uninitiated. "Literature," wrote M. Lemaître at the height of the symbolistic movement, "tends more and more to become a mysterious diversion of mandarins."

If such was the fate of a literature devoid of intellectual qualities, science, bereft of the succor of the imagination, fell only too often into arid analysis. In spite of their apparent divergence, however, the two classes, the æsthetes and the analysts, had one important point of resemblance. The artist pursued his æsthetic sensation and the scientist his analysis mechanically and as ends in themselves without reference to any aim that would have brought them into contact with life as a whole. They wanted respectively art for art's sake and science for the sake of science. They refused equally to take cognizance of that region of their own nature which is independent of both sensation and analysis, and thus cut themselves off from the insight which alone makes possible a belief in the freedom of the will. In this way it came to pass that Zola, one of the extreme representatives of a literature of pure sensation, was able to agree with Taine, an extreme scientific intellectualist, in the affirmation that virtue and vice are products no less than sugar and vitriol. "A whole subtle psychology utterly escapes him," says Brunetière of Zola, "the psychology of the forces of intellect and will which carry on the good fight against the shock of sensation and resist the assaults of desire. Do not speak to him of a liberty which is in some sort detached from the body, dominating it and imposing on it higher ends than the satisfaction of bodily cravings; he would not understand you." [1]

Brunetière thus attacked the æsthetic naturalists because of their disregard of those qualities which are most truly human, because of their attempt to reduce man to the plane of animal instinct. In defense likewise of the human self and of the discipline it imposes he attacked the "impudent knowingness" of the scientific naturalists, of a Berthelot, for example, who proclaimed that the answer to every question is to be sought in the laboratory and that there are "no more mysteries." Man, Brunetière insists, is more than nature. "The great error of the century, in morality as well as in science and art, has been to mingle and confound man

[1] *Le Roman naturaliste*, 207.

with nature without pausing to consider that in art as in science and morality he is a man only in so far as he distinguishes himself from nature and makes himself an exception in it."[1] One of the most pernicious doctrines of Rousseau is also one of the most widely spread — that of the natural goodness of man.[2] Man becomes good in reality not by obeying but by resisting "nature."

Brunetière's work, then, in one of its main aspects may be defined as a reaction against nineteenth-century naturalism; a protest against the absorption of man into nature. "There is surely," says Sir Thomas Browne, "a piece of divinity in us; something that was before the elements and owes no homage unto the Sun." Brunetière differs from Sir Thomas Browne in that he seems to have arrived at the notion of this supersensuous self more by logic than by direct vision. His idealism, resting as it does on ratiocination rather than on insight, remains essentially negative, and so failed to bring consolation.

Brunetière was fond of speaking of Christianity and Buddhism as the great pessimistic religions, and of identifying their doctrines with those of Schopenhauer. In one of his essays, indeed, he seems to put the system of Schopenhauer above Christianity and Buddhism. He failed, on the one hand, to feel the essentially negative character of the philosophy of Schopenhauer; and on the other hand, to appreciate that positive principle of joy and illumination which is the saving element of

[1] *Nouvelles questions de critique*, 343. [2] *Ibid.*, 345, 370.

both Christianity and Buddhism. "Let us live happily, then, though we call nothing our own; for so shall we be like to the bright gods feeding on happiness."[1] There is something in the ring of this passage which will serve once for all to mark the difference between the temper of Buddhism and the acrid disillusion of Schopenhauer; and what is true of Buddhism is at least equally true of Christianity.

III

Before considering, however, more fully Brunetière's relation to religion let us take up his third and most important polemic — that with the advocates of impressionistic criticism. Here again he championed the ideal as he understood it. He maintained against M. Lemaître and M. France that in addition to an apparent self of sensations and impressions there exists in each man a real self that he possesses in common with other men. He threw himself with special ardor into a conflict that seemed to him to be *pro aris et focis* and to involve the very life of criticism. The cultivation of literary criticism for several centuries in France has had the somewhat paradoxical result of producing critics who deny its very possibility. "As for myself," says M. France in the preface to the fourth volume of his critical studies, "I am not in the least a critic. I have no talent for working the threshing-machines into which ingenious persons put the literary harvest in order to separate the grain from the chaff." His utmost

[1] *Dhammapāda.*

endeavor, he adds elsewhere, is to tell pleasantly of the "adventures" of his soul in the midst of masterpieces.[1] M. France, it may be noted in passing, is fond of talking of his "soul," when he means in reality his nerves and sensibility. M. Lemaître and M. France are both *des féminins*. To the personality of M. France in particular there attaches something of that elusive charm which makes its possessor a baffling problem to others, and very often to himself. The debate between him and Brunetière took on at times the aspect of a warfare between the masculine and feminine principles. Strength was pitted against charm, and reason arrayed against sensibility.

A philosophical point of view always reflects in some measure the temperament of its propounder. The impressionists assert that it can reflect nothing else. Unfortunately M. Lemaître and M. France justified their assertion too much by their practice and Brunetière did not disprove it sufficiently by his. In the case of all three men we have the feeling of temperamental qualities that are quarrelling with one another simply because they are not, as Goethe says of his Tasso and Antonio, united in one person. But even such a union of qualities would not give all that is needful for the best criticism. There would still be lacking the type of intuition that Joubert possessed more completely perhaps than any other modern French critic.

M. Lemaître and M. France have, as a matter of fact, worked rather far apart since the polemic with

[1] *La Vie littéraire*, I, p. iii.

Brunetière in the early nineties, and even at the time they were perhaps not so close together as Brunetière supposed. They both, indeed, have a greater degree of æsthetic perceptiveness than Brunetière, of that gusto, as we may say, which is the necessary basis, though not the whole, of taste. M. Lemaître is not only superior to Brunetière in gusto, but at the time of his polemic with him displayed a special gusto for that contemporary literature from which Brunetière drew back with almost ascetic distrust. M. Lemaître says that such is his love for the literature of the second half of the nineteenth century — "so intelligent, so restless, so mad, so morose, so morbid, so subtle" — that at times it makes him "quiver with delight and penetrates him with pleasure to his very marrow."[1]

In his literary sensitiveness M. Lemaître reminds one of Sainte-Beuve and has written pages that Sainte-Beuve would probably have been more willing to sign than those of any other recent French critic. Animation, sprightliness, sparkling wit, and at the same time the power to insinuate deep and penetrating reflection under cover of an airy irresponsibility — these and other literary virtues abound in M. Lemaître. Yet the total impression that disengages itself from the work of what one may term his first period is a sort of spiritual bewilderment. He evidently finds no counterpoise in himself to an infinitely mobile intellect and sensibility. He reminds one of the Jesuit father in Pascal who would undertake to make any point of view look "prob-

[1] *Contemporains*, I, 239.

able." "It is delightful to see this learned casuist enter into the pros and cons of the same question and discover good reasons everywhere — such is his subtlety and ingenuity." M. Lemaître is ready to argue a question from two, four or six points of view, avoiding the odd number as savoring too much of a conclusion.

Yet we must be careful not to exaggerate the spiritual bewilderment and lack of standards of M. Lemaître, even when he was most impressionistic. He may have quivered responsive in his inmost fibres to the appeal of the ultra-modern, but ultra-modern writers like Zola and Huysmans and Verlaine had no special reason to be elated by his verdicts on them. He reacts upon writers of this kind in a way to show that he has not merely gusto but taste. In lieu of the logic that so superabounds in Brunetière he has instinctive good sense, which is an extremely classical virtue. "No, I shall not speak of them," he says of the verses of the symbolists, "because I find them unintelligible and that bores me. It is n't my fault. A simple native of Touraine, child of a sensible, moderate and mocking race, with the stamp upon me of twenty years of classic habits, I am ill prepared to understand their gospel." [1]

M. Lemaître, in short, had from the beginning a hold on literary tradition that balanced the keenness of his relish for contemporaries; and though he lacked inner standards he plainly suffered from the lack and did not delight, like M. France, in mere mocking detachment. The attack on Renan that first attracted attention to

[1] *Contemporains*, IV, 66.

M. Lemaître as a critic, though it doubtless seemed somewhat naïve to him later, and though he himself abounds in irony, and above all in true Gallic malice and irreverence, is yet significant. "This man," he imagines a somewhat rhetorical opponent saying of Renan, "passed through the most terrible moral crisis that a soul can traverse. He was forced at the age of twenty, and under conditions which made the choice especially painful and dramatic, to choose between faith and science, . . . and he is gay. For a rent that was more superficial (for perhaps he was only a rhetorician) Lamennais died in final despair; for a great deal less than that Jouffroy remained incurably sad. For still less, for merely having feared that he might doubt, Pascal went mad,[1] and M. Renan is gay! No, no; M. Renan has not the right to be gay; he can be so only by the most audacious of inconsistencies. Even as Macbeth murdered sleep, so M. Renan twenty times, a hundred times over in every one of his books, has murdered joy, has murdered action, has murdered spiritual peace and the tranquillity of the moral life."[2] It is therefore not surprising that under the stress of the Dreyfus affair M. Lemaître should, in lieu of the inner standards he lacked, have fallen back on traditional standards; in other words, should have allied himself, though in a less degree than Brunetière, with the reactionaries. Yet the gap between the Lemaître of to-day and the Lemaître whom Brunetière attacked as an impressionist is not so wide as one might suppose.

[1] This conception of Pascal is now discredited.

[2] *Contemporains*, I, 203.

In his book on Racine he defends the classical point of view with a sort of impressionistic trepidation. The result is piquant and in some respects delectable. In the "Rousseau," we have an impressionist attacking the father of impressionism, and this too is not without piquancy. But here we are more sensible to the defects than to the virtues of the method, especially to the lack of that large intellectual structure for which no amount of cleverness in single pages can atone. The sense of a contraction of horizon that one nearly always has in French reactionaries is reinforced in this case by M. Lemaître's insufficient knowledge of Rousseau's total influence abroad as well as in France. It will be noted also that during his reactionary period M. Lemaître has been drawn, whether in attack or defense, to writers, who, like himself, have a highly developed if not predominant sensibility, — Racine, Fénelon, Rousseau, Chateaubriand. He still believes that the critic is governed by his own changing sensibility and that criticism is therefore a "chimera."[1]

IV

M. France began by denying the possibility of fixed standards far more radically than M. Lemaître and has persisted in his denial. One finds in him the culmination and extreme expression of a main form of the critical spirit which he identifies with criticism itself — the form which, as he says, had for its creators Montaigne, Saint-Evremond and Bayle; the last in date of all the literary forms and destined perhaps to absorb all the

[1] *Chateaubriand*, 223.

others. In our day of absolute intellectual liberty, when curiosity is the chief virtue, this form has taken the place of theology and has found its Saint Thomas Aquinas in Sainte-Beuve.[1]

M. France as a matter of fact has simply developed to the ultimate stage the germs of relativity in his masters Sainte-Beuve and Renan. The substitution of the notion of the relative for the notion of the absolute — this, indeed, seems to have been the characteristic achievement of the nineteenth century not only in literary criticism, but in all departments of thought. From Hegel to Darwin, the idea of "becoming," of growth and development, has, in a hundred forms, so penetrated and transformed the mental habits of the modern man as to make it increasingly difficult for him to look upon anything as fixed and final. "The absolute is dead!" exclaimed Edmond Scherer in 1860. But the heart, as we have seen, refused to ratify this verdict of the head. Renan's attempt to reconcile in himself the old man with the new resulted in his theory of a God who does not yet exist, but is in process of "becoming." It was left for M. Anatole France to rid himself of these weak scruples, and to arrive at what may be termed the doctrine of the absolutely relative. The affirmation of M. France that he is absolutely imprisoned in his own personality, that there is no standard to which he may refer either his own opinions or those of others, has as its corollary a doctrine of universal illusion. The immense indulgence he professes comes in part, indeed,

[1] *La Vie lit.*, I, p. v.

from his power of sympathy, but even more from a tranquil contempt for human nature thus looked upon as the mere puppet of illusion. Health and disease are vain entities;[1] so are sanity and madness.[2] The new sect of "flowing" philosophers to which M. France belongs has arrived at a conception of life closely corresponding to that of the "flowing" philosophers of old: —

> "All thoughts, all creeds, all dreams are true,
> All visions wild and strange;
> Man is the measure of all truth
> Unto himself. All truth is change."

The Oriental doctrine of illusion has thus appeared in Western thought, but not accompanied, as it was in the mind of the Hindu, by a vision of the One. Leconte de Lisle, who is the poet of this modern doctrine of illusion, excels in seizing and rendering with extraordinary intensity the most fugitive appearances of space and time, and all without the slightest sentiment of a spiritual reality either in man or behind the shows of nature. There has passed into his verse something of the horror and vertigo that come from thus contemplating the meaningless flow of phenomena as they start up from vacancy, stand out for a moment on a background of deepest black, and then vanish into the void: —

> "Eclair, rêve sinistre, éternité qui ment,
> La Vie antique est faite inépuisablement
> Du tourbillon sans fin des apparences vaines."

The sense of universal illusion does not result, in the case of M. France, so much in metaphysical anguish

[1] *La Vie lit.*, II, p. viii. [2] *Ibid.*, I, 183.

as in an extreme form of the romantic irony that abounds in the later work of Renan — the irony of the man who hovers over all points of view and refuses to be bound by any because every point of view is necessarily relative and transitory. M. France, however, could cease from his detachment and become militant enough when, as in the Dreyfus affair, the liberties of the ironist seemed to be threatened by a reversion to the past and its intolerant attempt to confine the spirit within certain definite moulds. But even here his irony did not spare his companions in the cause so far as they themselves had any definite constructive programme. His underlying mood is always that of contemptuous pity for beings who even in their most serious concerns are the dupes of mobile appearances.

> "Les petites marionnettes
> Font, font, font
> Trois petits tours,
> Et puis s'en vont." [1]

But the little marionettes, as M. France sees them, are thoroughly vicious and depraved, the playthings of hunger and the reproductive instinct. At bottom his view of life is at least as brutally naturalistic as that of Zola. "The substance of human nature," he affirms, "does not change, and this substance is harsh, egotistical, jealous, sensual, ferocious." [2] One may say, in his own words and with his own works in mind, that there is something strangely acrid in contemporary thought; our literature no longer believes in the goodness of

[1] See *La Vie lit.*, I, 58. [2] *Ibid.*, IV, 48.

things.[1] His irony, which is at its blandest in "Le Crime de Sylvestre Bonnard," becomes in later works, like "L'Ile des Pingouins," positively corrosive.

It was therefore not inappropriate that M. France should have pronounced a eulogy over Zola's grave, in spite of the fact that a few years before he had spoken of him with a bitterness in strange contrast to the habitual appreciativeness of his critical writing. "His work is bad," he had said of Zola, "and he is one of those wretches of whom one may say it would have been better if they had never been born."[2] The explanation of the contradiction is simple enough: if M. France does not differ from Zola in his naturalistic view of life (except that on the whole he is less optimistic), he does differ from him infinitely in form and in his conception of the rôle of form. Be like the Greeks, is the sum of M. France's message; since all is illusion and truth escapes us, let us pursue beauty[3] (he should have said, be like certain Greeks, especially certain Greek sophists). About the only inheritance of the past that his irony spares, and that he is even ready to defend, is the ancient classics and the education founded upon them. His own style is richly reminiscent of the past and in its fusion of traditional elements has been compared to Corinthian metal. It has all the Alexandrian graces, however much it may fall short of the truly classical vigor. It is the extreme flower of the Latin genius, says M. Lemaître. We may add that it is also the extreme flower of romantic æstheticism. M. France puts more

[1] *La Vie lit.*, IV, 14. [2] *Ibid.*, I 236. [3] *Ibid.*, I, 343 f.

emphasis than most modern æsthetes, however, on the side of beauty that is related to symmetry as compared with the side that is related to expression. He is more enamored of the purity of the line both in art and language than M. Lemaître, for example, who pursues the vivid and the expressive even at the risk of narrowing unduly the gap between the written and the spoken word. He is not only more intuitive of form than most of his contemporaries, but has in some measure that sense of the human that has been so conspicuously absent in many of the writers and critics of our naturalistic period. "You are saddened," he says of Hugo, "and at the same time frightened not to encounter in his enormous work, in the midst of so many monsters, a single human figure." [1]

M. France may perhaps best be defined as a humanistic æsthete — the definition I have already applied to Walter Pater, who is indeed the writer with whom the English or American reader almost inevitably compares him. Pater's prose has, however, less purity of contour than M. France's, nor would he have been capable, I believe, of reacting so humanistically on Hugo. Though quite as æsthetic in his point of view as M. France, Pater was, to do him justice, less profoundly voluptuous. I remember having seen a volume of M. France from which a distinguished American scholar, who valued him greatly on his humanistic side, had nevertheless torn out a whole series of pages — the same treatment that Joubert accorded so liberally to his library of

[1] *La Vie lit.*, I, 115.

eighteenth-century authors. The contrast is also less sharp in Pater than in M. France between a sensibility that is steeped in romantic religiosity and an intellect that is increasingly impious. M. France's heart revels in Saint Francis at the same time that his head demands Voltaire. One is equally conscious, however, in Pater and M. France of an epicurean relaxation that is combined in both writers with a great suavity. In both writers we feel "to the full," in Pater's own phrase, "that subtle and delicate sweetness which belongs to a refined and comely decadence." Pater has been a doubtful influence in England. As to M. France's influence, Gréard accused him to his face, on receiving him into the Academy, of having encouraged *les songeries malsaines et les dilettantismes dissolvants*.

The dangers of a humanism that has deserted the character and will and taken refuge in the sensibility are indeed obvious. Some of the utterances[1] of M. France fall very little short of the ultimate stage of æsthetic deliquescence, as embodied in the precious dictum of the anarchistic Laurent Tailhade, "What matters the act provided the gesture be beautiful?" One feels that M. France would not balk at any corruption if it were expressed with sufficient artistry. On the other hand, he is almost capable of a certain pharisaism of taste in dealing with the vulgar and the commonplace. "He has no taste," he says of Zola, "and that I have finally come to believe is the mysterious sin spoken of in Holy Writ, the greatest of sins, the only

[1] See, for example, *La Vie lit.*, II, p. iii.

one that will not be pardoned."[1] Perhaps the best example of his tendency towards a pharisaism of taste is his onslaught on Georges Ohnet.[2] M. Lemaître was at least as effective when he prefaced his article on the same subject by the remark that ordinarily he regaled his readers with literary subjects, and that he hoped they would pardon him if to-day he spoke to them of the novels of M. Georges Ohnet.

M. France, in thus giving expression to an occasional violent antipathy, differs from Pater, who virtually never departs from the note of appreciation. But in general M. France would reduce his rôle as a critic to an expression of "gentle wonderment at the beauty of things." He is a dreamer, as he tells us, and interested in things less for themselves than for what they can suggest to him. "All books, even the most admirable, appear to me vastly less precious for what they contain than for what the reader puts into them."[3] The wondrous dream suggested to Pater by Mona Lisa and her smile is perhaps the best example in English of a critic narrating the adventures of his soul in the presence of a masterpiece. We have the method at its worst in the passage of M. France that so scandalized Brunetière; the passage in which he sets out to give us a criticism of Renan's "History of the People of Israel," and indulges instead in a revery on the Noah's ark with which he played as a child.

The whole procedure implies a certain confusion of the *genres*, an unwillingness to discriminate between

[1] *La Vie lit.*, I, 233. [2] *La Vie lit.*, II, 56 ff. [3] *La Vie lit.*, II, p. xi.

criticism and creation. M. Lemaître, though he has also had ambitions as a creator, keeps far more distinct the creative and critical attitudes. Possibly M. France would have done more with criticism if he had felt more keenly its separate justification. As it is, in his total career as a writer, the literary criticism, at least in the narrower sense of the word, is little more than episodic.

V

Brunetière at any rate gave no divided allegiance to criticism, and more than any man of his generation cultivated it as a clear-cut type. M. France's depreciation of judgment in criticism and indeed of the very *genre* itself arose, as I have tried to show, from his extreme sense of relativity, which is in turn a product of naturalism. The force of this naturalistic movement is shown by the fact that Brunetière, who fought it in so many ways, was himself anxious to enlist in its service on its scientific if not on its æsthetic side. He battled for the integrity of the type, yet granted that it was involved in the flux.

Sainte-Beuve, almost alone of modern critics, succeeded in practising criticism both as a science and as an art; or, as he himself puts it, in combining poetry with physiology. Taine attempted to make of criticism a pure science, while others, like M. Lemaître, have cultivated it almost entirely as an art. Brunetière also aimed to make of criticism both a science and an art, but it is evident at a first glance that his art is not the art of Sainte-Beuve. By his dogmatic temper he seemed fitted to keep alive the tradition which, begun in Latin by Scaliger, was continued in French by a series of critics extending from Malherbe and Boileau to Nisard; though from the outset he was, in virtue of his historic sense, nearer than these men to the relativists. In 1889, in the lectures he gave at the Normal School, he announced his intention of becoming scientific as well as historical, of seeking the same help from the doctrines of Haeckel and Darwin that Taine had sought from the doctrines of Cuvier and Geoffroy Saint-Hilaire. This literary Darwinism of Brunetière is in general an attempt to demonstrate that the different literary *genres* evolve in much the same way as the animal species. He proposes to show "in virtue of what circumstances of time and place they originate; how they grow after the manner of living beings, adapting or assimilating all that helps their development; how they perish; and how their disintegrated elements enter into the formation of a new *genre*."[1] For instance, the mediæval Chansons de Geste ramified into prose chronicles and Round Table romances and these romances in the course of evolution passed over into the modern novel.

Brunetière's evolutionary theory is defensible when thus stated in general terms. We feel, however, that in the working-out of his system, scholasticism has often got the better of science, and that he has been led astray by his love of logical symmetry. For example, Darwin attempted to account for the origin of species by sup-

[1] *L'Evolution de la poésie lyrique*, I, 5.

posing that certain animals tend, for some unexplained reason, even under the same influences of environment, to diverge and become different from others of their kind. In the same way, Brunetière tells us, individuals appear from time to time who have the power to modify the course of literature and to originate new literary *genres*. He thus uses a doubtful analogy with what is itself hypothetical in Darwin's doctrine to explain the one supremely important event in art, namely, the rise of a creator. If Brunetière's parallel be exact, the individual who innovates in literature does so in obedience to a blind cosmic impulse rather than by a deliberate act of his own will. The *genres*, as M. Lemaître points out, become in his hands pure scholastic entities, vegetative abstractions, evolving in virtue of a life of their own, and with little reference to the authors through whose brains they pass. The valuable germ of truth in Brunetière's evolutionary theory is already contained in a simple phrase of Aristotle's "Poetics": "Tragedy after passing through various transformations finally attained its true nature and there it stopped." The danger of pushing too far the biological analogy in dealing with the literary *genres* may best be stated in Brunetière's own words: "We should take special care not to transform what are, after all, simple metaphors into sovereign laws of criticism. In the midst of these ambitious generalizations the sense of the individual is lost. We become accustomed to value the men and works of the past only as they can be made to serve our own theories, and life in its diversity and rich complexity escapes us, and eludes the rigid formulæ in which we seek to confine it." His failure to carry through his evolutionary programme may have been due in some measure to the perception on his part that it was not possible to do so, at least in detail, without falling into pseudo-science.

But how does Brunetière, after thus abandoning to evolution, to the region of the relative, nearly everything that was regarded by old-time critics as fixed and stationary, manage to find a basis for "dogmatic" criticism? What standard is there raised above the realm of flux and change, with reference to which a work of art may be ranked as good or bad? How are we to escape in our literary judgments from the web of illusion thrown about us by our own temperaments, and from the fancies and passing fashions of the society in which we live? How, finally, are we to be rescued from the impressions of M. Anatole France? Brunetière's immediate answer to these questions, is that we must subordinate our sensations and emotions to reason. If we enter more deeply into his thought, we find that he was led in the search for an absolute to what may be termed the belief in an absolute man, to the Platonic, or the scholastic conception of "humanity." He would measure the value of a work of art according as it expresses this universal and essential humanity; according as it unites the power of giving a high degree of æsthetic pleasure with that of suggesting truly human thoughts and emotions.

The doctrine of the absolute man is in itself only a

metaphysical abstraction, and Brunetière refused to rest his criticism directly upon it. For an absolute based on this speculative unity of the human spirit he substituted in practice an absolute based on the unity of the human spirit as it has manifested itself in history. To the personal preferences and impressions of any particular man he opposes the testimony and experience of all men as embodied in tradition. That writer is most truly human, and consequently most worthy of praise, who has appealed through successive generations to the largest number of men. An opinion carries weight with Brunetière in proportion as it is ancient and universal. He did not hesitate to curtail the individual's right of independent judgmen, as he curtailed the individual's right of independent creation, and all to the greater glory and profit of human nature in general. The question at issue between Brunetière and the impressionists is so fundamental that I have reserved the full discussion of it for the closing chapter.

VI

Enough has been said to make clear that the great problem of Brunetière's life was that of finding standards to oppose to the universal laxity and self-indulgence of his time, — to what he called the "morbid and monstrous development of the me"[1]; and that his solution of this problem was from the outset extremely conservative. The reactionary tendencies of the last ten years of his life follow naturally enough from his earlier assumptions, especially the assumption that

[1] *Questions de Critique*, 214.

there is needed a principle of restraint in human nature (*un principe refrénant*), and that this principle cannot be evolved by the individual himself, but must be "exterior, anterior and superior" to the individual. As a result of its loss of traditional standards, modern society seemed to him to be plunging into a bottomless morass of impressionism. Of course the modern school gets around Brunetière's difficulty by offering as a substitute for the principle of restraint the principle of brotherhood; each man is to give a loose rein to his own instincts and "originality," and then temper this explosion of egoism by sympathy with an equally free play of individual impulse in others. This is the theory of fraternal anarchy found in Rousseau, and in his American congener, Walt Whitman. But modern France, according to Brunetière, has, in following Rousseau, taken a madman for its guide. He thinks we may make fine distinctions about different kinds of individualism, but in practice they are all synonyms for egoism; they all offer an undue opening to "the mobility of our impressions, the unruliness of our individual sense, and the vagrancy of our thought." [1]

In other words, Brunetière fails to escape from the vicious dilemma of nineteenth-century thought which would either sacrifice the individual to society or society to the individual; which fails to find a middle ground between anarchical self-assertion and a collectivism that would crush individual initiative. We may at least agree with him that a society that discards all the tra-

[1] *Discours de combat*, 2e série, 151.

ditional ways of unifying life, and then thinks it can get on without working out any new unity to oppose to individual impulse, may turn out to be strangely deluded. The opposing attitudes of Brunetière and M. France towards this problem have at least the merit of reflecting faithfully a main line of cleavage in contemporary French thought. Indeed, one can scarcely speak of the need of respect, authority and discipline in France without at once being set down as a reactionary. If France does not get beyond this stage, and yet prospers in a large way, all the sages of the past will have been convicted of error in their views of human nature; and this in itself will be a result of considerable interest.

The reasons that led Brunetière into the Catholic Church should now be clear. It alone seemed to him to afford the discipline and the definite standards that could protect society against the individual. The motives for his conversion, as he himself says, were "social"; they are certainly as far removed as possible from the motives of those who are drawn into the Church by the æsthetic charm of its ritual. Of this form of epicureanism he remarks contemptuously that "sensuality is not religion." He turned to Catholicism simply because it seemed to him to hold out the hope of a better-ordered social progress, of a more thoroughly disciplined collectivism. It is misleading to say, as is often done, that Brunetière had a "seventeenth-century soul," or, like M. de Vogüé, to compare him with Bossuet and Pascal. Brunetière's constant preoccupation with the humanitarian problem

— the future of society and the relations of man to his fellow-man — savors of Auguste Comte rather than of Bossuet. In his inner mood, again, he has more in common with Schopenhauer than with Pascal. It is enough to compare Brunetière's "social reasons" with the bit of parchment found sewn into Pascal's coat, on which he had recorded the details of his conversion (night of November 23, 1654). Pascal sums up this sudden illumination in the words, often repeated, "Joy, certainty, peace." Brunetière was a true child of his age in that he sought salvation in work and not in meditation; or rather, for the stoic Brunetière as for the epicurean Sainte-Beuve, work was, by their own avowal, a means of escape from the abyss of metaphysical despair. Brunetière was accused of being out of touch with his time. On the contrary, if his work fails to wear well, it may be because he was in too close touch with his time. He lacked the intuitions by which alone one can escape from the spirit of the age into the spirit of the ages. He had little experience of that wisdom which Joubert defines as "repose in the light." He is also very inferior to Sainte-Beuve and even to M. Lemaître in æsthetic perceptiveness. To this poverty in the two main types of intuition is to be attributed his small power of either emotional or intellectual suggestion. He is always lucid but rarely luminous. "He sets such great store," says M. Lemaître, "on precision, that nothing exists for him which cannot be expressed with rigorous exactness."[1] (This is the trait, it will be re-

[1] *Contemporains*, I, 225.

membered, that Charles Lamb discovered in Scotchmen and that led him to say that his own mind was in its constitution essentially anti-Caledonian.)

Brunetière's lack of intuitiveness impairs not only his defence of religious tradition, — it impairs also his defence of tradition in literature. He did not take sufficiently into account in either religion or literature the aristocratic elements that make directly for the perfecting of the individual and only indirectly for the perfecting of society. What Sainte-Beuve lamented in the decay of humane letters was the disappearance from the world of delicacy and distinction, and not simply the weakening of a discipline. The point may be made clear by comparing the attitude of the two men towards Balzac. Both Balzac and Hugo are indeed veritable touchstones for the critic, being as they are writers of immense power, but a power Titanic and Cyclopean rather than human. Brunetière ascribes Sainte-Beuve's hostility to Balzac to personal pique and jealousy. Personal pique there certainly was, but the underlying ground of Sainte-Beuve's hostility, as I have tried to show elsewhere, was his humanism — the fact, as he himself says, that "he still belongs in spite of everything to the classical school." Sainte-Beuve shows himself a better humanist than Brunetière, when he admires Balzac's exuberant creative energy, but at the same time is repelled by his violence and lack of measure.

Many readers of Brunetière's volume on Balzac have doubtless been puzzled by his warmth of admiration for a writer who, as he truly says, had immense influence in promoting the whole French naturalistic movement from Taine to Zola, and was himself an unchained force of nature.[1] Did not Brunetière begin his career as a critic by an onslaught on the naturalistic novel, and is he not always urging us to react against the "naturalism that we still have in our blood," and become "idealists"? The difficulty will be at least partly solved if we remember that Balzac and Brunetière both became Catholics and for somewhat similar reasons. Balzac failed to find in the individual life any resource against itself; he depicted it not as a struggle between a higher and a lower nature, but merely as the unfolding of a master impulse that is determined in turn by the pressure of an infinitely complex environment; he was unable to conceive of any inner avenue of escape for the individual from his own egoism and subjectivity, and so he opposed to individualism a social solidarity that receives its ultimate sanction from the Church. Like Brunetière he sides with society against the individual. In their return to the discipline of the past, Brunetière and Balzac both take their point of departure in naturalistic pessimism. If we had no other evidence in the case of Brunetière his sympathetic study of Schopenhauer would suffice.

An inevitable question arises in dealing with this difficult relationship between Brunetière's "naturalism," and his "idealism": How did he reconcile his keen sense of historical relativity with the need imposed by his logic of an outer absolute? His most evident ambi-

[1] *Le Roman naturaliste,* 165.

tion as a thinker is to combine the faith of the past in what is stable with the modern idea of development. Even dogma itself evolves, he asserts, and in all this part of his thought it is easy enough to trace the influence of Cardinal Newman. His plea for a Catholicism that would develop in harmony with some of the aspirations of modern democracy found favor with Leo XIII, but has been far less acceptable to the present Pope. Brunetière entered the Church to escape from individualism and then towards the end found himself treated as a heretic. The final impression, as in the case of Taine and so many other eminent personalities of the last century, is that of a great spiritual solitude.

Some of the arguments Brunetière brings to the defence of tradition are certainly surprising. In fact one suspects in him a violent love of paradox which he gratifies not by attacking the general sense of mankind, but by the means he employs in defending it. It is, he confesses, an undertaking at once hazardous and novel to press into the service of Catholic orthodoxy Comte's "Positive Philosophy" and the "Origin of Species." He identifies the scientific doctrine of heredity and the dogma of original sin, draws a parallel between the American Constitution and the Roman Church, and brings Darwin to the aid of St. Vincent de Lérins. We may well refuse to follow him in these bizarre associations; yet we must recognize that he is wrestling manfully all the while with what is the central problem of contemporary thought, the problem how to adjust the rival claims of "being" and "becoming"; how to retain the conquests of naturalism and at the same time assert the integrity of that part of man which is above phenomenal nature.

Brunetière, indeed, has an almost unerring instinct for the large and vital questions, even when he misses the right solution of them. He is instructive in his errors, even in his failure to recognize that the remedy for the excesses of individualism must be a saner individualism, that the lance of Achilles can alone heal the wound it has made. There are few more effective antidotes to impressionism than to read him through with a view to refuting him. He may be recommended as a corrective to those who suffer from epicurean indolence and unwillingness to think. It is some distinction to have attained, as Brunetière did, even to a logical cosmos in an age whose current philosophy would seem to be what a Harvard undergraduate, replying to a question as to the religion of China, described as *confusionism*. The atmosphere that surrounds his work has the stoic bleakness; yet he is tonic by the very faith he feels in the virtues of clear and consistent reasoning. "Who of us," says Brunetière, "is without his weaknesses? Mine — one of mine — has always been to love doctrinaires; and see how indulgent I am towards them: I pardon them not only for having had doctrines and for having defended them sturdily, but for having changed doctrines, every time they have given good reasons for so doing, — I mean good doctrinal ones."[1] He is convinced that "ideas govern the world."[2] Herein he differs from M.

[1] *Nouveaux essais de lit. cont.*, 314. [2] *Discours de combat*, 2e série, 172.

Faguet, a really distinguished thinker, who has no belief in the practical efficacy of thought; and that is perhaps why much of M. Faguet's work, brilliant as it undoubtedly is, fails to leave its sting. "Take Rousseau from the history of the eighteenth century," writes Brunetière, "and you put off the Revolution by perhaps twenty or twenty-five years; take from his writings the 'Social Contract' and you make the Jacobin programme impossible; take from the 'Social Contract' itself merely the sixth and seventh chapters of the fourth book, and you suppress Robespierre." Fortunately the connection between logic and life is not always so close.

Brunetière had only contempt for those who would divorce scholarship from ideas, or who, having ideas, fail to subordinate them to some serious end; contempt for the dilettantes and impressionists who see in literature only the occasion for an agreeable vagabondage of the intellect or sensibility; likewise for those who lose themselves in over-minute investigations: for instance, the man who devoted a volume of five hundred pages to proving that Molière died at No. 40 and not at No. 34 Rue Richelieu; or the man who searched through the records of Paris churches — eighty manuscript volumes — in order to determine the exact date of the birth of Ninon de Lenclos! In one of his most vigorous papers ("La Fureur de l'Inédit") he assails what is perhaps the main fetish of modern scholarship, — "original" research. "Science and conscientiousness," he exclaims, "delicacy of taste, tact, the art of selection and composition, feeling for style, felicity of expression, art or grace, eloquence or strength, all that formerly went under the name of talent or even genius,—do any of these qualities really count in the eyes of a decipherer of texts or an editor of unpublished documents? And public opinion, which they have already more than half corrupted, seems likely soon to side with them."[1] Brunetière waged continuous war on this tendency of scholarship towards Alexandrianism, towards what Bacon termed, in speaking of spelling reform, "unprofitable subtleties." No one in his generation so emphasized the relationship between literature and thought, the relationship between thought itself and life.

"Le vrai Dieu, le Dieu fort, est le Dieu des idées."

It is a pity that the needed example he sets in this respect should be compromised by the reactionary trend of his thinking; that men who are his inferiors in the scholarship of ideas and even in the scholarship of facts should yet have the advantage, in attacking him, of at least seeming to be champions of the modern spirit.

[1] *Nouvelles questions de critique*, 28.

XI

CONCLUSION

We are told that Louis XIV once submitted a sonnet he had written to the judgment of Boileau, who said, after reading it: "Sire, nothing is impossible for your Majesty. You set out to write some bad verses and you have succeeded." The point of this story for the modern reader lies not so much in the courage of the critic as in the meekness of the king. With the progress of democracy one man's opinion in literature has come to be as good as another's, — a deal better, too, the Irishman would add, — and such words as deference and humility are in a fair way to become obsolete. We can scarcely conceive to what an extent men once allowed their personal impressions to be overawed and held in check by a body of outer prescriptions. Only a century ago an Edinburgh reviewer could write: "Poetry has thus much at least in common with religion, that its standards were fixed long ago by certain inspired writers whose authority it is no longer lawful to question."[1] Racine tells us that the audience was afraid at the first performance of his comedy "Les Plaideurs," that "it had not laughed according to the rules."

The revolt came at last from this tyranny of the "rules," and the romantic critics opposed to the neo-

[1] Article on Southey, *Edinburgh Review*, October, 1802.

classic narrowness their plea for wider knowledge and wider sympathy; they would see before they began to oversee, and be historical rather than dogmatic; they would neither exclude nor conclude, but explain; above all, they would be appreciative, and substitute the fruitful criticism of beauties for the barren criticism of faults. The weakness of this whole school has been its proneness to forget that knowledge and sympathy are after all only the feminine virtues of the critic. Hence the absence of the masculine note in so much modern criticism, hence the tendency of judgment to be swallowed up completely in sympathy and comprehension — *tout comprendre, c'est tout pardonner*. Renan, one of the most perfect embodiments of the ideal of wider knowledge and wider sympathy, says that when any one was presented to him he tried to enter into this person's point of view, and serve up to him his own ideas in advance. One thinks almost involuntarily of Dr. Johnson and how, when people disagreed with him, he "roared them down"; how men like Reynolds and Gibbon and Burke ventured to present their protest to him only in the form of a Round Robin so that the awful Aristarch might not know on whom first to visit his wrath. It is of course well, and indeed indispensable, that the critic should cultivate the feminine virtues, but on condition, as Tennyson has put it, that he be man-woman and not woman-man. Through neglect of this truth criticism has tended in its development during the past century to become first a form of history, and then a form of biography, and finally a form of gossip. History and biography remind us in their gradual encroachments upon critical judgment of those mayors of the palace in Merovingian times who insinuated themselves under cover of the services they rendered and at last thrust themselves into their masters' place. It is true that judgment would not have been thus dispossessed if it had not first shown itself a *roi fainéant*.

I

Sainte-Beuve himself, as we saw, labored during the latter part of his life to correct, or one might more fairly say to complete, his earlier method and to assert once more the supremacy of judgment. It is curious to trace the transformation of the militant romanticist of 1830 into the conservative who finally extols as the true type of the critic Malherbe and Boileau and Dr. Johnson. He follows these men in founding his own judgments for the most part on the traditional standards of the classicist, yet no one knew better than Sainte-Beuve that these standards were doomed. "Let us be the last of our kind," he exclaims, "before the great confusion."[1]

The "great confusion" that Sainte-Beuve foresaw is now upon us. I pointed out that he himself has been correctly defined in his influence on his successors, not as a defender of standards and judgment, but as a great doctor of relativity. Now nearly all recent criticism, so far as it is anything more than a form of gossip and small talk, may be roughly classified as either impressionistic or scientific; and it is in this doctrine of rela-

[1] *Portraits littéraires*, III, 550.

tivity that both impressionistic and scientific critics unite. The impressionist is interested in a book only as it relates itself to his sensibility, and his manner of praising anything that makes this appeal to him is to say that it is "suggestive." The scientific critic for his part is interested solely in the way a book is related as a phenomenon to other phenomena, and when it is the culminating point or the point of departure of a large number of these relationships, he says that it is "significant" (the favorite word of Goethe). If the impressionist is asked to rise above his sensibility and judge by a more impersonal standard, he answers that there is no such impersonal element in art, but only "suggestiveness," and is almost ready to define art with a recent French writer as an "attenuated hypnosis." If the scientific critic in turn is urged to get behind the phenomena and rate a book with reference to a scale of absolute values, he absconds into his theory of the "unknowable."

We may illustrate by a familiar passage from Taine, who is easily the most eminent of those who have attempted to make criticism scientific. "What do we see," he says in his English Literature, "under the fair glazed pages of a modern poem? A modern poet who has studied and travelled, a man like Alfred de Musset, Victor Hugo, Lamartine or Heine, in a black coat and gloves, welcomed by the ladies, and making every evening his fifty bows and his score of *bons-mots* in society; reading the papers in the morning, lodging as a rule on a second floor; not over gay, because he has nerves, and especially because, in this dense democracy where we stifle one another, the discredit of official dignities has exaggerated his pretensions, while increasing his importance, and because the keenness of his feelings in general rather disposes him to think himself a god."

Now in the first place the results of this attempt to infer from a poem the life and personality of the poet are strangely uncertain. We read in the recently published letters of John Richard Green that when Taine was in England getting information for the last volume of his "English Literature," he began talking about Tennyson with Palgrave, a great friend of the laureate. "Was n't he in early youth rich, luxurious, fond of pleasure, self-indulgent?" Taine asked. "I see it all in his early poems — his riot, his adoration of physical beauty, his delight in jewels, in the abandonment of all to pleasure, in wine, and . . ." "Stop! stop!" said Palgrave, out of all patience. "As a young man Tennyson was poor — he had little more than one hundred pounds a year, his habits were, as they still are, simple and reserved, he cared then as he cares now for little more than a chat and a pipe; he has never known luxury in your sense." Taine thanked Palgrave for his information — and when the book came out Tennyson was found still painted as the young voluptuary of the critic's fancy.[1]

Even assuming that Taine's inferences could be drawn correctly, he would have us fix our attention on precisely

[1] *Letters of John Richard Green*, 372. Green's anecdote is perhaps not entirely fair to Taine's account of Tennyson as it finally appeared.

those features of a poem that are least poetical. The very prosaic facts he is looking for would be at least as visible in the writing of some mediocrity as in a work of the first order. It is, indeed, when Taine starts out to deal in this fashion with a poet of genius like Milton, to reduce "Paradise Lost" to a mere "sign," that the whole method is seen to be grotesquely inadequate. "Adam," says Taine in his critique of Milton, "is your true pater-familias with a vote, an M.P., an old Oxford man," etc. He listens to the conversation of Adam and Eve, the first pair, only to hear "an English household, two reasoners of the period—Colonel Hutchinson and his wife. Good heavens! dress them at once"; and he continues in this vein for pages.

But, says M. Bourget, speaking for the impressionists, there is another way of approaching the volume of verse that Taine would treat solely from the point of view of its "significance"; and in rendering the "suggestiveness" of the volume to the impressionist sensibility, M. Bourget proceeds to employ a luxuriance of epithet that lack of space forbids our quoting. He asks us to imagine a young woman alone in her boudoir on an overcast winter afternoon. A vague melancholy steals upon her as she reclines at ease in her long chair; all a-quiver with ineffable longing, she turns to her favorite poet. She does not surmise behind the delicately tinted pages of the beloved book the prosaic facts of environment, the obscure animal origins of talent that are so visible to Taine. What she does perceive is the dream of the poet—"the inexpressible and mysterious beyond that he has succeeded in throwing like a halo round his verses." For Taine the stanzas are a result; for the young woman "who intoxicates her heart with them so deliciously," they are a cause. "She does not care for the alembic in which the magic philter has been distilled, provided only this magic is operative, provided her reading culminates in an exquisite and trembling exaltation," and "suggests to her dreams either sweet or sad, but always productive of ecstasy." Who does not see, concludes M. Bourget, that entirely different theories of art are implied in the two ways of approaching the volume of verse? [1]

The two theories are different, indeed; yet they are alike in this, that neither the "significance" of the volume to Taine nor its "suggestiveness" to M. Bourget affords any real means of escape from the quicksands of relativity to some firm ground of judgment. We may be sure that a third-rate bit of contemporary sentimentality will "suggest" more ineffable dreams to the young woman in the long chair than a play of Sophocles. To state the case more generally, how many books there are that were once infinitely suggestive and are still of the highest significance in literary history which yet intrinsically are now seen to be of very inferior value! This is eminently true of certain writings of Rousseau, to whom much of the peculiar exaggeration of the *sens propre*, or individual sense that one finds in the impressionists, can ultimately be traced.[2] If the special modes of sensibility that

[1] Abridged from the chapter on Taine in *Essais de Psychologie contemporaine.*

[2] "Voici enfin Jean-Jacques, précurseur du XIXe siècle, qui dans l'indi-

impressionism exhibits go back to Rousseau, its philosophical theory may best be considered as a reappearance in modern thought of the ancient maxim that man is the measure of all things. This celebrated dictum became current at a decisive moment in Greek life and would indeed seem to sum up almost necessarily the point of view of any age that has cast off traditional standards. The all-important question is whether one interprets the maxim in the spirit of the sophists or in that of Socrates. The resemblance between the impressionistic and the sophistical understanding of the maxim is unmistakable; not only the individual man, but his present sensations and impressions are to be made the measure of all things. "All of us," says M. Anatole France, "judge everything by our own measure. How could we do otherwise, since to judge is to compare, and we have only one measure, which is ourselves; and this measure is constantly changing? We are all of us the sport and playthings of mobile appearances."[1] Perhaps no recent writer has shown more of the Socratic spirit in his use of the maxim than Emerson. "A true man," he says, "belongs to no other time and place, but is the centre of things. Where he is, there is nature. He measures you and all men and all events." Though Emerson thus asserts the maxim, he has not therefore succumbed, like M. France, to the doctrine of relativity and the feeling of universal illusion that accompanies it; on the contrary, he has attained to

vidu, c'est-à-dire dans le Moi affectif et passionnel, voit la mesure unique de toute chose." Pellissier, *Etudes de Littérature contemporaine.* Cf. Brunetière, *Nouvelles questions de critique*, 214.

[1] *Vie lit.*, I, 318.

a new sense of the unity of human nature — a unity founded, not on tradition, but on insight. He says somewhere that he finds such an identity both of thought and sentiment in the best books of the world, that they seem to him to be the work of "one all-seeing, all-hearing gentleman." Now it is evidently this one all-seeing, all-hearing gentleman who is for Emerson the measure of all things. The individual man is the measure of all things only in so far as he has realized in himself this essential human nature. To be sure, the line is often hard to draw in practice between the two types of individualist. There were persons in ancient Athens — for example, Aristophanes in the "Clouds" — who treated Socrates as an ordinary sophist. In the same way, there are persons to-day who fail to see the difference between Emerson and an ordinary impressionist. "The source of Emerson's power," says Professor Santayana, "lay not in his doctrine but in his temperament."[1]

Emerson's language is often indistinguishable from that of the impressionist. "I would write on the lintels of my doorpost, *whim*." "Dream delivers us to dream, and there is no end to illusion." "Life is a flux of moods." But he is careful to add that "there is that in us which changes not and which ranks all sensations and states of mind." The impressionist denies this element of absolute judgment and so feels free to indulge his temperament with epicurean indolence; at the same time he has the contemptuous indulgence for others that befits beings who are the "sport and playthings of

[1] *Poetry and Religion*, 218.

mobile appearances." M. France says that he "despises men tenderly." We would reply in the words of Burke that the "species of benevolence which arises from contempt is no true charity." Impressionism has led to a strange increase in the number of dilettantes and *jouisseurs littéraires*, who to the precept *de gustibus non* have given developments that would certainly have surprised its author. The Horatian plea for an honest liberty of taste has its necessary corrective in the truth that is very bluntly stated in a Spanish proverb: "There are tastes that deserve the cudgel."[1] We are told that Sainte-Beuve was once so offended by an outrageous offence to good taste in a remark of Nicolardot's, that, yielding to an irresistible impulse, he kicked him out of the room. Dante, in replying to a certain opponent, says, with the instinct of a true Italian, that he would like to answer such "bestiality not with words but with a knife." We must remember that "good taste" as formerly understood was made up of two distinct elements: first, one's individual sensibility, and secondly, a code of outer rules by which this sensibility was disciplined and held in check. The observance of these rules became for the community of well-bred people a sort of *noblesse oblige*, and taste in this sense has been rightly defined by Rivarol as a man's literary honor. Now that the outer code has been abrogated, taste is not therefore delivered over to the caprices of a vagrant sensibility; taste is attained only when this sensibility is rectified with reference to

[1] "Hay gustos que merecen palos."

standards inwardly apprehended, and in this sense may be defined as a man's literary conscience; it is, in short, only one aspect of the struggle between our lower and higher selves. Some, indeed, would maintain that taste is not a thing thus to be won by any effort of the will, but is rather an inborn and incommunicable tact, a sort of mysterious election, a free gift of the muses to a predestined few; that in literature many are called and few are chosen. In the article "Goût" of the "Philosophical Dictionary," Voltaire discourses on the small number of the elect in matters of taste, and in almost the next article ("Grâce") turns all his powers of mockery on those who assert the same doctrine in religion. Not only individuals but whole nations were once held to be under the reprobation of the muses. As Voltaire says sadly, *presque tout l'univers est barbare.* Perhaps even to-day persons might be found who would regard as legitimate the famous query of Father Bouhours whether a German can have wit. There are only too many examples in Germany and elsewhere of how far infinite industry and good intentions are from sufficing for the attainment of taste. However it may be in theology, it remains true in literature, as Gautier remarks, that works without grace are of no avail.

But one may recognize an element of predestination in the problem of taste and not therefore acquiesce in the impressionist's preaching of the fatality and finality of temperament. Every one, to be sure, has an initial or temperamental taste, but it is hard to say how far this taste may be transformed by subordinating it to the higher claims of our nature. Dr. Johnson says that if he had no duties and no reference to futurity he should spend his life in driving briskly in a post-chaise with a pretty woman. Here then is the temperamental taste of Dr. Johnson, and if he had been a disciple of M. France, he might have accepted it as final. Boswell reports an outburst of Johnson on this very subject: "Do not, Sir, accustom yourself to trust to *impressions*. By trusting to impressions, a man may gradually come to yield to them, and at length be subject to them, so as not to be a free agent, or what is the same thing in effect, to *suppose* that he is not a free agent. A man who is in that state should not be suffered to live; . . . there can be no confidence in him, no more than in a tiger."

Johnson would evidently have agreed with the Buddhists in looking on the indolent settling down of a man in his own temperament[1] as the chief of all the deadly sins. A fulmination like the foregoing is good to clear the air after the debilitating sophistries of M. France. Yet we feel that Johnson's point of view implies an undue denial of the individual's right to his own impressions and that therefore it has become in some measure obsolete. It is well for us, after all, to have fresh and vivid and personal impressions; it is well for us, in short, to awaken our senses; but we should "awaken our senses that we may the better

[1] This is the full meaning of the Pâli term *pamâda*. The opposite quality, *appamâda*, or strenuousness, — the unremitting exercise of the active will, — is the chief of the Buddhist virtues; this Oriental strenuousness, one should hasten to add, is directed towards self-conquest and not, like the Occidental variety, towards the conquest of the outer world.

judge" — and not simply that we may the better enjoy. For instance, Walter Pater continually dwells on the need of awakening our senses, but when he speaks of "living in the full stream of refined sensation," when he urges us to gather ourselves together "into one desperate effort to see and touch," there is a hedonistic flavor in these utterances that can escape no one. On the other hand, there should be no ascetic denial of the value of the impression in itself. Brunetière is reported to have said to another critic, whom he suspected of intellectual epicureanism, "*You* always praise what pleases you, *I* never do."[1] This is an asceticism of taste worthy of the spectator of Racine's comedy who wished to laugh according to the rules. And so Brunetière was led naturally into his reactionary attitude; seeing only the evil possibilities of individualism, he would have the modern man forego his claim to be the measure of all things, and submit once more to outer authority. A certain type of seventeenth-century critic attempted to establish a standard that was entirely outside the individual. The impressionist has gone to the opposite extreme and set up a standard that is entirely within the individual. The problem is to find some middle ground between Procrustes and Proteus; and this right mean would seem to lie in a standard that is in the individual and yet is felt by him to transcend his personal self and lay hold of that part of his nature that he possesses in common with other men.

[1] See Lemaître, *Contemporains*, VI, p. xi. Cf. Brunetière, *L'Evolution de la poésie lyrique*, 25.

The impressionist not only refuses the individual man any such principle of judgment to which he may appeal from his fleeting impressions; he goes farther and refuses men collectively any avenue of escape from universal illusion and relativity; he denies in short the doctrine embodied in the old church maxim, *Securus judicat orbis terrarum*, a doctrine so fundamental, we may note in passing, that in the form attributed to Lincoln it has become the cornerstone of democracy: "You cannot fool all the people all the time." M. Anatole France is fond of insisting, like Sainte-Beuve before him, that there inheres in mankind as a whole no such power of righting itself and triumphing over its own errors and illusions. A whole chapter might be made up of passages from Sainte-Beuve on the vanity of fame. "Posterity has allowed three fourths of the works of antiquity to perish," says M. France in turn; "it has allowed the rest to be frightfully corrupted. . . . In the little that it has kept there are detestable books which are none the less immortal. Varius, we are told, was the equal of Virgil. He has perished. Ælian was an ass, and he survives. There is posterity for you,"[1] etc. Here again the contrast between the two types of individualist is absolute. "There is no luck in literary reputation," says Emerson. "They who make up the final verdict for every book are not the partial and noisy public of the hour, but a court as of angels; a public not to be bribed, not to be entreated, and not to be overawed decides upon every man's title to fame. Only those books come

[1] *Vie littéraire*, I, 111.

down which deserve to last. Blackmore, Kotzebue, or Pollock may endure for a night, but Moses and Homer stand forever. The permanence of all books is fixed by no effort friendly or hostile, but by their own specific gravity or the intrinsic importance of their contents to the constant mind of man."

We should add, then, in order to define our critical standard completely, that the judgment of the keen-sighted few in the present needs to be ratified by the verdict of posterity.[1]

II

Such being in brief outline our critical standard, it remains to consider it more fully in its bearings on the main trend of contemporary life in France and elsewhere. It is evident that under existing conditions we can scarcely emphasize the first part of our definition too strongly (the keen-sighted few!). If it is not possible in literature to fool all the public all the time, it is only too possible to fool all or nearly all the public some of the time, and some of the public all the time. The opposite opinion is encouraged by the force now most active in the world and definable as Rousseauistic democracy. The Rousseauist, or, as I should not hesitate to call him, the pseudo-democrat (I am sorry I need so many "pseudos" in describing our modern activities), would eliminate from the norm the humanistic or aris-

[1] The appeal to the judgment of the keen-sighted few, as opposed to that of the many, appears in Aristotle, who always assumes an ideal reader, whom he refers to variously as ὁ σπουδαῖος, ὁ φρόνιμος, ὁ εὐφυής. The principle of universal consent as applied to literature is first clearly stated by Longinus (περὶ ὕψους, cap. VII).

tocratic element. He would value a book, not by its appeal to the keen-sighted few, but by its immediate effect on the average man. Tolstoy, it will be remembered, defends an extreme form of this fallacy, the humanitarian fallacy as we may term it, in his book on Art, and concludes that the masterpiece of nineteenth-century literature is "Uncle Tom's Cabin." Emerson, who has been our guide thus far, can be of little service to us here. He had humanitarian illusions of his own — illusions that he shared with his whole generation. "We," says Emerson, giving fresh expression to his favorite doctrine that man is the measure of all things, "We are the photometers, we the irritable gold-leaf and tinfoil that measure the accumulations of the subtle element. We know the authentic effects of the true fire through every one of its million disguises." One is naturally prompted to inquire whom Emerson means by this "we." Granting that man is a photometer or measure of light, it is yet absurd to add, as Emerson at times comes dangerously near doing, that this ideal measure exists unimpaired in the ordinary untrained individual. Elsewhere Emerson says of Goethe: "He hates to be trifled with and to repeat some old wife's fable that has had possession of men's faith these thousand years. I am here, he would say, to be the measure and judge of these things. Why should I take them on trust?" This may do very well for Goethe, but when the man in the street thus sets up to be the measure of all things, the result is often hard to distinguish from vulgar presumption. The humanitarian fallacy would be comparatively harmless if it did not fit in so perfectly with a commercialism which finds its profit in flattering the taste of the average man, and an impressionism that has lost the restraining sense of tradition and encourages us to steep and saturate our minds in the purely contemporaneous. As it is, these elements have combined in a way that is a menace to all high and severe standards of taste. To use words as disagreeable as the things they describe, literature is in danger of being vulgarized and commercialized and journalized. There are critics who have founded a considerable reputation on the relationship that exists between their own mediocrity and the mediocrity of their readers. Sainte-Beuve says that in writing "we should ask ourselves from time to time with our brows uplifted towards the hilltops and our eyes fixed on the group of revered mortals: What would they say of us?" We may contrast this advice with the familiar story of the American magazine editor who told his young contributor that there was an old lady out in Oshkosh and that he must always have her in mind and be careful to write nothing that would not be clear to her. It evidently makes a difference whether one writes in the ideal presence of the masters or in that of the old lady in Oshkosh.

Plainly the humanitarian fallacy threatens to subvert utterly our critical standard, based as this standard is on the judgment of the keen-sighted few in the present supported by the judgment of the keen-sighted few in the past as embodied in the *catena aurea* of tradition. We also have to face the fact that Emerson, who has emphasized more happily perhaps than any other recent writer the need of selectiveness in the individual (as, for example, in his poem "Days"), and also the wisdom of the selections embodied in tradition, nevertheless gave undue encouragement to the ordinary man, to the man who is undisciplined and unselective and untraditional. His influence has in important respects been undeniably dubious. "Almost all the 'perky' people one knows," says Mr. Brownell, "are Emersonians." If we are to avoid misunderstandings we need to inquire carefully into the nature of this "perkiness," and point out why it is possible to cherish Emerson, or at least one side of Emerson, and at the same time look with extreme suspicion on the Emersonians.

In an earlier chapter I insisted on various resemblances between Joubert and Emerson, and in the same chapter contrasted Joubert and Madame de Staël as clear-cut types respectively of the Platonic and Rousseauistic enthusiast. The question arises whether Emerson is, like Joubert, purely Platonic in his enthusiasm. Many of his admirers would not hesitate to answer affirmatively. A whole book has in fact recently been written to prove that Emerson derives almost entirely from Plato.[1] On the other hand, another writer declares that Emerson is the most creditable disciple Rousseau ever had.[2] As a matter of fact, if many of Emerson's sayings have their counterpart in Joubert, even more of these sayings, perhaps, run parallel to Rousseau.

[1] See J. S. Harrison: *The Teachers of Emerson.*
[2] See *Rousseau,* by Thomas Davidson, 231.

Without attempting to impose our formulæ too pedantically upon Emerson, we may say that we find coexisting in him the psychological traits that exist separately in Joubert and in Rousseau (as well as in Rousseau's disciple, Madame de Staël); a blend so curious as to make of Emerson one of the figures in literature most difficult to place.

An obvious point of contact between Emerson and Rousseau is the doctrine of self-reliance, which is expounded in so many passages of the "Emile" and is generally recognized as the central doctrine of Emerson. But what does Emerson mean by the *self* in his self-reliance? In his own words, "what is the aboriginal self on which a universal reliance may be grounded?" And he goes on to reply that it is "that source at once the essence of genius, of virtue, and of life which we call Spontaneity or Instinct. We denote this primary wisdom as Intuition," etc. The derivation of this theory of spontaneity from Rousseau through various German and New England channels is sufficiently plain. But does Emerson, like Rousseau, use the word "spontaneity" and similar terms to connote a pure process of expansion, a triumph of impulse over outer barriers and restraints? Does he above all employ the word "intuition" Rousseauistically or Platonically? At this point appears that strange mingling of elements in his genius of which I have spoken. He plainly has the Platonic perception of unity with the elevation and serenity that go with it. At the same time he exalts and puts on the same level with this perception the purely centrifugal powers of personality. He quotes approvingly the Oriental definition of God as the inner check (a definition that would never have occurred to Rousseau), and almost in the same breath he speaks of "divine expansion." Instinct is equally honored with intuition and often identified with it. One wonders at times why a human nature whose expansive instincts are so divine needs any inner check, why a God thus defined might not safely be reduced to the rôle of the gods of Epicurus. Is there not some principle of perversity in the human heart that leads in an entirely different direction from the Self on which we may rely, and which it is the business of this Self to discipline and subdue? "The entertainment of the proposition of depravity," replies Emerson, "is the last profligacy and profanation."

Emerson is thus at one with Rousseau in denying intrinsic evil in human nature. His main weakness, as it seems to me, from which all his other weaknesses derive, is that, like Wordsworth and so many other Rousseauists, he thus "averts his ken from half of human fate."[1] This attitude towards the problem of perversity is so contrary to the ascertained facts, so opposed to all hard and clear and honest thinking, that it may compromise gravely in the long run the reputations of all those who have taken it. A curious reflection occurs at this point. The reputation of Jonathan Edwards, probably the most original thinker America produced before Emerson, has

[1] This central weakness in Emerson and its consequences have been pointed out by Madame Dugard in her monograph, and by P. E. More in *Shelburne Essays*, I, 71 ff.

been gravely compromised by precisely the opposite excess in dealing with the problem of perversity. Historically Emerson's denial of perversity merely marks the extreme recoil from the Enfield Discourse on "Sinners in the Hands of an Angry God,"—from Edwards's use of perversity to establish a spiritual reign of terror which was to serve in turn to prop and buttress a tottering theology. Edwards, however, in his dealings with sin and its reality is only exaggerating the facts, exaggerating them it must be granted with an almost maniacal insistency, whereas Emerson and the Rousseauists are simply repudiating the facts. Possibly that is one reason for the contrast between the tremendous logical grip of Edwards and the dialectical feebleness of Emerson.

It is doubtful whether any one who is so weak in dialectic as Emerson may properly be called a Platonist at all. We can imagine how Socrates would have pursued Emerson in one of Plato's dialogues, exacting from him sharp and discriminating definitions and multiplying distinctions about words like "nature" and "instinct," which Emerson, as it is, employs so vaguely. He is not merely deficient in the more obvious technique of thinking, a deficiency that has led many of the professional philosophers to refuse him recognition entirely, but he lacks that more essential consistency which would have enabled him to knit together the two main aspects of his work—on the one hand, the insistence on the unique and the individual which he possessed in common with his century, and on the other, the spiritual concentration and perception of unity which he possessed in common with the seers of all centuries. A serious thinker should not, according to Joubert, put forth a truth without at the same time putting forth the counter-truth that corrects and conditions it; otherwise the truth will cease to be wholesome and become an intoxicant. Now Emerson, as a rule, supplies both the truth and the counter-truth, but the two not being linked together by vital dialectic, as they would ordinarily be by a thinker of his class, it has been possible for his followers to take the intoxicant and leave the corrective. An "ideal" one might suppose that carries with it no discipline or obligation is not worth a straw, but it has been possible to extract from Emerson something that passes for idealism and is not disciplinary at all, but merely a vague optimistic exaltation. Instead of seeking to ascertain the laws of nature and human nature and then striving to adjust ourselves to them, we are filled under Emerson's influence and in his own phrase with "the delicious sense of indeterminate size" and become "elastic as the gas of gunpowder." We are, in short, encouraged to believe that the stern realities of sin and suffering may be charmed away by a sort of emotional intoxication. This side of Emerson is plainly related on the one hand to Rousseau, and on the other to that most dubious aspect of our American national temper which finds its extreme expression in Christian Science. "Man is good and nature is beautiful," says Rousseau in substance. "I am lovely and the world is lovely, too," is a recent formulation of the creed of the Christian Scientist.

This Rousseauistic side of Emerson not only obscures

the struggle between good and evil in the individual, it also obscures the need of culture, the aid the individual may derive in solving his problems from society and, in general, from the experience of other men both in the present and in the past. If the times suffer from squalid mediocrity, as Emerson assures us they do, the difficulty must be that the individual does not show sufficient confidence in opposing to this mediocrity his own infallible intuitions. Emerson never tires of insisting on the horrors of conformity. As manifested in the English Church, for example, it "glazes the eye, bloats the flesh, and gives the voice a stertorous clang." A certain type of Emersonian suggests to us rather the horrors of nonconformity. The examples are only too numerous of persons who in exclusive reliance on the inner oracle have thought themselves inspired when they were only peculiar. In the end, it is true, a man must walk by his own light, but one would never gather from Emerson how terribly difficult it is to make sure first that this light is not darkness. In his essay on "Quotation and Originality" Emerson dilates on how little the individual amounts to after all, and how the best he can do is to quote and imitate; and the individual is in a fair way to become humble and conscious of the danger, as Burke would put it, of trading on his own private capital of wit. But then Emerson adds, "to all that can be said of the preponderance of the Past the simple word Genius is a sufficient reply. . . . Genius believes its faintest presentiment against the testimony of all history." At this reassuring utterance the individual is in a fair way to lose his incipient humility and become once more as elastic as the gas of gunpowder. With such an inner oracle to rely on, why go through the severe effort of building up standards based on the assimilation of tradition?

Pascal would have said that Emerson's sense of man's grandeur was not sufficiently tempered by a sense of man's wretchedness. "The single man," according to Emerson, must "plant himself indomitably upon his instincts." A Chicago physician recently declared that the average man has the murder "instinct"; and if we are to trust statistics an increasing number of Americans are planting themselves upon it very indomitably. I am not trying, however, to establish a connection between Emersonianism and murder. The worst that is likely to befall the man who plants himself indomitably upon his own instincts is that he will plant himself indomitably upon his own crudity. "The affirmative principle of the recent philosophy," Emerson declares, "is trust in the private, self-supplied powers of the individual." "As though," says Goethe, who had seen the beginnings of the philosophy to which Emerson refers, the philosophy of original genius, and had almost been the victim of it, "as though a man gets anything from himself except his own awkwardness and stupidity."

Emerson, then, is a wise man whose influence often works against that humility which is the first mark of wisdom; a true sage who must yet be numbered among the sycophants of human nature; a somewhat baffling blend, as I have already said, of Rousseauism and insight;

impressing us at times as a truly religious spirit, a spirit living, as a theologian would say, in a state of grace, and at times reminding us only too strongly of that Rousseauistic caricature of the religious spirit, the "beautiful soul." But light, as Arnold remarks, is rare and must be treasured wherever found: we must, therefore, treasure it in Emerson, though often associated with an impossible optimism, just as we must treasure it in Jonathan Edwards, though associated with an impossible theology. The oversoul that Emerson perceives in his best moments is the true oversoul and not the undersoul that the Rousseauist sets up as a substitute. He can therefore supply elements that will help us in forming our critical standard. I have tried, however, to make clear that our use of these elements, if it is not to be misleading, must be hedged about with the sharp distinctions of which he was himself so sparing.

III

What we are seeking is a critic who rests his discipline and selection upon the past without being a mere traditionalist; whose holding of tradition involves a constant process of hard and clear thinking, a constant adjustment, in other words, of the experience of the past to the changing needs of the present.

Who are to be our models for this right critical interpretation of the past? They are curiously hard to find in the nineteenth century, in spite of the fact that it is commonly supposed to be the most historical of centuries. There prevailed during this period two main attitudes towards the past which may be defined, respectively, as the scientific and the romantic. The man with the scientific attitude is chiefly concerned with investigating and establishing the facts of the past. The romanticist, for his part, revels in the mere picturesqueness of the facts or else takes refuge in the past from the present, uses it, as Taine would say, to create for himself an alibi. But the past should be regarded primarily neither as a laboratory for research nor as a bower of dreams, but as a school of experience. Where, then, is the man who has been fully initiated into tradition, and at the same time knows how to bring it to bear upon the present? Even Sainte-Beuve does not fully satisfy us here. He was one of the victims of that naturalistic fatalism that has lain like a blight upon the human spirit for the past fifty years or more. "Man," he says, "has the *illusion* of liberty." What is the use of knowing the past if one is not free to profit by the knowledge? We think by contrast of Goethe (whom Sainte-Beuve himself calls the king of critics), and of Goethe's saying that the chief benefit one may derive from a total study of his work is a "certain inner freedom."

Goethe, indeed, comes nearer than any other modern to what we are seeking; not the romantic or scientific Goethe, it should be added, but the humanistic Goethe, who is revealed in the conversations with Eckermann and others, and in the critical utterances of his later years. As an actual practitioner of the art of criticism, he seems to me inferior to the best of the Frenchmen;

but as an initiator into the critical habit of mind he is incomparable. He has, as Sainte-Beuve puts it, assimilated not merely tradition, but all traditions, and that without ceasing to be a modern of moderns; he keeps watch for every new sail on the horizon, but from the height of a Sunium. He would use the larger background and perspective to round out and support his individual insight and so make of the present what it should be — not the servile imitation, nor again the blank denial of the past, but its creative continuation. "To the errors and aberrations of the hour," he says, "we must oppose the masses of universal history." He would have us cease theorizing about the absolute and learn to recognize it in its actual manifestations. This particular form of the humanistic art of seeing the One in the Many would seem especially appropriate to an age like ours that differs above all from other ages, Greek and Roman antiquity, for example, in having at its command a vaster body of verified human experience.

I have said that the humanistic rather than the Rousseauistic Goethe is important for our purpose. But I should add that the process by which he passes from the Rousseauistic to the humanistic attitude is almost as instructive as the final result. The completeness of his reaction from the Rousseauistic theory of spontaneity or original genius, of which he was at the beginning the chief German exponent, may be inferred from a sentence I have already quoted. He did not go on, like Emerson, cultivating the delicious sense of indeterminate size, and feeling as elastic as the gas of gunpowder; he was not permanently satisfied, in short, with romantic megalomania; he discovered that man progresses by taking on limitations and not, as the Rousseauist would have us believe, by throwing them off. The lesson of "Wilhelm Meister," as of so much of his later writing, is that the individual must submit his temperament and impulses to something higher than themselves — in other words, he must renounce. The process of constant dying to one's self, that Goethe proclaims (*stirb und werde*), falls in, of course, with much that is most profound in religion; but Goethe's renunciation, it should be observed, is entirely unascetic. It seems the natural outgrowth of the experience of this life and not, as so often in religion, the violent contradiction of it.

What Goethe himself renounced was the world of Rousseauistic revery. He turned more and more from dreaming to doing. A man must, he says, combining the terminology of Leibnitz with that of Aristotle, raise himself by constant striving from a mere monad to an entelechy. Only in this way may he hope for happiness in this world and continuance in the next. We may take, as best summing up the central thought of Goethe, the lines at the end of the Second Faust in which the angels proclaim salvation by works: —

> "Wer immer strebend sich bemüht,
> Den können wir erlösen."

Yet it is just here in connection with this doctrine of works, especially as exemplified in the Second Faust, that our first doubts about Goethe arise. I have quoted

Goethe against Emerson. It is only fair to quote Emerson in return upon the limitations of Goethe. After praising Goethe heartily in his "Representative Men," he yet ends by saying that he did not worship the highest unity. So far as this judgment merely reflects the Rousseauistic side of Emerson, his suspicion of culture and his dislike of analysis, it is negligible. But Emerson was not only a Rousseauist but a seer, and his insight as well as his Rousseauism appears, as it seems to me, in the dictum that Goethe did not worship the highest unity.

Now to say of Goethe that he did not worship the highest unity is simply another way of saying that he lacked religious elevation. In any case he is less open than most men of the last century to the charge of confusing the planes of being. He kept his outlook open and unobstructed by scientific or other dogmatism even on the religious plane. He purged and purified himself very completely of the pseudo-spirituality of the Rousseauist, — of that shrinking back from outer reality coupled with that giddy gazing into the bottomless pit of the "heart" against which he utters a warning in his "Tasso."[1] He escaped in short from the world of romantic dreaming that is within us. We have it, however, on rather high authority that the kingdom of heaven is also within. Even in the inner life itself, it would ap-

[1] "Es liegt um uns herum
Gar mancher Abgrund, den das Schicksal grub;
Doch hier in unserm Herzen ist der tiefste,
Und reizend ist es, sich hinab zu stürzen."

pear, there may be a choice of direction, a parting of the ways. Goethe would not have hesitated to reply that he had aimed to escape, not only from the romantic, but also from the Christian morbidness. I have quoted Sainte-Beuve's saying that Goethe had assimilated, not merely tradition, but all traditions. How about the tradition that goes back to Judæa? The reply is by no means simple. We remember the impressive tribute he paid to Christianity[1] only a few weeks before his death, but then he also retained his early conviction that Pascal had done more harm to religion than all the deists and atheists of the eighteenth century. Now Pascal paints, though in somewhat less lurid hues, the same picture of human destiny as Jonathan Edwards: on the one hand, God in his absolute and arbitrary sovereignty; on the other, man weltering helplessly in his sin; the interval between only to be traversed by "thunderclaps and visible upsets of grace." This somewhat melodramatic form of Christianity, the tremendous spiritual romanticism of Saint Augustine, was undoubtedly distasteful to Goethe. As against this type of inwardness with its ascetic implications, he was for reconciling the flesh and the spirit, or as his detractors would say, for becoming a pagan. He had at least the advantage of being in accord in his attitude towards Augustinian Christianity with the main trend of the modern spirit. It would take almost unimaginable disasters to induce the world to give up its

[1] Conversation with Eckermann, 11 March, 1832. For the more important passages bearing on Goethe's religious opinions see Otto Harnack: *Goethe in der Epoche seiner Vollendung*, 50–90.

hard-won reconciliation of flesh and spirit, and once more go into sackcloth and ashes.

Goethe was, however, too great to deny entirely the truths of grace, or to lack the sense of man's helplessness in the hands of a higher power. He was capable of the obeisance of the spirit before this power and knew that if a man is not to remain a mere Titan his works must receive its blessing.[1] Yet he would have man dwell on works and the feasibility of works, and not on what is at bottom an insoluble mystery. No inconsiderable part of wisdom consists in just this: not to allow the mind to dwell on questions that are unprofitable in themselves or else entirely beyond its grasp.

I may myself seem to be straying at present into regions rather remote from my topic and therefore unprofitable. My reply is that the chief problem of criticism, namely, the search for standards to oppose to individual caprice, is also the chief problem of contemporary thought in general: so that any solution which does not get back to first principles will be worthless. If in a book on French criticism, again, I am devoting so much space to Emerson and Goethe, my purpose is to emphasize in this way my belief that this problem of discipline and standards is not to be solved in terms of French life alone, as a whole school of contemporary French thinkers[2] incline to believe, but is international. Finally,

[1] "Gross beginnet Ihr Titanen, aber leiten
Zu dem ewig Guten, ewig Schönen,
Ist der Götter Werk ; die lasst gewähren ! —"

[2] The so-called nationalists — Paul Bourget, Maurice Barrès, Charles Maurras, etc.

if my discussion of grace and good works seems to some to have an old-fashioned flavor, I would reply with Sainte-Beuve that simple psychological analysis when carried to a certain point encounters in other terms the same questions as theology. Both in a man's native gift as well as in the use of this gift to some adequate end there is an element of grace. In enumerating the various explanations of this mystery that have been attempted, Sainte-Beuve neglected, as I pointed out, the very interesting explanation embodied in the Oriental doctrine of karma. According to karma all that large part of a man's life which is so plainly independent of his own will and works is simply the result of his previous works. This doctrine must affect its devotees very differently from Augustinian Christianity, substituting as it does a strict causal nexus for the somewhat melodramatic intervention of a divine *bon plaisir*. Yet it only puts the difficulty a few steps farther back; the doctrine itself, along with the belief in reincarnation it implies, is just as unthinkable from the platform of the ordinary intellect as the doctrine of grace. We have the testimony of Buddha, the chief exponent of karma, on this very point. He puts it down in his list of the four "unthinkables."[1] In him who tries to grasp the workings of this law[2] directly, he says, grievous and vexatious mental habits will arise, which may even end in madness. The faith in karma is to remain in solution, as it were, in the background of our consciousness

[1] See *Aṅguttara Nikāya*, Part II, sect. 77.
[2] The Pāli word is "kammavipāko."

and from there to irradiate our action. Our actual attention should be fixed on the step in the "path" that is just ahead of us. We can infer what Buddha would have thought of the Augustinian[1] Christians who would have man turn away from works and brood everlastingly on the mystery of grace. He would have agreed with Holmes that the only decent thing for a consistent Calvinist to do is to go mad.

Goethe, then, to return to him, may simply have showed his supreme good sense, his instinct for a sound spiritual hygiene, in turning away from grace to works. He established his own list of "unthinkables," which is not so different from that of Buddha as one might suppose. We may note, for example, that both men dismissed as unprofitable speculations about personal immortality.[2] How many other questions there are that professional philosophers are fond of discussing and that may be profitably dismissed either because they are insoluble in themselves or because they do not, in Buddha's phrase, "make for edification"! Men do not fail, Goethe insisted, so much from lack of light on ultimate problems as from neglect of the very obvious and often very humble duty which is immediately before them; from not having met, as he puts it, the demands of the day (*die Forderung des Tages*). In thus looking to immediate practice Goethe is at one with Dr. Johnson, the fit

[1] I do not mean to say that St. Augustine did not put great emphasis on works, but merely that the side of Christianity which shows most clearly his influence has put an even greater emphasis on grace.

[2] For Goethe's admirable utterances on this subject see Eckermann, 24 February, 1824.

representative of a race that has shown a genius for conduct. All theory, says Johnson, makes against the freedom of the will and all experience in favor of it — the happiest utterance on this subject with which I am familiar. Like Goethe, Johnson simply refused, therefore, at the outset to enter into the metaphysical maze of either the dogmatic supernaturalist or the dogmatic naturalist. For the method of approach to the problem of a dogmatic naturalist like Taine involves, no less than that of the dogmatic supernaturalist, an attempt to think the unthinkable (as Buddha also pointed out).[1] Both the One and the Many as well as man's relation to them must forever elude final formulation.

Why, then, should we feel any doubt about Goethe's doctrine of work? The reply is that in his reaction from the romantic morbidness and what seemed to him the Christian morbidness he has transferred his work too much from the inner life of the individual to the outer world. This point may be made clear by comparing him with the great ancient of whom he is in some respects the disciple — Aristotle. For no one I presume, would deny that Goethe is in his general temper far more Aristotelian than Platonic. Now if Plato anticipates on one side of his thinking the doctrine of grace, as when he says that virtue is "neither natural nor acquired but comes to the virtuous by the gift of God" ("Meno"), Aristotle goes steadily on

[1] In the passage I have already quoted. The Pāli word for the attempt to grasp the material world intellectually (which Buddha deems impossible) is "lokacintā."

the assumption that virtue can be acquired, and is therefore a thoroughgoing partisan of works. The works he would have us perform, however, are not primarily utilitarian. He would have us work to redeem our own lower self from evil habits, and not, like Faust, to reclaim marsh lands from the sea. Moreover, the purpose that is imposed on the lower self and by which it is disciplined is linked by a series of intermediary purposes to the supreme and perfect End itself; in other words, it rests ultimately on an intuition of what Emerson calls the highest unity. Aristotle is indeed less habitually conscious of this unity than Plato. Though even Plato seems terribly "at ease in Zion" to the austere Christian, he has more sense of man's helplessness before the infinite, more of that humility, in short, that the man whose attention is turned too exclusively to works is constantly in danger of losing.

But though Aristotle is less preoccupied with the highest unity than Plato, I believe that he is more preoccupied with it than Goethe. Though far more than a mere naturalist, as I have tried to show, Goethe, in the last analysis, conceives of life more naturalistically, that is more expansively, than Aristotle. He was born into an enormously expansive age and was drawn into its main current. He found in the First Faust the happiest formulæ for the two main forces that were to dominate this age — scientific positivism (*Im Anfang war die Tat*) and Rousseauistic romanticism (*Gefühl ist alles*). The Aristotelian would object that the Deed and the Emotion do not by themselves suffice, that some adequate purpose must intervene to direct the Deed and discipline the Emotion. And Goethe himself became increasingly Aristotelian in this respect as he grew older. Yet even so, he still conceives at the end of the Second Faust of both the Deed and the Emotion too much in terms of expansion. I have already criticised from the Aristotelian point of view his conception of the Deed. Let us consider for a moment from the same point of view his conception of the Emotion. As is well known he praises as the most exalted form of emotion the "eternal Feminine" which "draws us upward." We are reminded here of Dante — a poet who will scarcely be accused of not having worshipped the highest unity — and his proclamation of that "primal love" that built the walls of hell.[1] Dante's conception implies a degree of selectiveness that makes us shudder. But is it not evident that to conceive of the highest love as Goethe did is to go to the opposite extreme, and eliminate from it the element of judgment and selection entirely; to forget that if the eternal Feminine draws us upward, only the eternal Masculine can keep us up? The supreme love, we may surmise, is not exclusively judicial or sympathetic, but a vital mediation between judgment and sympathy; it is selective love. It belongs to that superrational plane on which, in Goethe's phrase, the indescribable is accomplished.[2]

[1] *Inf.*, III, v. 6.

[2] "Das Unbeschreibliche,
Hier ist es gethan."

We can now begin to see in what sense Emerson may have been right in saying that Goethe did not worship the highest unity. His view of life in the Second Faust evidently tends to fly apart into the two extremes with which we have been so familiar during the past century — on the one hand, the idea of work conceived primarily in a utilitarian spirit, and on the other, diffusive, unselective sympathy. The supervention of the highest unity would have restored the work from the outer world to the breast of the individual and made the sympathy selective. We should then have had a point of view more humanistic and less humanitarian. To be sure, Goethe had no easy task in converting the mere romantic adventurer of the First Part (*der Unmensch ohne Zweck und Ruh*) into a good humanist or even into a good humanitarian. If we wish to do full justice to Goethe as a humanist we should not therefore confine ourselves too strictly to Faust.

The true humanist, that is the man who is sympathetically selective, has his standard within him — living, flexible, intuitive. Aristotle would make such a man the arbiter of all questions of taste and conduct — they are to be as he would decide.[1] A man may thus belong to the keen-sighted few, Aristotle admits, simply because he is born such.[2] In not trying to get behind this fact, Aristotle showed his good sense, if to do so would have been to run into insoluble mysteries. As the Greek poet says, there are three classes of men, (1) those who

[1] The σπουδαῖος is ὥσπερ κανὼν καὶ μέτρον . *Eth. Nic.*, III, 4, 1133 a 33

[2] He is a εὐφυής. Cf. *Eth. Nic.*, III, 5, 1114 b 6.

have insight, (2) those who, lacking insight themselves, have yet the wit to recognize it in others, and (3) those who have neither insight nor the wit to recognize it (and these last, he adds, are the truly useless men). The uncomfortable fact about life is that so many men belong to the third class, that there are so many men whose heads, in Joubert's quaint phrase, have no skylights in them. Men may be very eminent in other ways and yet lack the skylights; Taine, it seems to me, lacked them. Nor do we escape from the difficulty by putting our main emphasis with M. Bergson, not on the spiritual but on the æsthetic intuitions. The ordinary man can no more by any effort of his own be as æsthetically perceptive as Keats, let us say, than he can be as spiritually perceptive as Emerson. The undertaking in either case is of the same order as that of adding a cubit to one's stature. To be completely equipped for criticism one should possess in some measure both kinds of perceptiveness.

We must not, however, bear down too heavily, as Voltaire does, for example, in matters of taste, on the evident element of grace and predestination, for this is to neglect the truth of works; still less must we see the measure of all things in the man in the street, for this is to neglect the truths of both grace and works; least of all must we, like Tolstoy, seek our literary and artistic norm in the untutored peasant, for this is to set up a sort of inverted grace at the imminent risk of falling into bedlam delusion. The right use of grace and similar doctrines is to make us humble and not to make us morbid or discouraged. With due distrust of ourselves, a distrust that appears in our readiness to fortify our insight by tradition, with full admission that our works must be irradiated and guided from within and from above if they are not to prove vain, we must yet put our prime emphasis in literature, as elsewhere, on works. Now to perform works in the sense I have tried to define, that is, to feel in all one does the control of the highest unity, means in practice to select. All the knowledge and sympathy in the world can only prepare for the supreme, the distinctively human, act of selection. We must therefore train ourselves to feel that outer objects are, in the phrase of Epictetus, only the raw material for selection, and that it is possible to select. A great library, for example, is an infinite potentiality of selection, ranging from Zola to Plato. In our attitude towards it, as in our other concerns, we are to appeal from our moods of lazy self-indulgence to our moods of strenuous endeavor, from Philip drunk to Philip sober. Our reading enters as one element into that sum of choices that determines at last our rank in the scale of being. Here as elsewhere, if we neglect the opportunities that the "hypocritic Days" bring with them as they pass in their endless file, we shall "too late under their solemn fillets see the scorn."

We must select constantly and resolutely, though without sourness or asceticism. The romanticists have been busy for a century or more instilling into our heads the notion that to be selective is to be narrow and probably ill-natured. We must not select but admire — admire like a brute, Hugo would add. When Gautier averred that if he thought even one of Hugo's verses bad, he would not confess the fact to himself at midnight in a dark cellar without a candle, he must have come near fulfilling the master's ideal. Many authors would no doubt like to see criticism reduced, as a romantic dilettante recently defined it, to the "art of praise." A cat may, however, according to the adage, be killed with cream; and it has become only too evident that criticism may be killed by an excess of the appreciative temper. The true mark of barbarism, according to Goethe, is to have no organ for discerning the excellent. One may show that he lacks this organ just as surely by overpraising as by overblaming. What we see in America to-day, for instance, is an endless procession of bad or mediocre books, each one saluted on its way to oblivion by epithets that would be deserved only by a masterpiece. We have, in fact, been having so many masterpieces of late that we have almost ceased to have any literature. The critic is anxious like everybody else to show that he is overflowing with the milk of human kindness, that he is, in short, a "beautiful soul." Moreover, in a country where the belief is held that all things will turn out fortunately if only we feel lovely enough about them, it is commercially profitable to have a beautiful soul. The Christian Scientists, indeed, may be said to have put the art of feeling lovely on a dividend-paying basis. On the other hand, the man who has too many exclusions and disapprovals will fall under the suspicion of not being an optimist, and not to pass as an optimist is in many parts of America to be discredited. It is of course better to be a eupeptic than a merely dyspeptic critic. From this point of view we are better off than New Zealand if we are to believe a recent New Zealand writer, who, after comparing American critics to a "community of monthly nurses cooing and cackling over a succession of incomparable literary births," says that in New Zealand the comparison suggested is that of a "pack of incorrigible terriers watching for so many rats or rabbits to leave their holes." But it is not a question of being either eupeptic or dyspeptic, but of having standards and the courage to apply them. One may, as I have tried to show in the case of Joubert, be perfectly genial and good-natured, and at the same time extremely severe and selective.

The excess of the sympathetic and appreciative temper is of course nothing peculiar to America. As a matter of fact, Max Nordau cites certain German critics as the worst examples of the disease he calls superlativism, by which he means the facile outpour of epithets pushed to the verge of hysteria. Modern criticism, in getting rid of formalism and in becoming comprehensive and sympathetic, has performed only half, and that the less difficult half, of its task. The time would seem especially ripe for taking up the second half of the task — that of finding some new principle of judgment and selection. Renan says that "Goethe embraced the universe in the vast affirmation of love,"[1] — which is

[1] *Avenir de la science*, 448.

a somewhat hyperbolical way of saying that he is the worthy representative of a great era of expansion. But if Goethe were alive to-day, he might be less concerned with embracing the universe and more concerned with maintaining standards against the nightmare of an unselective democracy. We need not, again, admire Sainte-Beuve the less because we cannot admit, any more than in the case of Goethe, that the total emphasis of his criticism is just what we need at present. The *genre* in his hands, as I have tried to show, is expanding away from its centre. What seems desirable to-day is rather a movement that shall work in from the periphery of criticism in knowledge and sympathy to its heart and core in judgment. How peripheral criticism became during the nineteenth century may be inferred from the fact that Renan, for example, uses the word in a sense that is contrary to its very etymology.

What is most needed just now is not great doctors of relativity like Renan and Sainte-Beuve, but rather a critic who, without being at all rigid or reactionary, can yet carry into his work the sense of standards that are set above individual caprice and the flux of phenomena; who can, in short, oppose a genuine humanism to the pseudo-humanism of the pragmatists. A critic of this kind might be counted on to proclaim a philosophy, not of vital impulse, like M. Bergson, but of vital unity and vital restraint — restraint felt as an inner living law and not merely as a dead and mechanical outer rule. We may venture the paradox that criticism would derive less benefit at present from another Sainte-Beuve than from a second Boileau, that is, from a man who should work as effectively for the right kind of concentration in our own day as Boileau did in the seventeenth century. No sensible person would deny the narrowness of Boileau's range[1] or defend the formalism that appears so often in his theory. But his greatness, as Sainte-Beuve himself points out, lies elsewhere — in the native tact and almost infallible intuition he showed in his critical judgments.[2] All was not veto and restriction in his rôle, Sainte-Beuve goes on to say, yet the restrictive element predominated. A modern Boileau, if he were to be effective, would have to take up in himself the main results of the great expansion of the last century, but he would be primarily concerned, not with embracing the universe in the vast affirmation of love, but with making keen and crisp discriminations between different degrees of merit or demerit. He would also feel in his own way that hatred with which Boileau said he had been inspired from the age of fifteen — the hatred of a stupid book; and he would not lack material on which to exercise it. In other words, the age offers an opening for satire; but it must be constructive satire, satire that implies standards and is "purified," as Boileau claims of his own, "by a ray of good sense." Nothing could be more inspiriting than some twentieth-century equivalent for those first satires[3]

[1] Sainte-Beuve enumerates Boileau's limitations in *N. Lundis*, I, 300–02.

[2] See the important passage on the nature and rôle of the critic *Chateaubriand*, II, 114 ff.

[3] Especially the ninth satire which has been termed "a martyrology of bad books and bad authors," and which M. Lanson calls a "terrible and admirable slaughter of reputations."

of Boileau when the bad authors went down before his epigrams like the suitors before the shafts of Odysseus.

IV

What likelihood is there that we shall witness in contemporary France the rise of a selective and humanistic criticism of the kind I have just been trying to define? Any answer to this question must of course be provisional. Perhaps the most interesting development of recent years in criticism proper is the anti-romantic movement which has found notable expression in the volume of Lasserre.[1] This movement is open to some of the objections I have brought against Brunetière, whose influence is, indeed, very visible in it. A reaction against naturalism must take up into itself all that is legitimate in naturalism, after the fashion of Aristotle, and Goethe at his best. Though drawing vital nutriment from tradition, it must not dream of an impossible return to the past. It must not, in short, be reactionary in the French sense. The Frenchman has a way, partly as a result of his logical stringency, of connecting the literary problem with the religious problem and then running the religious problem in turn into the political problem. That is why, let me repeat, I have been discussing the literary problem in this chapter in terms of Emerson and Goethe. I could scarcely have avoided certain misunderstandings if I had discussed it in terms of some Frenchman (let us say, Joubert). The day much to be desired will doubtless come when it will dawn on

[1] *Le Romantisme français*, 1907.

the ordinary Frenchman that from the fact that a man is not a Jacobin, it does not follow that he must be a Jesuit, and that one may cease to be a clerical without therefore becoming an anti-clerical. This day, however, has not yet arrived, though there are signs that it is on the way. It may turn out that if France is to maintain her high place in civilization she will have to expel both the Jesuitical and the Jacobinical virus from her blood.

Another important French movement of to-day bearing directly on the question of critical standards is that in philosophy. M. Bergson is, of course, the most prominent internationally of the many representatives of this movement. If the main drift of the movement is to undermine scientific dogmatism, great confusion prevails as yet as to what is to be built on its ruins. I have made sufficiently clear in this volume my own belief that the philosophy of M. Bergson, whatever its merits as an attack on scholastic science, is on its constructive side not humanistic, but at most pseudo-humanistic. It is a late birth of romanticism, allied with all that is violent and extreme in contemporary life from syndicalism to "futurist" painting. M. Bergson's appeal to "intuition" in particular has been hailed with delight by romantic dilettantes the world over. It has confirmed them in their existing belief that they do not need to justify rationally their random impressions, that they may go on indefinitely luxuriating in a decadent æstheticism. The "Revue des Deux Mondes" suggests that M. Bergson may be a new Socrates. It is far more evident that he is a new Protagoras. His influence is making against the establishing of standards of judgment to-day just as the influence of Protagoras and the other sophists made against Socrates and his efforts to maintain rational standards in ancient Greece. Any attempt to base judgment on the flux is about as promising an undertaking as to seek to found a firm edifice on the waves of the sea.[1]

Finally if we are to understand the situation in France from the point of view of the present topic we must cast a glance at contemporary education. What is most obvious here is that for a number of years (especially since the "reform" of secondary education in 1902), a humanitarian reaction has been in progress against humanism. This French humanitarian movement, like all movements of the kind, breaks up when analyzed into two main aspects: first, the worship of the sovereignty of the Fact (*Im Anfang war die Tat*), the refusal to impose upon education other than utilitarian ends; secondly, the cult of diffusive unselective sympathy. Hand in hand with the undermining of the humanities in favor of scientific and utilitarian subjects in the *lycée*, has gone the exaltation of philological over literary scholarship at the Sorbonne. The old French education, it is asserted, gave too much encouragement to empty rhetoric; and we must recognize an element of truth in this

[1] Some of the most poisonous forms of impressionism are found among certain contemporary sociologists. It is easy to detect under the scientific or pseudo-scientific terminology the original Jacobinical assumption that mere impulse becomes august when multiplied by a million or by ten million. For instance, a prominent French sociologist claims that the Athenian jury was justified in condemning Socrates to death, being supported as it was by the "social conscience" of the time.

contention. For the humanism against which the French have been reacting is not humanism as it might be, but humanism as it was established in the *lycée* after the Revolution and under the patronage of Napoleon, a humanism that derives largely in turn from the somewhat formalistic scheme of education worked out by the Jesuits.

Perhaps the leader of the new movement at the Sorbonne has been M. Gustave Lanson. The admirable qualities of his "History of French Literature" should not blind us to the fact that he is a humanitarian rather than a humanist. He is especially unsound, it seems to me, in his solution of the infinitely delicate and important problem as to the right relationship between literature and science. He clings at present even more desperately to the Fact than he did at the beginning, he is even more convinced that to impose a human purpose on the Fact is either to become a reactionary or to be lost in the vaguely subjective. We may apply Sainte-Beuve's method to M. Lanson and study him in his disciples. We see dissertations issuing from the laboratory he has established at the Sorbonne which are immensely honest and thorough, but lacking in those finer qualities of selection and arrangement that have distinguished the best French scholarship in the past. This unselective worship of facts in literary study is what the French call *la fichomanie.*

In the meanwhile a lively counter-movement is beginning to declare itself, directed against both the "reform" of 1902 and the undue philologizing of the New

Sorbonne.[1] To those who have accused him of dehumanizing literary study, M. Lanson has replied with some acrimony [2] that they are only belletristic dabblers. We have had our own debates in America between the philologists and the humanists (or those who imagine themselves such), but the acrimony has been less. This is partly because we do not take ideas so seriously as the French (and herein we are their inferiors), partly because we do not mix the question up in their fashion with religion and politics (and herein we are their superiors). A man may set up as a humanist in this country without falling under any suspicion of being a Jesuit or a partisan of monarchical government. I should add that beside the more theoretical opposition to the new education there has been visible of late a sort of insurrection of common sense against it,[3] and the leaders of this latter movement are making a laudable effort to keep it clear of religion and politics: it is much as if the so-called "Amherst idea" in this country should spread and assume a national significance.

[1] The most brilliant of the recent attacks on the Sorbonne is that by Agathon in *L'Esprit de la Nouvelle Sorbonne* (3e ed., 1911; originally published as articles in *L'Opinion*, 1910). The book must be used with some caution. "Agathon" is the pen-name of two very young men who have, I understand, certain personal reasons for their animus. See also P. Leguay, *La Sorbonne* (2e ed., 1910).

[2] See for example his reply to M. Ch. Salomon in *Revue du Mois*, April, 1911.

[3] The "Ligue pour la Culture Française" was organized in 1911, and counts in its membership a majority of the different sections of the Institute (including the Academy). Interesting information as to the progress of the movement will be found in the *Bulletin* of the "League" (No. 1, December, 1911).

An insurrection of common sense is a good thing so far as it goes, but I do not believe that by itself it will prove sufficient. An effective revival of the humanities will have to rest on sound philosophical foundations, and these foundations do not at present exist. The points at issue between the New Sorbonne and its opponents are singularly complex and cannot be disposed of by labelling one side literary and the other scientific or philological. We are really helped very little in getting at a man's ultimate position by being told that he is "literary." The ancient sophists were also "literary," in fact they came out much more strongly for literature than Socrates. The important thing to know about a man is not whether he thinks himself literary, but whether his point of view is Socratic or sophistical. The professed champion of literature may be only a Bergsonian æsthete, who would have us get our vision of reality by "intuiting" the creative flux. M. Lanson is perfectly right in thinking that, as compared with that of many of his opponents, his own position is respectable. These opponents are undisciplined in themselves as well as lacking in the discipline that comes from the assimilation of tradition; whereas what M. Lanson has to offer may be a dehumanizing discipline, but it is a discipline. What is discrediting pure literature and literary study both in France and elsewhere is the intolerable flabbiness of most of those who claim to represent it. A naturalistic age, whatever it may set out to be, will end by being imperialistic; and the triumph of the scientific investigator even in the literary field is only one expression of the imperialistic idea. It is right that those who will not submit to any other discipline should at least have to submit to the discipline of the facts. The romantic dilettante who in order to enter the career of teaching is forced to bow his neck beneath the philological yoke is getting merely what he needs and deserves.

Still a discipline in facts and in scientific and historic method is no equivalent for a true humanistic discipline. France in particular will suffer an irreparable loss if the new education results in a loosening or severing of the bond that connects it with its great humanistic past. A literal return to this past or to the past in general is, I have said, out of the question. We must have standards and select, but it must be on different principles. No poet, for example, has treated the problem of selection, which means in practice the problem of the freedom of the will, more profoundly than Dante. Yet Dante could scarcely have conceived of a selection entirely independent of two outer standards — the Pope in matters spiritual, the Emperor in matters temporal.[1] Nowadays if we have standards they must be inner standards, and therefore, as I have said, our problem has more in common with the problem as it presented itself to Socrates and the sophists. The great effort of Socrates, we are told, was to recover that firm foundation for human life which a misuse of the new intellectual spirit was rendering impossible.[2] To the excessive mental suppleness of

[1] See especially his *De Monarchia*.

[2] See Arnold's *Speech at Eton* in *Mixed Essays*.

the sophists there is often added to-day an undue emotional pliancy. If some remedy is not found the modern world will, like the ancient Greek world, become the prey of its sophists. It will progress, not as our humanitarians would have us believe towards "some far-off divine event," but towards a decadent imperialism. What principle can set bounds to all this intellectual and emotional expansiveness? In the words of Cardinal Newman, "What must be the face-to-face antagonist by which to withstand and baffle the fierce energy of passion and the all-corroding, all-dissolving energy of the intellect" — what he calls elsewhere "the wild living intellect of man"? The reply would seem to be that this face-to-face antagonist will be found, if at all, not in a form of authority which has become impossible for so many moderns, but in the intuition of something at least as living as the intellect, which, in exact proportion as it is perceived, imposes, not merely on the intellect, but on man's whole being a controlling purpose. The world has been moving for some time past towards an entirely different order of intuitions, and in a philosophy like that of M. Bergson the pace has become headlong. I have, therefore, in my discussion of critical standards put considerable emphasis on a thinker like Emerson, who has a thoroughly modern view of authority, in some respects too modern a view, as I have tried to show, and is yet intuitive of the One rather than of the Many.

In Emerson's study at Concord, which remains as at the time of his death, almost the first object that meets one's eyes to the right on entering is a portrait of Sainte-Beuve. Emerson is said to have looked on this portrait as a special treasure. There is scarcely a single mention of Sainte-Beuve in Emerson's writings, and it is interesting to be able to connect even thus superficially men so different as the great doctor of relativity and the philosopher of the oversoul. The "Causeries du Lundi" and a book like "Representative Men" are at the opposite poles of nineteenth-century criticism; yet for this very reason and in spite of his humanitarian illusions, — in spite, we may add, of his curiously defective feeling for the formal side of art, — Emerson is the necessary corrective of Sainte-Beuve, who has infinite breadth and flexibility, but is lacking in elevation. This lack of elevation in Sainte-Beuve is not an accidental defect, but, as I have tried to show, bears a direct relation to his naturalistic method. The inadequacy of naturalism has been even more manifest in recent criticism. Sainte-Beuve himself maintained some balance between his regard for traditional standards and his aspiration towards wider sympathy and knowledge. This balance has not been preserved by his successors. Knowledge pursued as an end in itself and unsubordinated to any principle of judgment has degenerated into the narrowness of the specialist or into dilettanteism. A too exclusive emphasis on breadth and keenness of sympathy has led to the excesses of the impressionist. I have quoted Sainte-Beuve's description of the critics of the First Empire as the "small change" of Boileau. If the critics of to-day are to be anything more than the small change of Sainte-Beuve — or rather of one side of Sainte-Beuve — they need to cultivate, as a counterpoise to their use of the historical and biographical method, a feeling for absolute values; in short, they need to supplement Sainte-Beuve by what is best in a writer like Emerson. The point may be illustrated by two passages, each impressive in its own way.

The first passage is from the end of "Port-Royal" where Sainte-Beuve is commenting on his own efforts to attain the truth: "How little we can do after all! How bounded is our gaze — how much it resembles a pale torch lit up for a moment in the midst of a vast night! And how impotent even he feels who has most at heart the knowing of his object, who has made it his dearest ambition to grasp it, and his greatest pride to paint it — how impotent he feels and how inferior to his task on the day when, this task being almost terminated and the result obtained, the intoxication of his strength dies away, when the final exhaustion and inevitable disgust seize upon him, and he perceives in his turn that he is only one of the most fugitive of illusions in the bosom of the infinite illusion!"

This sense of universal flux and relativity can by itself result only in what I have called elsewhere a false disillusion, the disillusion of decadence. But there is another type of disillusion: the perception of unity may become so intense that everything else seems unreal by comparison. To illustrate this, we may turn to Emerson. "There is," he says, "no chance and no anarchy in the universe. All is system and gradation. Every god is there sitting in his sphere. The young mortal enters the hall of the firmament; there he is alone with them alone, they pouring on him benedictions and gifts and beckoning him up to their thrones. On the instant and incessantly fall snowstorms of illusions. He fancies himself in a vast crowd which sways this way and that and whose movements and doings he must obey. . . . Every moment new changes and new showers of deceptions to baffle and distract him. And when by and by for an instant the air clears and the cloud lifts for a little, there are the gods still sitting around him on their thrones — they alone with him alone."

In passages like this Emerson furnishes some hint of how it is possible to accept the doctrine of relativity without loss of one's feeling for absolute values, and without allowing one's self to be devoured by the sense of illusion, as Amiel was and Sainte-Beuve would have been if he had not found a sort of oblivion in unremitting toil. So far as Emerson does this, he aids criticism in its search for inner standards to take the place of the outer standards it has lost; he helps it to see in the present anarchy the potentialities of a higher order. What we need, he says, is a "coat woven of elastic steel," a critical canon, in short, that will restore to its rights the masculine judgment but without dogmatic narrowness. With such a canon, criticism might still cultivate the invaluable feminine virtues — it might be comprehensive and sympathetic without at the same time being invertebrate and gelatinous.

Our ideal critic, then, would need to combine the breadth and versatility and sense of differences of a Sainte-Beuve with the elevation and insight and sense of unity of an Emerson. It might be prudent to add of this critic in particular what Emerson has said of man in general, that he is a golden impossibility. But even though the full attainment of our standard should prove impossible, some progress might at least be made towards tempering with judgment the all-pervading impressionism of contemporary literature and life.

LIST OF CRITICS

LIST OF CRITICS

NOTE: This list makes no claim to completeness either in the names included or in the material given under each name. I have, however, aimed to record with some fulness the works of the more important writers who are primarily literary critics, but have in all cases been sparing in my references to books and articles on the authors I have listed. Those who wish more information may consult with profit H. P. Thieme's *Guide Bibliographique de la Littérature française de 1800 à 1906*, in spite of its numerous inaccuracies. The fourth volume of G. Lanson's *Manuel bibliographique de la littérature française moderne*, covering the nineteenth century, is, I understand, to appear shortly. Excellent bibliographical material will also be found in C. H. C. Wright's *History of French Literature* (1912), 883 ff.

Albert (Paul), 1827–1880.

Les poètes et la religion en Grèce, 1863. — *La poésie*, '68. — *La prose*, '69. — *Histoire de la littérature romaine*, 2 vols. '71. — *La littérature française des origines au XVIIe siècle*, '72. — *La littérature française au XVIIe siècle*, '73. — *La littérature française au XVIIIe siècle*, '74. — *Variétés morales et littéraires*, '79. — *Poètes et poésies*, '81. — *Histoire de la littérature française au XIXe siècle*, 2 vols. (prepared from his notes by his son, Maurice Albert), '82, '85.

See Sainte-Beuve, *N. Lundis*, XII, 1869.

Amiel (Henri-Frédéric), 1821–1881.

Caractéristique générale de Rousseau, in *J.-J. Rousseau jugé par les Génevois d'aujourd'hui*, 1879. — *Fragments d'un journal intime, précédés d'une étude par Edmond Scherer*, 2 vols., '83 (translated with introduction by Mrs. Humphry Ward, 2 vols., '85.)

See Bourget, *Nouveaux essais de psychologie contemporaine*, 1885. — Berthe Vadier, *H.F. Amiel;* '85. — Renan, *Feuilles détachées*, '87. — Matthew Arnold, *Essays in Criticism* (Second Series), '88. — Scherer, *Etudes critiques*, '89.

Ampère (Jean-Jacques), 1800–1864. Historian, etc. — Travels in Germany, Norway, etc. — Writes for *Globe*. — Professor of History and French Literature at Collège de France from 1833. — Elected to Academy, 1848.

De l'histoire de la poésie, 1830. — *Littérature et voyage*, '33. — *Histoire littéraire de la France avant le XIIe siècle*, '40. — *Histoire littéraire de la France sous Charlemagne et durant les Xe–XIe siècles*, '41. — *Histoire de la littérature française au moyen âge, comparée aux littératures étrangères*, '41. — *Ballanche*, 3 vols., '48. — *La Grèce, Rome et Dante*, '48. — *Littérature, voyages et poésies*, 2 vols., '50. — *Promenade en Amérique ; Etats-Unis, Cuba, Méxique*, 2 vols., '55. — *L'histoire romaine à Rome*, 4 vols., '65. — *La science et les lettres en Orient*, '65. — *Mélanges d'histoire littéraire et de littérature*, 2 vols., '67, etc.

See Sainte-Beuve, *Portraits littéraires*, II, 1844; *Portraits contemporains*, III, '46; *Nouveaux Lundis*, XIII, '68.

Angellier (Auguste), 1847–1911. Poet and critic.

Robert Burns, 2 vols., 1893, etc.

Aubertin (Charles), 1825–1908.

L'esprit public au XVIIIe siècle (1715–'89), 1873. — *Les origines de la langue et de la poésie françaises*, '74. — *Histoire de la littérature et de la langue françaises*, '76–'78. — *L'éloquence politique et parlementaire en France avant 1789*, '82. — *Origines et formation de la langue et de la métrique françaises*, '82. — *Les chroniqueurs fr. au moyen âge*, '96. — *La versification fr. et ses nouveaux théoriciens*, '98, etc.

Balzac (Honoré de), 1799–1850. — Balzac's chief attempts as a literary critic appeared in *La Revue parisienne*, 1840.

Lettre aux écrivains fr. du XIXe siècle, 1834. — *Etudes critiques publiées dans la Chronique de Paris*, '36. — *Code littéraire*, '56. — *Fragments inédits de la Revue parisienne*, '70.

See *Balzac critique littéraire*, in *Au temps du romantisme*, par A. Séché et Jules Bertaut, 1909.

Barante (Prosper-Brugière de), 1782–1866. Statesman, historian, etc. — Translates Schiller, 1821.

Tableau de la litt. fr. au XVIIIe siècle, 1809. — *Mélanges historiques et littéraires*, 3 vols., '35. — *Etudes de litt. et d'histoire*, '58. — *Souvenirs du baron de Barante*, 8 vols., '90–1901, etc.

See A. Michiels, *Histoire des idées littéraires*, 1842. — Sainte-Beuve, *Portraits contemporains*, IV, '43. — Brandes, *The Emigrant Literature*, '82. — A. France, *La vie littéraire*, IV, '92.

Barbey D'Aurevilly (Jules-Amédée), 1808–1889. Poet, novelist, etc. — A type of the Byronic dandy who survived into the second half of the nineteenth century; a master of flamboyant paradox. His tone of truculent opposition to the main tendencies of his time is very amusing if the reader does not get too much of it.

Les Misérables de V. Hugo, 1862. — *Les 40 médaillons de l'Académie*, '63. — — *Goethe et Diderot*, '80. — *Le théâtre contemporain*, 3 vols., '87–'92. — *Pensées détachées*, '88. — *Polémiques d'hier*, '89. — Most of Barbey's critical articles have been collected under the general title *Les Œuvres et les Hommes du XIXe siècle*, divided into three series, 17 vols., 1861–'99 (vol. IX missing). — *Critiques diverses*, 1910, etc.

See Bourget, *Etudes et portraits*, 1889. — Tissot, *Evolutions de la critique*, '90. — France, *La vie littéraire*, III, '91. — Lemaître, *Les contemporains*, IV, '93. — L. Gautier, *Portraits du XIXe siècle*, '94. — Levallois, *Mémoires d'un critique*, '96. — Doumic, *Hommes et idées*, 1903. — E. Grelé, *J. B. d'Aurevilly : sa vie et son œuvre*, '04. — E. Seillière, *Barbey d'Aurevilly*, '10.

Bardoux (Agénor), 1829–1897.

Notice sur la vie et les ouvrages d'Andrieux, 1868. — *Etudes sur la fin du XVIIIe siècle, Comtesse de Beaumont*, '84. — *Etudes sociales et littéraires, Madame de Custine*, '88. — *Etudes d'un autre temps*, '89. — *Chateaubriand*, '93. — *Guizot*, '94, etc.

Barine (Arvède), Mme. Vincens, 1840–1908.

Portraits de femmes, 1887. — *Essais et fantaisies*, 88. — *Princesses et grandes dames*, '90. — *Bernardin de St.-Pierre*, '91. — *Alfred de Musset*, '93. — *Bourgeois et gens de peu*, '94. — *Névrosés*, '98. — *Louis XIV et la Grande Mademoiselle*, 1905, etc.

Baudelaire (Charles), 1821–1867.

Most of B.'s critical writing will be found in Vol. II (*Curiosités esthétiques*) and in Vol. III (*L'Art romantique*) in the 7-volume édition Lemerre of 1870.

Beaunier (André), 1869. Novelist, journalist, critic.
La poésie nouvelle, 1902. —*Eloges*, '09, etc.

Bédier (Joseph), 1864. Professor at the Collège de France.
Le roman de Tristan et d'Yseult, traduit et restauré par J. Bédier, 1900. — *Etudes critiques*, '03. —*Les légendes épiques*, 2 vols., '08 (and numerous other studies on the Middle Ages).

Bersot (Ernest), 1816–1880. Philosopher and moralist.
La philosophie de Voltaire, 1848. —*Etudes sur la philosophie du XVIIIe siècle*, '52. —*Etudes sur le XVIIIe siècle*, 2 vols., '55. —*Litt. et morale*, '61. —*Questions actuelles*, '62.

Blaze de Bury (Henri), 1813–1888. Literary and musical critic, historian, etc. Translator of *Faust* and other works of Goethe.
Les écrivains et poètes modernes de l'Allemagne, 2 vols., 1846. —*Les écrivains modernes de l'Allemagne*, '68. — *Tableaux romantiques de litt. et d'art*, '78. — *A. Dumas, sa vie, son temps, son œuvre*, '85. — *Mes études et mes souvenirs*, '85. — *Goethe et Beethoven*, '92, etc.

Biré (Edmond), 1829–1907. A reactionary critic who investigated the details of Hugo's life with a somewhat malignant accuracy.
V. Hugo et la Restauration, 1869. — *V. Hugo avant 1830*, '83. — *V. de Laprade, sa vie et ses œuvres*, '86. — *Portraits littéraires*, '88. — *Causeries littéraires*, '89. — *V. Hugo après 1830*, 2 vols., '91. — *Portraits historiques et littéraires*, '92. — *V. Hugo après 1852. L'exil, les dernières années et la mort du poète*, '94. —*Histoire et litt.*, '95. —*Honoré de Balzac*, '97. —*Causeries historiques*, '97. —*Nouvelles causeries littéraires*, '97. — *Dernières causeries littéraires et historiques*, '98. —*Etudes d'histoire et de litt.*, 1900. —*La presse royaliste de 1830 à 1852*, '01. —*Les dernières années de Chateaubriand*, '02. —*Biographies contemporaines*, '05. — *Chateaubriand, V. Hugo, H. de Balzac*, '07. —*Ecrivains et soldats*, 2 vols., '07. — *Mes souvenirs*, '08. —*Romans et romanciers contemporains*, '08, etc.

Boissier (Gaston), 1823–1908. Professor of Latin Literature at the Collège de France; member of the Academy from 1876. Possibly the most gifted literary critic among the Latinists of the nineteenth century.
Le poète Attius, 1857.—*Etude sur la vie et les ouvrages de M. T. Varron*, '61.—*Recherches sur la manière dont furent recueillies les lettres de Cicéron*, '63. — *Cicéron et ses amis*, '65. —*La religion romaine d'Auguste aux Antonins*, 2 vols., '74. —*L'opposition sous les Césars*, '75. — *Discours de réception*, '77. — *Promenades archéologiques; Rome et Pompée*, '80. — *Le musée de St.-Germain*, '82. — *Nouvelles promenades archéologiques; Horace et Virgile*, '86. —*Mme. de Sévigné*, '87. —*La fin du paganisme*, 2 vols., '91. — *Saint-Simon*, '92. —*L'Afrique romaine*, '93.—*Tacite*, 1903. —*L'Académie fr. sous l'ancien régime*, '09, etc.

Bordeaux (Henry), 1870. Novelist and critic.
Villiers de l'Isle Adam, 1891. —*Edouard Rod*, '93. —*Teodor de Wyzewa*, '94. —*La vie et l'art, Ames modernes*, '94. —*La vie et l'art, Sentiments et idées de ce temps*, '97. —*Les écrivains et les mœurs*, (*'97–1900*), 1900. — *Portraits de femmes et d'enfants*, 1900. — *Les écrivains et les mœurs*, (*1900–'02*), '02. — *Pèlerinages littéraires*, '06, etc.

Bourget (Paul), 1852. At least as good a critic as he is novelist. The *Essais de psychologie contemporaine* in particular are a remarkable record of the spiritual maladies of the second half of the nineteenth century by one who has suffered from most of them.

Ernest Renan, 1883. —*Essais de psychologie contemporaine*, '83. — *Profils perdus*, '84. — *Nouveaux essais de psychologie contemporaine*, '85. —*Etudes et portraits*, 2 vols., '88, 3e vol., 1906. — *Discours de réception*, '95. —*Pages de critique et de doctrine*, '12.

Brisson (Adolphe), 1863. Editor of *Les Annales*.
Portraits intimes, 5 vols., 1894–1901. —*La comédie littéraire*, '95. — *Pointes sèches*, '98. — *Nos humoristes*, 1900. —*L'envers de la gloire*, 1905, etc.

Broglie (le duc Albert de), 1821–1901.
Etudes morales et littéraires, 1853. — *Nouvelles études de litt. et de morale*, '68. — *Malherbe*, '97. — *Voltaire avant et pendant la guerre de Sept Ans*, '98, etc.

Brunetière (Ferdinand), 1849—1906. — Unsuccessful in examination for Normal School, 1870. — Teaches at Pension Lelarge. — Begins to write for *Revue des Deux Mondes*, '75. — Maître de conférences at Normal School, '86. — Lectures at Odéon, '91, etc. — Elected to Academy, '93. — Editor-in-chief of *Revue des Deux Mondes*, '93. — Visits the Vatican, '94. — Lectures in the United States, '97. — Excites anger of the "intellectuels" by his attitude in the Dreyfus affair. — Announces his conversion to Catholicism, 1900. — Loses his position at Normal School and fails to be elected Deschanel's successor at Collège de France.

Etudes critiques sur l'histoire de la litt. fr., 8 vols., 1880–1907. —*Le roman naturaliste*, '83. — *Histoire et litt.*, 3 vols., '84–'86. —*Questions de critique*, '89. —*L' évolution des genres dans l'histoire de la litt.*, I: *Evolution de la critique depuis la Renaissance jusqu'à nos jours*, '90. —*Nouvelles questions de critique*, '90. —*Les époques du théâtre fr.* (*1636–1850*), '92. —*Essais sur la litt. contemporaine*, '92. — *Discours de réception*, '94. —*L'évolution de la poésie lyrique en France au XIXe siècle*, 2 vols., '94. —*Education et instruction*, '95. —*La science et la religion*, '95. — *Nouveaux essais sur la litt. contemporaine*,' 95. — *L'idée de patrie*, '96. —*La moralité de la doctrine évolutive*, '96. —*La Renaissance de l'idéalisme*, '96. — *Manuel de l'histoire de la litt. fr.*, '97. — *Après le procès. Réponse à quelques "Intellectuels,"* '98. —*L'art et la morale*, '98. —*Les ennemis de l'âme fr.* '99. —*Le génie latin*, '99. —*La nation et l'armée*, '99. — *Discours de combat*, 3 vols., 1900–'07. —*La liberté de l'enseignement*, '00.— *Discours académiques*, '01. — *Les raisons actuelles de croire*, '01. —*Les motifs d'espérer*, '02. — *V. Hugo. Leçons* (prepared, under B.'s editorship, by students of Normal School), '02. —*Cinq lettres sur E. Renan*, '03. —*L'action sociale du Christianisme*, '04. — *Sur les chemins de la croyance*, '04. — *Histoire de la litt. fr. classique* (*1515–1830*), vol. I (XVIe siècle), '05; vol. II (XVIIe siècle), '12. — *Variétés littéraires*, '05. — *H. de Balzac*, '06. —*Saint Vincent de Lérins*, '06. — *Questions actuelles*, '07. —*Etudes sur le XVIIIe siècle*, '11. —*Lettres de combat*, '12.

See J. Lemaître, *Les Contemporains*, I, '85; VI, '96. —Faguet, *Notes sur le théâtre contemporain*, II, '89; *Propos littéraires*, II, '04. — Doumic, *Ecrivains d'aujourd'hui*, '94. —Ed. Dowden, *New Studies in Literature*, '95. —A. Brisson, *Portraits intimes*, II, '96. — Albalat, *L'art d'écrire*, '96. —A. Darlu, *M. Brunetière et l'individualisme*, '98. — Pellissier, *Etudes de litt. et de morale*, '05. — V. Giraud, *F. Brunetière*, '07. —G. Fonsegrive, *Ferdinand Brunetière*, '08. — Faguet, *Ferdinand Brunetière*, '11.

Caro (Edme-Marie), 1826–1887. Philosopher, etc. He enjoyed a vogue in fashionable circles that reacted injuriously on his reputation. He is the original of Bellac in Pailleron's *Le Monde où l'on s'ennuie.* He is nevertheless a critic of real distinction.

La philosophie de Goethe, 1866. —*Le pessimisme au XIXe siècle,* '78. —*La fin du XVIIIe siècle,* 2 vols., '80. —*George Sand,* '88. — *Mélanges et portraits,* 2 vols., '88. — *Poètes et romanciers,* '88. — *Variétés littéraires,* '89, etc.

See Brunetière, *Questions de critiques,* 1888.

Cestre (Charles), 1871. Professor at the University of Bordeaux.

La Révolution fr. et les poètes anglais, 1906. —*Bernard Shaw,* '12, etc.

Chasles (V.- E.-Philarète), 1798–1873. Spent seven years as a young man in England. — One of the editors of the *Journal des Débats.* — Professor at the Collège de France from 1847.

Caractères et paysages, 1833. —*Le XVIIIe siècle en Angleterre,* '46. —*Etudes sur l'Espagne et sur les influences de la litt. espagnole en France et en Italie,* '47. — *Etudes sur le XVIe siècle en France,* '48. —*Etudes sur les hommes et les mœurs au XIXe siècle,* '50. —*Etudes sur la litt. et les mœurs en Angleterre au XIXe siècle,* '50. —*Etudes sur la litt. et les mœurs des Anglo-Américains au XIXe siècle,* '51. —*Etudes sur W. Shakspeare,* '52. —*Etude sur l'Allemagne ancienne et moderne,* '54. — *Voyages d'un critique à travers la vie et les livres,* 2 séries, '65–'68. —*Etudes contemporaines,* '66. —*Portraits contemporains,* '67. —*Questions du temps et problèmes d'autrefois,* '67. — *De l'Académie fr., de ses destinées et de son passé,* '68. —*Encore sur les contemporains, leurs œuvres et leurs mœurs,* '69. — *L'Arétin, vie et écrits,* '73. —*L'antiquité,* '75. —*La psychologie sociale des nouveaux peuples,* '75. —*Le moyen âge,* '76. — *Mémoires,* 2 vols., '76–'77. —*La France, l'Espagne et l'Italie au XVIIe siècle,* '77. —*L'Angleterre au XVIe siècle,* '79, etc.

Chateaubriand (François-René, vicomte de), 1768–1848. His literary opinions will be found scattered through the *Génie du Christianisme,* 1802 (originally had as subtitle *Les Beautés de la religion chrétienne*); in his *Itinéraire,* '11; in the essay *Sur la litt. anglaise,* '36; in the *Mémoires d'outre-tombe,* '49–'50, and the volume of his collected works known as *Mélanges littéraires;* finally in his *correspondance* now in course of publication (Vol. I, 1912).

See Sainte-Beuve, *Chateaubriand et son groupe littéraire,* 2 vols., 1860. — Scherer, *Etudes,* I, '63. — Brandes, *The Emigrant Literature,* '82. — Faguet, *Etudes sur le XIXe siècle.* — Brunetière, *L'évolution de la critique,* '90. — Vogüé, *Heures d'histoire,* '93. — Biré, *Etudes et portraits,* '94. — Doumic, *Etudes sur la litt. fr.,* II, '98.

Chénier (Marie-Joseph), 1764–1811.

Présentation à S. M. l'Empereur et roi du rapport historique sur l'état et les progrès de la litt., 1808. — *Tableau historique de l'état et des progrès de la litt. depuis 1789,* '16. —*Fragments du cours de litt. fait à l'Athénée de Paris en 1806–'07,* '18.

See A. Michiels, *Histoire des idées littéraires,* 1842.

Cherbuliez (Victor), 1829–1899. Novelist and critic.

A propos d'un cheval, ou Un cheval de Phidias, 1860. —*Etudes de litt. et d'art,* '73. — *Hommes et choses d'Allemagne,* '77. — *Hommes et choses du temps présent,* '83. — *Discours de réception,* '88. — *Profils étrangers,* '89. —*L'art et la nature,* '92. —*L'idéal romanesque en France de 1610 à 1816,* 1912, etc.

See Brunetière, *Discours académiques,* '01. — Faguet, *Propos littéraires,* I, '02.

Chuquet (Arthur), 1853. Professor at the Collège de France; editor of *Revue critique,* etc.

J.-J. Rousseau, 1893. — *Etudes de litt. allemande*, 2 vols., 1900–'02. — *Stendhal-Beyle*, '02. — *Litt. allemande*, '09, etc.

Cousin (Victor), 1792–1867. Philosopher and historian. — Professor at the Sorbonne. — Course discontinued by the Government, 1820. — Lectures again with great success in '28. — Engages in politics during July Monarchy. — Minister of Public Instruction in '40, etc.

Des pensées de Pascal, 1842 (*Etudes sur Pascal, 5ième édition, revues et augmentées*, '57). — *Fragments littéraires*, '43. — *Jacqueline Pascal*, '44. — *Mme. de Longueville pendant la Fronde, La Jeunesse de Mme. de Longueville*, 2 vols., '53. — *Mme. de Sablé*, '54. — *Mme. de Hautefort, La duchesse de Chevreuse*, 2 vols., '56. — *Fragments et souvenirs littéraires*, '57. — *La société fr. pendant le XVIIe siècle*, 2 vols., '58, etc.

See Sainte-Beuve, *Portraits littéraires*, III, 1844. — Cuvillier-Fleury, *Etudes historiques et littéraires*, II, '54. — Taine, *Les philosophes fr. au XIXe siècle*, '57. — Renan, *Essais de morale et de critique*, '59. — Charles Secrétan, *La philosophie de V. Cousin*, '68. — Scherer, *Etudes critiques sur la litt. contemporaine*, IV, '73. — Janet, *V. Cousin et son œuvre*, '85. — Caro, *Philosophie et philosophes*, '88. — Barthélemy St.-Hilaire, *M. V. Cousin et sa correspondance*, 3 vols., '95. — Faguet, *Politiques et moralistes au XIXe siècle*, II, '98.

Croiset (Alfred), 1845. — Professor of Greek at the Sorbonne.

Xénophon, son caractère et son talent, 1873. — *La Poésie de Pindare et les lois du lyrisme grec*, '80. — *Hist. de la litt. grecque* (in collaboration with his brother Maurice Croiset), 5 vols., '87–'99. — *Aristophane et les partis à Athènes*, '07, etc.

Cuvillier-Fleury (Alfred-Auguste), 1802–1887. Literary critic of the *Journal des Débats* from 1834. — Member of Academy from '66. — A critic of conservative taste. What he objected to in the romanticists was "le matérialisme du style."

Mélanges de critique et d'histoire, 11 vols., 1852–'65. — *Etudes historiques et littéraires*, 2 vols., '54. — *Nouvelles études historiques et littéraires*, '55. — *Dernières études historiques et littéraires*, 2 vols., '59. — *Historiens, poètes et romanciers*, 2 vols., '63. — *Etudes et portraits*, 2 vols., '65–'68. — *Posthumes et revenants*, '78. — *Journal intime*, 1900.

See Merlet, *Portraits d'hier et d'aujourd'hui*, '65. — A. France, *La vie littéraire*, I, '88.

Daunou (Pierre-Claude-François), 1761–1840. Historian, etc.

De l'influence de Boileau sur la litt. fr., 1787. — *Discours sur l'état des lettres au XIIIe siècle*, 1814. — Continues *Histoire littéraire de la France* and contributes many articles on writers of 12th and 13th centuries, etc.

Deschamps (Gaston), 1861.

La vie et les livres, 6 vols., 1894–1904. — *Marivaux*, '97, etc.

Deschanel (Emile), 1819–1904. The paradox on the "romanticism of the classics" that Deschanel maintained through several volumes does not seem of much significance for literary criticism.

Physiologie des écrivains et des artistes, ou essai de critique naturelle, 1864. — *Etudes sur Aristophane*, '67. — *A bâtons rompus, variétés morales et littéraires*, '68. — *Almanach des conférences et de la litt.*, '70. — *Benjamin Franklin*, '82. — *Le romantisme des classiques*, 5 vols., '82–'86. — *Lamartine*, 2 vols., '93. — *Les déformations de la langue fr.*, '98, etc.

See Sainte-Beuve, *Nouveaux lundis*, IX, '64. — Lemaître, *Les contemporains*, VII, '99. — G. Deschamps, *La vie et les livres*, V, 1900.

Desjardins (Paul), 1859.
La méthode des classiques fr., 1904.

Doudan (Ximénès), 1800–1872. Preceptor of Louis-Alphonse de Rocca, son of Mme. de Staël by her second marriage; later preceptor of Paul and Albert de Broglie. — Held a position in the Government under the duc de Broglie and spent the rest of his life in his household. — Doudan's letters to various friends, along with a few articles he had contributed to the *Revue française*, were published in 1876–'77, under the title of *Mélanges et Lettres* (4 vols.), with introductory notices by M. d'Haussonville, Silvestre de Sacy, and Cuvillier-Fleury. — Doudan is a type of the distinguished valetudinarian. He shows a delicacy and penetration in many of his literary judgments that remind one of Joubert.

Doumic (René), 1860. A regular contributor to the *Revue des Deux Mondes*. — Member of Academy from 1909.— Very conservative in his point of view. His special note may perhaps be best defined as a somewhat caustic good sense.
Eléments d'histoire littéraire, 1888. — *Portraits d'écrivains*, '92. — *Notice sur les écrivains maritimes et militaires*, '92. — *De Scribe à Ibsen*, '93. —*Etudes littéraires sur les auteurs fr. prescrits pour l'examen du brevet supérieur*, '93. — *Ecrivains d'aujourd'hui*, '94. —*La vie et les mœurs au jour le jour*, '95. —*Les jeunes*, '95. —*Essais sur le théâtre contemporain*, '96. —*Etudes sur la litt. fr.*, 6 vols., '96–1909. —*Histoire de la litt. fr.*, '00. —*Hommes et idées du XIXe siècle*, '03. —*Lettres d'Elvire à Lamartine*, '05. —*Le théâtre nouveau*, '08. —*George Sand*, '09. —*Lamartine*, '12, etc.

Du Camp (Maxime), 1822–1894. Novelist, traveller, soldier (one of Garibaldi's "Thousand"), etc.; intimate of Flaubert. — Member of Academy from 1880.
Souvenirs littéraires, 2 vols., 1882–'83. — *Théophile Gautier*, '90, etc.

Dumas fils (Alexandre), 1824–1895.
Discours de réception, 1875. —*Les préfaces*, '77. — *Réponse à M. Leconte de Lisle, successeur de V. Hugo*, '87.

Dupuy (Ernest), 1849.
Les grands maîtres de la litt. russe au XIXe siècle, 1885. — *Victor Hugo*, '86. — *Victor Hugo, son œuvre poétique*, '87. —*Bernard Palissy*, '94. — *Paradoxe sur le comédien de Diderot*, 1902, etc.

Ernest-Charles (Jean), 1875. Editor, literary and dramatic critic.
La litt. fr. d'aujourd'hui, 1902. —*Les Samedis littéraires*, 5 vols., '03–'07. — *La carrière de Maurice Barrès*, '07, etc.

Faguet (Emile), 1847. Professor of French Poetry at the Sorbonne from 1897; member of Academy from 1900. — The most prominent French critic of ideas now living. As a literary critic, he seems to me very inferior to M. Lemaître. His best and most characteristic work is probably found in his *Politiques et moralistes*. He shows here and elsewhere a brilliancy and intellectual ubiquity that is not sufficiently controlled by any vigorous synthesis of his own. Recently he has been pouring out volumes at a rate that suggests a certain intellectual incontinence.
La tragédie fr. au XVIe siècle, 1883. —*Les grands maîtres au XVIIe siècle*, '85. — *Notices littéraires sur les auteurs fr.*, '85. —*La Fontaine*, '85. — *Corneille*, '85. — *Recueil de textes des auteurs fr.*, '85. —*Etudes littéraires du XIXe siècle*, '87. — *Notes sur le théâtre contemporain*, 7 vols., '89–'95. —*Etudes littéraires*

du XVIIe siècle, '90. — *Etudes littéraires du XVIe siècle*, '93. — *Politiques et moralistes du XIXe siècle*, 3 vols., '91–'99. — *Voltaire*, '94. — *Cours de poésie fr. à l' Université de Paris*, '97. — *Drame ancien, drame moderne*, '98. — *Flaubert*, '99. — *Question politique*, '99. — *Histoire de la litt. fr.*, 2 vols., 1900. — *Problèmes politiques du temps présent*, '01. — *André Chénier*, '02. — *Le libéralisme*, '02. — *La politique comparée de Montesquieu, Rousseau et Voltaire*, '02. — *Propos littéraires*, I, '02; II, '04; III, '05; IV, '08; V, '09. — *Propos de théâtre*, I, '03; II, '05; III, IV, '06; V, '10. — *Zola*, '03.— *En lisant Nietzsche*, '04. — *Simplification simple de l'orthographe*, '05. — *Amours de gens de lettres*,' 06. —*L'anticléricalisme*, 06. — *Le socialisme en 1907*, '07. —*Le Pacifisme*, '08. —*Discussions politiques*, '09. —*Les dix commandements*, I, *De l' amour*. II, *De l'amitié*, 2 vols. '09. —*La démission de la morale*, '10. — *Madame de Sévigné*, '10. — *Le culte de l'incompétence*, 2 vols., '10. — *Vie de Rousseau*, '11. —*Ferdinand Brunetière*, '11. —*En lisant les beaux vieux livres*, '11. —*Les dix commandements : de la profession*, '11. —*Les dix commandements: de Dieu*, '11.—*Et l'horreur des responsabilités* (*suite au Culte de l'incompétence*), '11. —*Les préjugés nécessaires*, '11. —*Les amies de Rousseau*, '12. — *Rousseau contre Molière*, '12. — *Ce que disent les livres*, '12.

See M. Duval, *E. Faguet, le critique, le moraliste, le sociologue*, '11.

Fauriel (Claude-Charles), 1772-1844. Private secretary to Napoleon's police agent, Fouché, to 1802. — Professor at the Sorbonne from '30. — Member of Académie des Inscriptions from '36.

La Parthéneide, poème de J. Baggesen traduit de l'allemand par C. F. (with important preliminary discourse), 1810. —*Le comte de Carmagnola* et *Adelghis*, tragédies d'Alexandre Manzoni, traduites de l'italien par C. F.; *suivie d'un article de Goethe et de divers morceaux sur la théorie de l'art dramatique*, '23. — *Chants populaires de la Grèce moderne*, 2 vols., '24–'25. — *Histoire de la Gaule méridionale sous la domination des conquérants germains*, 4 vols., '36. — *Histoire de la croisade contre les hérétiques albigeois* (traduite du provençal), '37. — *Histoire de la poésie provençale*, 3 vols., '47. — *Dante et les origines de la langue et de la litt. italienne*, 2 vols., '54 (this work as well as the preceding was published from notes taken at his courses by J. Mohl). — *Les derniers jours du Consulat*, '85. — *Correspondance de Fauriel et Mary Clarke*, 1911.

See Sainte-Beuve, *Portraits contemporains*, IV, 1845. — A. Ozanam, *Mélanges*, II, '59. — J. B. Galley, *Claude Fauriel*, 1909 (for very full list of publications of Fauriel and works on him see 488 ff).

Féletz (Charles-Marie Dorimont, abbé de), 1767–1850. An editor of the *Journal des Débats* from 1801; member of Academy from 1827, etc. He is at once keen and amiable in his criticism.

Mélanges de philosophie, d'histoire, et de litt., 4 vols., 1828. — *Jugements historiques et littéraires sur quelques écrivains et sur quelques écrits du temps*, '40.

See Sainte-Beuve, *Causeries du lundi*, I, '50. — Villemain, *Souvenirs contemporains d'histoire et de litt.*, I, 1853.

Filon (Augustin), 1841.

Guy Patin, sa vie, sa correspondance, 1862. — *Etudes sur les lettres portugaises* (*1669*), '63. — *Histoire de la litt. anglaise*, '83. — *Profils anglais*, '93. — *Mérimée et ses amis*, '94. — *Le théâtre anglais. Hier, aujourd'hui, demain*, '96. — *De Dumas à Rostand*, '98. — *Mérimée*, '98. —*La caricature en Angleterre*, 1902 etc.

Flat (Paul), 1865. Novelist, art critic, etc.; editor of *Revue Bleue*.

Essais sur Balzac, 1893. — *Seconds essais sur Balzac*, '94. — *Nos femmes de lettres*, 1908, etc.

Fontanes (le comte Louis de), 1759–1821. Poet and critic. — Became acquainted with Chateaubriand when both were exiles in London. — Grand Master of the University from 1808.

Extraits critiques du Génie du Christianisme, 1802. — *Œuvres,* 2 vols., avec notices de Chateaubriand et de Sainte-Beuve, '39.

See Sainte-Beuve, *Chateaubriand et son groupe littéraire,* 1860.

France (Anatole), 1844. If M. France's criticism is often that of a creator, his creative writing (novels, etc.), on the other hand, is very much permeated by criticism.

Alfred de Vigny, 1868. — *B. de Saint-Pierre et Marie Miesnik,* '75. — *Lucile de Chateaubriand,* '79. — *La vie littéraire,* 4 vols., '88–'94. — *L'Elvire de Lamartine,* '93. — *Discours de réception,* '97. — *Discours prononcé à l'inauguration de la statue d'E. Renan à Tréguier,* 1903. — *Funérailles d'E. Zola,* '03, etc.

For controversy with Brunetière see prefaces to the four volumes of his *Vie littéraire;* also Brunetière, *Essais sur la littérature contemporaine* (*La Critique impressioniste*), '91, etc.

Gautier (Théophile), 1811–1872. Much of Gautier's critical writing was done as hack work for various newspapers (in his own phrase he turned the mill of the *feuilleton*), especially (from 1845), for the *Moniteur* and *Journal Officiel.* His criticism is remarkable for its extreme appreciativeness. He is a "creative" critic in the sense that is given to that phrase by certain neo-romanticists. A classicist would say that he confuses the *genres.*

Les Jeune-France, 1833. — Préface de *Mlle. de Maupin,* '35. — *Les grotesques,* 2 vols., '44. — *Zigzags,* '45. — *Le Salon de 1847,* '47. — *L'art moderne,* '52. — *Caprices et Zigzags,* '52. — *Histoire de l'art dramatique en France depuis 25 ans,* 6 vols., '58–'59. — *H. de Balzac,* '59. — *Trésors d'art de la Russie ancienne et moderne,* '61–'63. — *Les dieux et les demi-dieux de la peinture,* '63. — *Histoire du romantisme,* '74. — *Portraits contemporains,* '74. — *Portraits et souvenirs,* '75. — *Fusains et eaux-fortes,* '80. — *Souvenirs de théâtre, d'art et de critique,* '83.

See Sainte-Beuve, *Portraits contemporains,* II, 1838; *Premiers lundis,* II, '38. — Baudelaire, *Th. Gautier; Notice littéraire précédée d'une lettre de V. Hugo,* '59. — Brandes, *The Romantic School in France,* '82. — Montégut, *Nos morts contemporains,* II, '84. — Faguet, *Etudes sur le XIXe siècle,* '87.

Gazier (Augustin), 1844. Historian and critic. — Chiefly interested in Port-Royal.

Petite histoire de la litt. fr. depuis la Renaissance, 1891. — *Mélanges de litt. et d'histoire,* 1904. — *Port-Royal-des-Champs,* '05. — *Une suite à l'histoire de Port-Royal,* '06. — *Abrégé de l'histoire de Port-Royal,* '09. — *Port-Royal au XVIIe siècle,* '09, etc.

Gebhart (Emile), 1839–1908. Professor of Foreign Literature at the Sorbonne; Member of Academy, etc.

Histoire du sentiment poétique de la nature dans l'antiquité grecque et romaine, 1860. — *Praxitèle, essai sur l'histoire de l'art et du génie grecs,* '64. — *De l'Italie; essais de critique et d'histoire,* '76. — *Rabelais, la Renaissance et la Réforme,* '77. — *Les origines de la Renaissance en Italie,* '79. — *Introduction à l'histoire du sentiment religieux en Italie depuis la fin du XIIe siècle au Concile de Trente,* '84. — *Etudes méridionales; la Renaissance italienne, et la philosophie de l'histoire,* '87. — *L'Italie mystique,* '90. — *Autour d'une tiare* (1075–'85), '93. — *Rabelais,* '95. — *Le baccalauréat et les études classiques,* '99. — *Conteurs Florentins du moyen âge,* '01. — *Sandro Botticelli,* '07. — *Michel Ange,* '08, etc.

Geoffroy (Julien-Louis), 1743–1814. Pupil of Jesuits and professor at the Collège Louis-le-Grand. Collaborates with Fréron on *Année littéraire.* — In hiding during Revolution. — Creates literary *feuilleton* as dramatic critic of *Journal des Débats*, 1800–'14.

Discours sur la critique, 1779. — *Cours de litt. dramatique*, 6 vols., 1819–'20. — *Manuel dramatique*, '22, etc.

See Sainte-Beuve, *Causeries du lundi*, I, 1850. — Lemaître, *Geoffroy*, in *Livre du centenaire du Journal des Débats*, '89. — Des Granges, *Geoffroy et la littérature dramatique sous le consulat et l'empire*, '97.

Géruzez (Eugène-Nicolas), 1799–1865.

Histoire de l'éloquence politique et religieux, 2 vols., 1837–'38. — *Essais de litt. fr.*, 2 vols., '39. — *Essais d'histoire littéraire*, '39.— *Cours de litt. conforme au plan d'études des lycées*, '41. — *Nouveaux essais d'histoire littéraire*, '45. — *Etudes littéraires sur les ouvrages fr. prescrits pour les examens des baccalauréats ès lettres et ès science*, '49. — *Histoire de la litt. fr. du moyen âge aux temps modernes*, '52. — *Histoire de la litt. fr. pendant la Révolution (1789–1800)*, '59. — *Histoire de la litt. fr.*, 2 vols., '61. — *Histoire abrégée de la litt. fr.*, '62. — *Mélanges et pensées*, '66.

Gidel (Antoine-Charles), 1827–1899.

Etude sur la litt. grecque moderne, 1866. — *Les Français au XVIIe siècle*, '73. — *Histoire de la litt. fr.*, 4 vols., '74–'88. — *L'art d'écrire*, '78. — *Dictionnaire-Manuel illustré des écrivains et des litt.* (avec F. Loliée), '97.

Giraud (Victor), 1868.

Pascal, l'homme, l'œuvre, l'influence, 1898. — *Taine et le pessimisme*, '98. — *La philosophie de Taine*, '99. — *Essai sur Taine*, 1900. — *Taine (bibliographie)*, '02. — *Histoire des variations d'une page de Chateaubriand*, '03. — *La philosophie religieuse de Pascal et la pensée contemporaine*, '03. — *Chateaubriand. Etudes littéraires* '04. — *Anticléricalisme et catholicisme*, '06. — *Livres et questions d'aujourd'hui*, '06. — *Ferdinand Brunetière*, '07. — *Les Idées morales d'Horace*, '07. — *Les Maîtres de l'heure*, '11. — *Nouvelles études sur Chateaubriand*,'12, etc.

Les de Goncourt frères. Jules, 1830–1870. **Edmond**, 1822–1896. Novelists, etc.

Histoire de la société fr. pendant le Directoire, 1855. — *L'art au XVIIIe siècle*, 3 vols., '56–'65. — *Portraits intimes du XVIIIe siècle*, 2 vols., '57–'58. — *Le journal des Goncourt*, 7 vols., '87–'95. — *Préfaces et manifestes littéraires*, '88.

See Sainte-Beuve, *Nouveaux lundis*, IV, 1862; X, '66. — Bourget, *Nouveaux essais de psychologie contemporaine*, '85. — Lemaître, *Les Contemporains*, III, '88. — France, *La vie littéraire*, I, '88. — Doumic, *Portraits d'écrivains*, '92; *Etudes sur la litt. fr.*, II, '98.

Gourmont (Rémy de), 1860. Editor of *Mercure de France.* — Ultra-æsthetic in his point of view.

Le Latin mystique, 1892. — *La Poésie populaire*, '96. — *Esthétique de la langue fr.*, '99. — *La culture des idées*, '00. — *Le Problème du style*, '02. — *Promenades littéraires*, 3 vols., '05–'09. — *Dante, Béatrice et la poésie amoureuse*, '08, etc.

Gréard (Octave), 1828–1904. Exercised both by his writings and as an administrator an important influence on modern French education. — Member of Academy from 1886.

Précis de litt., 1875. — *Discours de réception*, '88. — *Edmond Scherer*, '90. — *Prévost-Paradol*, '94, etc.

Guizot (François-Pierre-Guillaume), 1787–1874. Historian, statesman, etc. — Begins lecturing at the Sorbonne, 1812. — Course suspended by Government in '22. — Begins lecturing again at same time as Cousin and Villemain in '28. — Appointed Minister of Interior by Louis-Philippe, '30. — Member of Academy from '36. — Virtually Premier from '40 to '48.

Shakespeare et son temps, 1852. — *Discours académiques*, '61. — *Mélanges biographiques et littéraires*, '68, etc.

See Sainte-Beuve, *Causeries du lundi*, I, 1850; *Nouveaux lundis*, I, '61; IX, '64. — Taine, *Essais de critique et d'histoire*, '58. — Scherer, *Etudes critiques sur la litt. contemporaine*, I, '63; IV, '73. — Faguet, *Politiques et moralistes au XIX*[e] *siècle*, '91.

Haussonville (le vicomte Othenin d'), 1843. — Member of Academy from 1888.

C.-A. Sainte-Beuve, sa vie et ses œuvres, 1875.— *Etudes biographiques et littéraires*, '79. — *Le salon de Mme. Necker*, 2 vols., '82. — *Prosper Mérimée*, '88. — *Mme. Ackermann, d'après des lettres et papiers inédits*, '92. — *Lacordaire*, '95. — *Souvenirs sur Mme. de Maintenon*, 3 vols., 1902–'05. — *A l'Académie française et autour de l'Académie*, '07, etc.

Hauvette (Henri), 1865. Professor of Italian at the Sorbonne.

Luigi Alamanni, 1903. — *Litt. italienne*, '06. — *Ghirlandaio*, '08. — *Dante*, '11, etc.

Hennequin (Emile), 1859–1888. Drowned while bathing in the Seine. The scientific theories of H., which attracted much attention a few years ago, are already beginning to seem pseudo-scientific. He has remarks of great penetration interspersed with remarks like the following: " Prédominance probable, dans l'organisme cérébral de Victor Hugo, . . . de la troisième circonvolution frontale."

La critique scientifique, 1888. — *Etudes de critique scientifique. Ecrivains francisés*, '89. — *Etudes de critique scientifique. Quelques écrivains fr.*, '90.

See Brunetière, *Questions de critique*, '88. — Tissot, *Les évolutions de la critique fr.*, '90. — Rod, *Nouvelles études sur le XIX*[e] *siècle*, '98.

Hugo (Victor), 1802–1885. His general outlook on life was uncritical or, one might say, anti-critical. For his literary opinions see various prefaces to *Odes et Ballades* (1822, '24, '26, '28, '53); also prefaces to his other volumes of verse (*Feuilles d'automne*, '34; *Chants du Crépuscule*, '35; *Les voix intérieures*, '37; *Les Rayons et les ombres*, '40; *Les Contemplations*, '56, etc.). His most important manifesto was his *Préface de Cromwell*, '27 (éd. M. Souriau, with very full introduction, '97). — See also prefaces to other plays (*Hernani*, '29; *Marion de Lorme*, '30; *Le Roi s'amuse*, '32; *Lucrèce Borgia*, '33; *Marie Tudor*, '33; *Angelo*, '35; *Ruy Blas*, 36; *Les Burgraves*, '43). — *Litt. et philosophie mêlées*, 2 vols., '34. — *William Shakespeare*, '64. — *Discours pour Voltaire*, '78, etc.

Janin (Jules), 1804–1874. Dramatic critic of *Journal des Débats* from 1830. Styled in his own day the " prince of critics." Expansive and superficial, a sort of bourgeois impressionist. He defined the *feuilleton* as " un petit cri de joie que nous arrache le spectacle du jour."

Histoire de la litt. dramatique, 6 vols., 1853–'58. — *Critiques, portraits et caractères contemporains*, '59. — *Variétés littéraires*, '59. — *Béranger et son temps*, 2 vols., '66. — *Œuvres diverses*, 12 vols., '76–'78. — *Œuvres de jeunesse*, 5 vols., '81–'83, etc.

See F. Pyat, *M. J. Chénier et le prince des critiques* (*J. Janin*), 1844. —

Planche, *Portraits littéraires*, '53. — Sainte-Beuve, *Causeries du lundi*, II, '50; V, '51. — B. d'Aurevilly, *Les œuvres et les hommes*, IV, '65. — Gautier, *Portraits contemporains*, '74.

Joubert (Joseph). Born at Montignac, 1754; died at Paris, 1824.— Student and professor in the Collège des Pères de la Doctrine Chrétienne (Toulouse). — Goes to Paris, 1778, and meets Diderot, La Harpe, etc. — Becomes intimate with Fontanes. — Elected Justice of Peace at Montignac, 1790. — Marriage, 1793. — Settles at Villeneuve-sur-Yonne. — Appointed "inspecteur et conseiller de l'Université," 1809.

Selection of *Pensées* published by Chateaubriand, 1838. — Enlarged edition published by nephew of Joubert, M. Paul de Raynal (*Pensées, Essais, Maximes et Correspondance*, 2 vols., 1842; 4e éd., augm., '64). — *Pensées de Joubert;* reproduction de l'édition originale. Introduction et notes par V. Giraud, 4e éd., 1911.

See Sainte-Beuve, *Portraits littéraires*, II, 1838; *Causeries du lundi*, I, '49. — Sacy, *Variétés littéraires*, I, '58. — Matthew Arnold, *Essays in Criticism*, '65. — P. de Raynal, *Les correspondants de Joubert (1785–1822)*, '83. — Lemaître, *Les contemporains*, VI, '96. — Pailhès, *Du Nouveau sur Joubert*, 1900.

Jusserand (Jules), 1855. French ambassador to United States from 1902.

Les Anglais au moyen âge. L'Epopée mystique de William Langland, 1893. — *Histoire littéraire du peuple anglais :* I, *Des origines à la Renaissance*, '94; II, *De la Renaissance à la guerre civile*, 1904. — *Histoire abrégée de la litt. anglaise*, '95. — *Shakespeare en France sous l'ancien régime*, '98, etc.

Lamartine (Alphonse), 1790–1869. Most of his literary criticism was written under pecuniary stress in his old age.

Des Destinées de la poésie, 1834. — *Cours familier de litt.*, 28 vols., '56–'69. — *Bossuet*, '64. — *Cicéron*, '64. — *Shakspeare et son œuvre*, '64. — *Balzac et son œuvre*, '65. — *Trois poètes italiens : Dante, Pétrarque, Le Tasse (extrait du cours de litt.)*, '92. — *Philosophie et litt.*, '94, etc.

Lanson (Gustave), 1857. Professor of French literature at the Sorbonne.

Principes de composition et de style, 1887. — *Nivelle de La Chaussée et la comédie larmoyante*, '88. — *Bossuet*, '90. — *Choix de lettres du XVIIe siècle*, '90. — *Conseils sur l'art d'écrire*, '90. — *Etudes pratiques de composition fr.*, '91. — *Boileau*, '92. — *Histoire de la litt. fr.*, '94. — *Hommes et livres*, '95. — *Corneille*, '95. — *L'université et la société moderne*, 1901. — *Voltaire*, '06. — *L'Art de la prose*, '08. — *Manuel bibliographique de la litt. fr.*, I (XVIe siècle), '09; II (XVIIe siècle), '10; III, (XVIIIe siècle), '11. — *Trois mois d'enseignement aux Etats-Unis*, '12, etc.

Laprade, Victor de, 1812–1883. Poet and critic. — Professor at University of Lyons. — Succeeds A. de Musset at Academy, '58.

Le génie littéraire de la France, 1848. — *Du sentiment de la nature dans la poésie d'Homère*, '48. — *Le sentiment de la nature avant le christianisme*, '66. — *Le sentiment de la nature chez les modernes*, '67. — *Essais de critique idéaliste*, '82. — *Histoire du sentiment de la nature*, '83.

Larroumet (Gustave), 1852–1904.

Marivaux, sa vie et ses œuvres, 1883. — *La Comédie de Molière. L'auteur et le Milieu*, '86. — *Salon de 1892*, '92. — *Notice sur le prince Napoléon Bonaparte*, '92. — *Etudes d'histoire et de critique dramatique*, '92. — *Etudes de litt. et d'art*, 4 vols., '93–'96. — *Meissonier*, '93. — *L'art et l'Etat en France*, '95. — *La maison de V. Hugo. Impressions de Guernesey*, '95. — *Petits portraits et notes d'art*, '97. —

La France en Orient, '98. — *Racine*, '98. — *Vers Athènes et Jérusalem. Journal de voyage en Grèce et en Syrie*, '98. — *Nouvelles études d'histoire et de critique dramatique*, '99. — *Derniers portraits*, 1904.

Lasserre (Pierre), 1867.
La crise chrétienne, 1891. — *Charles Maurras et la renaissance classique*, 1902. —*La morale de Nietzsche*, '02. —*Les idées de Nietzsche sur la musique*, '07. — *Le romantisme fr.*, '07. — *M. Croiset historien de la démocratic athénienne*, '09. —*La Doctrine officielle de l'Université*, '12, etc.

Leconte de Lisle, 1820–1894. His most important critical manifesto is the preface to his *Poèmes antiques*, 1852.

Lefranc (Abel), 1863. Professor at the Collège de France.
Les dernières poésies de Marguerite de Navarre, 1898 (and numerous other studies on the 16th century). —*La langue et la litt. fr. au Collège de France*, '04. — *Défense de Pascal*, 1907. —*Leçons sur Molière*, '04–'09. —*Etudes sur Maurice Guérin*, '08, etc.

Legouis (Emile), 1861. Professor of English literature at the Sorbonne.
Le général Michel Beaupuy (in collaboration with Georges Bussière), 1891. —*La jeunesse de William Wordsworth*, '96. —*Geoffrey Chaucer*, '11. — *Défense de la poésie française à l'usage des lecteurs anglais*, 1912, etc.

Lemaître (Jules), 1853.
La comédie après Molière et le théâtre de Dancourt, 1882. —*Quomodo Cornelius noster Aristotelis poeticam sit interpretatus*, '82. —*Les contemporains*, 7 vols., '85–'99. — *Impressions de théâtre*, 10 vols., '88–'98. — *Corneille et la poétique d'Aristote*, '88. —*Quatre discours*, 1900. — *Opinions à répandre*, '02. — *Théories et impressions*, '03. —*En marge des vieux livres*, '05; 2e série, '08. — *Rousseau*, '07. — *Racine*, '08. —*Fénelon*, '10. — *Chateaubriand*, '12, etc.
See A. France, *La vie littéraire*, I, 1888; II, '90. — Pellissier, *Nouveaux essais de litt. contemporaine*, '94; *Etu des de litt. contemporaine*, II, 1900. — Doumic, *Ecrivains d'aujourd'hui*, '95.

Lemercier (Népomucène), 1771–1840. Dramatist, etc.
Cours analytique de litt. générale, 4 vols., 1817.
See G. Vauthier, *Essai sur la vie et les œuvres de N. Lemercier*, '86. — M. Souriau, *N. Lemercier et ses correspondants*, '08.

Lenient (Charles), 1826–1906.
Etude sur Bayle, 1855. —*La satire en France au moyen âge*, '59. —*La satire en France ou la litt. militante au XVIe siècle*, '66. — *Conférences sur les œuvres poétiques de M. Pierre Lebrun*, '66. —*La comédie en France au XVIIIe siècle*, '88. —*La poésie patriotique en France au moyen âge*, '91. —*La poésie patriotique en France*, 2 vols.,'94. —*La comédie en France au XIXe siècle*, 2 vols., '98, etc.

Levallois (Jules), 1829–1903. Sainte-Beuve's secretary for a number of years.
Critique militante, 1862. —*Sainte-Beuve*, '72. —*Corneille inconnu*, '76. — *Un précurseur: Senancour*, '97, etc.

Lintilhac (Eugène),1854.
Beaumarchais et ses œuvres, 1887. — *Précis historique et critique de la litt. fr. depuis les origines à nos jours*, 2 vols., '91–'94. — *Supplément aux Etudes littéraires sur les classiques des classes supérieures et du baccalauréat ès lettres*, '92.

—*Lesage*, '93. —*Les félibres*, '94. —*Le miracle grec d'Homère à Aristote*, '96. — *Conférences dramatiques*, '98. — *Michelet*, '98. —*Le problème de l'enseignement secondaire*, '98. — *Histoire du théâtre en France*, I, 1904; II, '06; III, '08; IV, '09; V, '11.

Livet (Charles-Louis), 1828–1898.

La grammaire fr. et les grammairiens au XVIIe siècle, 1859. — *Précieux et précieuses*, '59. — *Portraits du grand siècle*, '85. —*Lexique de la langue de Molière*, 3 vols., '96–'97.

Loménie (Louis de), 1818–1878.

Galerie des contemporains illustres, 10 vols., 1840–'47. —*Beaumarchais et son temps*, 2 vols., '55. —*Les Mirabeau*, 5 vols., '78–'91. —*Esquisses historiques et littéraires*, '79.

Magnin (Charles), 1793–1862. A critic of romantic leaning. Dramatic critic on *Globe* and later on *National*. —Librarian at Bibliothèque nationale. — Substitutes for Fauriel at Sorbonne, etc.

Origines du théâtre en Europe, 1838. — *Causeries et Méditations*, '42. — *Théâtre de Hroswitha*, '45. —*Histoire des marionnettes en Europe*, '52, etc.

See Sainte-Beuve, *Portraits con.*, III, 1843; *N. Lundis*, V, '63.

Martha (Constant), 1820–1895. Professor of Latin at Sorbonne from 1869.

De la morale pratique dans les lettres de Senèque, 1854. —*Les moralistes sous l'Empire romain*, '64. —*Le poème de Lucrèce*, '69. —*Etudes morales sur l'antiquité*, '83. —*La délicatesse dans l'art*, '84. — *Mélanges de litt. ancienne*, '96.

Maurras (Charles-Marie-Photius), 1868. Has actively defended classicism against modern laxity and corruption of taste, in such a way, however, as to mix up the whole question of classic and romantic art with politics. — Besides numerous contributions to various newspapers and reviews (especially *L'Action française*), and books on social and political questions, has published: *Jean Moréas*, 1891. — *Trois Idées politiques: Chateaubriand, Michelet, Sainte-Beuve*, '98. —*Les amants de Venise, George Sand et Musset*, 1902. —*L'Avenir de l'intelligence*, '05, etc.

Mérimée (Prosper), 1803–1870. Novelist, archæologist, etc.

Mélanges historiques et littéraires, 1855. — *Portraits historiques et littéraires*, '75, etc.

Merlet (Gustave), 1828–1891. Exercised an important influence on numerous pupils as Professor of " Rhetoric " at Lycée Charlemagne and Lycée Louis-le-Grand.

Le réalisme et la fantaisie dans la litt., 1861. — *Portraits d'hier, etc.*, '63. — *Causeries sur les femmes et les livres*, '65. — *Hommes et livres*, '69. — *Saint-Evremond, étude historique, morale et littéraire*, '70. —*Etudes littéraires sur les classiques fr.*, '75. —*Etudes littéraires sur les classiques fr.* (*XVII–XVIIIe siècles*), '76. — *Tableau de la litt. fr.* (*1800–'15*), 3 vols., '77–'80. —*Etudes littéraires sur la Chanson de Roland*, '82. —*Etudes littéraires sur les grands classiques latins*, '84. —*Etudes littéraires sur les grands classiques grecs*, '85. — *Anthologie classique des poètes du XIXe siècle*, '90.

Mézières (Alfred), 1826. Professor at Sorbonne from 1863. — Member of Academy from 1874.

Shakespeare, ses œuvres et ses critiques, 1861. — *Les contemporains de Shakespeare*, '63. — *Prédécesseurs et contemporains de Shakespeare*, '63. — *Contemporains et successeurs de Shakespeare*, '64. — *Dante et l'Italie*, '65. —

Pétrarque, '67. —*La société fr. Le paysan, etc.*, '69. —*Goethe. Les œuvres expliquées par la vie*, 2 vols., '72–'73. — *Discours de réception*, '75. —*En France : XVIIIe et XIXe siècles*, '83. —*Réponse de M. Mézières au discours de Pierre Loti*, '92. — *Morts et vivants*, '97. — *Au temps passé*, '06. — *Hommes et femmes d'hier et d'avant-hier*, '09. — *De Tout un peu*, '09, etc.

Michiels (**Alfred-Joseph-Xavier**), 1813–1892. Art critic, historian, etc. An enemy of Sainte-Beuve.

Etudes sur l'Allemagne, 2 vols., 1839. — *Histoire des idées littéraires en France au XIXe siècle*, etc., 2 vols., '42. —*Souvenirs d'Angleterre*, '44. —*Le monde du comique et du rire*, '87, etc.

Monod (**Gabriel**), 1844. Historian; Professor at Collège de France, etc.

Jules Michelet, 1875. —*Les maîtres de l'histoire. Renan, Taine, Michelet*, '94. — *Portraits et souvenirs*, '97. —*Gaston Paris*, 1903, etc.

Montégut (**Emile**), 1826–1895. Historian, moralist, critic. — Succeeds Gustave Planche on *Revue des Deux Mondes* (his first article was on Emerson). One of the chief interpreters of foreign (especially English) literature to the French public during the second half of the 19th century, and a critic of delicacy and distinction.

Du génie fr., 1857. —*Essai sur l'époque actuelle*, '58. — *Poètes et artistes de l'Italie*, '81. — *Types littéraires et fantaisies esthétiques*, '82. —*Essais sur la litt. anglaise*, '83. — *Nos morts contemporains*, 2 vols., '83–'84. —*Ecrivains modernes de l'Angleterre*, 3 vols., '85. —*Livres et âmes du pays d'Orient*, '85. — *Choses du Nord et du Midi*, '86. — *Mélanges critiques*, '87. — *Dramaturges et romanciers*, '90. — *Heures de lectures d'un critique*, '91. —*Esquisses littéraires*, '93, etc.

Morice (**Charles**), 1861.

Paul Verlaine, 1887. — *Demain. Questions d'esthétique*, '88. —*La litt. de tout à l'heure*, '89. —*Opinions*, '95. — *Du sens religieux de la poésie. Sur le mot poésie. Le principe social de la beauté*, '98. —*Les textes de Rabelais et la critique contemporaine*, 1905, etc.

Musset (**Alfred de**), 1810–1857. Indulged in satire occasionally at the expense of his fellow romanticists especially in the *Lettres de Dupuis et Cotonet*.

Nettement (**Alfred-François**), 1805–1869. Strongly reactionary in his opinions.

Histoire de la litt. fr. sous la Restauration, 2 vols., 1853. — *Histoire de la litt. fr. sous le gouvernement de Juillet*, 2 vols., '55. — *Poètes et artistes contemporains*, '62. —*Le roman contemporain, etc.*, '64, etc.

Nisard (**Désiré**), 1806–1888. Writes for *Journal des Débats* and other periodicals. — "Inspector general" of Education. — Professor at the Sorbonne. — Director of Normal School, member of Academy, etc.

Etudes de mœurs et de critique sur les poètes latins de la décadence, 2 vols., 1834. — *Mélanges*, '38. — *Histoire de la litt. fr.*, 4 vols., '44–'61. —*Etudes sur la Renaissance*, '55. — *Souvenirs de voyages*, '55. —*Etudes de critique littéraire*, '58. — *Etudes d'histoire et de litt.*, '59. — *Nouvelles études d'histoire et de litt.*, '64. — *Mélanges d'histoire et de litt.*, '68. —*Les quatre grands historiens latins*, '74. — *Portraits et études d'histoire littéraire*, '74. — *Renaissance et Réforme*, 2 vols., '77. — *Discours académiques et universitaires*, '84. — *Nouveaux mélanges d'histoire et de litt.*, '86. — *Considérations sur la Révolution fr. et Napoléon I*, '87. — *Souvenirs et notes biographiques*, 2 vols., '88. —*Ægri somnia*, '89. —*Essais sur l'école romantique*, '91.

See Sainte-Beuve, *Portraits contemporains*, III, 1836; *Causeries du lundi*, XV, '64. — Scherer, *Etudes sur la litt. contemporaine*, I, '63. — Dowden, *New Studies in Literature*, '95. — Mézières, *Pensées choisies de D. Nisard (centenaire)*, '06.

Ozanam (Alphonse-Frédéric), 1813–1853. Succeeds Fauriel, whose influence is very marked upon him, as professor at the Sorbonne (1845). — A distinguished student of Dante and an important figure in French catholicism of the 19th century.

Essai sur la philosophie de Dante, 1838. — *Dante et la philosophie catholique au XIIIe siècle*, '39. — *Etudes germaniques*, 2 vols., '47–'49. — *Documents inédits pour servir à l'histoire littéraire de l'Italie du VIIIe–XIIIe siècles*, '50. — *Œuvres complètes, préface par M. Ampère*, 11 vols., '62–'65. — *Les poètes franciscains en Italie au XIIIe siècle*, '72.

See Veuillot, *Mélanges religieux*, etc., IV, 1847–'50. — Lacordaire, *Frédéric Ozanam*, '57. — Ampère, *Mélanges d'histoire littéraire et de litt.*, II, '67. — A. Ozanam, *Vie de F. Ozanam*, '79. — B. Faulquier, *F. Ozanam*, '03.

Parigot (Hippolyte), 1861.

Emile Augier, 1890. — *Le théâtre d'hier*, '93. — *Génie et métier*, '94. — *Le drame d'Alexandre Dumas*, '99. — *Alexandre Dumas, père*, 1900. — *Renan*, '09, etc.

Paris (Gaston), 1839–1903. Perhaps the most eminent of French mediæval philologists, and also a literary critic of distinction. — Professor at Collège de France from 1872; member of Academy from 1896.

La poésie du moyen âge, 2 vols., 1885–'95. — *Les origines de la poésie lyrique en France au moyen âge*, '92. — *François Villon*, 1901. — *Esquisse historique de la litt. fr. du moyen âge*, '07, etc.

Patin (Henri-Joseph-Guillaume), 1793–1876. Professor of Latin at the Sorbonne from 1833; member of Academy from 1843.

Mélanges de litt. ancienne et moderne, 1840. — *Etudes sur les tragiques grecs*, 3 vols., '41–'43. — *Etudes sur la poésie latine*, 2 vols., '69. — *Discours et Mélanges littéraires*, '76.

Pellissier (Georges), 1852.

Traité théorique et historique de versification fr., 1882. — *Les écrivains politiques en France avant la Révolution*, '82. — *De sexti decimi sæculi in Francia artibus poeticis*, '83. — *La vie et les œuvres de Du Bartas*, '83. — *Le mouvement littéraire au XIXe siècle*, '89. — *Essais de litt. contemporaine*, '93. — *Nouveaux essais de litt. contemporaine*, '95. — *Morceaux choisis des poètes du XVIe siècle*, '96. — *Etudes de litt. contemporaine*, '98. — *Le mouvement littéraire contemporain*, 1901. — *Précis d'histoire de la litt. fr.*, '02. — *Etudes de litt. et de morale cont.*, '05. — *Voltaire philosophe*, '08. — *Le Réalisme du romantisme*, '12, etc.

Petit de Julleville (Louis), 1841–1900. Professor at the Sorbonne.

Le discours fr. et la dissertation fr., 1868. — *L'Ecole d'Athènes au IVe siècle après Jésus-Christ*, '68. — *Histoire du théâtre en France: les mystères*, '80. — *Histoire littéraire*, 2 vols., '84. — *Histoire du théâtre en France: les comédiens en France au moyen âge*, '85. — *Histoire du théâtre en France: La comédie et les mœurs en France au moyen âge*, '86. — *Histoire du théâtre en France: Répertoire du théâtre comique en France au moyen âge*, '86. — *Le théâtre en France. Histoire de la litt. dramatique depuis les origines à nos jours*, '89. — General editor of *Histoire de la litt. et de la langue fr.*, 8 vols., '96–'99. — *Histoire de la litt. fr. des origines à nos jours*, '99.

Pichot (Amédée), 1796–1877. Historian, novelist, poet; active as a translator of Byron and other English writers.

Notice sur Walter Scott et ses écrits, 1821. — *Essai sur le génie et le caractère de Lord Byron*, '24. — *Voyage historique et littéraire en Angleterre et en Ecosse*, 3 vols., '25, etc.

Planche (Gustave), 1808–1857. Contributes to *Revue des Deux Mondes* from 1831. — Remarkable for the severity of his judgments on contemporary artists and writers with many of whom he was personally intimate. " A critic of the very first order," according to Matthew Arnold. The ordinary French view is that P. was a sort of critical Alceste — more temperamental than judicial in his severity.

Salon de 1831, 1831. — *Portraits littéraires*, 2 vols., '36. — *Nouveaux portraits littéraires*, 2 vols., '54. — *Etudes sur les arts*, '55. — *Etudes sur l'école fr. (1831–'52). Peinture et sculpture*, 2 vols., '55, etc.

See Michiels, *Histoire des idées littéraires*, etc., II, 1842. — Montégut, *Esquisses littéraires*, '93.

Pontmartin (Armand de), 1811–1890. A reactionary critic who had some lively skirmishes with Sainte-Beuve. The literary satire in *Les Jeudis de Madame Charbonneau* had a " succès de scandale."

Causeries littéraires, 1854. — *Nouveaux causeries littéraires*, '55. — *Dernières causeries littéraires*, '56. — *Causeries du samedi*, '57. — *Nouvelles causeries du samedi*, '59. — *Dernières causeries du samedi*, '60. — *Les semaines littéraires*, '61. — *Les jeudis de Mme. Charbonneau*, '62. — *Les nouvelles semaines littéraires*, '63. — *Les dernières semaines littéraires*, '64. — *Nouveaux samedis*, 20 vols., '65–'81. — *Souvenirs d'un vieux critique*, 10 vols., '81–'90. — *Mes mémoires : enfance et jeunesse*, '85. — *Mes mémoires : seconde jeunesse*, '86. — *Episodes littéraires*, '90. — *Derniers samedis*, 3 vols., '91–'92.

See Veuillot, *Mélanges religieux*, etc., II, 1859. — Sainte-Beuve, *Nouveaux Lundis*, II, III, '62. — Biré, *Etudes et portraits*, '94.

Prévost-Paradol (Lucien-Anatole), 1829–1870. A comrade of Taine's at the Normal School. One of the most brilliant publicists of the Second Empire. After years of opposition, he rallied to the Empire and was sent as minister to the United States, but committed suicide at Washington on the outbreak of the war with Germany.

Jonathan Swift, 1856. — *Essais de politique et de litt.*, 3 vols., '59–'63. — *Etude sur Etienne de La Boétie*, '64. — *Etudes sur les moralistes fr.*, '65.

See Sainte-Beuve, *Nouveaux Lundis*, I, 1861. — Scherer, *Etudes sur la litt. contemporaine*, I, '63; III, '66; IV, '73. — Gréard, *Prévost-Paradol*, '94. — *Lettres de Prévost-Paradol*, '94, etc.

Rémusat (Charles de), 1797–1875. Philosopher, etc. — Contributes to *Globe* from 1824. — Member of Academy, '46. — Minister of Foreign Affairs, '71–'73.

Abélard, 2 vols., 1845. — *De la philosophie allemande*, '45. — *Critiques et études littéraires*, 2 vols., '47. — *Passé et présent. Mélanges*, 2 vols., '47. — *L'Angleterre au XVIIIe siècle*, 2 vols., '56. — *Bacon*, '57. — *Channing*, '57. — *Lord Herbert de Cherbury*, '74, etc.

See Sainte-Beuve, *Portraits littéraires*, III, 1847. — Albert, *La litt. fr. au XIXe siècle*, II, '85, etc.

Renan (Ernest), 1823–1892. — The points of chief interest in Renan's life are those that he himself has given in his *Souvenirs*, — his birth at Tréguier, in

Brittany, his education at the Collège de Tréguier, and Saint-Nicolas du Chardonnet at Paris, his preparation for the priesthood at the Séminaire d'Issy and Saint-Sulpice, his growing skepticism as the result of historical and philological research, and his final rupture with Saint-Sulpice and Catholicism (October, 1845). — Renan spends the next three years and a half as a tutor in the Pension Crouzet, where he makes the acquaintance of Berthelot. — Receives a scientific mission from the government and travels for eight months in Italy ('49); his democratic illusions of '48 disappear, and the world of art is revealed to him. — Meets in '50 his sister Henriette, after a ten-years' separation, and has her constant companionship and counsel during the ten years following. (See *Ma Sœur Henriette*, p. 32 ff). — Is employed in the department of Oriental MSS. at the Bibliothèque Nationale, '51–'60. — Elected to the Académie des Inscriptions, '56. — Marries in the same year Mademoiselle Scheffer, niece of the painter Ary Scheffer. — Goes on a scientific mission to ancient Phœnicia, accompanied by his sister, '60. — They both fall ill of fever in Syria, and Henriette dies, '61. — Composes during his Eastern trip his *Vie de Jésus*. — Appointed Professor of Hebrew at the Collège de France ('62), but the government first suspends his course, because of his unorthodox attitude, and two years later deprives him of his professorship. — Unsuccessful candidate for deputy in the electoral district of Meaux, '69. — Travels with Prince Napoleon in Scandinavia, '70. — Reinstated in his professorship at the Collège de France on the fall of the Empire, '70. — Elected to the Academy, '78. — President of the Asiatic Society, '82. — Administrator of the Collège de France, '84. — After a long illness, borne with great fortitude, Renan dies in his apartment at the Collège de France, October 2, '92.

L'Avenir de la science, 1848 (published in '90). — *Averroès et l'Averroïsme* and *De philosophia peripatetica apud Syros*, '52. — *Histoire générale et système comparé des langues sémitiques*, '55. — *Etudes d'histoire religieuse*, '57. — *De l'origine du langage*, '58. — *Essais de morale et de critique*, '59. — Translations: *Le livre de Job*, '59; *Le Cantique des cantiques*, '60. — *Ma Sœur Henriette*, '62 (published, '95). — *Vie de Jésus*, '63. — Various contributions to the *Histoire littéraire de la France*, vols. XXIV to XXXI (especially the *Discours sur l'état des beaux-arts en France au XIVe siècle*, in vol. XXIV). — *Mission de Phénicie*, '64. — *Les Apôtres*, '66. — *Questions contemporaines*, '68. — *Saint-Paul*, '69. — *La réforme intellectuelle et morale*, '71. — *L'Antéchrist*, '73. — *Dialogues et fragments philosophiques*, '76. — *Les Evangiles*, '77. — *Mélanges d'histoire et de voyages*, '78. — *L'église chrétienne*, '79. — *Conférences d'Angleterre*, '80. — *Marc-Aurèle*, '82. — Translation: *l'Ecclésiaste*, '82. — *Souvenirs d'enfance et de jeunesse*, '83. — *Nouvelles études d'histoire religieuse*, '84. — *Discours et conférences*, '87. — *Histoire du peuple d'Israël*, 5 vols., '87–'94. — *Drames philosophiques*, '88. — *Feuilles détachées*, '92. — *Lettres intimes*, '96. — *Correspondance* (between Renan and Berthelot), '98. — *Cahiers de jeunesse*, '06. — *Nouveaux cahiers de jeunesse*, '07.

See Scherer, *Mélanges de critique religieuse*, '60; *Etudes sur la litt. contemporaine*, IV, VII, VIII, IX, and X, '63–'95; *Mélanges d'histoire religieuse*, '64. — Sainte-Beuve, *Nouveaux lundis*, II, '62; VI, '63. — Bourget, *Essais de psychologie contemporaine*, '83. — Lemaître, *Les Contemporains*, I, '84; IV, '89. — *Impressions de théâtre*, I, '89. — A. France, *La vie littéraire*, I, '89; II, '94. — E. M. de Vogüé, *Heures d'histoire*, '93. — Pellissier, *Le Mouvement littéraire au XIXe siècle* (p. 314 ff), '94. — G. Monod, *Renan, Taine et Michelet*, '94. — Séailles, *Ernest Renan*, '95. — F. Espinasse, *Life of Renan*, 95. — Brunetière, *Nou-*

veaux essais sur la litt. contemporaine, '95; *Library of the World's Best Literature*, XXI, '97.

Renard (Georges), 1847.

Vie de Voltaire, 1883. — *Etudes sur la France contemporaine*, '88. — *Les princes de la jeune critique*, '90. — *Critique de combat*, 3 vols., '94–'97. — *La méthode scientifique de l'histoire littéraire*, 1900, etc.

Rigault (Hippolyte), 1821–1858.

La querelle des Anciens et des Modernes, '56. — *Œuvres complètes*, 4 vols., '59.

Rod (Edouard), 1857–1910. Novelist, etc.

De la litt. comparée, 1886. — *Etudes sur le XIXe siècle*, '88. — *Les idées morales du temps présent*, '91. — *Dante*, '91. — *Stendhal*, '91. — *Essai sur Goethe*, '98. — *Nouvelles études sur le XIXe siècle*, '98. — *L'Affaire J.-J. Rousseau*, 1906. — *La Pensée d'Edouard Rod*, '11, etc.

Sacy (Samuel-Ustazade-Silvestre de), 1801–1879. Contributor of literary and political articles to *Journal des Débats* from 1828. — Member of Academy from 1854. — An attractive mixture of humanist and bibliophile.

Variétés littéraires, morales et historiques, 2 vols., 1858. — *Rapport sur le progrès des lettres, par de Sacy, Féval, Gautier, et Ed. Thierry*, '68.

See Sainte-Beuve, *Causeries du lundi*, XIV, 1858. — Renan, *Essais de morale et de critique*, '59. — Prévost-Paradol, *Essais de politique et de litt.*, III, '63. — Taine, *Nouveaux essais de critique et d'histoire*, '65; *Dernièrs essais de critique et d'histoire*, '94. — Scherer, *Etudes critiques sur la litt. contemporaine*, VII, '82.

Sainte-Beuve (Charles-Augustin), 1804–1869. Born at Boulogne-sur-Mer two months after the death of his father, a government official, who at the age of fifty-two married a woman of forty (English on her mother's side). — S.-B. studies at Blériot Institution at Boulogne. — In 1818 enters the Pension Landry at Paris. — Studies medicine, '23–'27. — Begins to write for *Globe* (founded by his old teacher, M. Dubois, '24). — As a result of his review of *Odes et Ballades* in the *Globe* (Jan., '27) gets acquainted with Hugo. — Rehabilitates Ronsard and the Pléiade as a part of his pro-romantic campaign. — Begins writing for *Revue de Paris*. — Has close relations with followers of Saint-Simon, '30–'31. — Writes for *National;* for newly founded *Revue des Deux Mondes*. — Goes to Switzerland. — Meets Vinet and lectures at Lausanne on Port-Royal, '37–'38. — Appointed by Cousin to a position in the Bibliothèque Mazarine, '40. — Elected to Academy, '44. — Leaves Paris after the Revolution of '48 and spends a year as professor of French literature at Liège, Belgium. (For circumstances see preface to his *Chateaubriand*.) — On return to Paris (Sept., '49), begins his *Lundis* in the *Constitutionnel*. — Passes over to the *Moniteur*, '53. — Appointed professor of Latin poetry at the Collège de France, '54; but is prevented by students, incensed at his political attitude, from giving more than two lectures. — Lectures at the Normal School, '58–'61. — Returns to the *Constitutionnel* and begins the *Nouveaux lundis*, '61. — Appointed senator, '65.

Tableau historique et critique de la poésie fr. et du théâtre fr. au XVIe siècle, 1828 (definitive ed., '76). — *Œuvres choisies de Pierre de Ronsard avec notices, notes, et commentaires*, '28. — *Vie, poésie et pensées de Joseph Delorme*, '29. — *Les Consolations*, '30. — *Volupté*, 2 vols., '34. — *Pensées d 'Août*, '37. — *Port-Royal*, 5 vols., '40–'59 (3^d ed., 7 vols., '69–'71). — *Livre d'amour*, '43. — *Causeries du lundi*, 16 vols., '51–'62 (3^d ed., revised, '57–'72). — *Etude sur Virgile*,

'57 (revised ed., '70). — *Chateaubriand et son groupe littéraire sous l'Empire*, 2 vols., '60 (revised ed., '73). — *Portraits littéraires*, 3 vols., '62–'64. — *Nouveaux lundis*, 13 vols., '63–'70 (2d ed., revised, '64–'78.) — *Portraits contemporains*, 5 vols., '69–'71. — *Portraits de femmes*, '70. — *P.-J. Proudhon, sa vie et sa correspondance*, '72. — *Lettres à la princesse*, '73. — *Premiers lundis*, 3 vols., '74–'75. — *Cahiers de Sainte-Beuve*, '76. — *Chroniques parisiennes*, '76. — *Correspondance de Sainte-Beuve*, 2 vols., '77–'78. — *Nouvelle Correspondance*, '80. — *Lettres inédites de Sainte-Beuve à Collombet*, 1903. — *Correspondance inédite de Sainte-Beuve avec M. et Mme. Juste Olivier*, '04. — *Lettres de Sainte-Beuve à Victor Hugo et à Mme. Victor Hugo*, *Revue de Paris*, Dec., Jan. and Feb., '05. — *Lettres inédites à Charles Labitte*, '12.

See Scherer, *Etudes sur la litt. contemporaine*, I, 1863; IV, '73; VII, '82. — Haussonville, *Sainte-Beuve, sa vie et ses œuvres*, '75. — Levallois, *Sainte-Beuve*, '72. — Troubat, *Souvenirs et Indiscrétions du dernier secrétaire de Sainte-Beuve*, '72; *Vie de Sainte-Beuve*, '76; *Souvenirs du dernier secrétaire de Sainte-Beuve*, '90. — M. Arnold, in *Encyclopædia Britannica*. — Brunetière, *L'évolution des genres*, '90. — Taine, *Derniers essais de critique et d'histoire*, '94. — Faguet, *Politiques et Moralistes du XIXe siècle*, 3d series, '99. — Spoelberch de Lovenjoul, *Sainte-Beuve inconnu*, 1901. — Giraud, *Table alphabétique et analytique des Premiers lundis*, etc., *avec une étude sur Sainte-Beuve et son œuvre critique*, '03. — Michaut, *Sainte-Beuve avant les Lundis*, '03; *Le Livre d'Amour de Sainte-Beuve*, '05; *Etudes sur Sainte-Beuve*, '05. — Séché, *Etudes d'histoire romantique: Sainte-Beuve*, 2 vols., '04. — G. M. Harper, *Sainte-Beuve*, '09. — P. E. More, *Shelburne Essays*, 3d series, '06. — F. Voizard, *Sainte-Beuve: L'homme et l'œuvre*, '12.

Saint-Marc Girardin, 1801–1873. Exercised a wide influence as professor of French poetry at the Sorbonne from 1834. — Member of Academy from 1844. — A keen and witty opponent of romantic extravagance; a moralist even more than a literary critic. He has been accused of having a somewhat bourgeois mental habit, and of being a brilliant improviser even more than a born writer (an " écrivain de race " as the French say).

Eloge de Lesage, 1822. — *Eloge de Bossuet*, '27. — *Tableau de la litt. fr. au XVIe siècle*, '28. — *Notices littéraires et politiques sur l'Allemagne*, '34. — *Cours de litt. dramatique*, 4 vols., '43. — *Essais de litt. et de morale*, 2 vols., '45. — *Souvenirs de voyages et d'études*, 2 vols., '52–'53. — *La Fontaine et les fabulistes*, 2 vols., '67. — *J.-J. Rousseau, sa vie et ses ouvrages*, 2 vols., '70.

See Vinet, *Etudes sur la litt. fr.*, III, 1851. — Nisard, *Etudes de critique littéraire*, '58; *Portraits et études d'histoire littéraire*, '74; *Souvenirs et notes biographiques*, '88.

Saint-Victor (le comte Paul de), 1827–1881. A romanticist whose style was admired by Taine and others for its warmth of coloring, a merit that does not compensate for its lack of intellectual content.

Hommes et dieux, 1867. — *Les femmes de Goethe*, '69. — *Lamartine*, '69. — *Victor Hugo*, '85. — *Anciens et modernes*, '86. — *Le théâtre contemporain*, '89.

See Sainte-Beuve, *Nouveaux lundis*, x, 1867. — Scherer, *Etudes critiques sur la litt. contemporaine*, IV, '73; VII, '82. — Taine, *Derniers essais de critique et d'histoire*, '94.

Sand (George), 1804–1876. For her critical views see her *Souvenirs et impressions littéraires*, 1862.— *Impressions et Souvenirs*, '73.— *Questions d'art et de litt.*, '78.— *Correspondance*, 6 vols., '82–84 (especially the letters to Flaubert), etc.

Sarcey (Francisque), 1828–1899. The most influential dramatic critic of his time. Writer for the *Temps* newspaper from 1867. A technician and advocate of bourgeois good sense.

Comédiens et comédiennes, '78. — *Souvenirs de jeunesse*, '84. — *Souvenirs d'âge mûr*, '92. — *Quarante ans de théâtre*, 8 vols., 1900–'02, etc.

See Lemaître, *Les Contemporains*, II, '89. — Faguet, *Propos de théâtre*, '03.

Sayous (André), 1808–1870.

Etude littéraire sur Calvin, 1839. — *Etudes littéraires sur les écrivains fr. de la Réformation*, 2 vols., '42. — *Histoire de la litt. fr. à l'étranger*, 2 vols., '53. — *Le XVIIIe siècle à l'étranger*, 2 vols., '61.

See Vinet, *Etudes sur la litt. fr.*, III, 1851. — S. de Sacy, *Variétés littéraires*, I, II, '58. — Sainte-Beuve, *Causeries du lundi*, XV, '61.

Scherer (Edmond), 1815–1889. Born at Paris of Swiss, Dutch and English ancestry. — Boards at Monmouth, England, with an evangelical clergyman from Aug. 10, 1831. — Returns to Paris, '33. — Theological student Strasbourg, '36–'39. — Teaches at *Ecole libre de Théologie*, Geneva. — Resigns from the School, Dec., '49. — Gives independent courses on theology at Geneva, '50–'59. — Leaves for Paris, '60. — Joins the staff of the *Temps* newspaper, for which it is estimated he wrote 3500 articles. — Elected member of National Assembly, '71. — Elected to Senate, '75.

Dogmatique de l'école réformée, 1843. — *De l'état actuel de l'église réformée en France*, '44. — *Esquisse d'une théorie de l'église chrétienne*, '45. — *La critique et la foi*, '50. — *Alex. Vinet*, '53. — *Lettres à mon curé*, '53. — *Mélanges de critique religieuse*, '60. — *Etudes critiques sur la litt. contemporaine*, 10 vols., '63–'95. — *Mélanges d'histoire religieuse*, '64. — *Diderot*, '80. — *La révision de la constitution*, '81. — *La démocratie et la France*, '83. — *Melchior Grimm*, '87. — *Etudes sur la litt. au XVIIIe siècle*, '91.

See Sainte-Beuve, *Causeries du lundi*, XV, 1860. — Gréard, *Ed. Scherer*, '90. — Tissot, *Les évolutions de la critique*, '90. — Dowden, *New Studies in Literature*, '95. — Boutmy, *Taine, Scherer, Laboulaye*, 1901.

Séché (Léon), 1848. Ultra-biographical in his point of view.

Port-Royal des Champs, 1899. — *Volney (1757–1820)*, '99. — *Sainte-Beuve*, 2 vols., 1904–05. — *A. de Musset*, '07. — *Le Cénacle de la "Muse française,"* '08. — *Hortense Allart de Méritens*, '08. — *Le Roman de Lamartine*, '09. — *Madame d'Arbouville*, '09. — *Muses romantiques*, '10. — *La Jeunesse dorée sous Louis Philippe*, '11. — *Le Cénacle de Joseph Delorme*, 2 vols., '12, etc.

Seillière (Ernest), 1866. Is developing the relationship between the expansive, romantic attitude towards life and imperialism (*La Philosophie de l'impérialisme*).

Etudes sur Ferdinand Lassalle, 1897. — *Litt. et morale dans le parti socialiste allemand*, '98. — *Le comte de Gobineau et l'aryanisme historique*, 1903. — *Apollon ou Dionysos?* '05. — *L'impérialisme démocratique*, '07. — *Le mal romantique. Essai sur l'impérialisme irrationnel*, '08. — *Une tragédie d'amour au temps du romantisme*, '09. — *Introduction à la philosophie de l'impérialisme*, '10. — *Barbey d'Aurevilly*, '10. — *Les mystiques du néo-romantisme*, '11. — *Schopenhauer*, '11, etc.

Simonde de Sismondi (Jean-Charles-Léonard), 1773–1842. Historian, etc.; an intimate of Madame de Staël's. — His work *De la litt. du Midi de l'Europe* (4 vols., 1813) is an underlying influence on the romantic movement. Like Madame de Staël he has little sense of form.

See Sainte-Beuve, *Nouveaux lundis*, VI, 1863. — Scherer, *Etudes critiques sur la litt. contemporaine*, II, '65.

Staël, Mme. de (*née* **Germaine Necker**), 1766–1817. Only child of rich Swiss banker, Necker, minister of Louis XVI, etc. — Meets in her mother's drawing-room La Harpe, Buffon, etc. Marries Baron de Staël, Swedish Ambassador at Paris, 1786. — Joins Talleyrand and other friends in England during the Revolution. — Meets Benjamin Constant, Sept., '94. — Opens salon at Paris, May, '95, but returns to Coppet same year. — Opens salon again, April, '97. — Enters into opposition to Napoleon. — Death of Baron de Staël, '02. — Receives order to keep at a distance of forty leagues from Paris, Oct., 1803. — Leaves for Germany (at Weimar from Dec., '03, to Feb., '04). Appoints A. W. Schlegel tutor to her son, '04. — Returns in haste from Germany on learning of the death of her father. — Sets out for Italy, Nov., '04. — Spends winter '07–'08 at Munich and Vienna. — Confiscation of French edition of the *Germany*, '10 (printed at London, '13, and at Leipzig, '14). — Marries Genevan officer of twenty-three, named de Rocca, '11. — Persecuted by Napoleon, she flees from Coppet, May 22, '12. — Reaches Russia by way of Vienna and Warsaw. — Visits Sweden and later England (June, '13). — Stricken with paralysis at a ball, Feb., '17, and dies July 14, of the same year.

Lettres sur le caractère et les écrits de J.-J. Rousseau, 1788. — *Essai sur les fictions*, '95. — *De l'influence des passions sur le bonheur des individus et des nations*, '96. — *De la litt. considérée dans ses rapports avec les institutions sociales*, 2 vols., 1800. — *Delphine*, 4 vols., '02. — *Corinne*, 3 vols., '07. — *De l'Allemagne*, 3 vols., '10. — *Réflexions sur le suicide*, '13. — *Considérations sur la Révolution fr.*, 3 vols., '18. — *Dix années d'exil*, '21.

See Sainte-Beuve, *Portraits de femmes*, 1835. — Brandes, *Emigrant literature*, '82. — Lady Blennerhassett, *Frau von Staël* (French and English translations), '87. — Pellissier, *Le mouvement littéraire au XIXe siècle*, '89. — Brunetière, *Etudes de critique sur la litt. fr.*, IV, '90.; *L'évolution des genres*, '90.; *L'évolution de la poésie lyrique*, '95. — Dejob, *Mme. de Staël et l'Italie*, '90. — Sorel, *Mme. de Staël*, '90. — Faguet, *Politiques et moralistes du XIXe siècle*, I, '91. — Doumic, *Hommes et idées du XIXe siècle*, 1903.

Stapfer (Paul), 1840.

Petite comédie de la critique littéraire, ou Molière selon les trois écoles philosophiques, 1865. — *Laurence Sterne*, '70. — *Les artistes juges et parties*, '72. — *Shakespeare et l'antiquité*, 2 vols., '79. — *Etudes sur la litt. fr. moderne et contemporaine*, '80. — *Molière et Shakespeare*, '80. — *Goethe et ses deux chefs-d'œuvre classiques*, '81. — *Variétés littéraires et morales*, '81. — *Racine et V. Hugo*, '86. — *Rabelais*, '89. — *Les réputations littéraires*, '93. — *Montaigne*, '94. — *La famille et les amis de Montaigne*, '95. — *La grande prédication chrétienne en France*, '98. — *Paradoxes et truismes d'un ancien doyen*, 1904. — *Humour et humoristes*, '11, etc.

Stendhal (Henri Beyle), 1783–1842. Important as an underlying influence on writers like Taine and Bourget rather than for his specific opinions on literature. His definition of romanticism in *Racine et Shakespeare* is impossible. It would follow from this definition, as M. Faguet points out, that the most unromantic of writers are the romanticists of 1830. The argument against the unities in the same book coincides with that of Dr. Johnson in his Preface to Shakespeare.

Racine et Shakespeare, 1823. — *Mélanges d'art et de litt.*, '67, etc.

See A. Paupe, *Hist. des œuvres de Stendhal*, 1904. — J. Mélia, *Les Idées de Stendhal*, '10.

Taillandier (René-Gaspard-Ernest), known as **Saint-René Taillandier,** 1817–79. Contributed articles for many years, chiefly on foreign literatures, to *Revue des Deux Mondes*.

Novalis, 1847. — *Histoire de la jeune Allemagne. Etudes littéraires*, '49. — *Poète du Caucase: Michel Lermontoff*, '56. — *Litt. étrangère*, '61. — *Lettres inédites de J. C. S. de Sismondi*, '63. — *Corneille et ses contemporains*, '64. — *Drames et romans de la vie littéraire*, '70. — *Introduction aux fables de La Fontaine*, '73. — *Les destinées de la nouvelle poésie provençale*, '76. — *Etudes littéraires*, '81, etc.

See Sainte-Beuve, *Nouveaux lundis*, v, 1863. — Montégut, *Nos morts contemporains*, '89.

Taine (Hippolyte-Adolphe), 1828–1893. Studies at Collège Bourbon and Ecole normale, 1841-'51. — Incurs displeasure of Government because of his determinist doctrines, and is forced to give up his position as teacher in Lycée at Poitiers, '52. — Receives doctor's degree, '53. — Attains notoriety by his attack in *Philosophes français au XIXe siècle* on the official philosophy of Cousin, '57. — Becomes professor at Ecole des beaux-arts, '64. — Marriage, '68. — Lectures at Oxford, '71. — Elected to the Academy, '78.

De Personis platonicis and *Essai sur les fables de La Fontaine*, theses presented for doctorate, 1853 (the latter recast and published under the title *La Fontaine et ses fables*, '60). — *Voyage aux Pyrénées*, '55. — *Essai sur Tite-Live*, '56. — *Philosophes français au XIXe siècle*, '57 (revised edition under title *Les philosophes classiques au XIXe siècle en France*, '68). — *Essais de critique et d'histoire*, '58. — *Histoire de la littérature anglaise*, 5 vols., '63–'67. — *Nouveaux essais de critique et d'histoire*, '65. — *Voyage en Italie*, 2 vols., '66. — *Philosophie de l'art*, '65; *Philosophie de l'art en Italie*, '66; *l'Idéal dans l'art*, '67; *Philosophie de l'art dans les Pays-Bas*, '68; *Philosophie de l'art en Grèce*, '69 (last five volumes united into two, under general title, *Philosophie de l'art*, '80). — *Vie et opinions de Thomas Graindorge*, '68. — *De l'intelligence*, 2 vols., '70. — *Du Suffrage universal*, '71. — *Notes sur l'Angleterre*, '72. — *Un séjour en France, 1792–1795*, '72. — *Origines de la France contemporaine*, 6 vols., '76–'93. — *Derniers essais de critique et d'histoire*, '94. — *Carnet de voyage*, '96. — *Vie et correspondance*, 4 vols., 1903–'07.

See Sainte-Beuve, *Causeries du lundi*, XIII, 1857; *Nouveaux lundis*, VIII, '64. — Scherer, *Mélanges de critique religieuse*, '58; *Etudes*, IV, '66; VI, VII, '78; VIII, '84. — Montégut, *Essais sur la litt. anglaise*, '63. — Caro, *L'Idée de Dieu et ses nouveaux critiques*, '64. — Bourget, *Essais de psychologie contemporaine*, '83. — Hennequin, *La critique scientifique*, '88. — Brunetière, *L'évolution de la critique*, '90. — Monod, *Renan, Taine et Michelet*, '94. — A. de Margerie, *H. Taine*, '94. — G. Barzellotti, *Ippolito Taine*, '95 (French translation by Dietrich, 1901). — Pellissier, *Nouveaux essais de litt. contemporaine*, '95. — Giraud, *Essai sur Taine*, 1901; *Bibliographie des œuvres de Taine*, '02. — Aulard, *Taine historien de la Révolution*, '07.

Texte (Joseph), 1865–1900.

J.-J. Rousseau et les origines du cosmopolitisme littéraire, '95. — *Etudes de litt. européenne*, '98.

Veuillot (Louis), 1813–1883. A writer who put an extraordinary gift for expression (manifested especially in satire and invective) into the service of a very ultramontane type of Catholicism. His organ was the newspaper *L'Univers* (suppressed, 1860–'67).

Mélanges religieux, historiques, politiques et littéraires, 18 vols., 1856–'75. —*Les odeurs de Paris*, '66. — *Molière et Bourdaloue*, '77. —*Etudes sur V. Hugo*, '85, etc.

See Sainte-Beuve, *Nouveaux lundis*, I, 1861. — Scherer, *Etudes*, I '63.; IV, '74. — Lemaître, *Les contemporains*, 6e série, '96.

Villemain (Abel-François), 1790–1870. Maître de conférences at Normal School, 1810. —Professor at the Sorbonne from '16. —Succeeds Fontanes at Academy, '21. —Becomes active politically. —Villèle Ministry suspends his course at the Sorbonne, '21. —Prominent politically during July Monarchy. —Minister of Education, '39–'44.

Eloge de Montaigne, 1812. —*Choix d'oraisons funèbres*, '13. —*Discours sur les avantages et les inconvénients de la critique*, '14. —*Eloge de Montesquieu*, '16. —*Essai sur les romanciers grecs*, '22. — *Discours et mélanges littéraires*, '23. *Nouveaux mélanges historiques et littéraires*, 27.— *Cours de litt. fr.*, 6 vols., '28. — *Considérations sur la langue fr.*, '35. — *Œuvres*, 10 vols., '40–'49. — *Cours de litt. fr.: Le tableau de la litt. fr. au XVIIIe siècle et du moyen-âge en France, en Italie, en Espagne et en Angleterre*, 6 vols., '40–'46. —*Etudes de litt. ancienne et étrangère*, '46. — *Discours et mélanges littéraires*, '46. —*Tableau de l'éloquence chrétienne au IVe siècle*, 49. — *Souvenirs contemporains d'histoire et de litt.*, 2 vols., '53–'55. —*Choix d'études sur la litt. contemporaine*, '57. —*La tribune moderne*, '58. —*Essai sur le génie de Pindare et sur la poésie lyrique*, '59, etc.

See Sainte-Beuve, *Portraits contemporains*, II, '36. — *Causeries du lundi*, I, '49; VI, '52. — Nisard, *Etudes d'histoire et de litt.*, '59. — Renan, *Discours et conférences*, '87. — Brunetière, *L'évolution de la critique*, '90.

Vinet (Alexandre-Rodolphe), 1797–1847. Professor of French literature at Basle from 1817–37; professor of theology at Lausanne, '37–'45. — A moralist and critic of rare insight and elevation. — Exercised a marked influence on men so different as Matthew Arnold, Sainte-Beuve, Scherer, Brunetière, etc. — The form of his work is inferior to the substance, an inferiority that may militate against its survival. "Le style," says Sainte-Beuve, "est un sceptre d'or à qui reste, en définitive, le royaume de ce monde."

Chrestomathie fr., 3 vols., 1829. —*Etudes sur Pascal*, '47. —*Etudes sur la litt. fr. au XIXe siècle*, 3 vols., '49 (vol. I, of a new and more complete ed., '12). —*Histoire littéraire fr. au XVIIIe siècle*, 2 vols., '53. — *Moralistes des XVIe–XVIIe siècles*, '59. —*Esprit d'Alex. Vinet*, 2 vols., '61. — *Poètes du siècle de Louis XIV*, '62. — *Mélanges*, '69.

See Sainte-Beuve, *Portraits contemporains*, III, 1837; *Portraits littéraires*, III, '47. —Scherer, *A. Vinet. Notice sur sa vie et ses écrits*, '53; *Etudes*, I, '63. — Rambert, *A. Vinet, sa vie et son œuvre*, '75. — Brunetière, *Essais sur la litt. contemporaine*, '92.

Vitet (Ludovic), 1802–1873. Literary critic on *Globe* from 1824. Later distinguished himself as art critic.

Essais historiques et littéraires, 1862. —*Etudes philosophiques et littéraires*, '74, etc.

See Sainte-Beuve, *Portraits littéraires*, III, 1846.

Weiss (J.-J.), 1827–1891. An unsystematic critic, but conservative in his general instincts. He had a marked gift for epigram. The title of an article he published in the *Revue contemporaine* in 1858 (*La Littérature brutale*) gave a phrase to criticism.

Essai sur Hermann et Dorothée, 1856. — *Essai sur l'histoire de la litt. fr.*, '65. — *Au pays du Rhin*, '86. — *Le théâtre et les mœurs*, '89. — *Autour de la Comédie Fr.*, '92. — *Sur Goethe*, '92. — *Le drame historique et le drame passionnel*, '94. — *Trois années de théâtre (1883–'85)*, 4 vols., '92–'96.

See Lemaître, *Impressions de théâtre*, VII, '91. — De Vogüé, *Regards historiques et littéraires*, '91. — Doumic, *Portraits d'écrivains*, '92. — France, *La vie littéraire*, IV, '92. — Pellissier, *Essais sur la litt. contemporaine*, '93. — E. Lovinesco, *J.-J. Weiss*, 1909. — G. Stirbey, *J.-J. Weiss*, '11.

Wyzewa (T. de), 1862. Has for many years contributed articles on foreign literatures and art to *Revue des Deux Mondes*.

Nos maîtres, 1895. — *Ecrivains étrangers*, 3 vols.,'96–'99, etc.

Zola (Emile), 1840–1903. Defends for the most part in his critical writing his own conception of the novel (a conception that involves a radical confusion of the *genres*).

Mes haines, 1866. — *Le roman expérimental*, '80. — *Le naturalisme au théâtre*, '81. — *Nos auteurs dramatiques*, '81. — *Les romanciers naturalistes*, '81. — *Documents littéraires*, '81.

INDEX OF NAMES

INDEX OF NAMES